THE PRESS IN THE
FRENCH REVOLUTION

The Press in the French Revolution

A Selection of Documents taken from the
Press of the Revolution for the years 1789–1794

J. GILCHRIST
W. J. MURRAY

Cheshire
Ginn

First published in Australia in 1971
by F. W. Cheshire Publishing Pty Ltd
346 St. Kilda Road Melbourne
First published in Great Britain in 1971
by Ginn and Company Ltd
18 Bedford Row London WC1
© J. Gilchrist, W. J. Murray 1971

ISBN 0 7015 0467 6
ISBN 0 602 21922 1
37104

Printed in Great Britain by
Western Printing Services Ltd Bristol

Contents

Contents

Contents

Contents

Preface

In the early years of the French Revolution the press played an important and active role. Despite its importance, however, the revolutionary press has not been studied at any length by English historians. A survey of the standard commentaries and anthologies shows that, with one or two exceptions, the press is little used either as a source of material illustrative of the events of the Revolution or as a force in the making of those events. One such exception is L. G. W. Legg, *Select Documents Illustrative of the French Revolution: The Constituent Assembly* (Clarendon Press 1905), 2 vols., who uses the newspapers extensively, citing the originals with commentary in English. This work has useful introductory material, especially as a guide to documentary references, but the commentary is excessively biased towards the political notions of Legg's own time. E. L. Higgins, *The French Revolution as told by Contemporaries* (Cambridge, Mass. 1938)–with the documents translated–makes only occasional use of the press, e.g. of the *Révolutions de Paris* and of Marat's *Ami du peuple*. Nor will the reader, who is looking for material illustrative of the press, find much of use in the excellent collection edited and translated by John Hall Stewart, *A Documentary Survey of the French Revolution* (New York, 1951, reprinted 1964), which concentrates on official documents. J. M. Roberts and R. C. Cobb, *French Revolution Documents*, vol. I (Oxford 1966)–with more volumes to come–which replaces J. M. Thompson's *French Revolution Documents 1789–94* (Blackwell 1933, reprinted 1948)–makes very little use of the newspapers, and the documents are not translated. Nor does P. Dawson, *The French Revolution* (Prentice-Hall 1967), use the press in his selection of translated documents. Almost all the extracts in the present work are therefore appearing for the first time in English.

By contrast, French historians have made ample use of the newspapers. First there is the monumental collection of documents by P. J. B. Buchez and P. C. Roux in their *Histoire parlementaire de la Révolution française* (Paris 1834–8), 40 vols., which contains many extracts from the press and which the authors used extensively. The standard work on the press itself remains that of L. E. Hatin, *Histoire politique et littéraire de la presse en France* (Paris 1859–61), 8 vols. In addition to citing a number of documents from Hatin, we found him invaluable when writing the introduction. For a bibliographical survey of the press, there

xiii

is the important work by M. Tourneux, *Bibliographie de l'histoire de Paris pendant la Révolution française*, of which vol. II (Paris 1894) deals with the press. At the turn of the century A. Söderhjelm published *La Régime de la presse pendant la Révolution française* (Paris 1900), of which the authors made some use, but it is concerned mainly with the issue of press freedom and is not without error. Among more recent studies special mention must be made of G. Walter, *La Révolution française vue par ses journaux* (Paris 1948). This is an impressive collection of documents, extensively commented on, one that provides references to a number of newspapers that were not easily accessible. This together with Walter's biographies of individual journalists (Hébert, Marat, Chénier) and his catalogue of the newspaper holdings in the *Bibliothèque nationale*, supplied much useful information. There have been several general works on the press, but these will all be superseded by the *Histoire générale de la presse française*.*
J. L. Godechot has contributed the section on the Revolution and Empire in vol. I, covering a vast amount of material in a masterly fashion. His bibliography is excellent, including unpublished as well as published material. For the scholar working in French this work is indispensable. Professor Godechot very kindly allowed us to read his text before publication. As our manuscript had already been prepared, we used his work mainly to correct certain emphases and to add details relating to subscription figures and profitability of newspapers. It also enabled us to correct some errors. Finally, the reader may care to consult individual biographies of such leaders of the Revolution as Marat, Hébert, Desmoulins, and others, where their role in the press is treated as only one aspect of their career.

The absence of any comparable work in English to those of Walter or Godechot prompted the authors to make this initial excursion into a field that may well prove more fruitful to others. Although there is next to nothing in English on the French press in the period of the Revolution, it is or, we hope, it will become, fairly obvious that the press is worth studying. There seem to be two main reasons for considering the newspaper press of revolutionary France of importance: first, since France between 1789–92 allowed an unprecedented freedom to the press, the press provides a remarkably varied and rich source of contemporary comment, exposition of ideas, and illustration of events. Second, the press was one of the prime movers of the Revolution, and one of the most important organs of both revolutionary and counter-revolutionary propaganda. It could, for example, be argued that the unlimited freedom of the press was one of the reasons for the breakdown of some of the achievements of the Constituent Assembly.

* Published by Presses Universitaires de France. Vol. I (1969) covers the period from Origins to 1815; vol. II (1969), 1815–71; vol. III (in preparation), 1871–1940; vol. IV (in preparation), 1940 to the present day.

Therefore the present work seeks both to examine the role of the press–hence the somewhat lengthy introduction, which has been made doubly necessary because of the complete absence of anything in English on the press–and to illustrate events of the day from the newspapers. Some thirty newspapers have been used, which, although a large enough number, is still only a small proportion of the total number of titles available. For this the authors make no apologies. As a matter of policy, it was decided better to capture the flavour of a number of journals than lose the sense of them all. Most of the generally known titles have been cited, and some heavily. The exception is the *Gazette nationale*, better known under the title *Le Moniteur*. It is so well known and so readily available in most libraries that the authors have taken from it only one extract. However, it was used extensively in preparing the Introduction. Moreover, the most noteworthy feature of the *Moniteur* is its impartiality; this makes it an excellent source for the historian, but it does not give an accurate reflection of the temper of the times.

The extracts are presented in translation. This has not been an easy task considering the great variety of styles and language used by the various editors and contributors. The authors have tried to convey the differing styles of the originals, but they are conscious of the immense difficulty caused by such a writer as Hébert or Lemaire. The translation of certain words, e.g. *bougre, foutre,* has only been generally covered for it is quite impossible to restore to such words the significance and import they had in the late eighteenth century: thus *foutre* was a word in the Revolution that when used was bad enough to cause horror and consternation and was usually printed in shortened form f*****, although Hébert and Lemaire used it in full. In setting out the documents, spelling, headings, capitals and so forth have generally been standardised to accord with modern forms. The widespread and somewhat arbitrary use of capital letters in the originals has not been retained, except where they are clearly called for in headings.

This work could not have been completed without the cooperation and help of a number of institutions and individuals. We are above all indebted to the staff of the Barr Smith Library, the University of Adelaide, especially to Mrs Anne Bockman of the Inter-Library Loan Service; to Mr Ivan Page, Officer-in-Charge of Rare Books at the National Library, Canberra; and to Mrs Enderby and Mrs Featherston of the School of General Studies Library, also in Canberra. In Melbourne we received valuable help from both the State Library of Victoria and from the Baillieu Library, University of Melbourne.

Our especial thanks belong to the Department of History, the University of Adelaide, South Australia, where the greater part of this work was completed. The department generously provided funds for microfilms, Xerox articles, and research visits to other capital cities. The authors recall the forbearance of their former colleagues with gratitude. Mrs Gwen Rice, departmental secretary, handled the various drafts of the MS extremely capably and enabled us to meet the deadlines.

John Gilchrist would also like to record his own personal thanks to Trent University's generous grant-in-aid that enabled him to return to Australia for consultations with his co-author W. J. Murray.

Special mention should be made of those whose advice we sought at various stages of the preparation of the MS. Dr Alison Patrick of the History Department of the University of Melbourne generously offered us material and information on the early period of the Convention; Mr Alan Sykes of the Adelaide History Department assisted in the initial stages of the work. W. J. Murray also records his special thanks to Professor J. Godechot for his help in the area of his own research, research which is in part connected with this work as evidenced by the Introduction and documentary commentaries for which Murray was especially responsible.

Our former colleague Professor G. Rudé at a very early stage advised us about the worst pitfalls, which subsequently we learnt were legion. The mistakes and errors remain our own.

In bringing the MS to the press we are pleased to acknowledge the co-operation and help of Miss Sandra Forbes and Mr Charles Casement.

J. G.
W.J.M.

Introduction

The Press and the Early Years of the French Revolution

In the three years between the fall of the Bastille on 14 July 1789 and the fall of the monarchy on 10 August 1792, the press in France enjoyed a freedom not only unprecedented at that time, but a freedom that probably has not been tolerated since. Free from the restraints of law, uninhibited by boards of directors or the need to mollify advertisers, and unhindered by heavy overheads, it was a freedom that often degenerated into licence, as the press was used to slander individuals, to vent personal grievances, or to further the interests of a faction. But this is only part of the picture: out of this freedom emerged figures who were to make their names through their newspapers, Marat and Hébert being the most famous, while the prominent revolutionary leaders usually had an interest in at least one newspaper.

The newspaper of 1789 would in many instances scarcely pass for such today. In quality of production and of style there was an infinite variety; many short-lived news-sheets appeared and disappeared, while clumsily written editorials appeared at the same time as passages of great literary merit; between the bitter but beautiful polemics of André Chénier and the chatter of the 'Aristocratic hiccup' (*Le Hoquet aristocrate*) there were many gradations.

The press of the Revolution was overwhelmingly political. Its influence on the events of the time has been variously estimated, with no definite conclusions being drawn. But it can be said that despite widespread illiteracy and difficulties of circulation the press did make an impact at all levels of society, and contributed in large measure to that atmosphere of recrimination and uncertainty that added to the already difficult task of the Assemblies, keeping France, and more particularly Paris, in a state of incipient revolt. What can be said with more certainty is that the press of the early period of the Revolution allows insights into the mind of revolutionary France and provides the background of fire and violence that gives meaning to the cold print of the governments' impersonal decrees. The French press has been called both the child and the father of the Revolution; the press preparing for the fall of the Bastille, and the fall of the Bastille clearing the way for a torrent of free and unsolicited opinion. Part of the social and political revolution of 1789 was the revolution in the press.

I

The Growth of the Political Press — the Early Stages to 1789

Prior to the French Revolution the growth of the political press in France had been slow and under the strict authority of the royal court. This authority goes back to the efforts of the government under Francis I to prevent the spread of the Reformation. In 1521 he ruled that all books be licensed before printing, the University being the authorising body. In 1563 under Charles IX, and even as late as 1757, royal edicts reaffirmed the heaviest penalties for unlicensed printing. In part to protect authors and publishers from piracy, the licence or *privilège* was seen by the University mainly as a political weapon. It was partly to attack this growing independence of the University that Richelieu issued a *privilège* to Théophraste Renaudot to found the first French newspaper, the *Gazette,* in May 1631. In addition to clipping the wings of the University printers, Richelieu saw in this innovation a means of controlling the publication of news. Both he and Louis XIII often contributed entire articles to the *Gazette,* and ensured that its readers learned only what the government wanted them to learn. It was not until 1762, however, that the *Gazette* became the official organ for expressing royal opinion: on that date it came under the Minister for Foreign Affairs and changed its title to the *Gazette de France.*

To Renaudot, on the contrary, the idea of a newspaper owed nothing to motives of politics or propaganda: it came from a more humane consideration. Prior to 1631 Renaudot had been in charge of an institution for the sick and needy. In his efforts to ease their plight he sought work and other forms of relief by means of a *Bureau d'adresse et de rencontre,* which performed the function of what today would be called 'small ads'. He thought also that by circulating stories and news he might distract his charges from their plight. These two concerns came together to suggest the idea of a newspaper.

In claiming that Renaudot founded the first French newspaper, it should be borne in mind that by newspaper is meant a publication that appears regularly and undertakes to give details of all items of interest as soon as possible after they come to hand. Before this, news had been disseminated by various means, usually, when not orally, by occasional news-sheets or *canards.* A feature of these *canards* was the long 'headline' designed to rouse the curiosity of the public. Thus when Renaudot took to publishing his newspaper he was careful to distinguish it from these *canards* by omitting sensationalism from the front page. Instead he started with news of events furthest from Paris and ended with events in the capital. Except for a few exceptions, notably during the Revolution, the idea of using 'headlines' was not revived until late in the nineteenth century.

During the Frondes there sprang up that myriad of libels known as

2

mazarinades, from the title of the most famous of them, issued in March 1651. Mazarin himself took no action against the authors, and France at this time was said to be 'an absolute monarchy tempered by songs'. The excesses of the Frondes killed this liberty of the press, and with the restoration of order censorship was re-enforced.

Some of the *gazettes en vers*, which were broadsheets written entirely in verse and a special feature of this period, persisted. In 1672 they formed the basis of the new *Mercure galant*, the prototype of the *petite presse* which specialised in comment in a lighter vein, combining prose and verse and including articles of universal interest–but no politics. The *Mercure galant* came under its better-known title of *Mercure de France* in 1724, when it added to its front page the notification 'Dedicated to the King'.

Seven years prior to the founding of the *Mercure*, the prototype of the literary and scientific newspaper had been launched when Denis de Sallo was granted the *privilège exclusif* for his *Journal des savants*. The fame of this paper spread well beyond France, and Voltaire called it the 'father of all similar works to be found everywhere in Europe today'.

By extending the *privilège* to these latter papers, the way was opened for the introduction of other papers of a specialist nature, without intruding on the *Gazette*'s political monopoly. In the eighteenth century such specialist newspapers became widespread: e.g. for medicine, religion, jurisprudence, economics, agriculture, finance, theatre, music, education, etc. They might also be a cover for more seditious writings. Despite the interest in, and commercial advantages of, the buying of newspaper space, it was not until 1751 that a newspaper developed the 'advertising' side of Renaudot's *Gazette* when the *Feuille de bureau d'adresse* devoted itself exclusively to this function. In England the *Public Advertiser* had appeared in 1657. France was later too in introducing its first daily; the *Journal de Paris* appeared on 1 January 1777, 75 years after its British counterpart, the *Daily Courant*. Nevertheless, if not always the first in the field and acknowledged as backward in terms of its political press, the French press surpassed the British press in most other fields of journalism.

The system of *privilège* that was the basis of this backwardness was resented by the liberal thinkers who were challenging the basic structure of French society at this time. It was a resentment that was in some measure dampened by the practice of the censorship, which allowed the growth of an influential clandestine press, a press that was to contribute in no small way to the events that led up to the Revolution of 1789. The two masters of the press in France in the decades before the Revolution were the *directeur de la librairie* (director-general of the book trade) and the *lieutenant de police*. The former nominated inspectors and could suspend the distribution of books: he could also correct the excesses of the law. Following the death of Louis XIV he often accorded the 'tacit permission' to print and sell, whereby books which did not have the king's *privilège* were allowed to be published in France under the imprint of a foreign place of publication. The *lieutenant* also had wide powers, which included the seizure of books at will. Responsible to these authorities were the censors, whose abilities and qualifications were constantly under fire. If they approved a book they were said to issue a 'certificate of stupidity'; if they refused, this was noted as an act of pusillanimity. To these taunts were added the accusation that their censorship enriched Holland, Britain and Switzerland at the expense of France. Nor were they treated any more justly by their superiors.

In the closing years of the old régime the public disdained the official or tolerated newspapers, preferring the foreign *Gazette de Leyde* or the *Courrier de l'Europe*. Only three French newspapers competed with the foreign newspapers: Linguet's *Annales*, which boldly attacked the Academy and the *parlements*; the *Journal de Paris*, under the patronage of 'Papa Grand-homme', enjoying the support of 3,000 subscribers; and the *Journal français*, equally popular but of a quite different stamp—its main desire was to see the *philosophes* bled and purged. However, it was mainly from the clandestine brochures that the public informed itself on the news it wanted; only in these pamphlets could you read a diatribe against the Church, details of a scandal at court, or a satire against a leading public figure. Then as ever censorship was the key to a best-seller. Forbidden pamphlets were the fashion, and their concealment a game.

In the late 1780s there existed veritable dens of pamphlet producers, of which that at the house of the banker Kornmann had a great influence on public opinion. To his house came individuals intent on the destruction of the existing institutions; among these individuals were figures who were later to achieve fame in the Revolution, not least through the influence of their newspapers; these included Brissot, Carra, Gorsas and the comte de Mirabeau.

Affairs in the book trade were showing that the old régime could not go on unreformed. The agents of the government were always ready to betray it, whether they were customs officers who allowed booksellers to bribe them, or superintendents of police who seized pamphlets only to sell them to their own profit. The inspectors too thought nothing of deceiving their chief, the director-general. This clandestine press, encouraged by those with an interest in maintaining the existing institutions, was proving to be one of the main solvents of the old order. Each rivalled the other in destroying its own supports.

The existence of activities such as this gives some plausibility to the scheme announced by Mercier in his celebrated *Tableau de Paris*, the twelve volumes of which appeared between 1781 and 1788. Under

his scheme the fiscal problems of the government, the political pre-
tentions of the writers, and the needs of the reading public, would be
solved at the same time. He claimed that French journals and other
publications had little interest, that they did not give the public what
it wanted, that their prose was insipid and their verse even worse. These
publications, he claimed, were full of acrimonious disputes among men
of letters, while editors, watching their subscribers fall away daily,
went around in circles trying to rearrange their material in a vain
effort to please their readers. Not only the editors but the paper
manufacturers and the printers were feeling this loss. His solution was
that all *privilège* be suppressed for journals, gazettes and other publications, and that every news-sheet pay a tax on condition that the press
be free. Then, he said, newspapers without number would burst into
being to rejoice the nation and enrich the treasury.

The first part of Mercier's prediction might be said to have become
a fact; the second was never implemented; but his third prognostication
about the type of press that would emerge takes on an ironical ring
when the newspapers of the Revolution are considered. For the press
that Mercier saw arising was to be in conformity with the nature of the
French people–it would necessarily be humorous. Every laugh was to
raise by so much the net profit. The clink of the coins in the treasury
and the hearty laughs of the reading public were to increase in ever-
growing harmony. The king would have his money, the people would
have their fun.

Perhaps in other circumstances Mercier's ideas might have been more
appropriate, but by 5 July 1788, when the king inadvertently opened
the way to the abolition of the *privilège*, the nation was not in the mood
for joking. On that date the king invited all 'erudite and educated
people' to express their opinions on the convocation of the Estates-
General and to send these opinions to the Keeper of the Seals. This
decree gave courage to those hitherto fearful of expressing their ideas,
but instead of addressing themselves to the Keeper of the Seals they
addressed themselves to the public. They sought not to enlighten the
king but the whole nation, nor did they feel restrained by a lack of
'erudition'. At this time of France's great economic and fiscal crisis,
they issued a flood of pamphlets to a public roused to optimism by the
forthcoming meeting of the Estates-General. Necker and the king tried
to stem the flood but police action was so clumsy and severe that it
succeeded only in rousing indignation.

In any case they were powerless to act against the crowds that
gathered in the open or the groups that met in cafés to discuss the events
of the day. These 'oral gazetteers' (*gazétiers de la bouche*) became well-
organised groups and took on themselves the task of giving information
to the crowd. In this, and in the elections to the Estates-General,

demands for freedom of the press were prominent. In the *cahiers* only a minority of the nobles and clergy did not demand this freedom. Even before his famous *Qu'est-ce-que le Tiers État?* Sieyès had released a pamphlet, in November 1788, entitled *Essai sur les privilèges*, that raised quite a stir. The conclusion to this pamphlet was that to give as an exclusive privilege to one that which belonged to all was to wrong the whole for the sake of the part–an absurdity and an injustice.

In the first fortnight of April 1789 Brissot challenged the authority of the *directeur* when he issued a prospectus for a bi-weekly newspaper to appear in that month. His challenge was met. On the 16th the authorities forbade the distribution of Brissot's projected newspaper 'for which no permission had been granted or accorded' and a circular to this effect was distributed among the officers concerned.

It appears that a first edition of Brissot's proposed paper did appear in early May, but in any case the challenge to the authorities had by then been taken up by a more redoubtable opponent. A few days before the opening of the Estates-General, Mirabeau issued a prospectus for a newspaper to be sold three times a week, which would deal with, first, the various matters arising from the meeting of the Estates-General; second, a faithful analysis of the most distinguished writings of the day; third, letters to the editor, provided they discussed only truly public affairs and the national interest.

On 5 May the first edition, under the title of *États-généraux*, appeared. On the following day a second number was issued, severely criticising the procedures being adopted at the Assembly. The *Conseil d'État* countered with two successive decrees on the 6th and 7th. The first decree forbade the 'printing, publishing, or distributing of any prospectus, journal or other periodical, whatever its denomination'. The second was aimed specifically at Mirabeau's *États-généraux*, which was denounced as injurious, hiding under the mantle of liberty the elements of licence. Undeterred, Mirabeau used his rights as a parliamentarian, being the representative of the Third Estate from Provence, to send 'open letters' to his constituents. He merely changed the title of his paper to the *Lettres du comte de Mirabeau à ses commettants*. Thus the authorities were thwarted, and Mirabeau continued to publish his paper unhindered by official sanctions.

On 8 May the assembly of the electors of the Third Estate of Paris, in what can be considered the first opposition of the Municipality against the government, had protested against the decree of the *Conseil* which attempted to muzzle Mirabeau, denouncing it as violating 'the liberty of the press being demanded by the whole of France'. In part yielding to such pressures, in part to re-assert its authority, the administration invited, on 19 May, the 'authorised' papers–the *Gazette*, the *Mercure* and the *Journal de Paris*–to report on the meetings of the

Estates-General 'but limiting themselves to the facts of which they have exact knowledge, and without allowing themselves any reflections or commentaries'. At the same time circulation of some other newspapers was tolerated: notably Barère's *Point du jour*, Le Hodey's *Journal des États-généraux* (from 1 June) and Poncelin's *Courrier français*. None of these papers did more than give as closely as they could a verbatim account of the debates at Versailles.

On 23 May the king requested that the Estates-General examine and make known to him 'the most appropriate means of reconciling the liberty of the press with the respect due to religion, custom and the honour of the citizen'. The request was never carried out. Events decided the question of the freedom of the press. It was seized following the fall of the Bastille and the new ruling powers were unable or unwilling to do anything about it. On 19 July the *Révolutions de Paris* made its auspicious entry on the Paris scene, heralding the opening of a new era in the history of the French press. For the next four and a half years the *Révolutions de Paris* would hold competently and virtually continuously its position in the first ranks of the Parisian press.

The Growth of the Political Press—1789–94

Between July and December 1789 no fewer than 250 newspapers were offered to the public, many of them to be forgotten as soon as they appeared, but already Marat's growling suspicions and Desmoulins' biting humour were making themselves felt; the *Annales patriotiques* was being received joyfully by the people of Paris; Brissot's long-announced paper appeared under the title *Patriote français* on 28 July; while Gorsas' *Courrier de Versailles à Paris*, which had first appeared on 5 July, gained a new spirit after the fall of the Bastille on the 14th.

The main papers of the old régime were at first little affected. The *Gazette* did not report the fall of the Bastille, perhaps in the belief that any mention of the changes operating might in some way condone them. The *Journal de Paris* continued in its cautious, circumspect reporting, pleasing its growing liberal clientele, but rousing the wrath of the radicals. At the offices of the *Mercure*, Mallet du Pan could now wield his pen with the freedom he desired, although he was soon to turn against what he considered the excesses of the Revolution. The *Journal général de France* would by the end of the year appear daily instead of three times a week, but without a consequent increase in influence.

The opponents of the Revolution were slow to react to the new political power wielded by the democratic press; indeed, it was not until later in the year that they began to group their forces. However, on the eve of the fall of the Bastille, one of the most bitter critics of the changing social and political scene began to make his voice felt in a regular paper. On 12 July Antoine de Rivarol, together with the ineffectual abbé Sabbatier, launched the *Journal politique national*, which was in fact a pamphlet of sustained hostility to the Revolution and to all those who, in the author's estimation, had brought it about. For Rivarol the Revolution began with the calling of the Estates-General. Later in the year, on 15 September, Brune issued the first number of what eventually became the ultra-right-wing *Journal de la Cour et de la Ville*. But it was not until Brune was replaced by Gautier de Syonnet, and the paper became known as the *Petit-Gautier*, that it won its reputation for violence against the Revolution. The *Gazette de Paris* was another extreme right-wing paper that started out as a supporter of the Revolution, yet by 1790 was an implacable enemy. It first appeared, written by the poet *manqué* Durosoi, on 1 October, praising the Revolution, royalty and aristocracy—a combination of principles that would become increasingly difficult to maintain. The next month, on 2 November, aristocratic resistance of a unique kind was put into operation with the *Actes des Apôtres*. The founder of the paper was Peltier, who turned against the Revolution after the October days, and the main contributors were a group of several-talented and witty young men who had been successful in the old régime. It may be noted that one of the most extreme of the opponents of the Revolution, the *Ami du Roi*, did not appear until June of 1790.

These are just some of the more important newspapers that helped to influence the events of the next few years. In the rush of new publications the search for a suitable title was considered important if the attention of the public was to be caught. The titles varied greatly. There were many *Amis*, *Annales*, *Journals*, *Gazettes*, *Courriers*, *Défenseurs*, *Bulletins* and *Chroniques*; a spate of *Anti*'s and *Contre*'s. Others, in their search for 'gimmicky' titles, might settle for 'The Aristocratic Vomit' (*Le Vomissement aristocratique*), 'The Patriotic Hen' (*La Poule patriotique*)— named in opposition to 'The Cock's Crow' (*Le Chant du coq*)–'The Stupidities of the Week' (*Les Sottises de la Semaine*), or 'The National Denouncer' (*Le Dénonciateur national*). The use of a title was fought over on more than one occasion, the most notable being that between Lemaire and Hébert over the *Père Duchesne*, while there were often attempts by counterfeiters to use the fame of other titles to their own advantage–Marat in particular was plagued by these 'false friends'. It was common for a paper to be headed by a motto, which might be inspiring or instructive: the aristocratic press delighted in dating its publications 'year 0 of liberty', 'the year of equality in misery', 'the year 1 of anarchy' and so on.

Almost all the major dailies were a single sheet folded over once to make a newspaper of 4 quarto pages. They often added supplements of

2, 4 or even more pages, either to report events of special interest, or to allow a correspondent to print a private opinion. The weeklies, on the other hand, were generally in-octavo, and the extent varied from paper to paper: Desmoulins' *Révolutions de France et de Brabant* appeared regularly with 48 pages; Prudhomme's *Révolution de Paris* varied from 32 to 56 pages; the *Feuille villageoise* from 16 to 24. The *Mercure de France* was a notable exception. It came out in duodecimo, but made up for its minuscule size by the number of pages–a regular 72 for the political section alone. The *Moniteur* coming out in-folio was also exceptional. The satirical papers, and those bearing the imprint of one author, such as Marat's or Hébert's, were mainly in-octavo and irregular in appearance, if not in extent. Of the satirical papers, for example, the *Actes des Apôtres* was supposed to appear every two days, but often it had more than one number compressed into one issue, while in length it varied from 8 to 64 pages. Other papers appeared regularly twice and three times weekly.

As was the custom in France, unlike Britain, newspapers were bought by subscription. Nevertheless, during the Revolution street-sellers became common, and posed a problem to the Municipality, which objected to the swarms of vendors proclaiming the latest events from newspapers of which they knew nothing. Many of these papers (since in practice there was no restriction on publication except the cost of a press, paper, ink and type) were badly printed and shockingly written, and their existence ceased when the author had satisfied his grievance. With such publications circulation was usually in keeping with their origins; but among the more influential papers were works of some magnitude– such as the *Moniteur*, the *Patriote français*, the *Révolutions de Paris*, the *Point du jour*, the *Mercure de France*, the *Gazette universelle*, the *Journal du Soir*, the *Journal de Paris* and *Chronique de Paris*. The usual circulation was 2,000 to 5,000, but the figure of 200,000 was claimed for the *Révolutions de Paris* at the funeral oration of its most famous writer, Elysée Loustallot, and the *Père Duchesne* was said to have reached a million when it was sub-sidised and distributed to the army in 1793. It is possible that the readers of the *Révolutions de Paris* reached 200,000; of the *Père Duchesne* it can be said that at the height of its fame it was the best-known paper in France.

The provincial press was considerably smaller. The *Courrier d'Avignon* reached a subscription figure of 3,000 during the Revolution, but more typical was the *Journal de Marseilles*, which could make a profit out of 300 subscribers before the Revolution, yet in 1792 had increased this figure to only 500. The Parisian press was dominant throughout France; Fontenay's right-wing *Journal général*, although barely known in Paris, sold 7,000 copies in the provinces.

For many editors, publishers and writers the newspaper was a lucrative source of income. This was despite, although in some ways because of (for it reduced overheads), the primitive stage of development of the printing-press in France at that time. The social and political revolution was not accompanied by a technological one. The presses were manually operated, and it required 24 hours for one press to print 3,000 sheets. Thus a daily with a circulation of 12,000 needed to have four presses working continuously to keep up with the demand. Most dailies charged 30 to 36 livres for an annual subscription–about two sous a copy. The *Révolutions de Paris*, a weekly, charged 14 sous a copy. It has been calculated that the *Patriote français*, selling more than 5,000, could, even with a subscription figure of 3,000, make an annual profit of 30,500 livres. Out of this the director Brissot received no more than 6,000 livres. Durosoi, whose enterprise was more fully controlled by himself, could make 6,000 livres a year from his *Gazette de Paris*. The editors of two of the most substantial papers, Mallet du Pan of the *Mercure de France* and D-J Garat of the *Journal de Paris*, received salaries of more than 12,000 livres a year for their work. In Garat's case this was in addition to the 18 livres a day he received as a deputy in the National Assembly. This was at a time when a worker's wage was about one livre a day, or the annual income of a clerk 1,500 to 2,400 livres, and that of a chief-officer in the ministry 5,000 to 6,000. Advertising space was sold, but a more substantial boost to profits might come from subsidies by an interested faction or individual–perhaps the king or the Duke of Orléans.

The Press and the Revolution

The press of the Revolution can be fitted into three broad categories. First, those papers created to propagate the author's own opinions: often they consisted of one article written by the sole editor. While most such papers were short lived, two of the most famous, those of Marat and Hébert, belonged to this class. Second, there were those most concerned with giving information, often an evening paper and essentially a commercial enterprise. For the latter reason they might change their opinions in the course of the Revolution. Third were the specialised papers, founded by a society, club or ministerial department.

The history of the press of the Revolution can be fitted into even more clearly defined categories. Between 14 July 1789 and 10 August 1792 the press was free for all shades of opinion; the tenth of August eliminated the royalists, leaving the differences of the Jacobins and of the Girondins to keep alive the freedom of the press. The victory of the Jacobins as a result of the insurrection of 31 May–2 June 1793 left them, in alliance with the sans-culottes, with a monopoly of the field–with a few notable exceptions. The events of 9 Thermidor restored the freedom of the press, but even before the advent of Napoleon this freedom had been dealt a severe blow by the Directory's decree of 18 Fructidor, Year V (4 September 1797).

In this first period, to the fall of the monarchy, the press played its most significant role. The freedom of the press, taken and not granted, was recognised on 24 August 1789 when Robespierre had inserted in the Declaration of the Rights of Man that it was the right of every individual to 'speak, write and print freely, on his own responsibility for the abuse of this liberty in cases determined by law'.

At first the press was hesitant in the face of this new-found freedom. But as the aristocratic press got under way with its mockery of the reforms of the Assembly, and as the decrees of the Assembly did not meet the approval of the radicals, the war of words developed in intensity.

The counter-revolutionary press, although in a minority in the early months, was more united, had in its employ some of the most skilful writers, and enjoyed more substantial financial backing. For some papers this meant subsidies out of the king's Civil List. The 'patriot' press, on the other hand, was more divided against itself, reflecting the disagreements that started to divide the revolutionaries from as early as the debates on the prerogatives of the king in the new constitution. Following the flight of the king and the 'massacre' on the Champ de Mars in mid-1791 the divisions among the Third Estate came into the open. The Assembly issued a decree, on 18 July, against what it considered the most inflammatory papers, but after a period of vigorous activity this decree was relaxed. At this time the device of 'placarding' the walls of the city with newspapers became very popular. The *Chant du coq*, paid for out of the Civil List to de-popularise the republicans, especially Brissot, was often posted over Tallien's *Ami des citoyens*. A new method of reply, noted the *Chronique de Paris*, that does not entail long discussion. As the popularity of this method of broadcasting opinion grew, the *Chronique* added the further remark that 'the walls seemed to sweat calumny'.

In 1792 the press was giving way to the clubs as one of the main influences in forming public opinion. As internal and external crisis deepened, the press became more and more purely destructive in its criticisms. The counter-revolutionaries re-doubled their fury, and continued to call on insurrection from within and foreign aid from abroad, and unhesitatingly indicated to France's enemies the best points for an invasion of the country. In reply the patriots demanded reprisals, but they were still divided among themselves. Brissot accused Marat of being an accomplice of Royou, the arch-royalist, with his attacks on the Assembly. Marat retaliated with details of scandals from Brissot's past. The 'great joys' and 'great angers' of the *Père Duchesne* gained in popularity, but, like Marat, it was not until after 10 August that his peak of popularity would be reached.

Following 10 August, the arrest of all counter-revolutionary authors was ordered and their presses distributed among the patriots. Marat, Gorsas, Hébert, Carra and some others were the main beneficiaries in the share of these spoils. Durosoi of the *Gazette de Paris* was executed on 25 August–the first journalist to be condemned to death by the new Revolutionary Tribunal.

Between 10 August 1792 and 31 May 1793, the press was not much more than an echo of the disputes raging in clubs and in the Convention between the Girondins and the Jacobins. Press reports, usually concentrated on the work of the Convention, often developed into mere personal abuse, and the impeachments of Marat and Hébert in 1793 were not so much attacks on the press as attacks by Girondins on Jacobin opponents. In the Girondin ranks the main protagonists were the *Patriote français*–since the autumn of 1791 edited by Girey-Dupré, but still following the principles of Brissot–Gorsas' *Courrier des départements*, the *Chronique de Paris* and Carra's *Annales patriotiques*. While Roland held the position of Minister of the Interior, Louvet's *Sentinelle* was financed out of the public funds to placard Paris with Girondin ideas, and other newspapers enjoyed to a lesser extent this government assistance: for example, the *Patriote*, the *Courrier*, and Dulaure's professedly impartial *Thermomètre du jour*. The *Révolutions de Paris* maintained an uneasy impartiality, as it had done throughout 1792. By comparison, the Jacobin papers were less imposing but more powerful, with the popularity approaching fanaticism that was held by Marat and Hébert among the sans-culottes of Paris. The second of June spelled the 'tenth of August' of the Girondins.

The field now remained to the Jacobins and the sans-culottes, but under the strict censorship of a government fighting a desperate war. One lone voice cried out against the 'committee of public misfortune', the 'men of prey', the 'scoundrels of the Mountain'–a voice which labelled Robespierre the 'king of the Jacobins', a 'fox' and a '*tartuffe*'. This was Roch-Marcandier, the *Véritable ami du peuple*, who, from his hiding place in a barn, printed his paper and had his wife placard it in the night. His paper ceased to appear after 28 June and almost a year later he and his wife were discovered and executed. His publication, Hatin says, was not so much a newspaper as an act of courage.

In December 1793 there appeared another great act of courage –one which was also a brilliant piece of journalism. This was the *Vieux Cordelier* of Camille Desmoulins. This paper, from the man who had played such a prominent role in the early days of the Revolution and who was now questioning the direction it was taking, was an impassioned plea for clemency for suspects and for a general relaxation of the Terror. Inspired in part by Danton, it was nevertheless written and presented by Desmoulins, costing him his life three months later.

On 28 February 1794, Prudhomme announced that 'due to the breakdown of [his] health' he would have to bring his *Révolutions de Paris* to a close. In March 1794 Hébert too was executed, and Desmoulins a fortnight later. With the deaths of these prominent journalists and the end of the *Révolutions de Paris* an era in the history of the press was closed. G. Walter, the author of many works concerning the French press, says that the press of 1794 until the fall of Robespierre underwent a total debasement, that after the fall of Hébert there appeared only 'living corpses'. Mention should be made, however, of Guffroy's *Rougyff* (an anagram on his name) *ou le Franc en vedette*. With his paper appearing twice a week, Guffroy saw himself as the successor to Marat and the emulator of the style of Hébert: he called for an end to all nobles–'too bad for the good ones–if there is such a thing'–and demanded that the guillotine 'be in permanence throughout the land', for, according to his estimation, 'France can get by quite well with five million inhabitants'. As an 'ultra-revolutionary', he was rendered suspect and had to cease publication in Prairial, Year II.

The fall of Robespierre on 9 Thermidor, Year II, brought a complete reaction and resurgence of the press, and the Constitution of the Year III consecrated once more the principle of freedom of the press. Yet even before Napoleon swept out the Directory and imposed the strictest controls on the press, the press had already been dealt a mortal blow. On 18 Fructidor, Year V (4 September 1797), following the coup which returned France to dictatorship, the walls of the capital were placarded with the warning that anyone recalling royalty or the Constitution of 1793 would be shot. Napoleon did not kill the press: he merely delivered the *coup de grâce*.

Editors and Newspapers: a consideration of the better known journals

(i) Pro-revolutionary

Mirabeau and Brissot are the most familiar of the first champions of the press. Mirabeau's *Courrier de Provence*, appearing three times a week, continued until the close of the Constituent Assembly–six months after his death. Long before then Mirabeau had ceased to play an active role in the paper, whose main importance is in the early months of the Revolution, when, as echoing Mirabeau's powerful eloquence, it defended the newly won freedoms of the people. The chief of these freedoms, claimed Mirabeau, was the freedom of thought, without which other liberties could not be conquered. The greatest of the orators at the Constituent Assembly and the initiator of many important reforms, Mirabeau's part at the Assembly is related in detail in his paper. The object of ridicule of the aristocrats, who lampooned him ferociously in their papers, Mirabeau's popularity with the people was saved by his timely death in April 1791. For although his financial dealings and conspiracies with the court were mainly suspicions, the radical press was beginning to turn cool towards him.

Brissot the politician has in many ways overshadowed the role of Brissot the journalist. Nevertheless his *Patriote français* ranks as one of the most important papers of the Revolution. Destined by his bourgeois father for the law, Brissot, 'avid for glory', embarked on a career as a writer. His talents as a translator took him to London in 1786 where he became involved in the anti-slavery movement, and a business deal on his return to France involved a trip to the United States where he studied the problem at first hand. At the same time he met Washington and Franklin, and after four months in the States he returned to France fired with enthusiasm for the young republic. These and other liberal ideals he promoted in his *Patriote français*, to which Condorcet, Pétion, Thomas Paine and the abbé Grégoire were some of the more prominent contributors.

The young man who took over from Brissot in the autumn of 1791, Girey-Dupré, continued to edit it on the principles established by its founder. The *Patriote* of late 1792 and 1793 is of great importance for the Jacobin-Girondin faction fights. By then the *Patriote* was placing more emphasis on the latter half of its motto: 'The scourge of the courts and the terror of the terrorists.' Girey-Dupré died with the other Girondins in October 1793. At his trial he proudly told his judges, 'I knew Brissot, and I attest that he lived like Aristeides and that he died like Sidney, a martyr of liberty.'

The *Révolutions de Paris* is one of the most distinguished papers of the Revolution. Founded and controlled by J. L. Prudhomme, it was written by authors who largely remained anonymous, or were only vaguely known. Headed by its famous epigram:

The great appear such	(*Les grands ne nous paraissent grand*
Only because we are on our knees:	*Que parce que nous sommes à genoux:*
Let us stand up!	*Levons-nous!*)

it came out weekly replete with details of all the events in and around Paris. Free from the influence of factions or powerful individuals, it is for this reason a comparatively impartial paper. Not that it was moderate; on the contrary it is a paper that bristles with indignation against what it considered injustices. But it is reasonably free from the virulence of the extremists of left and right. The circulation figure of 200,000 claimed for it, if exaggerated, at least points to a better than usual circulation. Like Brissot's *Patriote* it was sold overseas. Other papers might give more details of the deliberations of the Assemblies, or present more light on the decisions of the clubs; but none gives a more complete and judicious account of the first few years of the Revolution, especially so far as Paris is concerned. Desmoulins called it the 'encyclopaedia of the Revolution'.

If little is known of the later writers for Prudhomme's *Révolutions* at least the fame of his first main writer was acclaimed at the time. The early death of this young man, Elysée Loustallot, sent both the Jacobin and Cordelier Clubs into mourning for three days, and cut short the flowering of the writer whom Michelet considered the first of all the revolutionary journalists.

Loustallot's life was marked by modesty and untiring concern for the interests of the less fortunate sections of the community. Not content with just decrying the fate of the poor, he worked in their midst. In his paper, rather than make just vague cries for justice, he would quote the price of bread and equate it to a worker's wage. A severe critic of any decree that attacked the sovereignty of the people, which he interpreted in the broadest terms, he was beginning to despair at the turn events were taking in 1790 when the news of the 'massacre' at Nancy* is said to have struck him a mortal blow. Reporting his funeral, and reprinting the funeral oration that he himself delivered, Desmoulins quoted Loustallot's No. 60 referring to the massacre: 'How can I narrate with a leaden heart? How can I reflect when my feelings are torn with despair? I see them there, these corpses strewn about the streets of Nancy. . . . Await rascals, the press that uncovers all crimes and dispels all errors will deprive you of your joy and of your strength: how sweet it would be to be your last victim!' To which Desmoulins added the comment, 'Certainly one could die more usefully for one's country, but not more gloriously.'

Marat's assessment of Loustallot, whom he thought would 'live for ever in the glorious annals of the Revolution', typically included an attack on the apathy of the people: 'Endowed with a calm spirit,' he wrote, 'just, methodical, matured in the fullness of time, he would have been marvellously fitted to shape the liberty of a new people; in a happy nation, his loss would have been appreciable; it would have been disheartening in an oppressed nation; but in a nation menaced with servitude his loss is bitter and cruel.'

Prudhomme did not allow the fortunes of his newspaper to fade. To

* Throughout 1790, division between the rank and file in the army and its aristocratic officers had resulted in endemic rebellion. With discipline suffering, the situation seemed to be reaching a crisis. When Bouillé, cousin of the commander-in-chief of the army, Lafayette, crushed a rebellion of the garrison at Nancy in August 1790 and followed it up with harsh punishments, Lafayette endorsed his prompt action and the Assembly added its approval. Bouillé, within a year to be a declared enemy of the Revolution, was in August 1790 already strongly suspected of aristocratic sympathies.

his credit he maintained it in the principles established by Loustallot. Among the known later writers for the *Révolutions de Paris* are Chaumette, Sylvain Maréchal, Fabre d'Eglantine and Saintonax.

Although he managed to avoid involvement in the Jacobin-Girondin disputes, Prudhomme was arrested after 2 June 1793. He was released almost immediately, and later claimed that his arrest was due to the personal animosity of Lacroix of the Unité Section, who had been denounced in his paper.

Between 3 August 1793 and 28 October 1793 there was a break in the publication of the *Révolutions*. On its resumption Prudhomme explained the interruption in terms of his ill-health, caused by his 'arduous labours over the last four years'. A constant upholder of the principle of the freedom of the press, Prudhomme was finding it increasingly difficult to survive the régime of the Terror. Again pleading the state of his health, and adding that his mission was complete because the people were 'on their feet', Prudhomme closed down his enterprise on 28 February 1794.

Mirabeau, Brissot and the *Révolutions de Paris* each occupies a special place in the history of the revolutionary press, yet to most people it is the names of Marat's *Ami du peuple* and Hébert's *Père Duchesne* that are most closely associated with the press of this period. Add to these Desmoulins, first with his *Révolutions de France et de Brabant* and later with his *Vieux Cordelier*, and we have the three best known of the journalists of the Revolution.

Before the Revolution *Marat* had been variously engaged in medicine, science, philosophy, politics and literature and had visited London, Edinburgh, Madrid, Stockholm and Saint Petersburg. On his own account he had been in search of glory since his first day at school—a goal which eluded him until the Revolution. The means of achieving this goal was his newspaper, begun as the *Publiciste parisien* on 12 September 1789, but better known by the name it adopted on the 16th of that month, the *Ami du peuple*. Even with the further changes of title on 25 September 1792 to the *Journal de la République française* and after 9 March 1793 to the *Publiciste de la République française*, Marat was always the 'Friend of the people'!

Violence is Marat's mark of distinction. He perhaps anticipated this when he wrote in the prospectus announcing his paper that 'The reader will often be surprised at the boldness of the ideas [expressed]; but he will always find in them liberty without licence, vigour without violence; wisdom without deviation.' This was Marat's opinion. Others thought differently, and of the journalists of the Revolution none was more harried by the authorities than Marat. Signs of his often fugitive existence are in the frequent changes of printers for the paper, the poor quality of the paper itself, and the host of typographical errors that Marat eventually gave up trying to rectify. For a brief spell in October and November 1789 no edition of the *Ami du peuple* appeared, as the Municipality sought Marat's arrest. Similar persecution forced him to leave France, and between 22 January 1790 and 18 May 1790 publication of the *Ami du peuple* was suspended while its author spent an enforced stay in Britain. Following the Champ de Mars affair Marat's presses were broken and he was again forced into hiding. In December 1791, having roused the wrath of the Legislative Assembly, which he claimed was as much an enemy of the people as its predecessor, Marat felt obliged to go for a second time to Great Britain, but for a much shorter period. His return to writing was solicited by the Cordelier Club, and on 12 April 1792 he again took up his pen in what he thought was the interest of the Revolution. Once more the authorities thought otherwise and on 4 May, just three weeks later, his arrest was ordered–along with that of the abbé Royou–for inciting the army to revolt and to murder its leaders.

It was not until after 10 August 1792, and particularly during 1793, that Marat won the undisputed popularity of the people of Paris. Before that he was distrusted by many, while some even considered him an imaginary character. However that may be, his writings were never far from the public eye and behind the threats and the suspicions, and even his at times barely concealed contempt for the people, there was a realism that gained credence as the threat to the Revolution increased. The more disastrous the turn of events, the more the people were pushed to the conclusion that Marat was, as he kept telling them he was, the truest defender of the Revolution.

Marat's vocabulary, if clear cut, tends to repetition; 'traitors', 'cheats', 'rogues' being some of the words he was fondest of using. To Marat the authorities were invariably corrupt and poisoned with aristocracy. He was continually calling on the people to insurrection, berating them for their apathy, and with the outbreak of war he urged the soldiers to assassinate their aristocratic officers. Uncompromisingly suspicious, some of his suspicions were bound to prove well founded; persons were spared no less than institutions, and Marat did not shrink from giving the name and address of any traitor in need of correction. Towards the heroes of 1789–Necker, Bailly and Lafayette–he maintained a campaign of unflagging hatred. Because of his continual fury Marat's attacks, often founded on fact and good sense, lack balance. Unlike the *Père Duchesne*, with his 'great joys' as well as his 'great angers', the friend of the people was always in a rage.

Some of Marat's solutions to the problems of the nation show signs of paranoia; he often called for a dictatorship as the sole means of salvation: the people had to be saved despite themselves. Other solutions he suggested to bring about the completion of the constitution were to parade a few heads outside the Assembly or to stone the unfaithful deputies to death. One of his more spectacular ideas for getting rid of counter-revolutionary deputies was to lock them up in the National Assembly and then set fire to it.

Marat's death, stabbed in his bath by Charlotte Corday, has been immortalised in the painting by David. It is fitting that Corday gained entry to Marat's house by promising to disclose more plots; it is fitting too that Marat should then have been engaged in the compilation of his newspaper. On 14 July 1793, the day after Marat's death, the last number of the 'Friend of the People' appeared.

On 28 November 1789 *Camille Desmoulins*, already famous as one of the orators who called the people in the Palais-Royal to arms on 12 July and as the author of the pamphlets *La France libre* and the *Discours de la lanterne aux Parisiens*, issued the first number of his weekly *Révolutions de France et de Brabant*. The Brabant part of the title refers to the revolution which, it was hoped, would break out in the Belgian provinces. Almost from the outset it was one of the most eagerly read of the Parisian papers.

Like many other journalists of this time Desmoulins had been fired by an anxiety to become famous. Following a brilliant college career, and despite a bad stammer, he had at first hoped to shine at the bar. However, his college success did not repeat itself in the law courts, and Desmoulins took to haunting the cafés where, to his delight, he gained great popularity, being called simply 'Camille'. He revealed a similar delight when following the success of his two pamphlets he was referred to as 'Desmoulins' and not 'the writer Desmoulins'. This youthful desire for praise is obvious in many of his writings.

Although his success as a writer seemed assured, Desmoulins was still faced with financial difficulties. Two events solved this problem. One was his marriage to Lucille Duplessis which brought him more than 100,000 livres, the other was the reception of his *Révolutions de France et de Brabant* by the public. Under the terms of his contract with the book-dealer Garnery, Desmoulins had been promised 4,000 crowns if the number of his subscribers passed 3,000. This figure was passed easily.

Eloquence is the main feature of Desmoulins' paper. Although he lacked the profundity of Marat and the originality of Hébert, he possessed a spontaneity and quick wit designed to please the public. A contemporary in 1790 called Desmoulins 'a charming democrat who calls a spade a spade and Favras a vile traitor'. By the middle of 1791, however, Desmoulins' paper was starting to lose influence. Following the events of 17 July, Desmoulins was forced to cease writing. To fulfil his obligations to his subscribers, he passed the succession of his paper to the *Révolutions de Paris*, 'which leaves nothing to be desired', advising his subscribers that his number 86 should be followed by number 108 of the *Révolutions de Paris*. However J. F. N. Dusaulchoy took over the paper and continued it under the same title, but in a more moderate tone. From 19 December 1791 to 30 April 1792 Dusaulchoy changed the title to *Semaine politique et littéraire*.

In April and May 1792 Desmoulins collaborated with Fréron on the *Tribun des patriotes*, of which only four numbers appeared. Then between October and December of that year he produced with Merlin de Thionville a 'second half' to the *Révolutions de France et de Brabant*.

Elected to the Convention, Desmoulins' speech defect prevented him playing an active role. Apart from a pamphlet attacking the Girondins, which he later regretted having written, it was not until December 1793 that he again took to journalism, and once more figured prominently in the events of the Revolution. On this occasion he got himself embroiled on the side of Danton in the clash developing between Danton, Robespierre and Hébert. Desmoulins' contribution was the *Vieux Cordelier*, the organ of the Dantonist plea for clemency.

The success of this paper was astonishing. Following the third number, in which he made an appeal for a 'committee of clemency' to be set up to release anyone held in prison unnecessarily, crowds gathered around the Convention demanding the release of suspects. On 20 December queues formed to buy copies of the fourth issue, and those unable to buy copies from the shop attempted to outbid one another for second-hand copies.

The *Vieux Cordelier* raised a storm. The Jacobins wanted to have Desmoulins expelled from the club. But Robespierre defended him, saying: 'We must deal severely with his numbers . . . and keep Camille among us. I demand that as a lesson Camille's numbers be burned.' Desmoulins' rejoinder did not help his cause: 'That is all very well,' he replied, 'but I answer you like Rousseau: to burn is not to reply.'

Perhaps the best summary of the worth and influence of Desmoulins' *Vieux Cordelier* comes from Robespierre himself, who in the end had to watch Desmoulins mount the scaffold: 'You see in these works the most revolutionary principles alongside the most pernicious moderatism. Here he inspires the courage of patriotism; there he feeds the hope of aristocracy . . . with the aid of his redoubtable club he wields the most terrible blows against our enemies; with the aid of his biting satire he destroys the best patriots. Camille is a strange mixture of truth and lies, of political sense and absurdity, of sane ideas and of characteristic and chimerical schemes . . .' But, despite Robespierre, Desmoulins could not be saved. The Cordeliers Club, incensed by the attack on Hébert made by Desmoulins in his *Vieux Cordelier*, pressed for his punishment. On 5 April 1794 Desmoulins was executed with Danton and his friends. Of the newspapers of the Revolution the *Vieux Cordelier* stands out as a work of eloquence and courage.

Hébert occupies a unique role in the history of the Revolution. Yet although Hébert the man played a prominent role in the Cordelier Club and gave his name to a faction, this practical role was nothing compared to that of the Père Duchesne, the rough-mannered, rough-spoken '*marchand de fourneaux*' who became the voice of the sans-culottes. A historian and contemporary of Hébert, Paganel, writing a few years after the Revolution, made this observation: 'At the very name of the *Père Duchesne* two-thirds of France was paralysed with terror, yet even those who execrated his doctrines the most, and to whom his style was the most unfamiliar, were equally anxious to buy his obscene paper; they asked for it with a sort of ostentation, and spoke of it with a simulated joy; this was their means of avoiding the ranks of the suspects, and, to use the expression of the *Père Duchesne*, of "sans-culottising" themselves.' This was in 1793. The *Père Duchesne* had not always struck terror: indeed in his early pamphlets and in the first editions of the *Grandes joies* . . . and the *Grandes colères du Père Duchesne* Hébert had shown himself to be a moderate constitutionalist.

At this time too he was involved in disputes with another 'Père Duchesne', that of Lemaire, over which was the '*véritable*'. The name 'Père Duchesne' was used to describe a particular type of individual, and had been used as early as 1745. In 1790 several papers appeared using this title–there being no legal protection or copyright. Lemaire first used this name in his *Vitres cassées par le Père Duchêne*,* pamphlets that go back to 1789. In view of the success of these and other pamphlets, suitably laced with '*foutres*' and '*bougres*', Lemaire decided to make them a regular publication. The results were the 400 *Lettres bougrement patriotiques du véritable Père Duchêne*, which appeared between September 1790 and May 1792, and the *Trompette du Père Duchêne* which appeared between May 1792 and June 1793. In his paper Lemaire addressed himself to the soldiers in the army, using swear-words and his own peculiar neologisms, but without achieving the same success as Hébert. A moderate patriot, and later a Girondin, Lemaire declared his belief in 'the trinity' of 'the nation, the law, and the king'.

Hébert, then, was not the first to use swear-words as a point of style; nor was he the first to use obscenities–in this regard the aristocrats could easily compete with him–he was merely the most successful. As with Marat, Hébert's popularity increased as the danger to the Republic deepened, and he too was to be defended by the people of Paris when he was arrested, first in 1792, but more spectacularly in May 1793.

* Lemaire's spelling of 'Père Duchêne' differs from that of Hébert ('Père Duchesne').

By posterity Hébert has been almost universally judged with the same opprobrium he himself seemed to enjoy casting on others. Writing in 1912, Paul d'Estrée called Hébert such an object of execration that 'it would need a maniac to rehabilitate him'. Twenty-seven years later, G. Walter's biography of Hébert was greeted by one reviewer as the first apology for Hébert. This Walter denied. He saw Hébert mainly as the vehement and zealous interpreter of the popular wrath. He saw his success as being due to a remarkable facility to adapt himself to the events that followed the disastrous war of 1792. The *Père Duchesne*, insists Walter, should not be seen as a heap of vulgarities and insults; Hébert had one goal before him–to make himself understood by the people. Above all, the people wanted someone who spoke their own language. In Hébert they recognised themselves.

Hébert himself claimed that 'You must swear with those who swear.' On another occasion he pointed out that he did not write for the ladies. 'Anyone who appreciates frankness and probity,' he said, 'will not blush at the *foutres* and *bougres* that I insert here and there with my joys and my angers.' As many would-be imitators discovered, there was more to the style of Hébert than mere obscenity. The historian of the French language, Ferdinand Brunot, implicitly suggests one reason when he calls Hébert 'the Homer of filth'.

(*ii*) *Anti-revolutionary*

The first in the field of the opponents of the Revolution was Antoine, comte de Rivarol, idol of the pre-revolutionary café society, who wrote at first anonymously and then under a pseudonym in the *Journal politique national*. Although the paper was announced to appear three times a week from 12 July 1789, Rivarol's incurable lethargy defeated the promise of regularity. The first two subscriptions, each for three months, took nine months to fulfil, and the third petered out in November 1790 after only eight of the promised twenty-four numbers had been issued. Rivarol's admirers would no doubt have claimed that even only eight numbers at the full subscription cost of 12 livres was a bargain. His paper claimed to give reflections 'on the decrees of the National Assembly, on the faults of the government, and on the misfortunes of France'. His arguments anticipated those of Burke, the violence of his hatred that of Taine, but his grace of style remains his own. He stood for strictly limited monarchy, he feared the populace and hated the financiers. On 10 June 1792 he was forced to leave France, just seven days before a gang broke into his house to take revenge on him.

Rivarol's reputation as a writer has survived to the present day; his 'Dissertation on the Universality of the French Language' (1784) is still consulted, while his name has been given to a journal of the extreme right, which enjoys some success in present-day France.

The most entertaining of the aristocratic papers is the *Actes des Apôtres*. Written in an apparently frivolous fashion, concentrating on sharp wit and satire, it could also engage in serious polemics. For the most part, however, it is not essentially political in content. It devotes many of its pages to scurrilous attacks on individuals, respecting neither their public nor their private life, whether real or imagined. Among its more prominent contributors were Peltier, its founder, Suleau who would later take up his own paper, the younger Mirabeau, Montlosier, and Rivarol. Although only a few articles can be attributed to Rivarol, he seems to have been one of the main influences at work in the paper. The *Actes des Apôtres* appeared more or less regularly every two days. Although it lasted until just after the close of the Constituent Assembly, it had already lost much of its verve by 1791. Some of its best writers had gone elsewhere or had taken up their own publications; some of the members of the Assembly who supplied it with information had retired; many of its favourite Aunt Sallies in the Assembly were no longer there or their interest had expired. The editors were forced to repeat themselves; they ran into financial difficulties; they did not enjoy the support of the king. Claiming that he was obeying an order from Louis, Peltier closed his paper at the end of 1791.

At first the proprietors of the *Actes des Apôtres* did not open a subscription list, for they were 'aware of [their] laziness' and did not know how far the 'heroic and indefatigable activity of our honourable sovereigns' might lead, but several counterfeiters eventually forced them to open one. In a prospectus headed 'Liberty, Gaiety, Royal Democracy' they announced a 'national work whose reputation, bound up with that of our august legislators, is assured of a foundation as stable as the base of the new constitution that they have just imposed on France.'

The price of subscription was 9 livres and 10 sous. But assignats would not be accepted, a decision later revised when the concession was granted that assignats would be received 'when they forced the price of a salad up to 20,000 francs'.

The counterpart to the *Actes des Apôtres* was the *Journal général de la Cour et de la Ville*, less witty but more violent. It was founded by Brune— the future marshal of France and victim of the White Terror of 1815— who wrote the paper in a sense favourable to the Revolution from 15 September until 16 December 1789. In October, Brune had taken on Gautier de Syonnet as collaborator, but it appears that there was a conflict of interest, so that from 16 December two papers appeared under the title *Journal général de la Cour et de la Ville*, each with the same numeration, but one edited by Brune and the other by Gautier. Brune's paper disappeared on 2 January 1790. Gautier's, on the other hand, continued from strength to strength. At first favourable to the Revolution, by May 1790 it had radically altered to become one of its most extreme opponents.

By contrast, the *Gazette de Paris* made no pretensions to wit or gaiety, barbed or otherwise: it was an entirely serious paper. Under the sole direction of Farmin Durosoi, unsuccessful poet and playwright, it appeared daily, first in eight octavo pages, then in four quarto pages, from 1 October 1789. Of the right-wing press Durosoi most aroused the anger of the democrats, as much by his whimpering, patronising style as by his unconcealed desire for a return to the old régime. Yet he, too, at first welcomed the Revolution, and although by late 1789 he was casting caustic comment upon it, and was already well on the way to taking up his position of defiant intransigence, he could still find some words of praise for it in the early months of 1790. His change of opinion, apparently due to what he considered the excesses of a misled people against the monarch who loved them, the nobles who protected them, and the Church that offered them solace for the miseries of temporal existence, was also encouraged by financial subsidies from the enemies of the Revolution, notably the colonial proprietors of the *Club Massiac*. For Durosoi there could be no society where the king was not the centre of obedience and the pope the centre of faith. For this reason two races had to be subdued or exterminated—the Jacobins and the Protestants. Often carried away by his own rhetoric, Durosoi nevertheless made several efforts to carry out his beliefs. Thus he instituted the amazing scheme to buy back the king's lands. Following previous announcements in June 1790, he opened a subscription to which he invited his readers to give generously, with the object of buying the king's lands at the public auction and then returning them to him. The sole reward of the contributors was to be the happiness that would follow. This, and his Hostage Scheme that he thought up following the king's flight, could also be a rallying point for counter-revolution, a call that he made, if at first only implicitly, in the tear-soaked columns that filled his pages after the abolition of hereditary nobility and titles on 19 June 1790.

Accused of cowardice in his private life, Durosoi's paper, especially in 1792, showed a boldness and adhesion to principle that is at times quite startling. At his trial following the fall of the monarchy he faced his accusers bravely and accepted with equanimity the charges that he had invited invasion and called for counter-revolution in his paper. He met the death sentence and his execution with firmness and courage on 25 August 1792.

The most celebrated of the ultra-right-wing papers was the *Ami du Roi*, launched on 1 June 1790 under the title *Ami du Roi, des Français, de l'Ordre, et surtout de la Vérité*. The *Ami du Roi* issued from the *Année littéraire*, the paper founded by Fréron in 1754 to combat the opinions of the *philosophes*. As a result of the Revolution the proprietors of this paper had been forced to change from an essentially literary publication to a political one. In 1790 it was decided that, in order to combat the Revolution more effectively–a battle that was regarded as a continuation of the deceased Fréron's fight against the *philosophes*–a daily newspaper would be necessary. The result was the *Ami du Roi*. The *Année littéraire* continued to appear, but sporadically, and ceased publication in the middle of 1791.

The immediate success of the *Ami du Roi* was accompanied by domestic troubles. In August 1790 a prospectus for a new *Ami du Roi* was issued in which the writer, the abbé Royou, claimed credit for the success that the paper had been enjoying, but for which he received no due recognition.

The publisher Crapart, who had published both the *Année littéraire* and the *Ami du Roi*, did not treat the matter lightly. Claiming Royou to be an imposter, in the issue of 25 August he complained of the 'brigandage that the Revolution has made fashionable' and declared that the real author of the *Ami du Roi* was not an abbé nor was he named Royou. Although Crapart did not name him, the 'real author' whom he praised was Montjoye. To fill his cup of wrath to overflowing, Montjoye himself then issued a prospectus for a newspaper also to be called the *Ami du Roi* and also claiming to be a 'successor to Fréron'. To draw attention to his name, Montjoye boldly proclaimed, 'It is I, MONTJOYE, who am shepherd of this flock.' The exasperated Crapart bemoaned, 'Never has the prince had so many friends or Fréron so many successors.' Meanwhile the democrats enjoyed the insults that passed between 'an impostor named Montjoye' (from Royou), 'a rogue called Royou' (from Montjoye) and 'two brigands, one called Royou, the other called Montjoye' (from Crapart).

On 1 September as announced, three *Ami du Roi* appeared, each numbered 93, two with the same pagination,* and there continued to be three until 6 November when Crapart and Montjoye healed their differences and came together 'to give to the *Ami du Roi* every possible perfection'.

Montjoye and Royou had both worked on the *Année littéraire* and the *Ami du Roi*, but Royou was responsible for the majority of the lead articles in the *Ami du Roi* between 13 June and 6 August. These articles were a marked improvement on the first dozen which supposedly frightened Crapart into seeking a more trenchant writer. To contemporaries the real 'Friend of the King' was Royou, Fréron's brother-in-law, and a former teacher at the Collège Louis-le-Grand. His attacks on the legislators and on the popular writers 'vomited forth from Hell to

---

* Royou's edition was paginated 1–4.

ruin France', were maintained despite a severe illness, although it is not known to what extent the paper was written by his brother Corentin Royou, a lawyer, and his colleague Geoffroy, in the period following July 1791. Certainly Royou had the final say in the paper, and it was he alone whose arrest was ordered at the same time as Marat's by the decree of 3 May 1792. This was decisive to Royou's failing health, and he died a few weeks later on 21 June. Montjoye, 'the Brissot of royalty', continued his paper until 10 August. Although surpassed in violence and lacking the incisiveness of Royou, 'the Marat of royalty', his moderate expression of extreme right-wing opinion, presented with fine literary talent, ensures his place among anti-revolutionary journalists.

The royalist press had its Desmoulins too. This was Suleau, a prominent contributor to the *Actes des Apôtres*. Suleau's association with the *Actes des Apôtres* came as a result of the fame he achieved while being detained in the Châtelet prison in the first few months of 1790. His arrest had been ordered on suspicion of publishing incendiary brochures in his native Picardy in October 1789. He was eventually transferred to Paris, and at his trial in January 1790 his sharp wit continually rocked the public gallery with laughter, while even his interrogators were noted to be at times unable to suppress smiles. Even after his trial and during his detention, he continued to issue pamphlets that added to his reputation as an incorrigible aristocrat. He was released in April 1790, when he joined the *Actes des Apôtres*. From September of that year, however, he ceased active collaboration, and indeed retired from the public eye altogether until March 1791. He then announced that he would issue his own paper. This was the *Journal de M. Suleau*, which lasted from March 1791 to April 1792, being printed first at Paris and then from the émigrés' camp at Neuwied, before Suleau returned to Paris.

A Voltairian like Desmoulins, and sharing his friend's intemperance of language, Suleau also followed his goal tempestuously before coming to an abrupt reappraisal of opinion. In Suleau's case it was in the acceptance of the ideas of the *monarchiens* whom he had previously so violently denounced, and then in an attempt to win over Desmoulins to his cause. Through Desmoulins he also hoped to win over Danton and Robespierre. Already exasperated by Louis, Suleau had been disillusioned during his short stay with the émigrés; now he was rejected by Desmoulins. The death of the 'systematic temporiser', Leopold, returned Suleau to his former course, but in any case his paper came to an abrupt end in April 1792. Like Desmoulins too he died a violent death. On 10 August 1792, having rejected Desmoulins' offer of refuge on the evening of the ninth, he was massacred on the terrace of the Feuillants, attempting to stir up royalist resistance. It was a death he had in some ways sought from the beginning of the Revolution, both in word and in deed. He himself thought his continued existence 'a miracle sustained by the guardian fairy of the aristocracy', and remarked that every time he passed a lamp-post (*lanterne*), he saw it 'stretch out covetously' towards him.

(*iii*) *Four Radical Papers*

Among the other newspapers that first appeared at the beginning of the Revolution mention must be made of the *Annales patriotiques*, Gorsas' *Courrier*, the *Chronique de Paris* and Fréron's *Orateur du peuple*.

The *Annales patriotiques* was one of the most popular Paris papers in the early days of the Revolution. It appeared daily from 3 October 1789 in four quarto pages, listing as the editors L. S. Mercier and J. L. Carra. Mercier's name, as author of the *Tableau de Paris*, was given prominence, but Carra was soon to establish popularity in his own right. The self-taught son of poor parents, Carra tells us that he learned seven languages in his twelve years of travel throughout Europe prior to the Revolution in order that he could speak to and observe the common people. From this developed his hatred for kings and his 'tender love for humanity'. Carra's ideas were often extravagant, and were disdained by the more sober, but among the less discriminating he won many friends. A member of the Jacobin Club, he was one of the foremost protagonists for initiative in war in 1792, and from then on was allied with the Girondins. He suffered their fate in October 1793.

Mercier did not play such a big part in the *Annales* as Carra, nor did he play such an active political role. For this he escaped the proscription of the Girondins although he was imprisoned as a signatory to the 'protestation of the 73' against the insurrection of 31 May. He returned to the Convention after the fall of Robespierre, appeared in the Council of 500, but thereafter eschewed politics. Mercier maintained his association with the *Annales* until its demise on 22 Frimaire, Year VI (12 December 1797).

Gorsas' entry into journalism, as has been mentioned, was made before the fall of the Bastille. His paper was then called the *Courrier de Versailles à Paris et de Paris à Versailles*. It underwent several changes of title in its celebrated career, but each title began with the word *Courrier*. It is best known as the *Courrier des départements*.

In its early days the *Courrier* was best known for the speed with which Gorsas transcribed the speeches from the Assembly and converted them into the pages of his paper. He is also said to have read his issue of 4 October 1789 to a crowd in the Palais-Royal before heading a group of citizens on the march to Versailles. Nevertheless it is not until later in the Revolution that his paper achieved its greatest interest. Following the Champs de Mars affair Gorsas took the side of the radicals. He glorified the tenth of August and although he was later to inveigh against them he was one of the principal apologists for the September massacres.

Elected to the Convention, Gorsas sided with the Girondins, and in his paper carried out a systematic attack on Marat, a vendetta that went back to early 1790. His presses were wrecked on the night of 9 March 1793, and he barely escaped with his life. Undeterred, he took up his pen a few days later and continued his attacks on the Jacobins. Declared a traitor and outlawed on 28 July 1793, he escaped to the country but later returned to Paris, where he was recognised. Brought before the court, his trial was a simple matter of formal recognition, and he was executed on 17 October – the first *conventionnel* to be executed.

The *Chronique de Paris* is another paper which began as a moderate patriot but became radical after July 1791 and then sided with the Girondins. Under the editorship of A. L. Millin and J. P. Noël, it was introduced on 24 August 1789 to compete with the *Journal de Paris*. Judged by Desmoulins as the best-presented newspaper of the time, its collaborators included Condorcet and Rabaut-Saint-Étienne. As a supporter of the Girondins, its presses were wrecked by the same group that wrecked Gorsas' presses, interrupting publication until 14 March, 1793. Its publication was again interrupted following the events of 31 May. When it reappeared, with new editors, it no longer held the same interest, and publication ceased on 25 August 1793.

In May 1790 the demagogues were joined by Fréron's *Orateur du peuple*, which came out in eight octavo pages every second day. The radicalism of Fréron, the 'disciple and emulator of Marat', was in complete contrast to its owner's clerical and ultra-reactionary up-bringing. His father was the owner of the *Année littéraire*, and his uncle, the abbé Royou, its chief editor. At the Collège Louis-le-Grand Fréron was a class-mate of Desmoulins, and under his influence drew away from his family background. On the death of his father, in 1776, he inherited the wealth of the *Année littéraire*. It was partly with these funds that he founded his own newspaper, which he said was written by 'Martel'. The *Orateur du peuple* gained the full approval of Marat, who called Fréron his 'lieutenant' and his 'dear brother in arms', and often wrote entire editions for 'Martel'. With the close of the Constituent Assembly, Fréron passed the *Orateur du peuple* over to Labenette, who continued it in the same principles to the end of 1792.

Fréron's activities as a 'terrorist' and as a conspirator in the downfall of Robespierre brought him a certain notoriety. So too did his startling reversal of principle during the Thermidorian reaction. In this period he again took up his newspaper but this time as an organ of the most extreme reaction – the *Jeunesse dorée de Fréron*, whose favourite game was baiting suspected Jacobins. The close of the Convention brought an end to his political career; his fortune too ran out and he was forced to abandon his paper. His friendship with Pauline Bonaparte revived his fortunes when Napoleon came to power. He went to Santo Domingo as *sous-préfet*, but he died shortly after his arrival there in 1802.

(iv) Survivors from the Old Regime

The *Journal de Paris* continued to enjoy during the Revolution the commercial success that had made it an object of envy before the Revolution. Edited on the political side by D-J. Garat for the period of the Constituent Assembly, it was noted for its moderation and circumspection. Under Garat the *Journal de Paris* was unquestionably a supporter of the Revolution, although in the early months it was criticised by certain radicals for its pusillanimity and suspected connections with people in high office. The aristocrats found its exaggerated optimism an easy target for their mockery, and often linked Garat's name with Carra's and Marat's to refer to them as 'Camagara' or 'Carramaragara'. Granted leave to nominate his successor, Garat chose Condorcet. But the forthright views of the new editor, anti-papal and showing scant respect for the monarchy, shocked the *Journal*'s genteel subscribers and consequently the proprietors. After a fortnight Condorcet was replaced by Regnault de Saint Jean d'Angéley, an ex-constituent, and from then on the paper took a marked swing to the right.

This swing was given greater emphasis, understandably if unjustifiably, by the contributions of the poet André Chénier to the *Journal*'s 'supplements'. In these supplements, a feature of the paper since 1789, any writer could, at his own expense, set out his views on any subject. Thus the *Journal* could not be held responsible for the diatribes against the clubs penned by the poet who has since been claimed the greatest of the eighteenth century in France. To the men of 1792, however, the literary genius of the day was Marie-Joseph, Chénier's brother, the author of *Charles IX* and other 'patriotic' works. André was then no more than the anti-Jacobin, anti-demagogic polemicist whose writings were openly discountenanced by his popular brother.

The *Journal* appeared on 11 and 12 August 1792, but this affront to the revolutionaries was punished on 12 August, when its offices were broken into and its presses destroyed. Publication ceased for several weeks, and when it reappeared on 1 October – the 'fortunes of the fathers of many families depending on it' – the new editors included Garat, Condorcet, and Sieyès. To further emphasise its dissociation from its reactionary policies, the epithet NATIONAL was added. Thereafter the *Journal* does not hold comparable interest, re-establishing its reputation of bending before the prevailing wind, a policy that allowed it to survive through the political fluctuations of the Directory, Empire, and the Restoration–and thereafter under various titles–until May 1840.

The *Gazette de France* too survived the Revolution, Empire and Restoration. From being paid for out of the king's Civil List it passed to being an organ of the Girondin ministry, changing its title after the fall of the king to *Gazette nationale de France*, and then on 24 January 1793 to *Gazette de France nationale*. It was not a particularly influential paper during the Revolution.

Under the editorship of Mallet du Pan the *Mercure de France* became the leading exponent of those who welcomed the Revolution in its early phase but, standing for limited popular sovereignty and the retention of real power by the king, were soon alarmed by their failure to control the Revolution. The popularity of the *Mercure* can be judged from the figure of 13,000 subscribers reached in the first year of the Revolution, and its influence judged in some way by the domiciliary visits paid every now and then by patriots seeking to put Mallet on the proper path. Mallet went into temporary retreat following the flight of the king in June 1791, and as passions became inflamed in 1792 his position became increasingly difficult. Threatened by the democrats whom he assailed in the *Mercure*, and disliked by the émigrés whose plans for war he would not countenance, he found himself obliged to leave France after the outbreak of war in April 1792. The *Mercure*, with a slight break after 10 August 1792, continued until 1820.

(v) Some Special Cases

Towards the end of 1790 appeared the *Feuille villageoise*, a curious but rather charming paper, conceived and written in the purest of spirit, and which set out to act in accord with its motto: 'If an enslaved people must be held under the yoke of ignorance, a free people needs the restraint of instruction.' Particularly intended for the benefit of the peasants, in style and arrangement it resembles a school textbook. Every week it was despatched to the country in time to be read to the local parishioners after Mass on Sunday. Within a year it had a subscription list of over 16,000. It certainly influenced a much wider public, however, as it was regularly read aloud to 'classes' of interested peasants. The editors, chiefly Cérutti until his failing health in the middle of 1791 and death in February 1792, included Rabaut-Saint-Étienne, then the 'disciples' of Cérutti–Grouvelle and Guinguéné. Written in a tone of moderation, it survived until 23 Thermidor, Year IV (10 August 1796).

Some other papers worthy of note are Audouin's *Journal universel*, which Hatin says 'contributed a great deal to set the Revolution away from its principles and to degenerate from liberty into licence'; Feydel's *Observateur*, which took as its motto, 'Publicity is the safeguard of the people'; Dulaure's *Thermomètre du jour*, which did not come out until August 1791, and which although it was supposed to present the varieties of public opinion, leaned towards the Girondins and was subsidised by Roland; Dusaulchoy's and Étienne's *Contre-poison*, which in its brief existence in 1791 attacked the demagogues of left and right; the *Bouche de Fer*, organ of the masonic *Cercle social*, which owed its title to the collecting box outside its office into which the public was invited to deposit suggestions, comments, queries, advertisements, etc. It was in the printing presses of the *Cercle social* that the Champ de Mars petition was printed.

Three newspapers of interest because of the fame of their editors are: Barère's *Point du jour*, whose reports of the speeches in the Constituent Assembly show no signs of the future terrorist and are in some ways superior to those of the *Moniteur*; Robespierre's *Défenseur de la Constitution*, created by him to forward his own opinions in the disputes with the Brissotins in 1792; Tallien's *Ami des citoyens*, which appeared irregularly '*sous forme d'affiche*' and was adopted by the Jacobins as their official organ in September 1791. Each of these papers, whatever its intrinsic merits, has been overshadowed by the political careers of its editors. Nevertheless they were important publications in their day. In the case of Robespierre's paper this was openly a means of propagating private opinion.

Clubs as well as individuals had realised the value of a regular newspaper to advertise and propagate their principles, and from 1789 such papers appeared as the more or less official organs of the clubs. Among the host of papers of this type some of the best known are *Journal de la société de 1789*, the *Journal des Amis de la Constitution*, the *Journal du Club des Cordeliers*, the *Journal des débats des Jacobins* and the *Journal de la Montagne*. The Feuillant position was upheld by several papers, two of which had subscription figures of over 10,000: the *Gazette universelle* and the *Journal du Soir*. Indeed, there was probably a newspaper for every shade of opinion in these crowded years.

To round off this brief sketch of some of the more prominent news-papers of the Revolution, mention must be made of the *Moniteur*, the best known of all the revolutionary newspapers to later generations both for its value as a research source for the historian and for its ready availability as the *Réimpression de l'ancien Moniteur* in all major libraries. The *Moniteur*, or *Gazette nationale*, was founded on 24 November 1789 by C. J. Panckoucke.* Its editors, regarding themselves primarily as

* The most substantial newspaper owner of the time, employing over 800 workers. He had printed the Encyclopaedia, and also owned the *Mercure de France*.

historians of the Revolution, added no comment to their report of speeches or other items of news; nevertheless there were times when they showed themselves anxious to prove that they had favoured one individual or faction, insisting on the space allocated to certain speakers. Critics of the paper made similar complaints. It was not until Nivôse, Year VIII (December 1799), that the *Moniteur* became the official organ of the government. The introduction and coverage of events from 5 May 1789 were added later. Bearing in mind the qualifications that have been made elsewhere, the *Moniteur* remains, with its size, its completeness and its objectivity, the best single source of information on the events of the Revolution.

Press Freedom and Censorship

The question of freedom of the press was one that was brought up constantly in the period under consideration. Not only were there frequent clashes between writers and the authorities, but often the public intervened, now on the side of a popular writer against the authorities, now to take action against writers who incurred their displeasure. At the official level, however, there was a remarkable unwillingness to take action. This was apparent, too, in the absence of an official paper until 1800.

The idea of an official newspaper had been debated since the first days of the meeting of the Estates-General. On 20 May it was suggested that a means be found of ensuring that the provinces be acquainted with the information judged suitable for them by the Assembly. The motion was vigorously opposed. C. J. Panckoucke, ever open to a commercial proposition, asked on 23 May that he be the publisher of any such work. He claimed that his *Mercure de France* was the oldest French newspaper and that it had been the official depositary for the principal acts of the Estates-General of 1614. However, the matter was dropped. It was claimed that such a practice would give rise to a new aristocracy from among those preparing the matter for print; the Estates-General too would then become its own historian. Moreover it was thought that freedom of the press was the best means of ensuring that the acts of the Assembly be reported fairly.*

The matter was not taken up again for some time. Papers like the *Point du jour*, Le Hodey's *Journal des États-généraux* and, later, the *Gazette nationale*, specialised in reporting debates. From 27 April 1791 the *Logographe*, a newspaper that specialised in using the latest devices to allow, so it was claimed, every word of the speaker to be taken down—

---

* In September 1790 the *Chronique de Paris* regretted the absence of an official journal, and suggested that the government print four million copies of the Constitution, in several languages and dialects, so that every home in France should have a copy.

in this case, as the title suggests, by employing a succession of reporters to take down different parts of the speech–took on the appearance of being official, and was granted, as was the *Gazette nationale*, the privilege of a special box at the Assembly. However, its association with the king, who later subsidised it out of the Civil List, sealed its fate.* The issue of 17 August 1792 was the last.

The power of the written word could not be overlooked. Those in positions of authority realised that they would have to compromise with their liberal beliefs in so far as the free traffic of thought was concerned. Thus on 18 August 1792 the Girondins, with Roland, the Minister of the Interior, set up a *bureau d'esprit* to right wrong opinion, and put at the disposal of the Minister 100,000 livres for 'correspondence thought necessary, and for the distributions in the departments and in the army of all writings proper to enlighten people on the criminal plots of the enemies of the state'. On 22 May and 2 June 1793 funds were put at the disposal of the Minister of War to supply papers to the troops that would 'enlighten and animate their patriotism'. From this Hébert, among others, received 205,000 livres, the subject for later recriminations between the *Père Duchesne* and the *Vieux Cordelier* at the end of 1793.

Marat raged against the use of public funds by the Girondins, but mainly because he was not receiving what he thought his fair share, as well as being no doubt more than just a little put out by Roland's proviso that he furnish proof of his patriotism. Hébert, enjoying the full benefits of assistance from public funds, claimed that this was the 'cinders necessary to heat up' his furnaces. On 2 August 1793 the Committee of Public Safety had large sums put at its disposal, 50 millions of which went to forming public opinion. Deciding that a newspaper was the best means of doing this, but seeing the disadvantage of founding a paper specially for this purpose, the Committee took over Rousselin's *Feuille de salut public*, and transformed it into its own propagandist organ. In its anxiety to conceal the true nature of this paper the Committee went so far as to have banned any paper bearing the title 'Public Safety' (1 April 1794). Without altering its semi-official status the *Feuille de salut public* continued until 30 August 1795 under the title *Journal de la République*, and ceased publication on the 10 March 1796. Thus, although France did not adopt an official paper until 1800, the Government, whether Girondin, Jacobin or Directory, was never without a semi-official newspaper in support of its own interests.

* Or, according to another account, because it gave a too faithful account of the lapses of the orators.

(i) *Censorship and the Assembly*

The freedom of the press in France, inadvertently inaugurated on 5 July 1788, tolerated within certain limits from 19 May 1789, and seized after the fall of the Bastille, was officially recognised when it was written into the Declaration of Rights. Legal recognition came by its incorporation into the Constitution on 23 August 1791. Although this law imposed certain restrictions, the press was in fact completely free until 10 August 1792.

The most obvious aspect of this freedom was the abolition of the censorship system by which authors and publishers had to seek a licence before printing and have their work subjected to scrutiny by the police. Now the way was open for criticism of the authorities for the first time, whether they were local bosses, the nation's representatives or the monarch himself. Important sections of the *cahiers* had asked that, in granting freedom of expression, this would be in conformity with the respect due to religion and morals. Even this restriction was not observed: the Church was not protected from its opponents and the protective shell around conventional morality was shattered, so that neither respected institutions nor individual character were free from even the most vicious attacks. With the old régime struck in its vitals, and with the new régime yet to be established, a press law was not seen to be an urgent measure. On the occasions when attempts were made to introduce restrictions they were usually frustrated by appealing to the Declaration of the Rights of Man, or by pointing to the example of the old régime. Just as often such attempts were simply ignored. But they were not forgotten, and the matter of censorship and press freedom was periodically brought before the deputies.

On 20 January 1790, the irrepressible Sieyès tried to bring in a press law whereby press offences were to be presented not to an ordinary tribunal, but to a special jury. The proposition was not even discussed.

Malouet came closer to success when in the evening of 31 July 1790 he denounced Marat's pamphlet *C'en est fait de nous*. An article by Desmoulins was also denounced, as well as the slanders of the *Actes des Apôtres* and the *Gazette de Paris*. The representatives of the nation thought it beneath their dignity to worry about the mere personal insults of the aristocrats, but decided that the severest penalties had to be introduced for anyone who incited the people. Thus it was moved that 'all authors, printers and street-sellers of writings inciting the people to insurrection against the laws, to the spilling of blood, and to the overthrow of the constitution' were to be prosecuted as criminals against the state. The decision was not final, and Desmoulins touched on a sore point when he pointed out that: 'At the same time as the Assembly is proclaiming us as criminals against the state, the conquerors of the Bastille are proclaiming us as its most zealous defenders.' On 2 August Pétion raised the matter again. Holding up the example of pre-Bastille days, he argued that the decree was vague and hence open to abuse; it was said to aim at silencing the patriotic writers. The final result was amendments that left Marat's pamphlet the only object for reprisals.

At least Malouet did get his complaint listened to. The more typical attitude was that which greeted Moreau as reported in the *Moniteur* of 1 October 1790:

> *M. Moreau*–I denounce the number by Marat . . . (Murmuring breaks out in the Assembly. M. Moreau tries in vain to make himself heard; the harder he tries the louder the murmurs become. He carries to the bureau the number he wanted to denounce, and the Assembly decides to go on with the agenda).

The one occasion on which the Assembly took action against the press was following Champ de Mars. A decree of 18 July declared as sedition-mongers and disturbers of the peace any persons who 'incited murder, fire or pillage, or formally counselled disobedience to the law, either by placards, public writings or by speeches held in places of public assembly'. The *Moniteur* of 24 July will serve best to indicate the frenzy of activity that followed this decree as well as the papers it particularly affected.

Paris 22 July
M. Verrière, member of the Cordeliers Club and defender of M. Santerre against M. Lafayette, was arrested yesterday.

It is said that M. Verrière is the author of the paper entitled the *Ami du Peuple* by Marat. His presses and papers were seized. Mme Colombe, head of the printing-works, was also taken to prison.

They went to seize M. Fréron, author of the *Orateur du peuple*, but he was not at home.

M. Suleau, author of several aristocratic productions, is also under arrest.

M. Danton, Legendre, and Camille Desmoulins have left Paris; we are assured that there is an order for them to be taken prisoner. . . .

They have arrested the author of a work entitled the *Père Duchêne*. This paper must not be confused with that paper bearing the same title and which is written in a spirit of peace and patriotism that does honour to the heart of its author, an excellent citizen who enjoys the esteem of all good patriots. . . .

By virtue of an order of the *comité des recherches et des rapports*, the National Guard went to seize M. the abbé Royou; but he was not at home; seals were placed on part of his papers and the rest seized.

The *Ami du Roi*, the *Journal de la Cour et de la Ville* etc. and the *Gazette de Paris* did not appear today.

But the Assembly soon reverted to its inaction – and the press to its excesses.

In January 1791 indirect restriction on press freedom, by introducing a stamp tax, was postponed and finally abandoned. Later in the same year the Assembly prohibited the placarding of papers unless signed, and subsequently it ordered that coloured paper only must be used: official declarations alone were to be on white paper.

In August 1791 the Assembly dealt with the problem of press censorship as an article of the Constitution. Despite Robespierre's opposition, a decree introduced by the lawyer Thouret was passed enumerating crimes of the press. These included: provocation to break the law; incitement to destroy the constituted authorities, and to resist public authorities; gratuitous calumnies against public officials or against private citizens. In the case of violation of the law, the accused would appear before a jury, and if found guilty would then be handed over to the ordinary civil or criminal justice. The law was vague, however, both as to the composition of the jury and the selection of the judge.

In fact, the machinery of prosecution was not used, and the Legislative Assembly, despite the onset of war and the growing crisis of counter-revolutionary insurrection, made no further inroads on the freedom of the press. The only time it applied the law passed by its predecessors was in the decree of 3 May against Marat and Royou.

The fall of the monarchy meant the end of the royalist press although, in theory, the royalists could have continued their publications until 4 December 1792. On that day the Convention passed a law punishing anyone seeking the return of royalty. The law was at first vague, but when the deficiency was made up on 29 March 1793 it meant the beginning of the Terror for the journalists. The law imposed the death sentence for anyone publishing material favouring the return of royalty or for counselling murder and pillage. But by this time the royalist press was virtually dead, surviving only in a few clandestine pamphlets.

During the Convention it was again Marat, this time joined by Hébert, who drew the anger of the legislating body in disputes involving the press. But now the principle of freedom of the press was used as much as a defence of the Jacobins as of a sacred principle.

At the Convention on 26 February 1793, Salles read out an article by Marat in which he recommended the hanging of certain grocers from their shop-doorways. The *Moniteur* (in the issue of the 28th) noted that on the reading of this number the whole Assembly seemed alive with indignation, as people cried out for Marat's arrest. After Marat had leaped to the tribune in his own defence, Lejeune spoke up not 'as a friend of Marat' but in defence of the freedom of the press. After further interruptions it was decided to turn the matter over to the Minister of Justice 'to pursue the authors of these crimes and to make a report on them to the Convention every three days'.

When Duhem demanded on 8 March 1793 that journalists no longer be allowed to be present at the sessions of the Convention it was Marat whom he was attacking, but he generalised his accusation into an attack on the freedom of the press. These 'calumniating insects', he accused, 'are the sole and true obstacles to the progress of the Revolution'; and he demanded that the Convention 'clear out from its bosom all these filthy creatures' [greeted by cries of 'Yes! Yes!'] and that 'all the journalists be expelled from this room'.

The motion was not passed, but the issue was not dropped. It was decided on 11 March that since those deputies who published newspapers owed their every moment to the nation that paid them, deputies should no longer be allowed to write in newspapers. The decree did not last long. Marat made a mockery of it by simply changing the title of his paper from *Journal* to *Publiciste* and continued to make inflammatory statements for which he was brought to trial on 13 April. On this occasion he was acquitted and carried in triumph from the Revolutionary Tribunal to the Convention and thence to the Jacobin Club. Subsequently the decree was withdrawn.

The *Révolutions de Paris* took its accustomed stand on what it considered a violation of the rights of journalists, and in particular took Duhem to task for his diatribe: 'Duhem, you are a bad citizen or a coward, take your choice: a bad citizen by taking away from our legislators the only restraint capable of keeping them to their duty; a coward if you are incapable of braving the stilettos of calumny.'

On 18 May 1793 the newly formed *Commission des Douze*, composed entirely of convinced Girondins, took it on themselves to examine closely the acts of the Paris Commune. One of their first acts was to arrest Hébert. Immediately the Commune, feeling itself attacked by the arrest of one of its members, protested, invoking the rights of man and the liberty of the press. It declared against these 'acts of tyranny' and crimes against 'these [Varlet had been arrested at the same time as Hébert] apostles of liberty'. The Sections too, declared in favour of Hébert and demanded that he be freed. Proof of Hébert's innocence was forwarded by Chaumette, who visited him in his cell and found him asleep. Hébert could not be guilty, he decided, for 'crime does not sleep'; and he forthwith proclaimed that the cell where the martyr of truth was incarcerated be called the 'Chamber of the liberty of the press, as previously there was in the Bastille the "Tower of liberty" '.

Pressure on the Convention increased violently: Hébert was released and the *Commission* abandoned. A week later the Girondins were eliminated from the struggle.

The Constitution of 1793, issued after the fall of the Girondins, again proclaimed the freedom of thought and opinion, but this was immediately frozen as the government was declared exceptional and the freedom of the press incompatible with a state of war, whether civil or foreign. Thus from 2 June to the fall of Robespierre on 27 July 1794 there was no freedom of the press.

(ii) *Censorship and the Local Authorities*

While the Assembly allowed the press issue to drag on unresolved, the local authorities found themselves forced to take action against what they considered a serious practical problem. Before 10 August 1792 the Paris authorities were no more successful than the Assembly in their efforts to stem the journalistic anarchy. On 14 July the Paris Commune declared the press free, but just ten days later it forbade the crying of headlines except of a particular, sober type. It tried on 1 September to introduce controls on the new newspaper titles being proclaimed on the streets every day, by forbidding the sale of anonymous publications. Both decrees were virtual dead letters. On 24 December a more detailed ordinance confirmed the previous laws and, in addition, restricted the number of street-sellers to 300 and of bill-stickers to 60. Moreover, these street-sellers had to pass a literacy test. If they passed the test, they were granted a licence and received a badge that had to be worn. The badge bore the slogan: 'Publicity is the safeguard of the people.' The Commune passed these laws 'while waiting for the regulation that has to be made by the National Assembly'.

The Paris authorities soon took action against the authors of newspapers. Within a month of issuing his paper Marat was involved in the first of many head-on collisions with the new police force. On 5 October, in an article that he boasted helped to bring about the march to Versailles, Marat had called on the people to take action against their chiefs. The Municipality ordered his arrest, and although the *Ami du Peuple* disappeared for only a fortnight, Marat himself had to keep under cover for two months. Eventually brought before the *comité des recherches*, Marat was courteously released, even being offered a lift home by the officers. Encouraged, and undeterred by the order for his arrest, which had not been rescinded, Marat continued to assail the Municipality with threats and insults. He was again pursued, but this time the district of the Cordeliers took action to protect the liberty of an individual and the freedom of the press–the fact that the individual was Marat was not yet of great consequence.

There were several occasions when the Paris police swooped on 'incendiary' publications; not necessarily those of the left extremists, although on the whole the aristocrats were left freer to abuse the authorities. In March 1790, for example, the bookseller Pain was arrested in his shop in the Palais-Royal, following an edition of the *Sottises de la Semaine*. The *Révolutions de Paris* did not allow the incident to pass unnoticed, and in decrying the outrage, declared that the aristocrats too had to enjoy complete freedom of the press, an opinion that it upheld even on the eve of the monarchy's demise.

In September of that same year Marat and his 'lieutenant' Fréron were descended upon by Lafayette and his troops, in what Marat described as 'the patriotic expedition' by the 'general of the Parisian army . . . to violate the home of two citizens'. The *Révolutions de Paris* again protested:

> To see the persecutions being brought against the writers, printers and even street-sellers, one would be tempted to believe that liberty has gained nothing from the Revolution, and that the French have done no more than change their master. The police committees of some of the Paris Sections exercise over the press the most tyrannical inquisition. There is not a single district commissioner who does not arrogate to himself the right to seize or to have seized so-called incendiary brochures.

The anger of the democrats was further incensed by the sight of the armed guards protecting the persons and property of Durosoi, Royou and Gautier–an anomaly that they frequently pointed out in their papers.

A further example of the attempts by the Paris authorities to punish individuals for the boldness or sheer effrontery of their writings, and of the way in which such action was received by sections of the public, is vividly illustrated by the 'headlines' of two editions of Hébert's *Père Duchesne* that came out in early March 1792:

Great anger of the Père Duchesne against Madame Veto,* who offered him a pension out of the Civil List so that he would fool the people and mislead them, in order to re-establish the nobility and bring back the old régime.

For this Hébert was arrested, but according to him:

The arrest of the Père Duchesne under the orders of Madame Veto. His trial and interrogation before judge Brid'Oison. His great joy at seeing the brave sans-culottes come to his defence and take up their pikes to deliver him from the paws of the police pimps. Great judgement by which he is recognised as a brave bastard, and which orders his return to liberty.

---

* Marie Antoinette.

The democrats, the main upholders of freedom of the press, raised little protest when action was taken against the royalists in August 1792. On the 12th, the Commune of Paris decreed that 'the poisoners of public opinion, such as the authors of various papers, shall be arrested, and that their presses, type and equipment shall be distributed among the patriotic printers who shall be advised to this effect'. Ironically, the presses given to Gorsas and to the *Chronique de Paris* would be destroyed by a group hostile to the Girondins in March of the following year.

(iii) Popular Intervention and Press Freedom

A measure of questionable validity and of doubtful effect in curtailing press freedom was the use of force. The patriots of Paris resorted to it often enough, hence the granting of police protection to the aristocratic writers and their presses. On 2 August 1789, Rivarol had complained of the 'executions, fires and all the violent means used in France to establish liberty, which have intimidated the printers who have abandoned us one after the other at Versailles and at Paris'.

Of the royalists Durosoi was the individual most frequently insulted or threatened for what he said in his paper. After an attack on his presses in May 1790 he too was forced to leave Paris in order to continue his paper, complaining in his issue which he dated 26/27/28/29/31 May 1790 of the way the people were being led astray by their chiefs. The breaking of Durosoi's presses followed a burning of bundles of the *Actes des Apôtres* and other royalist literature, as a result of which the bookseller Gattey was forced to promise never again to sell aristocratic papers. On another occasion a complete edition of Gautier's paper was burned in the streets.

One of the main centres for these sorties, which had as their goal to exact retribution from an author who had displeased them, were the cafés, notably Zoppi and du Caveau. These cafés, the 'spoken press of the Revolution', usually did no more than ease their anger by a ritualistic burning of an offending newspaper. But as we have seen there were occasions on which they might also take the law into their own hands. The *Chronique de Paris* reports on 19 November 1790 how the patriots of the Café Zoppi signed a petition declaring that a deputation should visit certain counter-revolutionary journalists, and named the *Mercure de France*, the *Gazette de Paris*, the *Ami du Roi*, the *Chronique du Manège*, the *Actes des Apôtres*, and the *Journal général de la Cour et de la Ville*. The outcome was that on an admonition 'as moderate in appearance as it was vigorous in its proposals', the two writers encountered – Royou and Durosoi – promised to be less incendiary and to tell fewer lies and calumnies in future.

It is apparent that the failure of the government to define clearly the position of the press and to ensure its compatibility with the rights of the individual, in the end allowed this freedom to destroy itself. The aristocrats were scornful of this freedom and deliberately abused it to discredit the Revolution. Yet others, notably Brissot, argued that the solution to the licence of the press lay in its freedom. Individuals could, of course, have recourse to law, and Desmoulins was more than once forced to retract statements made in his paper or else face heavy damages. But such cases were exceptional. Threat of such action was even regarded as an attack on the freedom of the press. The isolated and ill-conceived attempts by the executive powers against individuals brought sympathy to the persecuted, whose still fresh freedom was being attacked. The hounding of Marat by the authorities while the counter-revolutionaries were left free to circulate their invitations to violence could only redound to the favour of Marat and to the distrust of the law.

In the failure of the government to legislate wisely and in the inconsistent and thus arbitrary actions of the executive powers, the people were encouraged or roused to act as law-makers themselves. In this as in every other field, the freedom of the individual soon developed into the rule of the strongest. In the final outcome it was deeds and not words that decided. Resort to violence was the logical outcome when words were exhausted.

When the despotism of thought endured under Napoleon gave way to the Restoration, and freedom of speech and thought was again a foremost demand as it had been before the Revolution, the example of Marat and Hébert was constantly recalled. Indeed, to contemporaries it was often writers who were praised or blamed for the turn of events. At all events no subsequent government could afford to ignore them.

The Influence of the Press

The influence of the press in the first years of the Revolution is difficult to ascertain. The most obvious restriction on the power of the press was the size of the reading public, while the difficulty of circulation could present a special problem, especially in some country regions. In the country illiteracy was general. The popularity of the *Feuille villageoise*, a paper with more than 16,000 subscribers and an estimated reading public of 200,000 to 300,000, indicates the keen hunger of any people for news of the world about them, especially when that world is in the throes of a revolution affecting every rank in society. But the groups who gathered to listen to readings from the *Feuille villageoise* were subjected to the censorship of the few who could read, and if these few were at all hostile to the Revolution, if they were for example non-juring priests, then the writings which favoured the Revolution could easily be ignored. Letters to the *Ami du Roi* and to the *Gazette de Paris* indicate that their readers were from among the more solidly established sections of society; often these letters would blame the popular writers for the indignities that they thought themselves exposed to.

In Paris, however, and to a lesser degree in the other main cities, literacy was considerably higher. If the clubs, popular societies, wine shops and cafés were the more important centres of revolutionary activity, it must nevertheless be agreed that each of these was influenced by the newspaper press, particularly in the first two years of the Revolution. On 21 August 1792, the Quinze-vingts Section, naming in particular Gorsas, Carra, Prudhomme, and Desmoulins, declared that the patriotic writers had prepared the French people to take the path of liberty and equality, and that 'their writings have spread throughout France the "electric fire" that will give a constitution to a people worthy of liberty'.

But almost certainly the influence of the press was given more importance by contemporaries than it merited. The cries of royalists, such as Royou, that a man could be hanged for six livres, and that it was the 'scandalous chronicles' and the 'barbarous hordes of bloody writers' whose unlimited liberty had brought France to ruin, is typical of the mind that will not grant genuine grievances in the complaints of the people, perhaps out of fear of the sacrifice that the solution to the problem might entail. It does, however, complement in some way the claims of the radicals on the power of the written word.

Georges Lefebvre sees fear, defensive reaction and punitive will as together forming one of the keys to the unfolding narrative of the French Revolution. Panic fears, or justified fears, of threats to life, property or means of subsistence, were at the basis of every major disturbance in the Revolution. The press was filled as much with rumours, not necessarily reported as such, as it was with facts. Every day fears were raised of 'aristocratic plots', of imminent foreign invasion, of treachery in high office, of hoarders bent on ruining the poor to their own advantage, of 'artificial scarcity'; alongside these reports went appeals and suggestions of means to overcome such problems, often in violent and emotional language. Such reporting often had a basis in fact, at least enough to give it credibility. These appeals could be overlooked in times of security, but they gained influence as security was threatened. Certainly they were not designed to ensure calm and stability. In view of recent scholarship that has shown the real basis of discontent in economic factors and in the personal experience of the individual, it would be unwise to over-stress the influence of the press. On the other hand it might be sensible not to overlook this influence. Napoleon stated that he would not have survived three months had he allowed freedom of the press. Napoleon, of course, was referring to the potential power of the press in a police state; but his remarks have relevance also to the régime of liberty that France allowed in the period of its first two Assemblies. 'Liberty' was then the catchword in every pronouncement. However, freedom soon develops into an injustice unless means are taken to ensure the equal chance for all to enjoy this freedom. In order to achieve such equality, liberty must be compromised. Liberty and equality as absolutes are thus contradictory: they can exist together only if tempered by 'fraternity' or wise laws. In the first years of the French Revolution the most influential of the Parisian newspapers showed little sign of this tempering quality; the authorities failed to introduce the alternative. On another occasion, Napoleon remarked that there was no stability in the liberty of libel: perhaps just a little of this Bonapartist philosophy on the part of the constituents might have helped ensure a longer life for France's first Constitution.

In conclusion let us quote the words of Lord Thompson of Fleet, spoken at the 1965 Assembly of the International Press Institute: his views concerned the position of the press in the developing nations of the contemporary world, but they could equally be applied to the emerging democracy that was France in 1789:

> In many of the new nations of the world the concept of complete freedom of the press as we understand it may not be entirely practical . . . in some of the new nations of the world, criticism of the governments may legitimately be subject to some degree of restriction. Some of the journalists in these developing countries do not have a sufficient background of knowledge, experience and judgement to enable them to restrain themselves from destructive or inflammatory criticism, which, exposed to populations that have not yet learned the art of political stability, could lead to serious unrest and even revolutionary activity. Admittedly many of the new governments make mistakes. Having regard to the enormous tasks facing them, it would not be surprising if their general level of effectiveness were sometimes low, or if the standard of conduct of their public services occasionally left something to be desired. But these difficulties would not be overcome by unreasonable and destructive criticism which might entirely disrupt the life of the country.
>
> Having regard to these circumstances, I believe we must accept the fact that new governments must on occasion take such steps as are necessary to ensure that irresponsible publications, which in developing nations may have an influence out of all proportion to their responsibility, do not cause chaos in the country. While we

must all of us work towards a full recognition of the basic principles of freedom of the press, we must be prepared to accept some degree of compromise in the interim period.

Quoted in *The Press in Developing Countries*, by E. Lloyd Sommerlad, Sydney University Press (1966), p. 143

PART ONE

1789

1789- one of the great years in history: the year of the first French Revolution that set the pattern for later revolutions in France as well as elsewhere in Europe. July and October of that year saw the first authentic popular insurrections, as the people of Paris, hungry, afraid and frustrated, saved the precariously constituted National Assembly from the counter-revolutionary forces that were emerging from conspiracy to an open display of force. At the same time the peasants in the country, oppressed and fearful, settled accounts with their overlords in the phenomena known as the 'Great Fear'. The immediate consequences of the peasant uprising was the attempt to forestall them by the concessions granted on the celebrated evening of 4 August. Following the second of the great urban upheavals, 'the October days', the king was brought back to Paris to virtual captivity under the watchful eyes of the Parisians. At the same time large sections of the right wing of the Assembly felt their security threatened, and left in large numbers. The victory of the revolutionaries seemed complete.

But already divisions had appeared within the ranks of the revolutionaries. If the absolutism of the king was unanimously rejected, how much power was he to retain? If the people were now sovereign, who was to exercise this sovereignty, and just what did this entail? If feudalism was to be abolished, what compensation was to be paid to the former seigneurs, many of whom were in fact influential bourgeois? If the 'people' had saved the Assembly from the aristocrats, and had their insurrection legalised in the Declaration of the Rights of Man, how could the Assembly prevent the 'sovereign will' being turned against itself? Indeed, how could the Declaration of Rights be implemented without frightening the delicate feelings of the property-minded bourgeoisie or inflaming the claims of the sovereign people proud of their part in securing victory, but as yet not enjoying the spoils?

Cutting across these broad problems were the more pressing necessities of stabilising the economy and restoring the finances, as well as reorganising the legal and civil administrative structure of the new France.

The press played an important part in publicising these issues, and although relatively cautious before 'the October days', the newspapers

44

of Paris thereafter boldly attacked, challenged or lauded every debate-able issue—and every issue of that crowded few months was subject to violent clashes of opinion. We have concentrated in Part One on the most famous events and debates of the early months of the Revolution, concluding with the views of three prominent individuals on what the Revolution stood for at the end of the momentous year 1789.

THE ESTATES-GENERAL: OPTIMISM UNFULFILLED

Following the first meeting of the Estates-General on 5 May 1789, the quarrel over procedure resulted in a deadlock broken only when the Third Estate declared itself the Nation (17 June) and three days later formally sealed its decision and determined never to revoke it, in the famous Tennis Court Oath. On 23 June they survived the king's attempt to cow them into submission, and on the 27th seemed to have secured victory when the king ordered the other two Estates to join the Third.

The documents in this section illustrate the writings of Brissot and Mirabeau that drew the wrath of the authorities, and close with samples from the authorised press, showing how even without editorial comment the tensions of the unfolding drama could be conveyed to the public.

1. Sentinel of the People

Brissot's prospectus for the *Patriote français* dated 1 April announced a new paper to appear on the 20th of that month. It criticised the prevailing system of censorship and announced the form of the proposed paper: these matters have been omitted from the extract given here.

A free press is an outpost that watches out unceasingly on behalf of the people.

Jebb

It would be an insult to the French nation if in the present circumstances we were to demonstrate at length the value and necessity of this journal. At the moment it [the French nation] is about to acquire a constitution that must ever assure its freedom: this constitution can only be the fruit of harmony among all the members of the state, and this harmony can only exist through universal education.

The mass of pamphlets that have appeared since the birth of the Revolution have begun that education, but these pamphlets cannot be read by everybody; there is a choice to be made, and that choice is impossible without reading the journals, and to read them you have to buy them; but all this costs money, and few people have the means; in any case, on every question the pamphlets will so grow in number, that our attention, despite its being held by a lively interest, will tend to flag. It is necessary therefore to find another means to instruct *all Frenchmen continuously at little cost, and in a form that will not bore them.* The way to do this is through a political journal or gazette. It is the only means of educating a large nation that is limited in its powers, unaccustomed to reading, and yet anxious to escape from the servitude of ignorance. Without the newspapers, the American Revolution, in which France played so glorious a part, would never have been achieved. They all, for example, reproduced the pamphlet 'Common Sense'. This article, in which reason triumphed, restored their shattered spirits; without the help of the papers, the article would have remained in the form of a pamphlet–unknown and without influence.

It is the newspapers that brought Ireland out of the apathy and abjection in which she was held by the English Parliament; it is the newspapers that keep alive what little political liberty remains in England. A newspaper, said Doctor Jebb, is a sentinel which is forever on the watch on behalf of the people.

It is a *free and independent* press to which Doctor Jebb was referring, for those newspapers that are submitted to any kind of censorship are marked out as untrustworthy. The authority that rules them avoids or (what comes to the same thing) is supposed to avoid the facts and reflections that could enlighten the nation, it is suspected of ordering them to print praises and satires. . . .

Written in the heart of the capital, at the centre of the movement towards enlightenment, and circulating rapidly, this newspaper will inform all the provinces, at the same time, of the latest event or important measure, that often demands a prompt and uniform resolution. It will put them in touch with one another, will instruct them mutually, and will thereby produce a unity of plan and action; it will be a means of avoiding renewed bloodshed, for these things only happen or re-occur through lack of understanding. It is known that *there is only one interest,* but a variety of opinions. The monarch who rules us is the friend of his people; his minister shows that he is the friend of the people; the nobility and clergy sacrifice every privilege that is opposed to the good of the people; there is then unity of purpose. What we need now is unity of opinion, but this can only be the fruit of gradual instruction, and this instruction can only be extended to all by a free and independent newspaper.

> Prospectus for *Le Patriote français*: issued 1 April 1789:
> cited in Hatin, *Histoire politique et littéraire de la presse en France*, vol. V, pp. 8–10.

2. Ministerial Manoeuvres

Mirabeau's second number briefly mentions the speech by the king and by the Keeper of the Seals: most of it, however, is taken up by an attack on Necker's speech, particularly on how the 'pillar of the people' upheld the vote *by Order*. The passage quoted is the final summing up.

Let us hope that the Finance Minister will at last realise that it is no longer a time for beating about the bush; that he can no longer go against the current of public opinion, that he must go with it or be submerged by it; that the reign of intrigue, like that of charlatanism, is past; that the cabals will die at his feet, if he stands by his principles, but they will speedily outsmart him if he forsakes them; that, supported by an unheard of popularity, he has nothing to fear other than the desertion of his own cause, and that, if, in the situation into which the kingdom is plunged, an unflagging patience is necessary, then an inflexible firmness is no less the necessary.

Let us hope that the nation's representatives will for the future have a better sense of the dignity of their functions, of their mission, of their character; that they will no longer give way to unbounded enthusiasm at any price and under any circumstances; that, finally, instead of presenting Europe with a picture of themselves as schoolboys who have escaped the rod and are drunk with joy because they have been promised an extra holiday each week, instead of this, they will show themselves to be men, and to be men of distinction in a nation, which, to be the world's leader, needs only a constitution.

> *Les États-généraux*, No. II, 5 May 1789, pp. 19–20.

3. The Service of Truth

Undeterred by the order issued against his *Etats-généraux* (see Introduction, p. 6), Mirabeau simply changed its title. Here is the first of his *Letters to my constituents*. Following an account of why he had to resort to this manoeuvre, he lashes out against what he considered an attack not only on himself but on one of his most cherished principles.

It is true then that, far from setting the nation free, they seek only to tighten its fetters! It is in the presence of the assembled nation that they dare to produce these aulic decrees in which they attack its most sacred rights, and that, adding insult to injury, they have the incredible gaucherie to have the nation believe that this act of despotism and ministerial iniquity is a measure in its own interest!

It is fortunate, gentlemen, that the monarch cannot be held responsible for these proscriptions, which circumstances make even more criminal. It is common knowledge that the decrees of the Council are *a succession of lies* to which the ministers take it upon themselves to fix the king's seal; they do not even take the trouble to disguise this strange malfeasance. To such a pass have things come that today the most despotic systems pass openly as legitimate government.

Twenty-five million voices clamour for the freedom of the press; the nation and the king unanimously call for the free interplay of every idea; that may well be, but after having deluded us with an illusory and treacherous tolerance, a so-called popular minister has the effrontery to put the seal on our thoughts, to give privilege for the traffic in lies, and to treat as an item of contraband the essential export of truth. . . .

But what crime has this paper committed that it should be singled out for special disapprobation? Doubtless it is not for having scoffed at the speech of a prelate who, in the seat of truth, allowed himself to proclaim the most false and absurd of principles; nor is it, despite what has been claimed, for having criticised the drawing-up of the benefice list, for is there anyone who does not know or say that the benefice list is one of the most powerful means of corruption? Would so trivial a truth need to have our attention drawn to it? No, gentlemen, the real crime of this paper, the one for which there is no pardon whatsoever, is for having proclaimed the strictest impartiality and freedom: it is above all for not having paid homage to the idol of the day, for having believed that truth is more vital to nations than praise, and that it mattered more, even to those in public office, whose position depends on their good conduct, to be of service than to be flattered.

Lettre du comte de Mirabeau à ses commettants,
10 May 1789, pp. 3–6.

4. Protest by the Nobility

Following the king's order of 27 June a protest of a minority of the
clergy was handed to the Assembly on 2 July; a similar protest,
drawn up and decreed in the chamber of the nobility on 3 July was
apparently not handed in. Mirabeau's insertion of this protest in
his 'Seventeenth Letter' had the comment: 'Here is this mystic, or
rather little-known piece, but whose authenticity is guaranteed!'

The Order of the Nobility in the Estates-General, whose members are
accountable to their constituents, to the entire nation and to posterity,
for the use they make of the powers confided in them, and for the sole
custody of the principles transmitted from one age to another under the
French monarchy,
   Declares that it has never ceased to regard as inviolable and constitutional maxims,
   The distinction of Orders;
   The independence of the Orders;
   The form of voting by Order;
   The need for the royal sanction for the establishment of laws;
   That these principles, as ancient as the monarchy, steadfastly
followed in the assemblies, expressly established in the solemn laws
proposed by the Estates-General and sanctioned by the king, such as
those of 1355, 1357 and 1561, are fundamental points of the constitution,
which are inviolable unless these same powers which gave them the
force of law freely come together to abrogate them;
   Announces that its intention was never to depart from these principles, when it adopted, for the present session of the Estates-General
only, and without drawing implications for the future, the king's
declaration of the 23rd June last, since the first article of that declaration
states and maintains the essential principles of the distinction of the
Orders, the independence and the separate voting by Orders;
   That reassured by this formal understanding, carried along by the
love of peace and by the desire to return to the Estates-General its suspended functions, eager to repair the error of one of the integral parts of
the Estates-General which had attributed to itself a name and powers
which can only belong to the three Orders acting together; wishing to
give to the king proof of their respectful deference to the invitations
repeated by his letter of the 27th June last, it has regarded itself as
permitted to accede to the partial and temporary derogations which the
aforesaid declaration brought against the constitutive principles;
   That it believes it can regard (according to the good pleasure of the
nobility of the *bailliages* and while waiting for further orders) this

exception as a confirmation of the principles which it is more than ever resolved to maintain for the future;

That it believes itself so much the more authorised in these matters, since the three Orders can when they judge it fitting take separately the resolution to re-unite in one and the same assembly.

For these reasons, the Order of the Nobility, without being bound by the form of the declaration read at the royal session of the 23rd June last, accepted it purely and simply; guided by circumstances imperative for any faithful servant of the king, it went, on the 27th June last, to the common room at the Estates-General, at the same time again inviting the other Orders to accept the king's declaration.

Moreover the Order of the Nobility makes the present declaration of the monarchical principle and of the rights of Orders to conserve them in their fullness and without in any way prejudicing their guarantee and their maintenance.

Le Mercure de France, 18 July 1789, p. 114: cited in Legg, *Select Documents illustrative of the French Revolution*, vol. I, pp. 37–38.

5. Alarm

On 30 June a crowd invaded the Abbaye prison to release members of the French Guard held there for insubordination. In the riots that accompanied this act, French soldiers, suffering with the Parisians from the high price of bread, refused to disperse the rioters. Shortly after this incident Louis brought in foreign troops to replace some of the French. Fear of 'counter-revolution' mounted.

(i) *Alarm dispersed*

Estates-General   *Thursday 9 July 1789*

. . . The reading of the address to the king, decreed yesterday, and which was to have been printed by the Drafting Committee, was expected; but it was no longer awaited with anxiety. The president of the National Assembly, summoned yesterday morning by His Majesty, had the honour of seeing him in the evening. His Majesty told him that he had had a look at the decree about to be presented by the Assembly, and that he wanted to assure the president in advance; that the troops who had been drawn up around the capital had no other object than to hold in check the people who might give themselves up to outbreaks of violence and that immediately he was informed that the people had returned to peace and order, then the troops would be withdrawn.

These promises and assurances by the king calmed all our fears. . . .

The president then announced that the Central Bureau had a report to make. This report also had a general success, most gratifying in its acceptance; it was approved equally by the three Orders.

What was mainly appreciated was its preamble, whose tenor was such as to encourage a spirit of moderation, peace and love in the great work of the constitution.

Here is the order in which the National Assembly will deal with the matters before it.

1st Declaration of the Rights of Man
2nd Principles of the Monarchy
3rd Rights of the Nation
4th Rights of the King
5th Rights of the Citizen
6th Organisation and rights of the National Assembly
7th Procedures required for the establishment of Laws
8th Organisation and functions of the Provincial Assemblies
9th Obligations and limits of the judiciary
10th Functions and duties of the military power.

All the Bureaux assembled after dinner to confer on this proposed order of work.

Le Journal de Paris, 11 July 1789.

(ii) *Alarm revived*

Estates-General   *Friday 10 July 1789*

Sire

You have invited the National Assembly to give you witness of its confidence: this was to anticipate the dearest of its wishes.

We come to place before Your Majesty our most pressing fears. If we were their object, if we were so weak as to be afraid for ourselves, your goodness would still serve to reassure us, and even whilst blaming us for having doubted your intentions you would still want to know what gave rise to our doubts; you would remove their cause: you would not leave the least doubt as to the position of the National Assembly.

But Sire, we in no way implore your protection; that would be to doubt your sense of justice: we have harboured fears; and, we dare say it, they stem from the purest patriotism, and concern for the interest of our electors, for public peace, and for the happiness of our beloved monarch, who, by making smooth the road to good fortune, well deserves to walk there himself unhindered.

Do as your heart commands, Sire, in this lies the true salvation of the French people. At this time when troops are approaching from all directions, when camps are being set up all around us, when the capital is besieged, we ask ourselves in amazement: does the king distrust the loyalty of his people? Had he doubted our loyalty ought he not to have told us of this fatherly distress? What does this display of force mean? Where are the enemies of the state and of the king, who must be crushed? Where are the rebels, the Ligueurs who must be mastered? As of one voice the reply is heard in the capital and throughout the breadth of the kingdom: 'We cherish our king, we bless heaven for the gift that he has given us, in his love.'

> The petition goes on to assure the king that the people in no way blame him for their ills, that his word is all that is necessary to avoid bloodshed. However it continues:

The danger, Sire, is pressing, it is universal and beyond all the calculations of man's prudence.

The danger is for the people of the provinces. Once alarmed for our liberty we know of no means of holding them back. Distance in itself enlarges things, exaggerates everything, doubles the unease, embitters, and finally envenoms them.

The danger is for the capital. How will the people in the depths of want, and tormented as they are by the most cruel anguish, look on the need to contend with a crowd of menacing soldiers for what remains of its subsistence? The presence of the troops will inflame them, cause them to riot, and produce universal unrest, and the first act of violence, delivered under pretext of police action, will set in motion a terrible succession of misfortunes.

The danger is for the troops. French soldiers, brought into the centre of discussions and joining in the passions and in the interests of the people, might forget that they are enlisted as soldiers, to remember only that nature made them men.

The danger, Sire, menaces the work which we have made our first duty . . .

The danger, Sire, is even more terrible; you can judge its extent by the fears which bring us before you. Great revolutions have been sparked off by less trivial causes than these; more than one enterprise fatal to nations has been ushered into the world in a manner less sinister and less formidable. . . .

Le Journal de Paris, 12 July 1789.

14 JULY: AN END TO DESPOTISM?

One event more than any other symbolises in the eyes of the world the French Revolution—the fall of the Bastille. At the time the more elated thought that with the fall of the symbol of despotism, despotism itself was destined to be eliminated. At first jubilation was muted to some extent by fear of foreign intervention and aristocratic counter-revolution, but this fear was in turn replaced by anxiety about the possibility of general lawlessness: fear of anarchy replaced horror of despotism, at least in some minds.

6. The Fall of the Bastille

(i) *A legend is born*

The *Révolutions de Paris* has been said to be responsible for giving rise to the legend of the taking of the Bastille as being a magnificent feat of arms carried out against terrible odds. Its description of the event should be read as it appeared to an actual participant in the event, rather than as an objective appraisal.

As soon as the city learnt of M. Necker's departure, there was general consternation; the people, in despair and seeking an end to its ills, set fire to several toll gates and dispersed in all directions, their aims uncertain, while the citizens, in gloomy silence, discussed the events among themselves and could not hide their tears. At five o'clock, on Sunday 12 July, some citizens, assembled at the Palais-Royal, despatched orders to close all the theatres; this was done without question. This mark of respect, given to so great a man, made known in no uncertain fashion the extent of the public grief . . .

Monday 13 July

The gun shots that were heard during the night of Sunday to Monday and which were mentioned in yesterday's news, had been fired by *the soldiers of the fatherland*; this is the title taken by the French Guards when presenting themselves at the camp of the regiments of Royal-Allemand and of Chateauvieux; but these refused to fight and the soldiers promised to lay down their arms. The cruel prince Lambesc threatened them with hanging; they rose up against him, and this detested person found himself forced to leave for Versailles the next day.

The National Assembly sent a deputation to the king, to set before him the state of the capital. The king replied that he intended to carry on with his plans as advised by his council. . . .

. . . in the evening the capital was quiet; bourgeois of the various districts, helped by some *soldiers of the fatherland,* were in arms and had orders to disarm all unauthorised persons, which they did with the strictest regularity.

We forgot to say that the majority of the national troops and even some of the foreign ones seemed to be on our side; and that at any moment we expected help from the provinces.

Tuesday 14 July

The night of Monday to Tuesday was extremely quiet, apart from the arrest by the citizen militia of some thirty-four unauthorised persons, who had plundered and caused a great deal of damage at St.-Lazare; they have been taken into custody . . .

But a victory of outstanding significance, and one which will perhaps astonish our descendants, was the taking of the Bastille, in four hours or so.

First, the people tried to enter this fortress by the Rue St.-Antoine, this fortress, which no one has ever penetrated against the wishes of this frightful despotism and where the monster still resided. The treacherous governor had put out a flag of peace. So a confident advance was made; a detachment of French Guards, with perhaps five to six thousand armed bourgeois, penetrated the Bastille's outer courtyards, but as soon as some six hundred persons had passed over the first drawbridge, the bridge was raised and artillery fire mowed down several French Guards and some soldiers; the cannon fired on the town, and the people took fright; a large number of individuals were killed or wounded; but then they rallied and took shelter from the fire; a row of bayonets, fixed in the wall, enabled some brave individual to cut through a post that locked the drawbridge; immediately it fell and they came to the second ditch, near which lay the first victims; meanwhile, they tried to locate some cannon; they attacked from the water's edge through the gardens of the arsenal, and from there made an orderly siege; they advanced from various directions, beneath a ceaseless round of fire. It was a terrible scene. The brave French Guard did wonders. About three o'clock they captured the overseer of the gunpowder store, whose uniform made them mistake him for the Governor of the Bastille; he was manhandled and taken to the town, where he was recognised and set free. The fighting grew steadily more intense; the citizens had become hardened to the fire; from all directions they clambered onto the roofs or broke into the rooms; as soon as an enemy appeared among the turrets on the tower, he was fixed in the sights of a hundred guns and mown down in an instant; meanwhile cannon fire was hurriedly directed against the second drawbridge, which it pierced, breaking the chains; in vain did the cannon on the tower reply, for most people were sheltered from it; the fury was at its height; people bravely faced death and every danger; women, in their eagerness, helped us to the utmost; even the children, after the discharge of fire from the fortress, ran here and there picking up the bullets and shot; [and so the Bastille fell and the governor, De Launay, was captured] . . . they strip him of his badges of rank; they treat him shamelessly; he is dragged through the crowd . . . Serene and blessed liberty, for the first time, has at last been introduced into this abode of horrors, this frightful refuge of monstrous despotism and its crimes.

Meanwhile, they get ready to march; they leave amidst an enormous crowd; the applause, the outbursts of joy, the insults, the oaths hurled at the treacherous prisoners of war; everything is confused; cries of vengeance and of pleasure issue from every heart; the conquerors, glorious and covered in honour, carry their arms and the spoils of the conquered, the flags of victory, the militia mingling with the soldiers of the fatherland, the victory laurels offered them from every side, –all this created a frightening and splendid spectacle. On arriving at the square, the people, anxious to avenge themselves, allowed neither De Launay nor the other officers to reach the place of trial; they seized them from the hands of their conquerors, and trampled them underfoot one after the other. De Launay was struck by a thousand blows, his head was cut off and hoisted on the end of a pike with blood streaming down all sides. . . . This glorious day must amaze our enemies, and finally usher in for us the triumph of justice and liberty. In the evening, there were celebrations.

Les Révolutions de Paris, No. 1, 12–18 July 1789, pp. 3, 5, 9, 12–17.

(ii) *A word of warning*

On 22 July the intendant for Paris, Berthier, and his son-in-law Foulon, who had replaced Necker during the short period of his dismissal, were murdered in the street. Whilst offering to 'despots and ministers' and all other tyrants this 'terrible and revolting spectacle', the writer hopes that this will be only a temporary aberration–a recurring theme in the *Révolutions de Paris*.

Frenchmen, you destroy tyrants; your hate is frightening; it is shocking. . . . But you will be free! O my country, the rights of man will at last be respected among us! I know, O my fellow citizens, how deeply these turbulent scenes afflict your soul; like you, I am seized to the quick by such events; but think how ignominious it is to live and to be a slave; think with what torments one should punish crimes against humanity; think, finally, of what good, what satisfaction, what happiness awaits you, you and your children and your descendants, when august and blessed liberty will have set its temple among you! Yet do not forget that these proscriptions outrage humanity and make nature tremble.

Les Révolutions de Paris, No. 2, 18–25 July 1789, p. 25.

7. Palais-Royal: Centre of Revolution

Desmoulins' pamphlet *Discours de la lanterne*, was issued in September 1789, attacking the move made by certain deputies to grant the king an absolute veto. A curious sidelight of the controversy was the attempt by a group of Palais-Royal journalists to incite the Parisians to march to Versailles and bring the king back to Paris. As a result of this the Parisian authorities made an attempt to remove the threat posed by this trouble spot. In his criticism of this decision of the Municipality, Desmoulins evokes the glory of what he calls the 'foyer of patriotism'.

It is from the Palais-Royal that the loyal citizens set out to snatch from the Abbaye prison the French Guards who had been detained or had been presumed to be detained for the good cause. It is from the Palais-Royal that the orders were issued to close down the theatres and to go into mourning on 12 July.* It is at the Palais-Royal that on the same day the call to arms was made and the national cockade adopted. It is the Palais-Royal which for six months has inundated France with all the brochures that have made of everyone, even of the soldier, a philosopher. It is at the Palais-Royal that the patriots, mingling joyously with the cavalrymen, the Dragoons, the Horse-Guards, the Swiss Guards, and the cannoneers, embracing them, intoxicating them, and lavishing gold on them to drink the health of the nation, won over the whole army and thus upset all the infernal plans of these veritable Catilines. It is the Palais-Royal that saved the National Assembly and the ungrateful Parisians from a general massacre.

Discours de la Lanterne aux Parisiens, France,
1st Year of Liberty, pp. 50–51.

---

* On news of the dismissal of Necker.

8. The Depredations of Despotism

> The problems of public protest and government authority, of riot and repression, are inescapable in any democratic country. This debate was a live one from the first days of the Revolution. We have chosen Mirabeau to speak for the 'people' and Rivarol for 'authority'.

Let them compare the number of innocent people sacrificed by the abuses and bloody decisions of the tribunals, the ministerial acts of vengeance secretly carried out in the tower [*donjon*] of Vincennes, in the dungeons of the Bastille, let them compare these with the hasty and impetuous acts of vengeance on the part of the masses,* and then let them decide on which side lies barbarity . . . If the anger of the people is terrible, the cold-bloodedness of despotism is atrocious; its systematic cruelties result in more victims in one day than all those sacrificed by popular risings over a period of years.

Consider how many causes have prepared the material for this explosion! All the denials of justice, all the insults, all the scandals; popular ministers sent into exile; the failure to take notice of the public contempt for the leader of those who replace them; the sanctuary of laws defiled; the National Assembly compromised and threatened; foreign troops, and artillery; the capital about to be besieged or invaded; preparations for a civil war; and what does this mean! a butchery where all the friends of the people, known or suspected, must fall—surprised and disarmed–beneath the soldiers' sword; and, to put everything in one word, two hundred years of oppression–public and private, political and fiscal, feudal and judicial–crowned by the most terrible conspiracy whose memory the annals of the world will forever keep alive . . . that is what has provoked the people! . . . They have punished a small number of those whom public outcry denounced as the authors of its ills; but let them tell us if there would not have been more bloodshed had our enemies triumphed. . . . They often fear the people because of the harm they have done to them; they are forced to keep the people in chains because they oppress them and their persecutors slander them to salve their conscience. Those who had had things so arranged that they need not fear any court, now tremble before that of the people; there are still too many guilty parties for there to be no more terror. If the scenes recently enacted at Paris had taken place in Constantinople, the most timid of men would say: 'The people has done itself justice. The affair had come to a head; the punishment of one vizir will serve as a lesson to the others.' This event, far from appearing to us unusual,

---

* This was written just after the murder of Foulon and Berthier (22 July 1789).

should hardly attract our attention. It would need a whole volume for us to illustrate with examples that in times of crisis, such as the present, governments reap only the fruits of their own iniquities. They despise the people yet expect them to be always calm, always unmoved! No, there is a lesson to be drawn from these sad events: injustice perpetrated against the people by the other classes makes it seek justice even in its very barbarity.

But . . . these excesses are far from equalling the measured cruelties that the judiciary exercise against those unfortunates whose crime has been forced on them by the vices of governments. Let us congratulate ourselves that the people has not acquired all the refinements of barbarity, and that it has left to the savants the honour of discovering such abominable devices!

> *Dix-neuvième Lettre du comte de Mirabeau à ses commettants,*
> 9–24 July 1789, pp. 55–58.

9. New Masters for the Old

Amid vague cries of 'fatherland' and 'liberty', and in that merging of all the ranks which to the common gaze appears as a union of every interest, flight or silence have distinguished the true politicians, the true friends of order, and all those, finally, who can distinguish liberty from licence, courage from fanaticism, a blind insurrection from an enlightened constitution.

Moreover Paris has never merited the name of capital more than today: it raised the standard, and the whole kingdom fell in behind it; it took for itself the name *'patrie'*, its town hall called itself 'the nation', and this insolent sophism has aroused no-one's indignation. Paris absorbs all the state's revenue, it holds in its hands all the branches of authority, its Palais-Royal draws up the proscription lists, its populace carries them out, and flight is not always possible for those whose names are inscribed on these fatal lists. Three million armed peasants, from one end of the kingdom to the other, stop travellers, check their papers, and bring the victims back to Paris; the town hall cannot protect them from the fury of the patriotic hangmen; the National Assembly, in raising Paris, might well have been able to topple the throne, but it cannot save a single citizen. The time will come, and that time is not far off, when the National Assembly will say to the civil army: 'You have saved me from authority, but who will save me from you?' . . . If a flock of sheep summons tigers to save it from the dogs, who will be able to save it from its new defenders . . . How do you reply in fact to an armed people who say to you: 'I am master' . . .?

When authority has been overthrown, its power passes inevitably to the lowest classes of society since basically it is there that the executive power resides in all its fullness. Such is today the state of France and the capital.

Le Journal politique national (edition of 1790), No. 8, pp. 83–85.

4 AUGUST: AN END TO PRIVILEGE?

The calling of the Estates-General raised the hopes of the peasants for some improvement in their wretched situation. But their feudal superiors failed to respond. This intransigence increased the tension that had long existed between the two classes, and a dangerous situation evolved. To this ferment were added economic crises and fear of 'brigands' and 'aristocratic plots'. Even before 14 July there had been numerous riots in the country with peasants, armed to meet 'brigands' who never appeared, settling accounts with their overlord. In the second fortnight of July these riots became so widespread that the deputies had to leave off their work of constitution-making to meet the crisis. One solution was to make concessions rather than lose everything, and on the evening of 4 August the remarkable 'Saint Bartholomew's night of privilege' saw nobles trying to outdo each other in sacrificing their feudal rights.

10. The Electric Whirlwind

In his previous number Mirabeau had remarked on his failure to report the riots, burning and destruction in the countryside, which he considered was the inevitable outcome of two centuries of oppression.

There is no doubt that the session of 4 August presented an unusual sight to the onlookers. Men of distinguished rank, proposing the abolition of the feudal régime and the restitution of the people's fundamental rights (for it is not they who dishonoured these equitable acts by calling them *sacrifices*) provoked widespread acclaim; the kind of tribute that is paid every day to high-sounding phrases and which could not be denied to patriotic sentiments. For him who knows the full Assemblies, the dramatic emotions to which they are susceptible, the seduction of applause, the rivalry to outbid one's colleagues, the honour of personal disinterestedness, in short the kind of sublime intoxication that accompanies an outpouring of generosity; for him, in short, who reflects on the coming together of these causes, everything that seems extraordinary in this session belongs to the class of the ordinary. The Assembly was in an electric whirlwind, and the shocks succeeded each other without a break.

Why debate when everyone is in agreement? Did not the common good clearly manifest itself? The first to display a new tribute to the public interest did no more than express what the others already felt: there was no need for debate or fine speech to have adopted what had already been decided by the majority and commanded by the overwhelming authority of the nation's mandates.

Le Courrier de Provence, No. 24, pp. 2–3.

11. Immortal Night

The fourth of August is often seen as the date of 'the destruction of the feudal régime'. In fact while the remnants of serfdom, the *corvée*, were swept away, ecclesiastical tithes, though condemned in principle, were to be collected until provision for church worship was voted (April 1790), and some of the more onerous privileges and obligations were made redeemable by individual purchase. Nevertheless, the intention was belied by the deed. What the peasants had, they held; the compensation was never paid. The two sides of this question are brought out in the following documents.

Frenchmen, aren't you going to institute a fête in commemoration of that night when so many great things were done without the delays of scrutiny [*scrutin*] and as by inspiration? It is on that night, you must say, more so than that of Holy Saturday, that we came forth from the wretched bondage of Egypt. That night put an end to the wild boars, rabbits and game devouring our crops. That night abolished the tithe and the *casuel*. That night abolished annates and exemptions, took the keys of heaven from an Alexander VI to give them to individual conscience. . . . That night, from the great requisitor Séguier almost to the last tax collector, has destroyed the tyranny of the Robe; that night by suppressing the venality of the magistracy, has secured for France the inestimable benefit of the abolition of the *parlements*. That night has put down the seigneurial justices and the free duchies, has abolished *mainmorte, corvée* and crop-share rents, and effaced from the

land of the Franks all traces of slavery. That night restored Frenchmen
to the Rights of Man, and declared all citizens equal, equally admissible to all offices, places, and public employ; again, that night has
snatched all civil offices, ecclesiastical and military, from wealth, birth
and royalty, to give them to the nation as a whole on the basis of merit.
That night has taken from a Madame de Béarn her pension of 80,000
livres for having been so shameless as to introduce du Barry; has taken
from Madame d'Epr[émesnil] her pension of 20,000 livres for having
slept with a minister. That night has suppressed pluralism, has deprived
a Cardinal of Lorraine of his twenty-five or thirty bishoprics, a Prince of
Soubise his pension of 1,500,000 livres, a Baron de Besenval his seven
or eight provincial commands, and has forbidden the reunion of so
many places that one sees accumulated under one head in dedicatory
epistles and epitaphs . . . It is that night that suppressed mistresses
and exclusive privileges. Trade with the Indies is now open to anyone.
He who wishes may open a shop. The master tailor, the master shoe-
maker, the master wigmaker, will weep; but the journeymen will
rejoice and there will be lights in the garrets.

On that night finally, Justice cast out of the temple all the sellers in
order to listen freely to the poor, the innocent and the oppressed; that
night destroyed the exclusiveness of the legal classes, an order that
monopolised all suits, and with its monopoly of pleading, its claim
to exploit exclusively all the disputes of the realm. Now, any man who
has the ability and confidence of his clients can plead. Maître Erucius
will be included on the new register even though he is illegitimate;
Maître Jean-Baptiste Rousseau, even though he is the son of a shoe-
maker; and Maître Demosthènes, even though in his cellar there is no
suitable antechamber. O night disastrous for the grand chamber, the
clerks, the bailiffs, the procurers, the secretaries, under-secretaries,
soliciting 'beauties', the porters, the valets, the lawyers, the king's
followers, indeed, for all plunderers. Disastrous night for all the bloodsuckers of the state, the financiers, the courtisans, the cardinals, the
archbishops, abbots, canons, abbesses, priors and sub-priors.

But O wonderful night, O *vere beata nox*, for the thousand young
recluses, the Bernardines, Benedictines, and Visitandines, when they
are going to be visited by the monks—Bernardin, Benedictine, Carmelites
and Cordeliers, when the National Assembly will cast loose their bonds,
and when the abbé Fauchet, as a reward for his patriotism, and to
outrage the abbé Maury, after having been Patriarch of the new rite
and, in his turn, President of the National Assembly, will mark his
presidency with these words from Genesis, which the nuns no more
hoped to hear: *Increase and Multiply.* O happy night for the merchant,
who is assured of freedom of trade! happy for the artisan, whose
industry is free and given every incentive, who will no longer work for

his master but will receive his salary for himself! happy for the peasant, whose property finds itself increased by at least ten per cent with the suppression of tithes and feudal dues; happy indeed for everybody, since the barriers that excluded nearly everybody from the path of honours and employment have been forcibly thrown down for ever, and today there no longer exist among the French any distinctions but those of virtue and talent.

Discours de la Lanterne aux Parisiens, France,
1st Year of Liberty, pp. 5–9.

12. The Ruination of France

The twenty numbers of this paper, which appeared between 22 September 1789 and March 1790, were aimed at defending 'the rights of the nation against the tyranny of the Paris Communes and absurdities of the National Assembly, by showing in their true light the operations of these illustrious CONGRESSES.'

Since they met what have our 1,200 representatives done? The verification of powers, a verification already begun, a task which we found extremely tedious, and which is at last finished. Since that time what have they eventually decreed for the good of the state? This is what they have decreed: that they will continue to waste time in reading petitions. They love praise, our Seigneurs, . . .

They then decide to give their full attention to the Constitution; but will they precede it or follow it with a Declaration of the Rights of Man? . . . Another question: will the Declaration of Rights be accompanied by a declaration of duties?

And now after all these discussions what have you done? You spent a night which provoked a peal of laughter throughout half France; the next morning and within three days, all Paris, all the kingdom, learned that you had decreed part of the articles of the Constitution, but that they had not yet been sanctioned. Never mind! No sooner was word of these proposed articles which you are discussing today heard, than the people in the provinces regarded them as formally decreed; and they took every advantage which only they themselves can withdraw. They no longer pay taxes, they indulge in smuggling, protected by force of arms; they fix the price of salt, and it is rather nice of them that they have consented to pay a half of what it was formerly worth; they devastate the woods, forests, countryside, property, and destroy all the game, but their greatest wrong is to ruin the crops at the very time that they are most valuable to us. They refused to honour rights whose abolition was still under discussion; they no longer fear the ministers of justice, whose abolition in the villages has been recommended. They are acting, then, precisely like people who no longer fear the law, and the enjoyment of liberty goes to the strongest, whilst your mission is to give it to the weak as well as to those who possess brute force.

Ah! Do you think, then, only of one section of the citizens? Do you not see half of France ruined, reduced to wretchedness by your too hasty and too numerous suppressions? Carry out these suppressions, but by degrees, and if I have to live only on what I produce myself, do not ruin me with a wave of your wand; wait till I am dead before you do away with the position I occupy, or the modest pension I have obtained; do you think you can regenerate the kingdom by ruining those who nourish the people?

> *Le Fouet national*, No. 1, 22 September 1789, p. 3: cited in
> Legg, *Select Documents*, vol. I, pp. 111–12.

THE DECLARATION OF RIGHTS: DEADLOCK
AND EMERGENCE OF FACTIONS

With the municipal and rural disturbances apparently under control, the Assembly returned to the task from which it had been interrupted (see 5(i) Alarm dispersed, p. 50). The question of the Rights of Man was a subject that was to open up vast new fields of ridicule for the aristocrats to gambol in, while it left the moderates with some difficult problems to solve, of principle and practice. More immediately divisive was the question of the nature of the new parliament and the position of the king within it. The first question centred around whether there should be two houses as in Britain, the second around whether the king should have an absolute or modified veto or no veto at all. From this debate dates Mirabeau's alienation from the newly emerging Left, and the rise to prominence, on the extreme Left, of Robespierre and Pétion. The Left, or rather Left-centre, who supported the compromise of the suspensive veto, dominated the debates in the whole period of the Constituent Assembly. They became the Feuillants on their secession from the Jacobin Club on 16 July 1791.

13. Ban the Bible

Many of the passages of the *Actes des Apôtres* are not suitable for translation, partly because many of the satirical allusions refer to characters now forgotten, partly because the point of their barbs has become blunted with time; again many passages are just too scurrilous for printing. The pretensions of the leaders in the Assembly served as a butt for many of their jibes; the glorification of the 'people' was mocked in nearly every edition. This latter theme is developed in the following document.

The Abbey of St.-Germain-en-Laid,
28 April 1790.

Christians and Apostles My Brothers:
Gentlemen

I denounce an aristocratic book that has spread everywhere, that is found in the schools, in former religious houses, that is cited in sermons, sung at times at high mass; a book that the Jews will propagate even more so as they become our active brothers, and which some of those apostolic priests who have contributed so generously, so devoutly, to the destruction of the clergy, to obtain pensions that no one will pay them, still retain perhaps, without being aware of it, in the dust of their presbyteries. This book, in truth, was not written for that time of enlightenment, peace and prosperity, in which we live today, since it was translated from the Hebrew into Greek 131 years before Christ; but it is none the less dangerous for the principles it contains and for the insult it makes against all eligible citizens; its very title renders it suspect; it is called ECCLESIASTICUS. Indeed! Gentlemen, this book claims that the wisdom necessary for doctors of law is acquired only in retreat and meditation. It claims that farm-workers, tradesmen and craftsmen, are incapable of making laws; that, if they should stick to their job, they could make it perfect, but that to allow them to act as law-makers, to grant them membership of the assembly, is to allow prudence, justice and obedience to be eroded. What nonsense, Gentlemen! what anti-national prejudice! I appeal to all shoemakers, wigmakers, hosiers, tinsmiths, leather curers, and other merchants, who have all suddenly become Lycurguses or Solons, nay even a Condé or a Turenne. I appeal from this book to our sixty districts, from which have come forth so many regulations, so much advice, so many ordinances, so many provisional laws, tending to shape a *pure and royal* democracy, and the finest Constitution that has appeared on earth. The very walls of the capital bear witness to it: and the proof that the Parisians are a thinking people is that the opinion of one in no way resembles that of another, and that each remains buried in the depths of his own meditations. I do not speak of their great skill in forming peaceful battalions, in mounting assault by ladder, and in guarding one prisoner* with forty thousand men. . . .

It is, however, true that part of the nation that was formerly called the populace is today vested with all the executive power; that by it alone is the constituent power maintained, flattered, and applauded; but that contemptuous term must be excised from the French language. In being born and remaining thereafter equal in rights, receiving the same education, the same feelings, the same desire to show their talents and their virtues, all will be equally honest, equally polite, equally lofty of mind; and we shall see no more of those men such as we have known until now, who, through neglect, poverty, low birth, the faults of their parents and their own needs, retained uncouth manners, a language of their own, and feelings of bitterness and hostility towards those whom they saw better dressed and better fed than themselves. The schools will be opened to them, not at five louis a year as under the *aristocracy*, but free for love of the nation; and as this good people will be freed from the worry of having to earn a living, they will be able to attend punctiliously all the lessons and to acquire on their slates the new ideas, the sublime thoughts of their teachers. A splendid invention, which will make them happier than those religious principles that committed them to Providence, which consoled them in their inevitable but fleeting troubles, with the hope of eternal happiness that is the promised reward of virtue!

That is not all, Gentlemen, for this book that I denounce also claims that, to the wisdom and meditation, which are necessary to acquire the art of governing men, there must also be added pilgrimages and prayer [Ecclus. 39]. What a mistake! Go into the Manège, and if it is a time when the bell is quiet, when 'union and concord are followed by calm and tranquillity', examine the personalities who have put all France into a turmoil to unite it in a manner previously unknown. Are there many who have thought on other things than the means of advancing their own interests. . . . ?

Yet see with what facility these great men speak without thinking and destroy without consideration! See how they improvise the decrees and send them for the royal approval at the same time as they go to the printer! See how they give to *the first representative of the nation*, who no longer represents anything, the freedom of deferring his consent to the new laws until a third legislature, and see how they order him, midst the roll of drums, tinder alight, murderers in front, and cannons behind, to give it in twenty-four hours! What skill! What verve! . . .

* i.e. the King.

O France, how fortunate you are to have found in your midst so many creative geniuses, so many unquenchable orators, so many journalists full of ideas, so many pillars of wisdom, so many '*lanternes* to bring you to the true light'.

Your most humble and obedient servant, Dom Bouquin, active religious of a large library and a small refectory, which is sufficient for his existence and happiness, and soon to be a passive citizen, forced to perish of boredom and misery.

Long live liberty.

Les Actes des Apôtres, IV, No. 104, pp. 3–5, 8, 11, 14-15.

14. The Sceptre of Power

> Fear of the populace and the extension of their sovereignty to the 'dogma of absolute equality among men and so to equal partition of land', and a belief in the 'harmony of inequality' are behind Rivarol's interpretation of sovereignty as explained here.

The writers of the Third Estate, and, in general, all the *philosophes,* having pushed to its limits and drawn out the implications of the principle *that sovereignty resides in the people,* it was therefore necessary that the Revolution, written about in their books, should have come into play and been enacted in the capital and in the provinces. Could one, in fact, have stopped an Assembly which exercised the sovereignty of the people and which had won control of the army? Was it not at the same time a veritable display of power for deputies, the majority of whom had spent their lives in greeting the bailiff of their villages or in fawning upon the intendant of their provinces, was it not, I say, pure joy for them to trample underfoot one of the leading thrones in the world? Could the lawyers resist the pleasure of humiliating the sovereign courts? As for those who had nothing, were they not delighted to distribute the treasure of the Church to the vampires of the state?

One cannot insist too much on the evil that can result from a good principle when it is abused.

Sovereignty resides in the people. Yes, without a doubt; but it does so in an implicit manner, that is to say, the people will never exercise it except in nominating its representatives; and if it is a monarchy, then the king will be the first magistrate. Thus, although it is basically true that everything comes from the land, it is no less true that it is brought under control by cultivation, and likewise the people are brought under control by authority and law. Sovereignty resides in the people as much as fruit is in our fields, that is, in the abstract; the fruit has to come from the tree that produces it, and so must public authority come by the sceptre that rules. This maxim of the *sovereignty of the people* had, however, so turned men's heads that the Assembly, instead of prudently following the proposals of the Constitution Committee and building a sound and lasting edifice, gave themselves up entirely to the ebb and flow of the motions as well as to the fugue of its orators, who vied with one another in heaping decree upon decree, ruin upon ruin, in order to satisfy the people who swarmed through the alcoves of the Chamber, who raised their threats in the Palais-Royal, and created disturbances in the provinces.

Le Journal politique national (edition of 1790), vol. I,
No. 18, pp. 195–96.

15. Mirabeau on the Veto

Mirabeau has been called the 'democratic monarchist' for his upholding of royal prerogatives at the same time as he supported the rights of the people. His support of the absolute veto was his first major break with the 'patriots'.

Session of the first of September

GENTLEMEN

In the best organised monarchy, royal authority is always the object of fear on the part of the better citizens; he whom the law puts above them all too easily becomes the rival of the law. Sufficiently powerful in order to protect the constitution, he is often tempted to destroy it. The uniform path pursued everywhere by the authority of kings has taught us only too well the need to watch them. This suspicion, which is a good thing in itself, naturally leads us to want to restrict such a formidable power. A subconscious fear makes us turn away, despite ourselves, from the means with which it is necessary to equip the Supreme Leader of the Nation, so that he can fulfil the functions assigned to him.

Yet, if we consider dispassionately the principles and nature of monarchical government that has been established on the basis of the people's sovereignty, if we carefully examine the circumstances that give rise to its formation, we shall see that the monarchy ought to be regarded more as the protector of the people than as the enemy of their well-being.

Two powers are necessary for the existence and function of the Body
Politic: namely, the power to decree and the power to act. By the first,
society establishes the rules that must guide it towards the goal that it
lays down, which is without any doubt the common good. By the
second, these rules are executed; the public power serves to help society
to surmount the obstacles that this execution might meet in the opposition of individual wishes. In a great nation, these two powers cannot
be executed by the people as such; there is then the need for the
representatives of the people to exercise the faculty of the will, i.e. of the
legislative power; and again the need for another type of representatives,
for the exercise of the faculty of acting i.e. of the executive power.

The greater the nation, the more it matters that this last power be
viable; hence the need for a single and supreme head; hence the need
for monarchical government in great states, where the disturbances, the
excesses would be infinitely to be feared, if there did not exist a strong
enough power to unite under it all the factions and to direct their
activity to a common end.

Both these powers are equally necessary, equally valuable to the
nation. . . . No one protests against the *veto* of the National Assembly,
which, effectively, is only a right of the people entrusted to *its representatives* so as to oppose any proposal that would tend to re-establish
ministerial despotism. Why then protest against the *veto* of the prince,
which also is no other than a right of the people *specially entrusted to the
prince*, since the prince is as concerned as the people to prevent the
establishment of the aristocracy?

But, you say, the deputies of the people in the National Assembly
are invested with their power for a limited time, and they have no share
in the executive power, therefore the abuse that they could commit
through their veto, cannot have so serious a consequence as that which
an immovable prince would oppose to a just and reasonable law.

Firstly, if the prince does not have the *veto* who will prevent representatives of the people from prolonging and finally making their
positions permanent? It was in this way and not, as we have been told,
by the suppression of the House of Lords, that the Long Parliament
overthrew the political liberty of Great Britain. Who will prevent it
from even appropriating to itself the executive power's function, which
disposes of positions and favours? Will there lack pretexts to justify
this usurpation? Jobs being scandalously filled! Favours unworthily
prostituted! etc.

Secondly, the *veto*, whether of the prince or of the deputies to the
National Assembly, has no other function than to stop a proposal: the
only result of a *veto*, whatever it is, would be inaction on the part of the
executive power in this regard.

Thirdly, there is no doubt that the prince's *veto* can be opposed to a good law; but it can also protect us from a bad one, the possibility of which is not unlikely.

Fourthly, I will suppose that, in effect, the prince's *veto* prevents the establishment of a law that is the best and most advantageous to the nation; what will happen *if the* ANNUAL *return of the National Assembly is as firmly assured as the crown on the head of the prince who wears it*, that is to say, if the annual return of the National Assembly is assured by a law *truly constitutional* which forbids, under penalty of conviction of madness, from proposing either the grant of any kind of tax, or the establishment of the military force for more than a year. . . .

1. It wrongly supposes that it is impossible for a second legislature to fulfil the wishes of the people.

2. It wrongly supposes that the king will be tempted to continue his *veto* against the known wishes of the nation.

3. It supposes that the *suspensive veto* has no defects whatsoever, whereas in several respects it has the same defects as if the king had been granted no *veto* at all.

Le Courrier de Provence, No. 35, pp. 3–5, 10–12, 20.

16. 'Power Corrupts'

National Assembly   *Versailles, Saturday 12 September 1789*

For how many Legislatures or Sessions will the suspensive veto last?

This is what it was proposed should be decided in the National Assembly this morning; but it was pointed out, and it was quite obvious, that before decreeing for how many legislatures the power of veto should last, it should be determined how long the legislatures themselves should last. This question, which was surely of the greatest importance, was then debated. If the legislatures last too long they develop an aristocratic spirit; for a great authority always corrupts more or less those who exercise it. If the legislatures last too short a time they do not have time to get to know their business; the mediocre talents, always the most audacious, show themselves first and spoil everything, so that when real talent shows itself, the legislature is coming to an end. These are the two reefs, equally dangerous, to be avoided. It is known that the corruption so common in the English Parliament can largely be attributed to its having been changed from triennial to septennial.

Le Journal de Paris, 14 September 1789, p. 1163.

17. The Right to Rebel

The debates on the veto convinced Loustallot that the Assembly
was still dominated by aristocrats, only whereas they had formerly
'reigned over us like lions now they reign like foxes'.

The *suspensive veto*–which has been presented to the people as a good
measure, and which we could not avoid granting to the king, will put
the nation in chains on account of the intended length of its operation,
for one would have to be blind or a fool to doubt, following M. Necker's
note, that the suspension is valid for three legislatures, that is to say,
for six years, without doubt long enough for a Louis XI or a Richelieu
to recover a despotic authority.

Considering the influence of the ministerial party in the Assembly,
that is, the nobles, the clergy and some deputies of the commons who
have feudal property, or who aspire to the favours of the Court, we
cannot in any way expect to gain a constitution for the nation; it will
be for the Court. What then can be done? To despair or go to Versailles
and snatch from the Assembly the traitors to the fatherland? Neither
one nor the other is worthy of the majesty of the French people.

Our representatives are not, as in England, the sovereigns of the
nation. IT IS THE NATION THAT IS THE SOVEREIGN. Indeed, they have
tried to make themselves our masters, by declaring that their mandates
are not *imperative*. But their decision takes nothing from the people. It is
absurd that a representative can make law for his constituents; the
people, assembled in communes, has therefore the right to summon
back its representatives, to revise their work, to adopt, reject or to
amend it. Let us act promptly and make use of this right–indeed, we
must–for public opinion no longer means anything to certain deputies;
and we must do so, in accordance with a decree of the National
Assembly.

Les Révolutions de Paris, No. 11, 19–25 September 1789.

18. The Chains Replaced

The fears voiced here by Marat are typical of the political discontent
that helped prepare the way for the October days.

I beseech my readers to observe closely that the articles to be sanctioned, over which the king, or rather his ministers, have raised difficulties
are those that relate to making good the loss of financial dues, to the
suppression of tithes before having provided for the needs of the

prelates, to the abolition of venal charges, and the suppression of pensions etc. In refusing their sanction, they can only have in mind the formation of a formidable party, the clergy, the Order of Malta, the tribunals, the merchants, the financiers and the innumerable crowd of creatures that the prince buys with the state's money.

I beseech them also to observe that in refusing to enforce to the letter the decree on the movement and export of grain, they are seeking to find a means of continuing their monopoly of these and of reducing the people by famine.

Again I beseech them to observe that, in pressing for the financial measures, they are only awaiting the time when the public treasury is filled in order to stop the work of the National Assembly, to reduce to smoke the great work of the Constitution, and to return the people to its chains.

These then are my fears for the dangers arising from the wrong course followed by the Assembly in the past two months, fears which have been justified in the event and which have shown the correctness of my observations, unfortunately only too clearly proved.

Then there is the prince, who has become once more the supreme arbiter of the law, seeking to oppose the Constitution even before it is finished.

Then there are the ministers so ridiculously exalted, whose only thought is to return to the hands of the monarch the chains of despotism that the nation has taken from him.

Here then is the nation itself enchained by its representatives and delivered defenceless to an imperious master, who, forgetful of his powerlessness, violates his promises and oaths.

L'Ami du peuple, No. 10, 20 September 1789

OCTOBER DAYS

The insurrection of 5 and 6 October brought an end to the Versailles monarchy. The events preceding the march closely paralleled those of the previous July: economic distress, uncertainty as to the king's intention, and fear of counter-revolution. This time, however, initiation of the 'march' came from the women of the markets and faubourgs of Paris, with their demands for bread. They were followed by their menfolk, sections of the National Guard (officially formed on 10 August) and a hesitant Lafayette. On this occasion, too, the press played a significant part by criticising the Assembly's decrees and publishing the king's opposition to them. Marat boasted later that his paper played a major role in these events; Gorsas is said to have read his number of 4 October, which gave details of the celebrations of the king's troops, to a crowd in the Palais-Royal, so inciting them to action. The extracts that follow indicate attitudes after the event, varying from the lyrical Desmoulins to the conservative Mallet du Pan, driven to complain that 'moderation [has] become a crime'.

Following this event the Châtelet, already branded by the radicals as a refuge for aristocracy, conducted an inquiry to discover the instigators of the uprising. The radicals were incensed at this insult to their patriotism. When the results of the inquiry were published in March of the following year they served only further to confuse the issue. Mirabeau and Orléans were implicated but without substantial evidence.

19. Paris in Turmoil

The account by Desmoulins presented here was written a year after the event, complaining of the time spent investigating the affair when it was a simple matter of 'the price of bread'. Nevertheless he presents a vivid picture of events on the Saturday evening and Sunday preceding the march.

[Another banquet was held] on Saturday but with certain inflammatory incidents. Our patience was almost exhausted, and it could well be said that whatever patriotic onlookers there were at Versailles, they either left to take the news back to Paris personally, or at least sent off their despatches containing these details. The same day (Saturday evening), all Paris is in a turmoil. A woman, seeing that no-one in the district assembly had listened to her husband, is the first to come to the counter of the *Café de Foi* to denounce the anti-national cockades. M. Marat flies to Versailles, comes back like lightning, making by himself as much noise as the four trumpets of the last judgement, and shouts to us: '*O morts, levez-vous!*' Danton, for his part, rings the tocsin at the Cordeliers. On Sunday, this immortal district puts out its manifesto, and on that very day would have formed the advance guard of the Parisian army and marched to Versailles, if M. de Crèvecœur, its commander, had not restrained its martial fervour. People take up arms, and swarm into the streets, in search of the royal cockades. They take reprisals, tear off the cockades, trample them underfoot, and threaten to lynch anyone who should wear them again. One soldier who tries to recover his cockade is soon persuaded otherwise by a hundred cudgels raised against him. The whole of Sunday is spent making a clean sweep of the black and white cockades, and in plotting at the Palais-Royal, at the

Faubourg St.-Antoine, by the bridges and on the embankments . . .
It is noticed that secret meetings are being held in the mansions of the
aristocrats, that recruiting sergeants are active, and that people are
being secretly enrolled from outside the districts. It is noticed that at
Paris, as at Versailles, sinister uniforms, green with red facings, have
been seen; that a new body of troops is being fitted out to reinforce the
official bodyguard; that there is a plan afoot to bribe a certain number
of men in each district to spike the cannons that the Parisians have
seized. Rumour as well as established facts add to the general upheaval.
It is said that at night, invisible hands, which can't be caught in the act,
mark a number of houses in red and black. It is said that 1,500 uniforms
have been ordered from a tailor, 40,000 rifles from an armourer. It is
said that a miller has been paid 200 livres to stop grinding, and with the
promise of even more if he will remain arms folded in his mill . . .

Les Révolutions de France et de Brabant, No. 47, pp. 359–62.

20. Steps towards Liberty

The article by Loustallot from which this extract is taken was
headed: 'Conspiracy formed by the aristocrats against your liberty:
proofs and consequences of this affair'. The latter part of the article
has been omitted.

The insolent aristocracy has just been laid low a second time, and the
nation has taken another step towards liberty. 'What is needed is *a
second dose of revolution*', we were saying, a few days ago, '*and everything is
getting ready for it; the soul of the aristocratic party has not left the Court at all.*'
Citizens, what is the point in us giving ourselves over to the most
powerful hatreds, submerging ourselves in the most painful research,
ceaselessly guarding your interests, if you read us only to satisfy a
childish curiosity, if you do not take it on yourselves to follow the
course of events and to recognise their causes, and above all if you do
not profit from your own mistakes?

When you escaped from the scourges of every kind that the aristocrats set against you, famine, war, multiple dissensions, it must be
admitted more by the help of providence than by your own courage,
you determined never again to let yourselves be reduced to such
extremities; you undertook your own defence and the maintenance of
your own supplies; yet were you not a few days ago on the verge of
famine and of civil war with its attendant horrors?

A quick resolution, a moment of action, a choice resolutely taken to die or to be free, snuffed out the conspiracy in its cradle. But, citizens, do not rest on your success, as you did after the great event of 14 July, and fail to take the steps necessary to prevent the aristocracy hatching new plots and making new plans. At first this aristocracy of ours used force, then cunning; now it is reduced to despair.

Do not then allow indifference to prevent you seeking out the authors of this second conspiracy. . . .

Les Révolutions de Paris, No. 13, 3–9 October 1789, p. 2.

21. *Le Journal de Paris* breaks its Silence

The temperate journalism of the *Journal de Paris*, catering as it did for the educated and professional classes, had combined with the prudence of its proprietors to take a self-imposed vow of censorship on all political matters (28 June 1789). Under attack for its moderation by the radical press, this was its first comment on the 'recent upheavals'.

The anxiety which has been felt for some time about the capital's food supply, despite the ceaseless concern of the members of the Commune who had devoted themselves to this difficult and dangerous task, and the difficulty encountered for some days in getting bread, have aroused popular discontent and complaints, which the secret enemies of the re-establishment of law and order have doubtless not failed to stir up and intensify.

This popular feeling gained new force from the details which became known to the public of a military banquet given last week by the Royal Bodyguard to the Regimental Officers who are at Versailles. Some remarks, which were certainly indiscreet, and which were perhaps let slip in the warmth and intoxication of the table, especially the suggestion that the national cockades be replaced by black and white cockades, seemed to indicate that these military bodies had attitudes quite contrary to the public spirit and to the national interest.

These incidents have perhaps been exaggerated; but those which were true were sufficient to give rise to legitimate cause for concern and to re-awaken the suspicions and fears that were only just beginning to calm down. These feelings were intensified as the accounts from Versailles spread abroad; before long it aroused an almost universal unrest in the National Guard. On Sunday evening it was feared that there would be some disturbances amongst the people, but it is believed that the precaution taken on the spot by the Commandant-General forestalled them; however, on Monday morning at nine o'clock a large group of women were seen to arrive at the Place de Grève and present themselves at the Hôtel-de-Ville, shouting '*bread, bread*'. At first, it was thought desirable to prevent them coming in: but as their numbers were visibly increasing, it was thought that violence should not be used to keep them back.

They made their entry *en masse*, and soon they were followed by a crowd of men, armed for the most part with pikes or sticks. They broke down the doors, seized weapons and ammunition, and spread out from there to the various quarters of Paris. The ringing of the tocsin in most of the churches, the drum summoning to arms all the soldiers of the National Guard, and the general tumult soon set in motion a hundred detachments of armed citizens. No longer did they speak of bread; it was only a question of going to Versailles, but for reasons which were as vague as they were varied.

Le Journal de Paris, 8 October 1789.

22. A Letter from a Bourgeois

Paris, 7 October 1789.

Monsieur,

I am the father of six children, four boys and two girls. The two older boys wear the national uniform; on Monday they set out for Versailles, leaving me at home with my fears. Yesterday evening the joy of seeing them return in good health re-united my family, and we set about preparing a pleasant meal; the only one missing was my son who is an *abbé* and who usually comes home very early. We all love him dearly, because he is kind, learned, and good company. His mother and his two sisters were extremely alarmed; when at last he arrived home at half past nine his face was covered with blood and mud, his clothing in shreds. He had wanted to see the king pass by. But just because he was an abbé he had to suffer in silence, for more than two hours and in full view of the National Guard, the most disgusting jeers and insults. After this he was pursued by a crowd of madmen who beat him up. Ah! If this is freedom let us be returned to despotism with its spies and its soldiers, at least they will guarantee our safety. . . .

Les Révolutions de Paris, No. 13, 3–9 October 1789, pp. 34–35.

23. Rumour and Unrest

It is useless to speculate on the thousands of rumours that have more or less the appearance of truth. It has been said that several secret agents were distributing gold to make sure of supporters; that four thousand knights of St Louis were going to reinforce the batallion of the Guards; that their uniforms were either ordered, or ready to be ordered; that the summoning of the Flanders Regiment, under the pretext of relieving the national militia of Versailles, concealed ulterior motives; that a high price had been paid to bring the mills in the vicinity of Paris to a standstill; that a thousand infamous devices had been used to stop the movement of grain supplies etc. etc.

Without rashly giving too much credence to uncertain or exaggerated rumours, it is possible to believe that a number of men, driven to desperation by the Revolution, had joined forces to bring about its collapse. Corrupt enough to put all their faith in intrigue and favour, they knew only too well that the establishment of liberty would mean their own destruction. Their wretched minds, far from aspiring to the regeneration of the kingdom, are not even capable of forming a conspiracy.

Recent events are a new proof that, in times of unrest, there is nothing which is unimportant, or trivial in itself. An incident verging on the comic, an impropriety committed by drunken men, a ribbon of a particular colour, can bring about a revolution: a meal given on 1 October by the Royal Bodyguard to the Flanders Regiment (against military regulations) has caused the capital to explode. . . .

Le Courrier de Provence, No. L, 5–6 October 1789, p. 1.

24. The Price of Revolution

[How are we] to bring together the recent events, and get to their real causes . . .? Doubtless it is very easy to scribble off pages of calumnies, to proscribe those whom one can defame with impunity, and to pour acid on the bleeding wounds of the state. Let us leave these things to the host of writers who are good for nothing else, and let us try to present the less suspect reports which have come to us concerning the principal events of our recent political drama. . . .

. . . The incomprehensible shortage of bread and the military dinner at Versailles were the reason for its outbreak. The people suffering in every way, deprived of the help of many rich families now expatriated, out of work, lacking several of their ordinary resources, and, moreover, accustomed during the previous two months to independence and idleness, found it difficult to get even a poor-quality bread. It should be noted that bread was available; but it had to be fought for; the doors of the bakeries resembled those of the Discount Bank; and hunger waited for its food for hours on end, with fear its ready cash. For a fortnight there was an appearance of famine without actual scarcity. The 'popular' press which took upon itself to account for this state of affairs, embellished its accounts with so many contradictory details, that it became difficult for an intelligent person to make sense out of this scarcity of bread.

Several districts set themselves to discover the causes, but no two reports were the same; the roads were full of convoys, but the abundance disappeared as soon as the flour was converted into bread.

This shortage would ease off for a day or two only to reappear with greater effect. The people would ask themselves how it was that even in the middle of a freezing winter, supplies had been extremely regular, whilst at the end of summer, and following a good harvest, they were being held up. Murmurs became a clamour; from day to day a riot was expected. The public places were crowded with people, often even with strangers, who, adding their voice to the general complaints, joined with them in hurling curses against the Hôtel de Ville, against the majority in the National Assembly, against the ministers, against the most august personnages.

Le Mercure de France, 17 October 1789: Legg, *op. cit.*, vol. I, pp. 142–143.

REFLECTIONS

By the end of 1789 the Revolution seemed to many people to be completed–a hope that would continue to be expressed at intervals throughout the Revolution. The grumbling of Marat that the Revolution had failed because of lost opportunities to clean out the aristocrats once and for all made for no more popular reading than the cold water he had wanted to throw over the decrees of 4 August but for which he could not find a publisher. More to the popular taste was the hosannah to liberty gained and despotism destroyed that Mercier offered his readers in his last edition for 1789. To round off Part One we leave the debate to Mirabeau and Rivarol, who figured so prominently in the opening fusillades of the Revolution.

25. Mercier salutes 1789

Farewell, memorable year, the most illustrious of this century, a unique year when august Frenchmen brought back to the Gauls the equality, justice and liberty which aristocratic despotism had held captive. Farewell, immortal year, year that put an end to the degradation of the people, ennobling them even as it revealed to them rights whose title had been lost over the years! Farewell, most glorious year, year which through the courage and vigour of the Parisians, and with the death of the high, powerful and pompous clergy, and with the decease of the powerful and proud dame Nobility, ended its life in convulsions.

Marvellous year! Patriotism emerged fully armed from your generous loins, and it was patriotism that in one fell swoop put a host of enlightened citizens in their proper places, that brought to blossom unknown talents, and that gave to an attentive and astonished Europe great lessons from which she will doubtless profit.

Incomparable year! you have seen the end of a government of frightful memory which was so closely linked with the Bastille, its first favourite and the ugliest and most monstrous bitch that has ever been seen, a government that died of a sudden, violent attack; and it is in this way and on that very day that our brave and favoured compatriots saved the National Assembly (which was about to be cut down by red-hot shot), broke the chains of slavery, and terrified despotism's sword, which the Prince of Lambesc had already brandished, that treacherous blade placed in the hands of foreign troops, and who (whatever they say), wished to sacrifice us to save himself the trouble of paying us.

What unexpected events crowd into that year! In the space of a few months the misfortunes and abuses of several centuries have been remedied; man has recovered his first dignity, and that system of feudalism, of oppression, which outraged humanity and reason, is destroyed.

I offer you my homage, august year! You have altered *my Paris*, it is true, it is quite changed today; but grant us a short time and it will be the abode of freedom and happiness. Already I breathe there the mountain air of Switzerland; there I am a soldier, not as a warrior watch-dog sent out by despotism; but as a citizen who will joyfully give his life for the *true* cause of his country . . .

Les Annales patriotiques: cited in Hatin, *Histoire de la presse*, vol. VI, pp. 373–74.

26. Love of Liberty

One is constantly amazed to find men who although they lack neither good nor worthy sentiments, yet cannot be inspired with a sincere love of liberty. Their conscience never fails to be troubled by the powers attributed to the people; the present saddens them, the future chills them with fear; obstacles multiply beneath their very eyes, but benefits they never see. It is better to find oneself among the declared enemies of the Revolution: they are less discouraging than these prophets of doom.

It would seem that their scepticism about political freedom derives from a certain false association of ideas, facts wrongly observed and misinterpreted. In their mind they associate absolute government with tranquillity, peace and order; free government is associated, by contrast, with violence, disorder and turmoil: they are convinced that liberty is only maintained amidst storms, and that those who enjoy it walk on the edge of a volcano that threatens at any moment to erupt into violence.

From a distance, countries that are governed despotically present a calm enough surface; the sovereign speaks, he is obeyed. From this there follows an apparent order, an outward appearance of tranquillity that is at first sight deceptive. But this 'first sight' is what misleads a multitude of men. The revolutions in these countries are frequent, it is true, but sudden. The court is the centrepiece, and the people are rarely concerned; the next day, everything has returned to normal: this is another reason for superficial onlookers thinking that in these servile countries peace is a compensation for liberty.

But how deceptive appearances are! In a despotism, no one writes, there is little communication, and people are unwilling to associate with their neighbour: people are afraid to complain. . . .

No one dares count the victims; but does that mean to say that there are none? Can one weigh those silent tears, this dumb grief, those overlooked disasters whose ravages are so much the more terrible because nothing stops them? Does anyone keep a check on the judicial assassinations, the secret acts of vengeance, of spoliation, clandestine murders, of the victims given up to the torments of the state prisons? Public peace seems to exist but it is an illusion: in countless places at any one time, thousands of isolated individuals experience, within their own homes, in their relations with men more powerful than they, everything that civil war has at its worst. Imagine all these unfortunate creatures, all these oppressed slaves; listen to their dull mutterings, to the great weight of their despair, the voice that they do not have, and then say, if you dare, that despotism is a state of peace!

The picture of free countries is very different. There are no shrouds of mystery to cover the iniquities of the administration; everything is known. There, for fear of seeming to be a lover of power, the individual tends to turn a sense of disappointment into a mark of honour. This discontent, which is not unhappiness, is one of the characteristics of liberty. The free man seeks a perfection that can never be attained; in the matter of government, he is a sybarite wounded by rose leaves. No one waits for actual evils to occur in order to complain of them, but seeks to prevent them. Every opinion is a matter for division, any man endowed with great ability becomes a power in his own right and forms a party; but they all restrain one another, they all bend before the law. By contrast with despotic states, where much evil prevails and little noise is made, in the free states there is a great deal of noise and an even greater good: for, despite all these warring opinions, there is peace at the heart of the family; each member gathers the fruits of his industry, reaps where he has sown, enjoys himself without fear, gives himself freely to an exchange of confidences, and makes use, according to his abilities, of all the sources of public wealth, and willingly gives in to the sweetest instinct of nature, rejoicing at the hope of giving birth to future citizens.

It is often said: *Such people are free, yet never peaceful.* But do not judge from a distance; come closer and judge for yourself. You accuse liberty of an unrest whose principle is the very lack of liberty itself. . . . The reproach you make applies only to bad laws, to a defective constitution. Make liberty more pure, more strong, more general, and you will destroy the unwholesome seed of dissension and unrest. When the aristocrats in a republic complain about the disturbed spirit of the citizens, it is a case of the fever accusing the pulse of the speed and strength of its beating. . . .

Le Courrier de Provence, No. LXXIV, 2–3 December 1789, pp. 1–5.

27. Rivarol and the Revolution

The capitalists who gave you Paris have especially deserved their misfortune. They did not see that it was necessary to strengthen their debtor, not to weaken him; the king could never be too powerful if they were to get their money. They destroyed the old power to which their fortune was tied, in order to raise up a new power that owed them nothing, that was in no way beholden to them, and which could, after all, only make them bankrupt. Finally they played for the provinces, and capital lost the game. Paris, which has upturned the kingdom, will not restore it. M. Roederer* has just told us that the greatest of our mis-

---

* Deputy in the Assembly.

fortunes was the lack of circulation. The quip is a cruel one for people who had nothing to circulate. It is as good as saying to a man dying of hunger that he is dying from a defect in mastication. Here, in effect, is the sole incontrovertible truth: namely, that there is no money in Paris, and that money flows and disappears daily from the provinces: and this is the time that M. de Lameth in your midst has chosen to assure you that there is no nation whose finances are in such good order. You will say, perhaps, that M. de Lameth is only a child who is stuttering in the cradle of liberty. You must then reply for him, or you must answer for him; you must teach him to speak or you must get him to keep quiet. But you merit these words, since they do not astonish you. M. Robespierre takes advantage of your state, to add that *you can restore everything by reinforcing hope with patriotism and patriotism with hope. . . .* M. the Bishop of Autun speaks on our position with the dignity of a priest, and curses the bankruptcy in the name of a philosophic god. A priest of Calvin (M. Rabaud*), seeing the blessings rain down upon the nation on every side and bankruptcy truly cursed, takes the opportunity to get the better of a bishop of the Roman Church; he mounts the tribune and exorcises the bankruptcy: *Messieurs, he exclaims, you are in great danger; but, for you, what is one more danger? be reassured; bankruptcy is impossible; what can I say? Messieurs, it is eight times impossible. And he immediately starts the count and repeats, eight times in succession: bankruptcy is impossible.* But the demon of bankruptcy resists: despite Calvin, the Assembly and *the eight times*, it remains badly exorcised . . .

So many motions without purpose, so many requests without replies, and discussions without conclusions; so many voices that thunder without enlightening, and purposeless lists, that rain down from every side and gather about the National Assembly like a storm of absurdities; all that, I say, is only an abridged version of one of your sessions. And what purpose does it serve if I depict the Assembly as dividing into several groups, to form a conflict of blind men who dispute about reason—the 'blacks', on the one side, and the *enragés*, on the other; Mirabeau, blacker and more *enragé* than them all, leaping into the middle of the hall, with *all his armoury*, spewing his froth and his spirit upon the Assembly which remains terrified; the gallery, drunk on the fumes that drift up to it, and in the midst of this diseased cloud, hurling forth its anathemas indiscriminately on so many brows that blush only with anger?

. . . And I, I tell you that if my sketches, today so weak, seem one day too strong, other monuments, and monuments as durable as mine will survive your rages, and will bear witness with me: bankruptcy and its horrible consequences, the collapse of trade, the spectre of famine,

* Rabaut-Saint-Etienne.

poverty, the cries and tears within, borrowing and shame abroad: these are my witnesses; dare to contradict them . . .

. . . the capitalists said: *we want the constitution, but the sort that pays;* and the people: *we want the constitution, but the sort that exempts from taxation.* The position was critical, and you escaped from it by a treacherous and puerile artifice. 'We abolish,' you said, 'the tithe, the *gabelle*, the aids, the *franc fief*, costs of litigation, the one per cent tax on property, the right of conveyance, the gold mark, provisions, stamps, parchment, seal, registration, the five per cents, etc.' and the people trembled with joy at this patriotic nomenclature. But the capitalists shuddered at it, and said to you, in a doleful voice: *what will you now pay us with?* 'You must understand, was your reply; to take away is to impose: we abolish the tithe from the clergy's hands, but restore it into yours: as for the *gabelles*, we suppress only the word, which is barbaric. Be calm, and let us get on. We order a substitute of 40 millions: the constitution will have its dictionary and the royal treasury its money . . .'

. . . [The capitalists] saw especially that the people always stopped at the first part of your decree that *abolishes*, and never at the second part that *replaces*. Then you voted the *patriotic fourth;* and, in order not to scare people, you decreed that this contribution would be *voluntary*; but in order not to alienate the capitalists, you have just declared that it will be a *forced* one. Finally, since all these methods have been insufficient or illusory, you fell upon the property of the clergy and *expropriated* the Church. I will not trouble to investigate whether you had the right to do so; you had the need to do so, and I leave you the excuse of necessity, that grand protectress of all crimes; . . . do not say that I bring about bankruptcy, I do not advise its declaration; all I do is tell you it is a fact. The doctor does not bring on the illness; he diagnoses and names it. . . . You have broken all the bonds that united Frenchmen to the state. France is parcelled out into forty thousand petty republics, which still recognises your aristocracy: let them at least profit from the general dissolution: let them escape the clutches of this capital that has been for too long their vampire.

Le Journal politique national (edition of 1790), vol. II, No. 24, pp. 308–17, 323 *passim*.

PART TWO

The Church

In 1789 the bulk of the French people were no less devoted to Catholicism than they were passionate monarchists. Reform of the Church and removal of royal absolutism were two of the main aims of the revolutionaries, but neither the destruction of the monarchy nor the increasing manifestation of anti-Christian feeling was part of their plan. On the contrary, a Church wedded to the state and a constitutional monarchy were basic to their plans. In the reforms affecting the Church the Assembly called for flexibility and understanding; instead it was faced with rigidity and opposition. Nevertheless the decrees concerning the Church are frequently condemned as the worst mistake of the Assembly, while the liberal catholic Lord Acton goes so far as to claim that these decrees were 'hostile measures, carefully studied and long pursued'. In view of their disastrous effect these decrees do appear to be foolhardy, but it could be argued that they were drawn up out of expediency, that they were based on tradition and that they were in conformity with the principles of the Revolution.

The deputies acted out of expediency in that the bankruptcy they inherited from the old régime necessitated urgent measures. The most obvious solution seemed to be in the nationalisation of Church lands. This naturally met with the opposition of the higher clergy, but as the state promised to take over the Church's financial obligations, the lower orders welcomed this change. More general opposition greeted the Civil Constitution of the Clergy (July 1790), which introduced more democratic administration and, in the interests of streamlining, reduced clerical administration to conform with the civil. This move, however, engendered fear in more clerics than the bishops who were displaced when the number of bishoprics was reduced to eighty-three. These fears led to resistance to the decrees. Again the deputies were forced, as they thought, to weed out the dissidents by imposing an oath, on pain of deprivation of office, on all priests and bishops, of loyalty to the constitution and, implicitly, to the Civil Constitution of the Clergy. The imposition of the oath (27 November 1790) brought all discontent into the open, and served only to show to what extent the decrees of the Assembly, genuinely misunderstood or deliberately distorted, had resulted in general dissatisfaction.

In acting out of expediency, however, the Assembly tried to work within the Gallican tradition of the Catholic Church. This partly explains why the pope was not consulted before the reforms were instituted. This tradition, whilst not necessarily disputing the pope's supremacy in the Church, restrained his authority in favour of bishops and of the temporal ruler. By the Concordat of 1516, in return for a financial consideration, the King of France (Francis I) had been given the right to nominate bishops, who were only thereafter consecrated by the pope. In 1582 the 'four articles' of the Gallican Church, never officially refuted by Rome, definitely established that although the pope, through Saint Peter and his successors, had received dominion from God over things spiritual such as concern salvation, the king ruled over all things temporal and civil. They also postulated the superiority of General Councils as enunciated by the Council of Constance (1414) and claimed that all papal decrees had to be approved by the Assembly of the French clergy. This tradition of independence from Rome had allowed the 'calvinistic' Jansenists to flourish in France long after they were condemned by the pope in 1713. Headed by Camus, they were an important force in the Assembly. Support could be expected also from the *Richéristes*, a movement that aimed at greater autonomy among the lower clergy. In fact there was within the Church a microcosm of the Revolution. The same barriers to privilege and preferment that angered the bourgeoisie in the political field, irked the lower clergy in the religious. Indeed it was the support of the lower clergy for the bourgeoisie that had helped break the deadlock of June 1789. For these reasons then, the deputies felt free to introduce much-needed reform. The sovereignty of the nation had passed from the king to the people and with it his prerogatives. The representatives of the people thus felt free to interfere in the non-spiritual affairs of the Church.

The Assembly had to act out of principle in that its declared liberal philosophy and egalitarian principles had to be extended to religion. Outside the Catholic Church this meant the formal recognition of other forms of belief. The tolerance of other creeds by a Catholic country was not the least of a devout catholic's fears for the reforms of the Assembly but it was the logical extension of its principles.

However, on none of these matters was a council of the French Church called, nor was the opinion of the pope in any way sought, Certainly he had not objected to the reforms of Joseph II of Austria. nor to Catherine of Russia's reorganisation of her Polish dioceses. Between June 1790 and March 1791 the pope remained officially silent, concerned over the fate of his temporal power in Avignon, where the leaders of a revolt there sought union with France. But when he did speak out in March and April of 1791 he condemned ecclesiastical reforms of the National Assembly and the annexation of Avignon.

The Revolution was accompanied by a nationalistic fervour that at times took on all the appearance of religious worship with its symbols, its celebrations and its Altar of the Fatherland. At first this parallel development could only be confounded with the Catholic Church, but it also contained implicitly the basis for a civic religion. As the divisions between juring priests (who took the oath) and non-juring priests (who refused to take the oath) widened, and as the counter-revolution used this breach to its own advantage, measures against the non-juring clergy from November 1791 on became increasingly severe. Intransigence led to persecution, which in turn led to more determined intransigence. Hostility to religion in general became confused with hostility to counter-revolution. This hostility assumed a new form towards the end of 1793 with the de-christianisation movement of the Hébertists, particularly Chaumette and Fouché, and the enthronement of the 'goddess of reason'. Many were scandalised by this frenzy, not least Robespierre, who feared the threat the extreme Left posed to his government as well as the gratuitous insult that this represented to the majority of Christians who still held to the Revolution. Partly to off-set the disgust that this atheistic orgy aroused, and partly to institute his own beliefs in the Rousseauist Moral God, Robespierre introduced the Cult of the Supreme Being in May 1794. However, the immediate result of this civic religion was to anger those who saw in it a plot to restore catholicism, and to arouse fear in others that Robespierre intended to set himself up as the 'pontiff' of the new religion. Robespierre thus added to the enemies who were shortly to ensure his overthrow.

NATIONALISATION

The abolition of feudalism and the Declaration of the Rights of Man cleared the way for ecclesiastical reform. On 4 August tithes and fees were abolished, clerical offices were democratised, annates and other payments to Rome discontinued, and pluralism was declared illegal. This did not, however, solve the basic financial problem. Inevitably the nation had to turn to the Church. But was it to seize its property or merely use its revenues? On 2 November the wealth of the Church was declared 'at the disposal of the nation'.

The decrees of 4 August had meant a considerable loss of revenue to the papacy. Nevertheless, on neither this nor the nationalisation decree did the pope protest. Of more immediate concern to him were his rights and properties in Avignon and the Comtat Venaissin, where economic unrest and dislike of papal rule had resulted in a revolt in

August 1789. After much hesitation, and without consulting the pope, the first steps towards annexation were taken on 27 October 1790, when troops were sent to Avignon.

28. Mirabeau on the Nationalisation of Church Lands

In No. 60 of the *Courrier de Provence*, the speech that Mirabeau presented to the Assembly and which he 'considered feeble because moderate', was reported in full. A footnote advised that a second speech, prepared but not delivered, would be held over to a future publication. This extract is from the second, undelivered speech.

You are going to decide an important issue. It concerns religion and the state; the nation and Europe are waiting, yet we have until the present been engaged in frivolous and puerile objections.

It is I, Messieurs, who have the honour of proposing that you declare that the nation is the owner of the wealth of the clergy.

This is not a new right that I wanted you to acquire for the nation; I only wanted to affirm what it has, always has had, and always will have; and I wanted justice to be done to it, because it is principles that save peoples, and errors that destroy them . . .

. . . the law that permitted a corporation to be a proprietor, gave it this power only so that it could exercise it on behalf of its members; the law granted this right only on condition that it should be exercised on the nation's behalf.

But, Messieurs, do not deceive yourselves: it is for the entire nation that the clergy received its wealth; it is for the nation that the law allowed them to receive offerings; otherwise, without the liberality of the faithful, society itself would have been compelled to give the clergy some source of income, for which these properties, acquired with its consent, were only temporary substitutes. It is for that reason that the property of the Church has always had the character of reserved property.

M. the abbé Maury again raises an objection on this matter. A society, he says, can have only empire and sovereignty over the wealth of its members, and not at all ownership of the same goods. . . . It is easy to reply to M. the abbé Maury that it is not at all a question here of the rights of the prince but of the rights of the nation: that it is certainly true the prince has neither dominion nor empire over the goods of his subjects, but it is no less true that the French nation enjoys a right of ownership over a host of goods which, without actually possessing them, are destined for its needs and are administered in its name. . . .

It is therefore true that, outside this sovereignty, the nation as a body can have special property rights: it is then no longer a question of knowing if it is in the name of the nation that the Church enjoys its goods as it is for the nation that the king possesses his demesnes.

To decide this question, it is enough to compare the properties of the Church with all other kinds of property known to us.

> He goes on to point out that personal or private property held by non-clerics belongs to them as individuals and may be disposed of by them as they wish.

. . . Now, I ask whether one can say the same thing for the goods of the Church; they have not been given to individuals, but to a body, not to transfer them, but to administer them; not as a title of income, but as a trust; not for the particular use of those who must possess them, but in order to fulfil a public purpose, and to provide for those expenses that would otherwise have been a charge on the nation. The goods of the Church have then nothing in common with those of the nobility . . . the wealth [of the Church], like the lands of the Crown, are a major national resource. Ecclesiastics are neither the owners, nor even the usufructuaries; their income is destined for a public service; they take the place of the dues that would have had to be established for the service of the altars, for the maintenance of their ministers; [the property] exists then for the relief of the nation.

Here then, Messieurs, are two kinds of property, very much alike, and belonging entirely to the state; here are two kinds of property that have nothing in common with the property of individuals, nor with the individual property of bodies non-politic; nor with the fiefs of the nobility. . . . I will not bother, Messieurs, to reply to those who have attacked the motion that I have made, by delineating the consequences of such an attack; I will merely make two observations on the point, which seem to me important. The first is that it is not a question of taking the wealth of the clergy to pay the state's debt, as we have tried to make people understand. One can declare the principle of ownership by the nation, without the clergy ceasing to administer the property; these are in no way monies owing to the state: it is a security and a mortgage; it is a credit and a trust.

The second point is that there is no member of the clergy whose fortune would not be increased by the effect of more equal distribution . . . [with the exception of those who have ten times more than they need and who ought not to dread any sacrifice, since, even after the most stringent reductions, they would still have ten times more than they need].

Le Courrier de Provence, No. 62, pp. 22, 24, 32–34, 37, 38, 39, 44–45.

29. 'It is the People who will Suffer'

In its first few weeks the *Gazette de Paris* did not show itself hostile to Church reform–for example, Durosoi had shown himself to be an apostle of toleration and declared himself an ardent advocate of clerical marriage and of divorce. However, he did not support the nationalisation of Church land, although it was not until 1790 that he actively opposed it.

In an article continued over two issues, Durosoi extols the virtues and necessities of monarchy, nobility and Church. The extract presented here is from the conclusion and omits the sections on monarchy and nobility.

We tell you again: you need a religion, and if man has sometimes defaced that which is bound to the true Constitution of the French Empire, must it be rejected by you for that reason? Take heed of three great truths. If there was no God, it would be necessary to invent one for the peace of the whole earth: if there was no religion, it would be necessary to create one for the safety of the realm, of which you are the largest part; if you had no king, it would be necessary from tomorrow, from today, to elect one for the happiness of the citizens. Yet do you know what is happening? People have almost forgotten the idea of a God . . .

Prelates most respectable for their moral virtues, most distinguished by their learning, and by the splendour of their titles, said to the nation: 'Let our goods be at your disposal, but let us retain the ownership. We shall be your revenue collectors; ours will be yours. In exchange for this act of justice, which we call a favour, we offer the most complete tribute to prove our patriotism . . .' And concerning this tribute, good people, it is we who have the honour of showing you all its advantages, and above all of proving to you just how baneful are those systems that dare to deprive you of it.

The clergy offered: 1. to pay every year, for twenty years, a figure of 40 millions, a sum that you could estimate as a quarter of the gross proceeds of its wealth . . .; 2. to realise in two years the proceeds of a quarter of these twenty years; which would mean an effective 200 millions that could be disposed of immediately by assignats upon the clergy; 3. as the nation's justice must necessarily grant to the clergy the means of effecting this operation, which would immediately provide for the deficit in the finances, so should the clergy be left the power to alienate, by means of suppression or of reunion, such benefices as it should judge convenient . . .; 4. the clergy made no less an offer to fix the revenue of each priest at 1,200 livres minimum, and that of the vicars proportionately.

Apart from the incalculable advantages of having overcome the deficit, which is an ever-open gulf towards which the nation seems inexorably drawn, there resulted another advantage, which tied the happiness and security of generations yet to be born to the interests of the present generation; namely, of keeping for the state–through the continued existence of the whole of the clergy's property–an ever-growing source of revenue, for in twenty years' time, perhaps even in ten, the same operation could be repeated.

People, it is you that we wish to convince, since no part of the nation has suffered as much as you; see how they have contributed to your misfortune, instead of accepting the offer that would have cured so many ills.

They have suppressed the tithes, yet you do not profit from it, and when a substitute has to be found, it is upon you that will fall the tax created to replace it.

The sale of 400 millions of the clergy's property has been decreed. But it will be necessary to sell 800 millions before realising in real terms the 400 millions requested.

It is again you, good people, that will one day suffer for that scandalous transaction. But not everybody will lose by it as you will do. There will be profit in it for those vile brokers, those insatiable speculators, whose criminal cupidity glories in the fact that the clergy, deprived of the right to execute by itself either the reunion or the sale of its varied properties, cannot deprive [these speculators] of the pleasure of immersing themselves in these golden streams, of which it matters little to them that the source be dried up for posterity, provided that their unquenchable thirst may be steeped in it at will . . .

Country folk, see what future has been left to you. These nobles, in whose homes you used to shelter from the seasons' inclemency, you pursued from refuge to refuge; will you dare to ask them for bread, when you have not left them asylum? Those pastors, who lived with you, and through whom you lived, are now on wages; and one day perhaps, deprived even of this income, they will not have, like you, the spade and plough to fall back upon. Yet we now hear you slandering them; for you are daily being taught to become more unjust. They will have been deprived of the means of helping you, yet you will accuse them of being indifferent to your sufferings, when they are beggars like you. Your injustice will be the most severe of their punishments; and the most sacred, the most noble of callings will become the saddest and most wretched of these estates . . .

La Gazette de Paris, 30 March 1790.

30. Superstition and Despotism in Alliance

A common argument among the radicals and those writers of a 'philosophic' bent was that dispossession merely returned the Church to its 'primitive purity'.

Some eighteen centuries ago there appeared in Jerusalem a Divine Man; all his words were so many saintly precepts. Every step he took left the imprint of heavenly virtue. He forgave the woman caught in adultery, and showed himself relentless towards the bad priests. This man of exemplary justice, who did not like tyrants, died the death of guilty slaves; but before expiring on the cross of shame, he summoned together his beloved disciples, and said to them: 'I leave you to return to him who sent me; but I leave behind me my example for you to follow, and my lessons for you to preach to men of *good will*. Tell them that the mighty will be brought low; tell them that religion is a bond of peace, and that its ministers owe their first obedience to the laws of the country. Go then and preach the gospel throughout the earth. I say to you truly, that as long as you shall preach only a law of brotherly love, I say to you in truth, you shall work wonders: crowns will fall at your feet, the people will heap their blessings upon you. But woe to you or to your successors, if the spirit of intrigue and vanity takes hold of my church! I warn you, I shall abandon it to the anger of the people whom it shall have filled with its scandals. Go in peace, and I shall be with you always . . .'

If the striking promises of Christ have had their full effect, it has been kept for our time to see his threats also accomplished.

Supported in the early days by the charity of its followers, from the time that the priests became proprietors they began to lose their apostolic virtues. Rich in their landed possessions, they soon aspired to titles and honours; not being able to attain immediately to the first rank of public office, they set out towards achieving this by inventing the ecclesiastical hierarchy *with its pretensions*.

In enlarging upon his theme, the editor is careful to point out that he is not attacking 'the ineffable mysteries of religion', but its ceremonial that 'our bishops have borrowed from the Church of Rome'.

Then came the day that saw the dawn of reason. In a manner akin to those habitual liars whom nothing can disconcert, the upper clergy acted out their parts with effrontery and were unwilling to forgo any one of their pretensions. It paid its tribute to the kings and set itself at their feet to seek from them protection or vengeance. The two monsters, superstition and despotism, became as one, and from their impure embraces were born all the political scourges which afflicted the empire for several centuries; now that events have come to a head, the nation is holding its grand assizes.

Far from bending beneath the paternal hand of the fatherland, far from being at the head of reform that had become indispensable, the upper clergy allies itself with the nobility, and the priest, who makes a vow of Christian humility, stubbornly persists in maintaining the first rank in the state. The ministers of a poor God, who possessed nothing on this earth where he might lay his head, haggle and dispute over every square foot of that third of the land in the kingdom, of which they were no more than the beneficiaries. . . .

French prelates! if you had been allowed to act as judge in your own cause, and if these facts had been set before you, reply: is it the Gospel and the Acts of the Apostles that you would have consulted to restore to religion the innocence of its first days, and to its ministers the morality of the first Christians? Would you have done more than all the councils have been able to do? Would you have had the courage to reform yourselves, your harems and your studs? Would you have had the good faith to bring yourselves to accept the loss of your rights of ownership to the immense possessions that paid for your pleasures? . . .

What then is a priest? He is a citizen who, feeling himself endowed with gentleness and humility, consecrates himself in a special fashion to the cult of those virtues that tend towards the good of society. . . . Under the old régime and in times when we lacked energy, a good priest would ease our chains, and give us hope that sooner or later God, who had called us all to liberty, would give us the opportunity, and provide us with the means for breaking our chains. In this way Moses and Aaron were truly citizen-priests, since they restored the courage of their downtrodden countrymen, since they led them to a holy insurrection, and finally to cast off the yoke of the Egyptian aristocracy. . . .

My friends, my brothers! Three more months and the country will be saved. Have patience; take courage; the beginnings of liberty are not at all easy; put on a good face; let harmony reign in our midst. Let us remain united, and we shall stay free. Do not let the refusal of a few bishops and several priests [to take the oath] alarm you; that's their affair. God is on our side, for liberty is his beloved daughter. Liberty is the handmaid of religion. God repulses the incense of slaves. Servitude gives rise only to superstition. Let us then remain free to please God and to make ourselves respected among men.

Les Révolutions de Paris, No. 79, 8–15 January 1791,
pp. 8–12, 16, 17.

31. Maury on Avignon

The abbé Maury, one of the most eloquent of the right-wing deputies, was constantly eulogised in the ultra-right-wing press. In the biased reporting of the anti-revolutionaries he was given an inordinate amount of space, and often his speeches were reproduced in full. Malouet, and lesser figures, were afforded similar treatment.

This is the conclusion to the report of a speech given by the abbé Maury on 17 July 1790.

'The first thing is that our King Henry IV, who bought the town of Antibes in 1608, for the sum of 50,000 crowns that he paid to the Prince of Monaco, had copied, on the advice of Sully, when deliberating on the acquisition, the contract of sale of the town of Avignon. When you have decided whether a town has the right to dispose of its sovereignty, whether a forced compliance under armed threat really expresses the will of the people, you will decide if you must authorise, by a decree of strict parity, M. the Prince of Monaco to regain possession of and to be reimbursed for the alienation of Antibes.

'My second observation has for its object to remind you that Louis XIV occupied Avignon and the comtat in 1667, and again in 1688, and that Louis XV, who took possession of it in 1768, restored this province to the pope in 1774. Louis XIV restored the comtat at a time when he did not easily relinquish his conquests; but he paid this homage to justice, without being forced to it in any way by the pope who opposed him. His august successor imitated the same example of magnanimity. Thus these three enterprises of the kings of France, concerning Avignon and the comtat, far from weakening the rights of the pope, served only to state more solemnly the sovereignty of the Court of Rome. You are, gentlemen, the representatives of a nation just and generous; you will decide neither on the advice of interested parties nor by the abuse of force, the rights of a foreign sovereign, the rights of a sovereign whose political existence concerns every Christian power. You will not grant to a misguided faction the disposition of sovereignty; and the new enquiry to which France at this time submits the prosperity of the sovereign pontiff, will emerge from this Assembly, as it did from counsels of our last two monarchs, as the most authentic confirmation of the sovereignty of the pope over Avignon and the comtat.

'As for the proposal that has been put to you, . . . namely to institute a committee charged with examining the Avignon petitions, I ask by way of amendment that you will add to the proposed decree, which is designed to establish in this Assembly a committee of confiscation, that such a committee be organised on the plan of the *chambre d'union* that Louis XIV instituted in the town of Metz, to the general edification of all Europe, with a view to confiscating all the towns and provinces that it thought fit. . . .'

We desired to enter into the greatest detail on this matter in order to make known once and for all how much M. the abbé Maury, so slandered, is superior to his opponents, not only by his reasoning and eloquence, which is no longer challenged, but also by the wisdom and dignity of his sentiments. That session gave proof of it. For his erudition, the immensity of his knowledge, his facility of improvising with all the wealth of the art of oratory, he is, without contradiction, the foremost man of the century. Why is it that so many and such sublime talents should be lost? His opponents remained for a time dumbfounded; they even blushed. But soon, overcoming all shame, they speak as if he had not pulverised their principles and their sophistries.

L'Ami du Roi, 20 July 1790 pp. 203-4.

TOLERATION

De Brienne's Edict of Toleration (1787) proved still-born, but its objective was realised with the granting of religious liberty to Protestants on 24 December 1789. The Declaration of Rights included freedom of belief 'even in religion', a significant phrase indicating the special nature of the concession granted. Despite this the Jews did not have their rights granted to them as easily as the Protestants, and they had to wait until 28 January 1790 before being granted the first instalment of religious equality.

Not surprisingly, the new legislation collided with deep-rooted tradition and prejudice. In parts of France religious wars broke out that continued sporadically throughout the Revolution.

32. Overcoming Prejudice

On 23 and 24 December 1789 the Assembly discussed whether Jews, actors and hangmen should be admitted to the rights of citizenship.

It is only by cold, dispassionate reason, by the evidence of the good, that [the legislators] can establish their work; this is without a doubt a sound approach, but one which supposes a people composed of men equally enlightened and equally virtuous.

Such a people neither exists nor is ever likely to exist. The constitution then must be made for the people since the people cannot be made for the constitution; one must, following the example of Solon, put before it not the best laws possible, but the best they can uphold.

The spirit of legislation consists therefore in distinguishing the customs, abuses, and prejudices that one can attack openly, from those that must be quietly undermined. This spirit supposes not only knowledge of the human heart; it supposes a profound study of the people that is about to receive a constitution.

There exist against the Jews hatreds; against actors, opinions; against hangmen, prejudices. If it is not shown, in the eyes of the great majority of individuals composing the nation, that these hatreds, these opinions, these prejudices, are without foundation, then we run the risk of making laws that will not be executed at all; and, what would be even more dangerous, laws that could cast disfavour on the code in which they were to be found, on the laws that preceded or followed them.

It is not therefore for a legislator to say to a people *you will no longer have such an opinion*, nor to prescribe what is contrary to such a prejudice, unless it has been severely shaken; for a legislator does not lightly compromise his work; now if the National Assembly decided that the hangman could be mayor, judge and commandant, no one would dare to affirm that nineteen-twentieths of the nation do not regard their representatives as fools and that they should not take this decree as an atrocious insult, as the aristocratic deputies wanted the nation to do.

There was such a simple means of sounding their views that it is astonishing that it has not been used. Let us suppose that the National Assembly had defined that which constituted the citizen, which was the first thing that it had to do in order not to expose itself to risky discussions. Suppose that it had said: 'Permanent residence in the territories of the French monarchy, carries the obligation of contributing to the public taxes and confers rights of citizenship.' From that time, the Jew domiciled in France would have been reckoned a citizen; if chosen by his neighbours he could have been elected; his virtues, talents, and services would gradually make people forget the wrongs committed by those of his cult. These men would attach themselves to professions, to works by which they could conquer the general esteem; public hatred would be extinguished; the Israelite caste would be united to the great mass of the body politic; and the legislator would obtain without upheaval, without friction, without danger, the effect that will be tried perhaps vainly to be produced by another means.

Les Révolutions de Paris, No. 24, 19–26 December 1789, pp. 2–6.

33. Jews and the Suffrage

Just a few weeks prior to this number, Durosoi had lauded the abbé Grégoire for his support of various reforms. Grégoire, however, was soon (19 February 1790) to be contemptuously dismissed as 'that priest, that *curé*, who is the advocate of Jews, Protestants and Negroes'. When writing this article, Durosoi's 'conversion' to outright reaction was not quite complete.

As for the Jews it was doubtless a frightening thing that they should be punished almost every fifty years with every kind of torture that greed or fanaticism could conjure up. But while granting them, under the protection of the law, all the success that they could enjoy, should it not be noticed that, in the centuries when people were somewhat more convinced of the truths of Christian dogma, the whole Christian nation could and must only have regarded with a sort of horror, this people who had laid its bloody hands upon the divine founder of their religion, whose dogma was revered even though its ministers were criticised. Why such great interest in wanting the Jews to be active citizens, provided they are content? Has it not already been too often forgotten that the King of France was also His Most Christian Majesty? Can he not be King of the French, without being King of the Jews?

If the aim of this marked concern, which has been for some time accorded to the Jewish nation, is to be assured of bidders at a time when the sale of ecclesiastical property is about to begin, why not admit it? There are many innovations similar to this one, for which the least mudslinging citizens vainly seek an explanation. It would have been more loyal, more French, for the matter to be explained without any mystery. People would at least have been grateful for the frankness.

Finally, after the most stormy session of which the annals of the present legislature have conserved the memory, by reason of the schism that divides this senate of King-Legislators into two quite opposing parties, after a roll-call, begun and interrupted six times, the seventh finally resulted in 370 votes in favour of an amendment proposed by M. SEZE, made on the main motion, with 225 dissenting votes.

Then the following decree was passed: 'The National Assembly decrees that Jews, known in France under the names of Portuguese Jews, Spanish and Avignonese, will continue to enjoy the rights that they have enjoyed until the present and which have been consecrated in their favour by Letters-Patent; and, consequently, they shall enjoy the rights of active citizens, provided they fulfil in other respects the conditions laid down by the other decrees of the National Assembly.'

La Gazette de Paris, 31 January 1790.

34. Religious War

On 17 April 1790 trouble broke out in Nîmes, chief city of the Gard, over the ostentatious parade of the white cockade by the local National Guard. The mayor, who was also a right-wing deputy at the National Assembly, instead of quelling the affair sided with the 'white cockades' who were ardent Catholics, and so incited further troubles. He then followed this up by appointing only 'white cockades' to the main public offices.

This article, a letter to the *Ami du Roi*, opens with a complaint about the numerous ephemeral newspapers, spreading lies etc., quoting the *Journal de la Révolution*, as an example; it is with this quotation that the following document begins.

'After the horrible massacre of Saint Bartholomew's day, the court wrote to every province that the Huguenots had wanted to slaughter the Catholics; in the same way the enemies of the Revolution, calling themselves Catholics, are spreading lies everywhere in an attempt to persuade everyone that the Protestants of Nîmes had planned to murder their brothers, and urge the Catholics of Languedoc to unite and sack that town. The *camp fédératif*, 32,000 strong, at Vivarais, would have suffered the most disastrous consequences but for the prudence of its leaders. Detachments were seen under the command of priests, who, sword in hand, presented a novel sight for this century; others had at their head ecclesiastics carrying the cross. Are private interests going to renew the horrors of the religious wars?'

So many words, so many deceptions in that miserable article. Let us first of all, before replying, advise that the author copied it from other articles inserted in the *Courrier d'Avignon*, subsidised by the Huguenots, and from the *Moniteur*, controlled by the Huguenots. Let us add that the Huguenots are ill-advised continually to harp back to that terrible *Saint Bartholomew*, for they can always be successfully replied to on this matter, by saying that the massacres committed by them in 1562 and 1563, on several other occasions, and notably the *terrible Michelade* that took place at Nîmes in 1567, that is to say five years before *the horrible Saint Bartholomew*, compelled the unfortunate Charles IX to such a frightening extreme.

They are no less ill-advised to present the Catholics of Nîmes as the enemies of the Revolution, for that is a lie destroyed by the facts. . . .

The Catholics of Nîmes . . . are true friends of the constitution; they seek only peace and will maintain it at the risk of their lives. . . .

Let us reply now to the demand made by the author of the *Journal de la Révolution*, but in a quite different sense from how he would put it. '*Will private interests renew the horrors of the wars of religion?*' Yes, the *private interests* of the Protestants. Desperate at not getting into the municipality of Nîmes, they wanted to get their own back by forming the district of that town and by nominating only their own members to the department of the Gard; and it is this that has led to the renewing of these *horrors*; and they have renewed them by massacring six to seven hundred people, for the sole reason that they were Catholics, by pillaging more than a hundred catholic houses, by devastating the fields of the Catholics, murdering their priests, pillaging their convents, stealing the priestly ornaments, the sacred vessels, profaning in the churches that which we hold most worthy of respect in them; by practising, finally, cruelties beside which the worst tortures ordered by any tyrant pale into insignificance. Here then is what anyone could call, and with good reason, horrible *religious war*, and of which I offer the most clear and convincing proof, and which must bring down on the Protestants of Nîmes, until such time as the sword of the law hangs heavy over their guilty heads, the animadversion of every Frenchman,

I am, etc., signed, B***.

L'Ami du Roi, No. CIV, 12 September 1790.

THE CIVIL CONSTITUTION OF THE CLERGY

By taking over the Church's property, the state also had to take over certain of its duties. On 12 July 1790 the Civil Constitution of the Clergy was passed, incorporating the Church into the state. The administrative structure of the Church was streamlined to accord with the civil administration. It was ruled that bishops and clergy should in future be appointed by local election, stipends of bishops and clergy were fixed, and finally the movement of bishops and clergy outside their dioceses was restricted, while it was forbidden to hold certain secular offices that might interfere with clerical work. Punishment for violation of these regulations was given in charge of the departmental officers, thus putting the clergy under the disciplinary control of the state.

Opposition to the Civil Constitution precipitated a crisis: the deputies thought they could force the issue by requiring clerics to take an oath to the Constitution as was required of civil functionaries. The decree requiring the clerical oath was passed on 27 November 1790.

No exact figures can be given for the number of priests who took the oath and those who did not. To suggest averages would be misleading, for in the Vendée and the Lower Rhine there were more than 90 per cent refusals to take the oath while in the Var 96 per cent of the clergy took it; between these two extremes there were many variations. What can be said with certainty is that imposition of the oath brought schism into the open.

35. 'The Reign of Priests has Passed'

The reign of the priests has passed; and the more efforts they make to maintain the tottering remains of ecclesiastical power, the sooner will they hasten its collapse.

The National Assembly, in debating the Civil Constitution of the Clergy, has declared that each department will form a single diocese. It has established ten metropolitans and defined their area of authority. In reducing the number of bishoprics, it has assigned them new districts and has suppressed several of them. It has forbidden the recognition of the authority of a bishop whose see is under foreign control. It has established the election of bishops and curés, it has committed this election to the same electoral body as nominate the members of the departments and districts.

Such in brief are the decrees of the National Assembly on the Civil Constitution of the Clergy, and these decrees are constitutional.

If the clergy were less concerned with their past glory and wealth, if they did not wish to foment, at any possible price, civil war, they would no longer resist the lawful will of the nation. One would not see the majority of the bishops of France, in agreement with the curés, crying out that the Catholic religion is lost, because they have been deprived of the means of a display of wealth that is both insolent and absolutely opposed to the principles and spirit of the Gospel.

. . . It is most surprising that the bishops of France today regard the Roman pontiff as the voice of the universal Church, they, who, at all times, have affected to refuse him any other quality than that of the Bishop of Rome, and any supremacy other than what would be purely honorary.

Article 4 of the liberties of the Gallican Church says precisely that the pope can neither command nor ordain anything in France that pertains to temporal things. Now, if according to the admission of the aforementioned clergy, the pope can neither ordain nor command anything concerning temporal matters, he cannot then in any way interfere in the definition of the new dioceses; for this operation is purely temporal, purely political; it in no way touches upon the spiritual jurisdiction of the Church. . . .

The bishops deafen us with their claim to ecclesiastical power, which, they say, must co-operate with the civil power for the union and the suppression of benefices. What then is this ecclesiastical power? It is doubtless that of a council; but a council must concern itself only with matters of dogma and church morals. In civil affairs, it must not have more authority than any club whatsoever or than any other assembly of citizens. If the state were to recognise the ecclesiastical power with regard to matters other than of worship, then it would be acknowledging a corporation of priests independent of the agents of government, which would constitute a division of powers impracticable in a free state.

The National Assembly, in defining the limits of the dioceses of the kingdom, by no means injures the rights of the episcopacy; it does not set any limit on the spiritual authority of the bishop, it only declares what is within its competence, that is to say, it will recognise the exterior exercise of its jurisdiction only when this does not exceed such and such a limit.

. . . As long as they are not forced to an inconvenient place of living, as long as they are left to enjoy in peace the scandalous usurpations of their predecessors, they would tolerate the most impudent undertakings; their fervour has only been revived at the moment that one tried to bring them back to a life a little more in conformity with the spirit of the Gospel. Leave the priests their wealth and they will be amenable in matters of dogma and morals; but attack what they are pleased to call their properties, and they will cry out against the profanity, against the sacrilege; there is *your spirit of the Church.*

The bishops rise up against the entrusting of the election of priests and bishops to the people. But do they not know that in the ancient Church the people themselves elected the ministers of religion? . . . Almost all the bishops of the early Church were elected by the people; it is only after the relaxation of religious principles that the Church has concentrated on a government purely representative by excluding the people from the right of voting in elections. Moreover, how can the bishops prove themselves difficult on the institution of popular elections, when they are such who have calmly seen ecclesiastical offices distributed and sold in the most infamous fashion by unworthy courtesans, by valets and prostitutes? Ministers of the altars, be more sincere in your protests. It is not the changing of the ecclesiastical rule that arouses you against the new Constitution; you miss your scandalous wealth, your soft and sensuous life, so little suited to the successors of the apostles. Surrender with good grace the pretensions that you can no longer retain without risk. Submit while there is still time, or fear the just severity of a people whom you have for too long trampled underfoot.

Les Révolutions de Paris, No. 73, 27 November–
4 December 1790, pp. 390–94.

36. Election of Priests

This is one of the first Assembly reports by Royou in the *Ami du Roi*, only recently formed.

The question came up as to how priests would be elected. There was one who wanted the elections to be carried out only by the active citizens in a parish–as if they were the only ones interested in a good choice! But are they in a position to do so? Another wished to reserve this right to the district electors–because this form of election is closer to the constitution, but is it equally advantageous to religion? A third brought the opposite parties together by suggesting the combining of the active citizens of a parish, where the cure is vacant, with the district electors.

Everything was going well when M. the abbé Jacquemard stepped in to disturb this harmony; he ardently depicted intrigue and ambition forcing the door of the sanctuary; the debased priest (in order to capture votes) obliged to flatter passions, to conform to the grossest and most corrupt manners of those on whom he depended for his advancement; he depicted hidden merit and timid virtue condemned to languish eternally in a precarious state. And how, in fact, can district electors, drawn for the most part from the country, be expected to discover the virtuous man, the enlightened and modest pastor in his humble retreat? Are they in a position to appreciate the knowledge, the talent, the prudence that the pastoral duties demand? Will they before an election leave their plough to conduct an enquiry throughout the diocese of the vicars most worthy of their choice? Intrigue alone will decide. To leave the choice of priest to men unable to know those most worthy of being their pastors is to open the door to simony, to nepotism, to all types of intrigue and corruption.

Despite these and many other reasons, which would take too long to go into here, the constitutional spirit triumphed. . . .

There follows a discussion on the titles for the new civil functions, then on the question of appointments to cures, especially when they fall vacant before the time of re-election.

It was decided that there would be no nominations to cures falling vacant before the month of November, regardless of when they fall vacant. But how are the spiritual needs of the country people, who might be deprived of their pastors possibly for as long as a year, to be catered for? It is true that if religion will lose something by this suspension, the finances will gain, for the income from the vacant benefices is to be poured into the district coffers. It is a rule if not ecclesiastic, at least economic.

The choice of bad pastors being the surest means of destroying religion, it did not seem natural to confide this choice to its most deadly enemy; a priest demanded, therefore, that there be imposed on the electors an obligation to take an oath declaring that they are Catholic: but it was decided that there was no need to discuss this point.

M. le chevalier de Muriney proposes the subordination of priests to bishops. There are cries of 'Order!' and so it is; when one urges civil subordination, as well as ecclesiastical, there is nothing to discuss.

L'Ami du Roi, No. XVI, 16 June 1790.

37. The Wages of Schism

Royou's reporting is a continuous attack on the deputies and their work. Vitriolic for the most part, his criticisms do not lack irony.

The fourth article concerning the stipends of the vicars of cathedral churches was discussed.

M. de Robespierre wanted a fraternal equality among the vicars of the bishop, and proposed a scale somewhere between the *maximum* and the *minimum* recommended by the committee. When it comes to the salaries of judges and lawyers will M. de Robespierre still hold to his ideas of a fraternal equality among all those in the kingdom? However that may be, the Assembly seemed to fear too great an extension of the idea of fraternal equality when it might extend beyond the vicars to every citizen; it rejected the median scale of M. de Robespierre . . . and it decreed that the stipends in cathedral churches would be . . . [there follows a scale of the remuneration to be granted to the vicars depending on their rank and place of residence].

Session of Thursday morning, 17 June

This session opened as though it was a music hall or an academy, with the reading of snatches of verse in praise of the National Assembly; after consecrating some time in which to receive this homage, the Assembly took up the agenda. The stipends of the priests was the first matter to be discussed. [Figures are given for the new wage scale for priests.]

MM. the priests found that the scale of remuneration was not generous; one of them had called out on another occasion: '*When in the name of the God of peace you asked us to join you was it, then, to cut our throats?*' Another cried out today: '*This then is what comes of the magnificent promises that you made us!*' Why did they not foresee the consequences of their break with the higher clergy and of their excessive credulity! It is not, however, by way of reprisal that the Archbishop of Aix, the Bishop of Nancy, the Montesquieus, the Maurys, these celebrated orators, abandoned MM. the priests. It is known that they take no part in the deliberations of the clergy.

L'Ami du Roi, No. XVIII, 18 June 1790.

38. The Oath to the Constitution

(i) *Introduction of the Oath*

Montjoye, though just as critical of the Assembly as Royou, is much milder and less incisive.

There is so much uncertainty, inconsistency, even disorder, in the way in which so many diverse topics pass one after the other for deliberation by our legislators that rarely do they deal with the topic they have resolved to debate; the extraordinary session that we are about to report was especially called to hear the *comité des finances*; no other matter was to have been discussed. Well! Not one word was heard on finance.

But the topic that was substituted will none the less hold interest for our readers. Imagine a heavy storm, growling and menacing with all its thunderbolts, without however striking, the loftiest trees in a majestic forest; then you will have some idea of that which growled in this session over the loftiest heads of the French clergy.

The first thunderbolt particularly menaced M. the Bishop of Nantes. . . .

Soon the storm growled anew in the distance; M. Voidel, in the name of the four united committees of *recherches, rapport, aliénation* and *constitution*, presented a long list of complaints, imputed to the whole ecclesiastical body since the beginning of the Revolution.

Before getting down to his subject, and before launching his thunderbolt, he thought he would discourse skilfully on religion, whose superstition and fanaticism, he said, might pervert the mind, but could not change it; he described its progress from its inception to the present day; and showed how its ministers, according to him, knew how to gain the confidence and respect of men: he then thought to explain the causes for the progressive diminution of this confidence: then passing from these broad details he went into particular detail of deeds that are attributed, in our day, to the ecclesiastics, and which he called *a long rebellion against the laws*; he cited several instances. . . .

It is with the aids of a few facts of this nature that M. Voidel prepared his audience to approve the blow he wished to deliver. He proposed the following decree:

The bishops, former archbishops and priests who are absent shall be ordered to return to their residence and take the civil oath within a fortnight of their arrival. In the event of the civil oath not being taken, the said bishops and archbishops will be considered to have renounced their office, and steps will be taken to have them replaced. In cases where the oath is violated, they will be deprived of their stipends, forfeit their rights as citizens, and be declared incapable of exercising any public function; and in consequence they will be considered thus to have been tried and judged. Finally the *ci-devants* having suppressed titles or benefices, those who exercise any of the functions attached thereto will be punished as disturbers of the peace.

At this frightening project, needless to say, the applause from the left and from the tribunes was more significant than ever, and the printing of the speech, as of the proposed decree, was ordered. If this printing passes to posterity, will it then show that in this unhappy century it was proposed to bring to the scaffold all those titled ecclesiastics who addressed their prayers to heaven in the accustomed manner?

Discussion, however, was opened on this terrible project.

L'Ami du Roi, No. CLXXXI, 28 November 1790.

(ii) *Profession of Faith on the Oath*

When the Assembly abolished hereditary nobility and titles on 19 June 1790, the right-wing press opened its columns to individuals wishing to protest. It adopted similar manoeuvres following the imposition of the oath.

The most precious concern for every thinking being is his religion; all that is purely temporal can be sacrificed for the sake of peace, but when it is a question of the eternal truths, every concession becomes a crime.

I therefore declare, in the name of my constituents and on my own behalf, that the decree of 27 November of the Assembly, which has called itself national, is an impious and criminal attempt on the authority and liberty of the Gallican Church, since it seeks to separate France from the union and obedience owed by every Catholic to the pope as Vicar of Jesus Christ.

I wish to live and die in the Catholic, Apostolic and Roman faith, and if the Assembly, which has called itself national, revives the centuries of persecution, I ask God for the grace to be the first martyr either for my faith or for my king.

Signed le marquis de la Queuille, marshal of the king's camps and armies, deputy of the nobility of Auvergne, in the free and general states of France, retired at the end of my period of election.

Paris 28 November 1790.

L'Ami du Roi, No. CLXXXII, 29 November 1790.

(iii) *The Oath retracted*

It is no longer possible for me to struggle against the commanding voice of my conscience, to continue to exercise functions for which I no longer have authority from my lawful prelate, Monseigneur de Juigné, Archbishop of Paris. I must honestly admit that, when I took the oath of 9 January, I had the firm intention of excluding from it everything that could compromise the interests of religion and of the Church. I must now withdraw the unconditional oath that I took, and I must make it known that I at no time acknowledged any other authority than that of the Church, no other pastors than those who had been approved by the Church and confirmed by the Sovereign Pontiff, visible Head of the Church. I must now renew the promise that I made at the foot of the Altar of Martyrs, of being by the grace of God and until death, the defender and faithful disciple of the Catholic, Apostolic and Roman faith.

Cerveau, Doctor in Theology in the Paris Faculty, and Prior of the Parish of SS. James and Innocent.

La Gazette de Paris, 2 October 1791,

39. France in Division

LIST	LIST
Authorities who condemn the oath demanded of the clergy:	Partisans of the oath demanded of the clergy:
1. The pope	1. The comte de Mirabeau
2. The cardinals	2. The marquis de Condorcet and consorts
3. Thirty bishops in the National Assembly	3. Two bishops in the National Assembly
4. Ninety-six other French bishops	4. Three or four other French bishops

5. The majority of the clergy, representing the second Order

5. The minority of the clergy, representing the second Order

6. The greater part of the curés of the city of Paris

6. Fifteen or sixteen curés of the city of Paris, out of fifty-two

7. All the cathedral and collegiate chapters, all the worthy religious

7. Some apostate monks

8. The Sorbonne, the greater part of the University of Paris, the provincial Universities

8. A small number of M.A.s, almost all laymen; the academics of the current philosophies

9. All the directors of seminaries, almost all the Professors of Theology, of Philosophy and College regents

9. The hired madmen who bawl out their declamations in associations whose very name arouses horror, indignation and contempt

10. Fifty thousand curés or vicars

10. Seven to eight thousand curés or vicars–ambitious, troublesome, fanatical, ignorant, Jansenist

11. All the Catholic Churches of Europe, foreign nations, even the Protestants

11. The emissaries of the Jacobin Club, the propaganda missionaries, and the Geneva speculators

12. M. the Archbishop, one hundred and eighty-five ecclesiastics, and almost as many religious of the town of Avignon, where the revolutionaries have just exacted the oath

12. Several oratorians, Doctrinaires, Augustinians, Adherents of Jansenism

13. Three-quarters of the town of Paris

13. The Palais-Royal, the Rue Vivienne, the hired Galleries, the tigers of the Terrasse des Feuillants, and the infernal *phalanx* of c. de M.

14. The right wing of the National Assembly, or the élite of the defenders of religion and of the throne

14. The left wing, and the monstrous assembly of the principal enemies of the Church and of the monarchy, Jews, Protestants, Deists

15. All the papers, friends of order and of truth

15. All the newspapers in the pay of the factions, such as the execrable rags of Desmoulins,

Noël, Brissot, Marat, Mercier etc. and the imbecile ecclesiastical gazette

16. All good Frenchmen who love their country, their religion and the happiness of their brothers

16. All the brigands who burn the châteaux, pillage the mansions, set up gallows; all the scoundrels who have bathed France in blood, and yet still breathe, thanks to the impunity of their frightful instigators

17. All worthy and virtuous citizens

17. All the libertines, cheats, capitalists, Jews and Protestants

18. All sensible and righteous hearts who groan over the terrible decree that followed the crimes of the 5th and 6th of October 1789

18. Some factious republicans, to whom these crimes were necessary in order to complete the overthrow of the monarchy

19. Almost all the provinces whose protests in favour of religion and monarchy have been suppressed by means of bribery and threat of confiscations

19. The abominable inquisitors of the *comités de recherches*

20. Humanity and the Constitutional Decree which declares that 'no one is to suffer for his religious beliefs'

20. The most horrible intolerance, and the belief, as ferocious as it is absurd, in might

21. The will of our good king

21. The most detestable tyranny, which has taken his place, and exercises in his name a most frightful despotism

22. Finally, the comte de Mirabeau himself, who on leaving the session of 4 January, ever glorious for the Gallican Church, could not prevent himself from making this avowal: 'We have their money, their wealth, but theirs is the honour'.

22. Finally, the torches, the daggers, the bayonets and *la lanterne.*

L'Ami du Roi–Royou, No. CCCVI, 22 March 1791.

CONFLICT WITH ROME

The revolutionaries failed to consult the pope on any measure concerning the Church, refusing to admit the thin line dividing 'temporal and spiritual powers'. For his part the pope, concerned as much for his temporal power in Avignon as for his spiritual prerogatives in France, left the faithful in doubt as to his intentions. He secretly condemned the Declaration of Rights on 29 March 1790, and on 12 July 1790 issued two other briefs declaring the Civil Constitution unacceptable, but these were kept secret by the French bishops. Not until March and again in April 1791 did the public hear the decision of the pope; then he condemned the Declaration of the Rights of Man as well as the Civil Constitution. The seal was set on schism.

40. On the Pope's Delay

The prelates then are no longer permitted to instruct the people. Wretched adventurers have the right to preach impiety, for money, in all the public places; yet lawful pastors are silenced; their precepts are punished as crimes against the fatherland! The Bishop of Saintes is denounced by the department of the lower Garonne for having preached to the people of his diocese the message of the Gospel. The public prosecutor pursues him as an incendiary and a rebel. Thus do the new kings of France usurp for themselves an authority that our former monarchs never claimed. They are no longer the leaders of the left wing, they are the district administrators, and the municipal officials who set themselves up as doctors of law and as fathers of the Church. The least village mayor acts like a sovereign pontiff; he summons the bishop to his court and condemns him as a heretic: men who do not know how to read are now our theologians: you must obey even bad laws, they say; no doubt, but one must not obey laws that offend one's religion and conscience. Bishops, who refuse to submit to the decree of the Assembly, must if they are to avoid scandal explain to the people the reasons for their disobedience; they must teach the misused multitude that this law, which they oppose, is contrary to the law of God; they must prepare the people who are in their charge, against the dangers that threaten their religion: when they fulfil the most sacred of their duties, when they publish in their dioceses these wise and moderate instructions that contain only the purest doctrine of the Church, they are not at all incendiaries who seek to overturn the state, but they are shepherds who care for their flock and watch over its safety. Some complain that the head of the Catholic Church has delayed too long to give his views on this article; they think that his authority would impose on M. Camus, and that on the article of religion the administrators of the departments would not claim to know more than the pope.

That last view would at least console the oppressed bishops; it would strengthen them against the horrors of persecution; but perhaps the delay by the sovereign pontiff is only an excess of prudence. Certain of the steadfastness of our prelates, full of confidence in the loyalty of the French people to the faith of their fathers, he imagines that time will reunite the brethren, that the National Assembly will retrace its steps; he is afraid lest hasty action would force him to cast against the rebels the anathemas of the Church and thereby provoke a schism. Thanks to his moderation the Catholic faith will perhaps have no need of the use of violence to triumph against hatred and the devices of the Protestants in alliance with the philosophers.

L'Ami du Roi–Royou, No. CCXLXI [*sic*], 5 February 1791.

41. Pontiff, Canonists and Cardinals

Rome

The sovereign pontiff, embarrassed by the reply awaited from him concerning the Civil Constitution of the Clergy of France, has consulted in turn the cardinals and the Roman canonists. We call CANONISTS lawyers learned in the canon law, that is to say in the laws relating to ecclesiastical discipline and jurisprudence. These lawyers well versed in religious antiquities found a striking similarity between the early Church and the Civil Constitution of the Clergy of France; and consequently they invited the pope to approve it. The pope was disposed to do so by his feelings that were at one and the same time evangelical and pacifist. But the cardinals were of an opposite opinion, and for a very simple reason. Possessing the right to elect the popes, they regard the papacy as an inheritance that they can dispose of at will, and as a crown offered to their old age. Now, they risked losing this prerogative, if they approved a constitution granting the people the natural right to elect their pastors and their bishops, for the Roman people would reclaim this right at the first election of a pope, and the conclave, instead of being an antichamber of the Holy See, occupied by intriguers, would become as before, the electoral chamber of the Church, that is, of the assembled faithful. Thus do the canonists judge according to canon law; and the cardinals according to personal ambition.

La Feuille villageoise, No. 18, 27 January 1791, pp. 335–36.

42. 'Poor Braschi . . .'

This indignant outburst against Pope Pius VI followed publication of his condemnation of the Civil Constitution of the Clergy.

Since the Revolution, the Roman Church and Gallican Church no longer speak the same language; nor is it surprising that they misunderstand each other so badly. A constitutional bishop of France, and the Bishop of Rome have still the same corner-stone of the Gospel on which to found their institution, but that is all. . . .

Poor Braschi! Since your journey to Vienna, under the rule of Joseph II, your reputation in our eyes has been that of a wise pontiff who knew how to yield to circumstances, and prudently to give up something rather than lose everything.* Your letter in reply to the two letters of the Bishop of Sens, provided you were in good faith when dictating it, would earn for you a writ of reprieve; but if it is merely another example of Italian trickery, it will earn for you our utmost contempt.

The mere reading of the official papers, by informing Braschi of the circumstances of the French Revolution, must have taught him that an assembled nation finds within itself all the powers necessary for the reforms that it intends to carry out; that it has the right, in professing the same Gospel as the Vatican, to alter the limits of the dioceses that compose its territory, and to dethrone from their sees those bishops in France who persist in sticking to ultramontane principles; that all the councils together cannot restore to a refractory bishop the character of a public official of which he has been deprived by the whole nation assembled; that the full power of the people extends to bishops as to magistrates; that one and the other, made for it, must be elected by it; that heaven itself and its vice-God on earth cannot invalidate the national decrees, and that, finally, a Bishop of Rome shows extreme poor grace in finding fault with what happens at Paris. Poor Braschi! . . . Who does not see, and you yourself the first, poor Braschi, that a pope needs religion, but that religion, at least in France, can well do without a pope?

If there existed but a single copy of the Gospel and if that copy were under lock and key in the Vatican Library, we would have recourse to the pope to consult this divine book; but as its author has deigned that typographic art should multiply it an infinite number of times, it has dispensed us from endless voyages to Rome. There is not one family in its cottage that does not possess, at little expense, this religious treasure; and in the Gospel, who is not aware that he possesses

* Reference to Joseph II's detailed regulation of Church administration that was not opposed by the pope.

the quintessence of religion? Who, indeed, is not aware that it is only in reading the Gospels, with bowed head, that we have found the precious seed of the fortunate reforms that we have just decreed by so large a majority, indeed by the almost unanimous consent of the French clergy themselves?

So then, most holy father, stop penning your lengthy letters to our French cardinals, to our bishops and to the king. Our mind is made up, and it is irrevocable. For a long time you have passed as infallible; it is now the people's turn. . . .

Braschi! rather than casting at us from afar your bolts of lightning which are extinguished before arriving at their destination, leave the palace of Saint-Ange for a few weeks; the road to Paris is open to you and it will be more pleasant than that to Vienna. . . .

. . . Take part in the rebirth of an entire people; be amazed like us at the miraculous speed with which it has been achieved; and before re-taking the road for Italy, intone in the episcopal seat of ancient Lutèce, the canticle of holy Simeon: dismiss now your servant, O Lord . . . in peace, because my eyes have seen . . . the light . . . before the face of the people. Lord, you can now dismiss your servant in peace, because my eyes have at last seen the light of reason illuminate a nation of 25 million men.

Les Révolutions de Paris, No. 89, 19–26 March 1791,
pp. 551–54.

PERSECUTION

During the period of the Constituent Assembly, counter-revolution and the dissident clergy became welded ever closer together, leaving the Legislative Assembly to deal with this widening breach between Church and Revolution as one of its major problems. On 29 November 1791, following a report by the civil commissioners sent to investigate the uprisings in the Vendée, 'under pretext of religion', the Assembly passed a decree which required non-juring clergy to take the civic oath. This decree reaffirmed and added to the penalties of the decree of the previous year. It added the ominous clause that ecclesiastics refusing to take the oath 'shall be deemed suspect of revolt against the law and of sinister intent against the *patrie*, and as such more particularly subjected and recommended to the surveillance of all constituted authorities'. War between the Revolution and the refractory Church was being openly declared.

The king vetoed this decree, and on 27 May 1792 the Assembly substituted for it the first of the 'Revolutionary Decrees', which subjected non-juring priests to deportation. This decree the king also vetoed, but at the popular level feelings were increasingly embittered, and persecution and counter-persecution continued unabated.

43. An Anecdote

In the first part of 1790, threat of counter-revolution tended to be muted in the right-wing press.

It is well known that the pope reads nearly all the French newspapers. Seeing in some papers the vigorous replies of the former chevalier de Meude-Monpas,* he remarked to a French seigneur: 'I see there are still some French subjects who are courageous and faithful to their king'. Indeed! Could his Holiness have believed that the spirit of novelty and headiness had seized almost every single Frenchmen? Ah! There are a great number of them who, bowing before the needs of the moment, believe themselves forced to moderate the expression of their feelings; but a time will come, perhaps, when the unhappy people who are now being cheated in the cruellest way, will see their error; and it is then that the true partisans of religion, the faithful subjects, will be able to oppose with some success the perverse and dangerous maxims of our would-be politicians.

L'Ami du Roi, No. XXX, 30 June 1790.

44. The Apple of Discord

In the radical press, on the contrary, new plots were continually being discussed.

Paris, 13 April—New plot discovered

Citizens, do you not see the triumphant look of the aristocrats, and do you not hear their insulting talk? Are you not witness to their insolent joy? And do you know why they are like this? It is because they think that the counter-revolution is ripe, and that today it is they who will gather its fruits.

You know with what profusion they spread their libels against the constitution that makes you free and snatches you from the clutches of those brigands at court, from those brigands of the robe, from those

* Contributor of short satirical poems to some extreme right-wing papers, especially the *Petit-Gautier*.

brigands of the Church, who steeped themselves in your blood and in your sweat, and who devoured your livelihood; they infect the provinces with these libels, and the smallest villages see them arrive by the sackful.

They try to make the conspiracies that we disclose look like vain imaginings, and, at the same time, they plan crimes worthy of Saint Bartholomew; they want to make you cut each other's throats, in order to enjoy their spoils in peace.

The Bishops of Treguier, of Blois, of Ypres, and many others, issue inflammatory commands and, ministers of peace, they fan the fires of revolt; already this last named has seduced some of our citizens.

In Alsace, they try to set the Protestants against the Catholics, Jews against Christians; prelates, abbés, monks, try to foment disturbances and to excite a war of religion.

In Languedoc, the same attempts: scarcely had the appointment of the worthy Rabaut-Saint-Etienne, your friend and brother, been announced, than there appeared in the streets of Nîmes the following poster: *The infamous National Assembly has just climaxed its crimes by appointing a Protestant as its president.* The next day, four Protestants were assassinated. Can anyone fail to recognise in this the fury of the priests, the rage of the aristocrats?

In your frontier towns, they try to seduce your faithful friends, those worthy soldiers whose lot the National Assembly has just improved. At Metz, Vitry-le-Français, Saumur, etc. they have been excited to revolt; in other towns, people have tried to set one against the other, and to start a general war out of their private quarrels.

This is what these enemies of the people, these enemies of the king, have just done at Lille, Livarot and Noyelle: [The *Annales* then gives details of disturbances in these places].

Those, citizens, are the fears that a true friend of the public good has wished to expose to you. These are not empty terrors; yet there is nothing easier than to outmanoeuvre the aristocracy: let us not pick up the apple of discord that it seeks to cast among us, and all will go well.

> *Les Annales patriotiques*, No. 196: cited in Buchez and Roux, *Histoire parlementaire de la Révolution française*, vol. V, pp. 360–63.

45. Civil War

So the civil war has finally broken out; again we are going to see the horrors which dishonoured the reign of Charles IX. Already the Protestants have taken up arms against the Catholics, in the department of the Gard; already French blood has flowed; such is the bitter fruit of France's regenerative laws. For a long time wise men have trembled at the thought of the terrible consequences of so many abrupt and trenchant innovations. The administrators of the department are asking for troops, ammunition and artillery; in these we are feeding and not curing the civil fury. These disturbances are attributed to a letter from the Bishop of Uzès, which is no more than a faithful account of the famous session where the oath was demanded of the clergy. This letter, acknowledged by the Right, is criminal in the eyes of the demagogues only because it is too true. . . .

The Assembly could have prevented all these disturbances, by being more genuine and by making a greater show of its attachment to the Catholic and national religion, and by refusing Protestants the right to worship in public; a privilege which sound politics rejects, which is incompatible with the Catholic religion, and which will always sow the seeds of discord. . . .

L'Ami du Roi–Royou, No. CCLXXV, 24 February 1791.

46. Debasement of the Inheritance

The author of this extract, Mallet du Pan, was a Protestant and a foreigner.

Posterity will easily understand the expropriation of the clergy, the reduction of its revenues, the abolition of its privileges, the changes brought about in its discipline; thinking people will be divided in fifty years time, as they are today, on the need for that reform, but what will never be contemplated without a quiver of indignation is the resentful fury that persecutes the members of this unfortunate order. They arouse the compassion even of the ungodly; foreigners can react only with horror when they learn of the threats which have been hurled at them [the clergy] for the past twenty months. Is it conceivable that our self-indulgent morals can be so cruel; that at the instant when the charlatans smear their sheets with words like virtue, tolerance, humanity, liberty, they are not satisfied with the ruin of the clergy, with its debasement, with the loss of its influence and honour; that while enjoying its spoils they drag it down daily to the most ignominious of outrages, that the rogues dare to speak constantly of murdering at the slightest pretext those whom the nation has just disinherited?

Le Mercure de France: Hatin, *op. cit.*, vol. V, p. 62.

47. The Persecutors Persecuted

Since these *honest folk* are causing such a stir that we are forced to turn our attentions to them *again*, we must, damn it, say something on the matter. They have forced the National Assembly to take firm measures and you will see them cry out 'Tyranny', 'Persecution', as if it were not they who are the most determined persecutors of the people.

At the time of writing, the Assembly has not as yet taken a strong line, and perhaps it will be afraid to commit itself in this way. Could it not be said that, because some men are obligated by their vocation to a more saintly way of life, to a more exemplary conduct, to more edifying acts, they should be entitled to the kind of sympathetic consideration that we would refuse to culprits who are not bound by the same obligations? No, damn it, crime must not be sheltered. A calotte, a sash, a cimarre, a cross etc. must no longer be used to paralyse the law. If any one person on earth is singled out for special consideration, then society is badly organised; public order is ill-assured; justice is no more than a name; for far too long the worst criminals have sheltered behind a title or some bauble attached to their buttonhole. Religion is the enemy of disorder, it preaches only peace; therefore to strike all disturbers of the peace, even at the foot of the altar, with the lightning bolt of the law, is to serve religion, not, damn it, to debase or to destroy it, nor to go against the sacred principles that it teaches.

We have seen governments favour the corruption of priests, in order to weaken the hold given them by their mummeries, by their devout and atrocious advice, by their underhand dealings, their skilful and pernicious hypocrisy; do we then wish to tolerate for long among us that kind of impolitic management? The priests are well enough known; the good ones ought to be infinitely respected; but the holy agitators ought to be attacked from all sides at once, otherwise they shall push the people's patience to the limit, damn it; and they would do better to try the patience of the legislator. The vengeance of the laws will not be at all blind, that of the people will be; and innocent victims could, in the crushing débâcle, be confused perhaps with the guilty at the time of the disasters that will soon be upon us, if we do not put them in their place.

Those who do not wish to submit themselves to the laws of the majority must be transported to Italy or elsewhere without any remission. There they will not have to complain of being *persecuted*, although they are the ones who all this time have been the persecutors; there they will do what they want, and give themselves up to everything that will flatter their imbecile madness; it is a sure means of securing peace for them and for us. Actually they themselves must want us to export them, for if this measure displeases and kicks back at them, I will say that they like, as much by choice as by obstinacy, to be pestered by and to struggle against the authorities; I will say that they take a delight in going against the laws, in challenging and in insulting them. But let them be exiled to the Mississippi, if necessary, and if they do not find it to their satisfaction, we at least will find ours, namely, that of being at peace. And whose fault will it be? Their own!

La Trompette du Père Duchêne, No. 2, *s.d.* (May 1792), pp. 6–8.

DECHRISTIANISATION

One aspect of the Terror was the dechristianisation movement. On 20 October 1793 additional legislation was enacted against non-juring priests, following which many churches were closed and converted into Temples of Reason. The instigators of the anti-Christian measures were the Hébertists, whose *armées révolutionnaires* considered it their mission to spread their gospel of reason and nature worship as a sideline to their officially appointed task. On 10 November the 'goddess reason' was enthroned in the former metropolitan church of Paris, in a ceremony of the 'purest patriotism'; in fact of revolutionary idealism carried to its most ridiculous limits. Concurrently with these events the Convention was preparing the revolutionary calendar which would replace the 'superstition' attached to the Christian calendar with the 'exactness and simplicity' demanded by reason and philosophy.

The religion of reason was an autonomous movement, unconnected with the schism between the Catholic Church and the Revolution. It never gained root and died within a few months. Robespierre attacked the leaders of the 'dechristianisers' as 'diversionists' and passed a decree (8 December 1793) proclaiming religious liberty for all those who did not compromise the cause of liberty. In general the Convention was more concerned with destroying counter-revolutionary clergy than attacking the constitutional Church, but Robespierre did not discountenance the idea of a revolutionary religion: on 7 May 1794 his decree was passed establishing the Worship of the Supreme Being, which was to be celebrated annually at the festivals of 14 July 1789, 10 August 1792, 21 January 1793 and 31 May 1793.

48. Reform of Religion

Among the more important reforms that the Convention has carried out must be counted that of the calendar;* the common people see in this change merely a change of days, months and names; but anyone

* See also doc. 145, p. 264.

who stops to consider it, will see that it was without a doubt a magnificent idea to exorcise, as it were, all reference to former terms that were consecrated to despotism and superstition, by altering in a single stroke the whole nature of the French calendar, and by dating the new era from the beginning of the Republic. . . . What is more ridiculous than that the days of the week should bear the names of the moon, the sun, the gods of Mars, Mercury and Venus etc.? Alongside such names, the Catholic Church solemnly set the names of the saints, as if it had meant to say that it was merely replacing one superstition by another, or rather by a combination of them both.

Could anyone believe that sincere Catholics who had such an easy tolerance as to set, without scruple or regrets, the devil and the saints on the same level; could anyone believe, I say, that men who such a short while ago were so easygoing would see anything wrong in the recent calendar reforms? What especially shocks the priests is the suppression of the Sabbath, and several are already seeking, it is said, to arouse the simple-minded and credulous against this fine piece of reform, to persuade them that their religion is being directly attacked, whereas what has been promised them is full and complete freedom. . . . If they are truly attached to their religion, they ought to feel that it is by no means necessary to allow a conflict to develop between their religion and their liberty, for there is no middle way; if this conflict continues, it will be a fight to the finish. One or the other of these two cults must be annihilated. And can anyone doubt that liberty would not emerge victorious from amidst all the storms? Who can doubt that it will not rightfully avenge itself against all its enemies? . . .

For our part, we do not take it upon ourselves to convert by theological arguments ignorant Catholics; for a journal must be like the law, it must not appear to favour any particular religion, we shall content ourselves merely by saying that almost all the Catholic priests of Paris perform, on the *décadi*, or on the day of the *décade*, all the Sunday services. They have been quick to submit to the law. All the other churches will doubtless do the same. The Sabbath rest, the closing of the shops, and cessation of work was a real insult to the Jews and Mohammedans, and all non-Christians who had not adopted the same day of religious rest. The law must eliminate this line of division, and it has done so.

There is another outrage that the Catholic religion daily makes against other religions. Our streets, our highways, our buildings are covered with crosses and chapels. All the signs collectively seem to want to force passers-by to stop and to worship, despite themselves, so to speak, such and such a god, such and such a saint, just as the red letters of our calendar seem to force them to rest; they announce a domineering religion. Some representatives of the people have already made these things disappear in several departments. The Paris Commune has just followed their example in this great city. On its orders, the virgin of the Rue aux Ours has been removed. It has been decreed that all religious statues to be found in the various Paris districts should disappear, and that kings and saints of wood and stone should no longer stand freezing at the church entrances: as every individual is the master of creating for himself a deity according to his own desire, it has been felt that it is no longer necessary to retain in the open signs of the divine other than those provided by nature herself, the earth and the heavens; and that the Hindu and Persian ought to cross the whole of France, without meeting anything that would shock their religious susceptibilities. . . .

If anything can prove that we are little advanced in the Revolution, it is the prolongation of this abuse, that none of our National Assemblies has yet dared to eradicate; if one were to ask the Catholics whether they would consent to pay for the upkeep of the Protestant religion, of the Jews, of the Mohammedans etc. their reply would be immediately in the negative. How then can they consent that these others sects should defray the costs of the Catholic religion? Have not the Catholic priests already headed a large delegation to ask the National Convention that it cease to grant this odious privilege, and that it should not force all the sects to contribute towards the expenses of a single religion.

. . . Admit then that it is not your religion that you cherish but its revenues, the income whose enjoyment it gains for you. You still want the splendour of the processions and the pomp of the numerous feast-days to continue to bring into the collection box which you empty, the mite of the orphan and widow, and it is this that the new calendar has suppressed.

In all these reforms, commanded by reason and necessitated by circumstances, let us not forget to propose the abolition of confession. This measure is a pressing one in the present crisis. If we leave this means open to the priests, they will not fail to abuse it shamefully so as to hoard consciences and to establish for themselves a group that will constitute a hard core of blind counter-revolutionaries. This is neither the time nor the place to urge the principle of freedom of thought, it is a measure of general security that has to be taken, and the penalty of death would not be too much against those who confess and those who hear their confessions.

Confession is far from being of divine institution, and the secrecy that priests demand from their penitents clearly tells how perverse are their intentions. In the early Church, people confessed themselves aloud and clearly, in public, in the centre of the temples. . . .

To sum up, let us say that there is no longer need for priests in a republic founded on morality; however, to observe all the rules of justice, even towards those who have for so long violated them with impunity and impudence, let us leave to the old priests their emoluments to the end of their days; as for the young ones, let us pay them a pension for three years, which will be long enough time for them to acquire another occupation that will not cause them any shame.

Les Révolutions de Paris, No. 213, 7–14 Brumaire, Year II
(28 October–4 November 1793), pp. 140–45.

49. The Temple of Reason

. . . when you consider that there is no absurdity anywhere in the world that has not been seriously preached by the priests, what is the more surprising is not that we have suddenly given up all our superstitious mythology, but that we delayed so long in rejecting them as they deserved.

To celebrate this triumph of reason, that we have so long awaited, the department and Commune of Paris decreed that there should be a patriotic celebration the following *décadi*.

In the former metroplitan church of Paris, an immense crowd assembled. There they had erected a temple of simple but majestic architecture, on whose façade could be read the words: *to philosophy*; they had decorated the entrance of this temple with busts of the *philosophes* who had most contributed by their enlightenment to the advent of the present Revolution. The sacred temple was raised on the summit of a mountain. Towards the centre, upon a rock, was seen burning the torch of truth. All the constituted authorities were represented in this sanctuary. The only one not there was armed force, and the commandant general, in his order of the day, anticipated those who had noticed this, by pointing out that arms belonged only to battles, and not where brethren came to cleanse themselves of all their gothic prejudices, and to savour, in the joy of a soul fulfilled, the sweetness of equality.

As that ceremony had nothing that resembled Greek and Latin mummeries, so then did it enter directly into the soul. The music that was played did not sound in any way like that in churches. A republican band, placed at the foot of the mountain, played, in everyday language, a hymn that the people understood so much the better, because it expressed natural truths and not mystical and fanciful praises. During this splendid music, two rows of young girls, dressed in white and crowned with oak leaves, were seen to descend and cross the mountain, torch in hand, and then climb the mountain in the same direction. Liberty, represented by a beautiful woman, came out of the temple of philosophy, and taking her seat on the green sward, accepted the homage of the republican men and women, who sang a hymn in her honour, whilst stretching out their arms to her. Then liberty descended to re-enter the temple, but stopping before her entry to turn and cast a look of good-will upon her friends. As soon as she entered, their enthusiasm broke out in shouts of joy and oaths that they would never cease to be faithful to her.

As the National Convention was not able to be present at the morning ceremony, it was repeated in the evening in its presence.

Les Révolutions de Paris, No. 215, 23–30 Brumaire, Year II
(13–20 November 1793), pp. 214–15.

50. Festival of the Supreme Being

The public spirit developed, last *décadi*, at Paris, in a way that was as satisfying as it was powerful. Without contradiction, this day consecrated to the Supreme Being will be the finest day in the life of the virtuous man, and it will always be with renewed interest, with the most lively sentiment that he will recall this happy occasion. The fête, so imposing in its purpose, was celebrated with a simple ceremony, majestic and truly worthy of the eternal author of nature. One saw nothing here of the pomp of courts and the ruinous display of despots reflected on all our walls, one saw nothing of the sumptuous furnishings of the rich which insult the modesty of the poor; no, happy and touching uniformity prevailed in the exterior decoration of our houses, and good nature herself had paid all the expenses. Festoons, garlands of flowers, numerous foliages, trees planted before every door, everywhere the gay national colours fluttering in the breeze: at first sight, one would have said that Paris had changed into a vast and beautiful garden, into a smiling orchard. It is easier to sense than to convey the sweet and profound impression that the sight of this new and picturesque scene made on all sensible souls. The freshness of the universal decoration, the beauty of the day, the open joy of the people, the eternally repeated shouts of '*vive la République, vivent nos représentants, vive la Montagne*', announced to the aristocrats, in a way both terrible and eloquent, that their hour had come and that they must flee forever from a city where the entire people, who were loudly proclaiming the existence of the divinity, immortality of the soul and death of tyrants, no longer leaves to the scoundrels, to traitors and to conspirators any hope of escaping from its inexorable and vengeful justice.

Le Journal de la Montagne, 22 Prairial, Year II (10 June 1794):
cited in Walter, *La Révolution français vue par ses journaux*,
pp. 354–55.

PART THREE

The Monarchy

In 1789 Louis XVI enjoyed the adulation of most of his subjects; in August 1792 he was dethroned; in January of the following year he was beheaded. His personal weaknesses were the main factor contributing to this rapid decline in fortune. Whereas the Church met the reforms of the revolutionaries with rigidity and hostility, Louis met them with hypocrisy and deceit. From the fall of the Bastille Louis had to choose either to accept the Revolution, and his diminished personal role within it; to refuse to accept it and so provoke a further crisis; or to flee France and seek aid from abroad. His upbringing and the force of tradition made the first of these alternatives difficult for him to accept. His nature and the lack of a reliable force to back up such a stand ruled out the second. Wavering between these two alternatives Louis professed support for the Revolution at the same time as he engaged in a secret correspondence with the foreign courts of Europe, while his court became the main centre of counter-revolution within France. Eventually the third of these alternatives was tried and after some false starts Louis managed to escape from Paris on the evening of 20 June 1791, only to be halted at Varennes and brought back to Paris a few days later.

The king's flight forced on the Assembly its most serious crisis since 1789, but the danger it now saw came from a different direction. At the expense of their popularity with the people of Paris, which had been becoming increasingly strained in any case, especially throughout 1791, and despite the radicals within the Assembly, the deputies skilfully steered their way through the crisis with the fiction of the 'kidnapping', and two months later completed their work with its presumed keystone being the constitutional monarch.

On 1 October 1791 the Legislative Assembly met for the first time, to govern France according to the Constitution drawn up over the previous two years. One of the few powers granted to Louis was the suspensive veto. This concession was vigorously opposed by the radicals who resented what they claimed to be an infringement of the sovereignty of the people. To Louis the veto was the main means of him asserting his authority and blocking any measures he considered obnoxious. His over-use of this prerogative, together with his further incensing popular opinion by his choice and dismissal of ministers, helped ensure his downfall. The weakness in the keystone brought down the entire structure. In September 1792 the deputies at the Convention had to start building anew.

The question remained, however, of what to do with Louis. Alive he was a rallying centre of opposition to the Revolution; but his death might excite the vengeance of his fellow monarchs not yet at war with France. So far as Robespierre was concerned he had already been tried and sentenced; his guilt and death had been pronounced by the Parisians on 10 August. With this logic he attacked the Girondins who temporised on the sentence of death. Vacillation had sealed Louis' fate; vacillation by the Girondins was now to put them on the first step towards their own downfall a few months later.

CONCESSION, DISSIMULATION OR ABDICATION?

On the fall of the Bastille Louis had at first wanted to flee the country but he was dissuaded from doing so by Marshal Broglie. For some time thereafter he believed the chance to be passed and so refused to consider flight, despite the desires of his wife and the advice of part of his court. In the meantime he was forced to make an appearance of approving and appreciating the Revolution he hated.

Never a man to hold to the same course for too long, he eventually decided, his conscience outraged by his sanctioning of the clerical oath (26 December 1790), to accept the advice of those who counselled flight and foreign aid. Throughout 1791 plans were under way for his escape from France.

From as early as 1790 the patriot press was attacking Louis for his apparent vacillation, but little criticism was made directly of the French monarchy. By 1791, however, this issue was broached, although it did not receive full vent until after the Champ de Mars affray. (See also Part Four, Sovereignty of the People, pp. 158–64.) Despite these attacks by the press Louis remained largely a father figure to his people, and it was not until 1792 that republicanism became a popular movement.

51. Fading Respect

Among the radicals Loustallot was one of the shrewdest critics of the monarchy. The documents that follow show Loustallot's equivocation on the king's professed love of the Revolution, and also indicate how rapid was his fall from favour in the radical press.

(i) '*A great king*'

The remarks which follow were prompted by Louis' declaration in favour of the Revolution, a declaration to offset the adverse publicity of the Favras affair.*

It is impossible at such moments to allow oneself any reflections; it is entirely an emotional thing. We shall only say, and this from the bottom of our hearts: May this day extinguish the discord that has reigned among our citizens, and bring back to the nation those who have been unable to recognise its rights! And let us patriots, in the interests of peace, make all the sacrifices that are in keeping with liberty. Let us show ourselves worthy of being free, let us show ourselves to be worthy subjects of such a king.

> *Les Révolutions de Paris*, No. 30, 30 January–6 February 1790, p. 31.

(ii) '. . . *dear to his people*.'

Sire,

The conduct of your ministers slanders your devotion to the principles of the Revolution . . .

. . . the greatest possible misfortune that could befall us, after the dissolution of the National Assembly, would be for the people to fall back into the same state of perplexity as they were concerning your intentions, at the time of 12 July, a perplexity that was so fortunately dispelled by your acceptance and magnificent surrender. Never, in all the history of your reign, have you been so dear to the French people as you have been since that time; but, Sire, there is not one example even in the history of the most fickle nations, of a king who has regained the people's esteem, once he has lost it.

> *Les Révolutions de Paris*, No. 38, 30 March–6 April 1790, pp. 10–11.

* Executed 4 February 1790 for conspiring against the nation and plotting to get the king out of the country.

(iii) *Quiet joy*

On 29 May 1790, the king, on Bailly's advice, and to win popularity declared his solidarity with the Assembly, condemned all opposition to its decrees and prohibited the wearing of a favour other than the tricolour.

The people displayed a quiet joy and not a mad abandon. If, at some other time, you had said to the French: why do you shout *Long live the king*, what could they have replied? On Sunday, they would have said: 'We wish to see at our head for a long time a king who has finally listened to the voice of reason rather than to the senseless advice of his ministers; who has preferred to be our king by constitutional law rather than by virtue of a right for which he could not have brought forward any proof, and which could not be established except by fire and sword. To his credit, we must acknowledge the harm that he could have brought down upon us, despite our certainty that we would have made the general will prevail over that of the king and his court.'

Les Révolutions de Paris, No. 47, 29 May–
5 June 1790, p. 455.

(iv) *'His qualities, but . . .'*

A week later the king made a public appearance–a procession with the deputies and the National Guard.

I could dispute this affection for the person of Louis XVI, not only with all the members of the legislative body, but with all the other citizens. It was I who fixed the attention of the French people on his excellent qualities at a time when his refusal to accept the Constitution, a few days after the orgy at Versailles, gave some grounds for the calumnies by means of which the courtiers had, since his accession to the throne, degraded his officials in the eyes of the people. Since that time I have not ceased to distinguish, in all the acts of the government, ministerial decisions from those of the king, and to profess for him the most zealous respect and the most sincere affection. Must I then sacrifice to the *royalism of the moment* the interests of the people; must I neglect the interests of justice and of reason, in order not to appear to contradict myself? Should I be afraid to resist the enthusiasm that has fired the wise representatives of the people? Should I dread the charges of demagogy? Should I make myself the apostle of a *legal brigandage* which sacrifices to the false brilliance of a court (that can never be anything but the enemy of the public good) the blood, the sweat and the livelihood of our unfortunate citizens? No, no! . . .

Les Révolutions de Paris, No. 48, 5–12 June 1790, pp. 516–17.

(v) *All praise cancelled*

On 9 June the Assembly granted with acclamation and passed unanimously the sum which the king had estimated he would need to meet the needs, and uphold the dignity of his household. This was met by a storm of protest by the radical press: the *Révolutions de Paris* received the Assembly's decision with indignation, and from this time on maintained a constant attack on the 'frivolous deputies' and the person of the king, using the Civil List as its basis.

After a succession of serious offences against the nation, Louis XVI suddenly broke with his court; he threw himself into the midst of our representatives; he came alone into the midst of 300,000 men, armed, desperate and dying of hunger. This quality alone must have made us appreciate him; and since then all our efforts have tended to dispel the prejudice and calumny that had been poured down on him. Despite his refusal in the month of October to sanction the Constitution, despite his extremely ambiguous speech on 4 February, despite his continued confidence in the military chiefs, and in ambassadors who arrogantly profess the most shameless aristocratic sentiments, I have continued to speak well of him, without praising him.

But finally, his pen has set out the fatal *lettre-décret* for 25 millions; he has asked for 4 millions as a pension for the queen; he has deceived us into paying for the upkeep of his servants of which the state treasury has no records. As he signed that disastrous letter the king should have been able to see, despite himself, that neither his spirit had been touched nor his soul moved by the depredations of his and his predecessors' reign or by the utter poverty of the masses. Thus, caught between the diverse sentiments, which have provoked in us contradictory attitudes, and by no means wishing that our opinions should mislead the public, we ask you, citizens and soldiers, to accept our declaration, that all the praise which we have given to Louis XVI be regarded as cancelled, *until such time as*, divesting himself of more than *five hundred millions of landed possessions*, and of half the Civil List that he has had allocated to himself, he no longer forces us to doubt that he desires the alleviation of the ills of the people, and the liquidation of the public debt.

Les Révolutions de Paris, No. 52, 3–10 July 1790, pp. 741–42.

52. Gall and Humiliation

> While Loustallot condemned what wealth and power was left to
> Louis, the royalists saw only what was taken from him.

Some people are anxious to exclude from sale [of the *biens nationaux*]
the châteaux, residences, demesnes and woods reserved for the king.
Some members of the right wing demand that these words be inserted:
according to the choice of the king. But the left wing found it improper to
leave to the king the right of himself selecting from among the former
demesnes of his ancestors those whose use he wished to reserve to
himself. It is of the essence of the constitution, according to M. de
Robespierre, that it should be the National Assembly which assigns to
the king his quarters, his apartments, and where he should take his
walks; consequently, by the *question préalable*,* the demand of *freedom of
choice* claimed on the king's behalf has been rejected. They went even
further: on the motion of M. de Robespierre, in order that Europe could
not be deceived on the matter and so imagine that a free people left
their king the choice of his places of pleasure, after these words, *reserved
for the king*, they were careful to add: *by virtue of the decrees of the Assembly*.
Thus, his enjoyment is only precarious, submitted to the fickle will of
the Assembly; the same authority that today grants him a château,
may well tomorrow, on a thousand pretexts, take it away from him.
Will people then not grow weary of soaking with gall and humiliation
the best of kings; and will the nation not think itself debased in the
person of its august head?

> *L'Ami du Roi*, No. CXXIX: cited in Buchez and Roux,
> *Histoire parlementaire*, vol. VII, p. 353.

---

* The process by which the Assembly was called to decide if a matter ought to be
debated or not.

53. A Time for Congratulations?

The decree of 22 May 1790 referred to here is that which gave the king the right to initiate war and the legislature the right of veto. It was a compromise between leaving this matter entirely in the hands of either the legislature or the executive. It was greeted as a victory by the people and acclaimed by most of the radical press. Desmoulins, for whom *any* power in the hands of the king was an evil, never disguised his republican sentiments. The implications of this power in the hands of the king as being more important than the negative function of the legislature was more fully discussed by Loustallot in his paper.

In my opinion, the best touchstone as to whether a law is good is the dismay of the Tuileries and the long faces of the 'ministerials'. There are none–even down to the children of the *château*–whose looks do not warn the citizens of what they have to fear or to hope. For example, on Saturday 22 May, the young dauphin was applauding Mirabeau's decree* with a good sense beyond his years. The people for its part was also applauding and it escorted in triumph Barnave, Pétion, Lameth, d'Aiguillon, Duport, and all the illustrious Jacobins. It thought itself to have won a great victory, and those deputies were stupid enough to maintain them in their error. Robespierre was more frank. He said to the crowd who surrounded him and deafened him with their clapping: *Well, gentlemen, what have you to congratulate yourselves for? the decree is detestable, excessively detestable; let us leave this monkey to beat his hands at his window, he knows better than us what he is doing.*

Since that time the king has appeared more often in public. He goes to the hunt and in procession, he makes his thanks to the National Parisian Guard, he reviews it on the Champ de Mars, and, with sorrow, I have seen him gallop amidst endless cries of *Long live the king!* with me alone making myself hoarse by shouting in their ears *Long live the nation!* I recall some years ago, his wife, on one occasion entering Paris and meeting with a very cold reception, saying these highly comical words: *I think my people annoy me.* For close on a year, in her turn, Madame has been somewhat annoying her people, but she begins to smile at us in a less forced manner, and sometimes even with an infinite grace.

Les Révolutions de France et de Brabant, No. 28, pp. 665–66.

* On the right of war and peace.

54. Marat on Royalty

From December 1790 until the king's attempted escape, Marat constantly preached vigilance over his movements. His fears were partly due to the belief that despite Louis' faults France needed a king.

(i) *Critic*

Marat has been listing the corrupting influences surrounding Louis and in particular the vices inherent in absolutism, finally putting the question whether there is any reason to expect that Louis should have escaped these evils. From the general he turns to the specific.

No, I judge you by your past conduct; I judge you for yourself. Tell me, what confidence would we have in the word, in the protestations, in the oaths of a king who had summoned the nation only to engage it to fill the abyss dug by the wastefulness of his ministers, of the household princes, of his favourites, and of the other scoundrels of his court; of a king who tried to dissolve the National Assembly as soon as he found some opposition to his wishes; of a king who worked six weeks, and quite cold-bloodedly, at the execution of a terrible plan to put the capital to fire and sword, in order to punish its unfortunate inhabitants for the generous support that they seemed to promise the representatives of the nation against the attacks of despotism; of a king who was prepared to renounce his terrible plans, only when he saw the people up in arms, ready to take justice into their own hands; of a king who, in defiance of his most solemn oaths, and almost at the very time that he had just secured his pardon from a generous people, gave ear to the treacherous counsels of his court, in order to contrive a new conspiracy against the people who had become free; of a king who, forgetting that he had asked for pardon, dared to adopt the tone of a master, as soon as he believed himself to be strong enough, and who prepared himself to massacre the malcontents or to escape from them, afterwards, if fortune went against him; of a king who, reduced to asking for forgiveness a second time, had no sooner obtained his pardon, than he plotted anew; of a king who closed his ear to the denunciations that came from all quarters against his ministers, a thousand times traitors and prevaricators; of a king who, far from expelling them in disgrace, gave them his protection, as if he was himself the author of all their terrible plots, and who finally consented to accept their dismissal only when the people clamoured loud and strong for their guilty heads.

Such is the true account of your conduct for the past eighteen months. Be then your own judge, and tell us, if you dare to do so, whether such a king deserves names other than those of *stupid automaton* or *treacherous liar.* Yet you boast to us of your attachment to the constitution, and you remind us of your oaths of being true to the country, and you speak to us of the civic loyalty of your wife, and you ask us to trust ourselves to your word! Ah! would to God that we could indeed believe you; but we could not do so without passing as imbeciles ourselves, without betraying our duties as men and as citizens, without renouncing our liberty, our peace, our happiness; without sacrificing our friends, our parents, our brothers, our children, our wives, without indeed sacrificing ourselves! Sire, you are *the friend of our liberty*, as your wife is *the friend of the French*. The very tone with which you have expressed yourself on this matter serves only to arouse our suspicions. What then! is it part of the dignity of a king, who has not been accustomed to deception, to say to us *I will speak to you openly and frankly?* The truth that you owe us and which you hide from us, we are going to say it to you; have the courage to listen to it, and try to profit by it.

> There follows an account of 'cheating ministers' and an aristocratic plot to massacre the patriots, worded by Marat to deter Louis from becoming their 'docile organ'. Marat then goes on to warn Louis that if any dissenting prelate should escape from the obligations contained in the clerical oath that Louis had just sanctioned, and this because of Louis' negligence, then

. . . you would pass, Sire, for an enemy of the public liberty, for a treacherous conspirator, for the most cowardly of perjurers, for a prince without honour, without shame, for the lowest of men. May the fear of being covered with opprobrium in the eyes of all Europe close your heart to the counsels of the scoundrels who surround you; may it determine you to deliver them yourself to the sword of the law! Finally, fear to repel the truth that dares to draw near you. It is on this new proof that present generations and future races will judge you.

L'Ami du peuple, No. 324, 29 December 1790.

(ii) *Friend*

I do not know if the counter-revolutionaries will force us to change the form of government; but I do know that limited monarchy is the one that best suits us today, in view of the depravity and degradation of the upholders of the old régime, all so prone to abuse the powers entrusted to them. With such men, a federal republic would soon degenerate into oligarchy.

I have often been represented as a mortal enemy of royalty, yet I maintain that the king has no better friend than me. His mortal enemies are his relatives, his ministers, the 'blacks' and the 'ministerials' in the

National Assembly, the members of the *club monarchique*, the factious priests and other supporters of despotism: for by their machinations they continually expose him to losing the people's confidence, and they push him by their advice to risk losing his crown, which I fix firmly to his head by uncovering their plots, by pressing him to deliver them to the sword of the laws.

L'Ami du peuple, No. 374, 17 February 1791.

(iii) *Critic of the Court*

(a) The hostage aunts

On 4 February the king's devout aunts asked for passports to leave for Rome. They eventually left on 20 February, following a heated debate.

We are assured that the king's aunts raise the devil in order to leave. It would be extremely imprudent to permit them to do so. Despite all that the imbecile journalists have said on the matter, they are not at all free. We are at war with the enemies of the Revolution: it is necessary to keep these *béguines* as hostages, and it is necessary to set a triple guard over the rest of the family.

It is of the utmost importance to write a circular immediately to all the municipalities. . . . Observe carefully, citizens, that the king's aunts in leaving would leave behind three millions of debts, and that they would take away twelve millions of gold, which they have acquired by paying almost 29 livres for each louis; notice again that they would take with them the dauphin, and that they will leave at the Tuileries a child of the same age and looks, who has been brought up with him for the past eighteen months in order to perfect this premeditated abduction.

L'Ami du peuple, No. 371, 14 February 1791.

(b) 'Dagger Day'

On 28 February 1791 about a thousand workers from the Faubourg St.-Antoine marched to the castle at Vincennes to destroy the *donjon* which was being converted into a temporary overflow prison for the Châtelet. The press had been agitating against the restoration of what was regarded in the popular mind as another Bastille. On hearing of the march a crowd of nobles gathered at the Tuileries to protect the king from what rumour had enlarged into another 14 July or 5 October. The affair ended when Lafayette arrived and arrested sixty-four of the Parisians. Rumours of an abortive royal flight, of a plot to murder the patriots, filled the radical press. The court conspirators hurried ahead at even greater pace with their plans to get the king out of the country.

Let us conclude by an important reflection on the conspiracy that heaven has just made abortive. The secret grouping of armed counter-revolutionaries, in the king's appartments, presents a multitude of crimes rolled into one. One sees there treason towards the fatherland, offence to the National Guard, and insult to the king; an odious plot to overturn the constitution by kidnapping the king, and a plan to set aflame civil war by the assassination of the château guards; monstrous crimes, worthy of the worst punishment.

In revealing this conspiracy, in keeping the general* out of the way, and in summoning that day only the hired Grenadiers, it seemed that heaven had made it its business to muster the black swarm of conspirators under the sword of these brave warriors and had delivered it defenceless to their blows in order to free the country.

They had the right to massacre them, and they could do so with impunity. The true friends of liberty will always deplore that they let slip such a favourable opportunity, which will never come again; the Friend of the People is above all inconsolable.

L'Ami du peuple, No. 394, 9 March 1791.

55. Respect and Disrespect

A bulletin on the king's health signed by his doctors, like the one quoted below, appeared daily in many of the Parisian newspapers during the occasion of his 'bad cold'.

The king's sickness broke out last Friday with fits of fever and shivering. The fever, the bitter cough and the other symptoms of catarrh continued yesterday until four o'clock in the afternoon. In that time the king spat blood (three times). His evacuations have been bilious, brown and glaireous, his urine dark coloured and infrequent. The crisis began at eight o'clock, with an increase in hoarseness and inflammation of the throat. The night was often interrupted by coughing; the other symptoms have eased a little.

L'Ami du Roi, No. CCXCIV, 10 March 1791.

Desmoulins was particularly scornful of the exaggerated concern shown for the monarch.

---

* i.e. Lafayette.

For example, it is with good reason that J. P. Brissot makes fun of the good nature of our legislators, who every day allow the majesty of their meetings to be interrupted in order to listen to, on the occasion of the eldest of the Capets' cold, that ridiculous *technology of the diaphorous: that the king's urine has been clearer and more frequent, that his stools are glaireous etc.* Where is the citizen who is not indignant at the level to which our deputies have sunk when they applaud enough to bring the house down when a bishop mounts the tribune of the National Assembly to make the proclamation that the bowel movements of a citizen down with the cold *have been copious and that their matter is not so nauseous, but are indeed rather laudable.* I am amazed that MM. Lemonnier, Laservole, Vicq-d'Azir, Audouille and Lousteneau* do not enter in ceremony with the Prince's urinal and night-stool to pass them under the nose of the President of the National Assembly, and that the Assembly does not expressly create the position of patriarch of the Gauls to make proclamations on the quality of the bowel-movements of the Grand Lama. . . .

Les Révolutions de France et de Brabant, No. 69, p. 159.

FLIGHT

On 21 June 1791, Paris first learned that the king had fled. Consternation seized the people, hope filled the counter-revolutionaries. After its initial panic the Assembly acted calmly and with dignity: it suspended the king and took measures to have him recaptured, and after announcing the fiction of the 'kidnapping' carried on as though nothing serious had happened. In fact this was, with its far-reaching implications, one of the most crucial events of the Revolution.

56. The Royal Cannibal

Compare this piece with those in doc. 51 (i–v), pp. 122–24.

The worthiest man in the kingdom (You cowardly writers, incompetent or hired hacks, it is thus that you refer to Louis XVI). The worthiest man in the kingdom, this father of the French people, following the example of the hero of two worlds,† has deserted his post, and escapes in the hope of sending us, in exchange for his royal person, several years of

* The doctors.
† Lafayette.

foreign and domestic war. This conspiracy, worthy of the united houses of Bourbon and Austria, this cowardly, treacherous conspiracy, hatched for the last eighteen months, has at last been carried out.

Citizens: give us credit! Remember now, that we didn't wait until the dénouement of 21 June to tell you what kings are capable of. He has gone, this vile king, but he is no doubt the last to fool you. Let him go, never to return. To have kept him any longer at our head would have been far too much of an encumbrance.

But observe, citizens, how criminal are all the circumstances which have preceded, accompanied, and followed this flight. Has the author of noble deeds ever struck with his fatal weapons more accomplished villains than those who have just fled by night from the palace of the Tuileries? Julius Caesar, stabbed to death by the Romans, Charles I, executed by the English, these were innocents compared with Louis XVI.

Our former king (for Louis XVI is no longer king and can no longer be king) first greedily demands 25 millions on the Civil List and numerous estates. He wants his debts and those of his brothers paid off, even those of his wet-nurse whom he sends before the nation to be paid for the milk that she lavished on the royal wolf-cub; he orders the felling of his woods; he no longer has to pay his ministers; his guard is no longer maintained at his expense, and already he finds himself short. He needs advances; the royal cannibal devours all the cash; and when he has converted the people's bread into gold he is still ravenous for whatever money we have left.

Les Révolutions de Paris, No. 102, 18–25 June 1791, pp. 525–26.

57. The King is no more

Unlike the *Révolutions de Paris*, the king's flight called for a sudden reversal of opinion on the part of Hébert. On the occasion of the king's cold, for example, he had been unable to drink his wine, which had become bitter, or smoke his pipe, because the tobacco choked him, and all because 'My king, my good king, is ill . . . the restorer of French liberty is confined to bed'.

Now the Père Duchesne, in a conversation with the king, calls him a 'fat yokel'; and when told to remember to whom he is speaking, he replies . . .

You my king. You are no longer my king, no longer my king! You are nothing but a cowardly deserter; a king should be the father of the people, not its executioner. Now that the nation has resumed its rights it will not be so bloody stupid as to take back a coward like you. You, king? You are not even a citizen. You will be lucky to avoid leaving your head on a scaffold for having sought the slaughter of so many men. Ah, I don't doubt that once again you are going to pretend to be honest and that, supported by those scoundrels on the constitutional committee, you are going to promise miracles. They still want to stick the crown on the head of a stag; but no, damn it, that will not happen! From one end of France to the other, there is only an outcry against you, your debauched Messalina, and your whole bastard race.

No more Capet, this is what every citizen is shouting, and, besides, even if it were possible that they might want to pardon you all your crimes, what trust could now be placed in your remains? You vile perjurer, a man who has broken his oath again and again. We will stuff you into Charenton and your whore into the Hôpital. When you are finally walled up, both of you, and above all when you no longer have a Civil List, I'll be stuffed with an axe if you get away.

Le Père Duchesne, No. 61: Walter, *op. cit.*, p. 180.

58. The King Complains

Garat, the political editor of the *Journal de Paris*, was one of the most ardent supporters of the Constituent Assembly. His optimistic, often naïve, reporting had constantly praised the king and welcomed his declarations in favour of the Revolution. For him, then, the flight was a moment of disbelief, followed by despair when the contents of a note in which the king had recorded his feelings regarding the Revolution were made known. In two issues of the *Journal* he criticised this note.

This will be one occasion added to so many others to prove just how estranged are kings from the truth, and how impossible it is for them to form a clear conception of human affairs, of social institutions and of the place which a king should occupy in the constitution, of which he can be no more than one part. At every turn and in so many ways one shudders at this misfortune which is characteristic of kings, which puts a veil between them and reality, and which delivers their minds up to the fascination of a thousand cares and a thousand affections, none of which is natural.

The king complains of the acclaim lavished before him by a people intoxicated by a minister whom he had nominated, dismissed and recalled.* It is in this way that princes are accustomed to look on glory, won through talent and virtue, as a usurpation of their own power . . .

The king complains of not being properly looked after during his stay in Paris, yet he was lodged in a palace seemingly built by the love of luxury and pride of kings to display their pleasure and magnificence before the eyes of the world; and to furnish this palace at the Tuileries he had all the furniture of the Crown, that is to say, all that the centuries had accumulated in the palaces of the Kings of France to satisfy their taste for grandeur, their comfort, and their whims.

The king complains of having received only 25 millions for the Civil List . . . [yet] there are empires of world-wide importance which do not have for their general expenditure a revenue as considerable as that which has been granted Louis XVI for the household expenses.

The king complains of what has been excluded from the constitutional laws, of the small part remaining to him in the legislative function of the veto; the fact is that even the slightest part given to any one man in legislation is, in the eyes of a strict critic of political systems, a violation, or at least an alteration, of those rational principles that should not be changed except to be strengthened; and the fact is that peoples who submit their constitutional laws to the veto of the king would never have a constitution . . .

The king complains of how the Constitution has robbed royalty in order to transfer to the people the right to elect almost all public officials, judges, administrators etc. etc. etc. As if royalty could exist, and have some power independent of the Constitution! As if it wasn't more reasonable to have public officials elected by the people who know them, and who must suffer or profit according to their incapacity or their merit, than by the king and his ministers, who know only one small part of the kingdom, and whose happiness is never endangered by elections that have been fixed.

The king complains of the violence which in some parts of the kingdom, and even in his palace at Versailles, has covered the Revolution in blood: but what French citizen has not been horrified by it, has not been deeply disturbed by it? These crimes were committed against both the nation and its king . . . can they be justified in any way? When 26 million men take so great and unprecedented a step towards a new order of things, how is it humanly possible to avoid in such an upheaval a few acts which go wrong? Where is the justice in placing responsibility for a murder committed at Aix on the legislators at Paris, who are making a new constitution?

Le Journal de Paris, 24 June 1791.

* Necker. The *Journal de Paris* was always extremely lavish in its praise of Necker—as it was of most public figures.

59. Dictatorship or Defeat

Marat's warnings now appeared only too justified.

All France recalls the address that Louis XVI gave before the National Assembly on 18 April, complaining like a schoolboy that the people of the capital had prevented him going to Saint-Cloud,* that is to say to Brussels. All France will also recall that famous letter† written under his orders to his ambassadors abroad, and officially communicated to the National Assembly, which was designed to demonstrate his pretended loyalty, making himself out as the defender of public liberty and the upholder of the Constitution, complaining of the doubts that citizens had expressed as to the sincerity of his sentiments, decrying the rumours circulating that he was not a free agent, declaring that he had no intention whatever of fleeing, and protesting that he was in the midst of his children, his fellow citizens and his friends, to whom he was bound both by joy and affection.

In support of these declarations he invoked truth, loyalty, honour and his pledged oath. Pledged oath my foot! Remember Henry III and the Duke of Guise. Henry had appeared to be reconciled to the Duke; in order to lull him into a sense of false security, he appealed to heaven to witness the sincerity of his oaths; he ate at the same table, promised to put aside all resentments, and swore eternal friendship upon the altar, at the same instant as he was plotting in his mind the heinous deed of having him assassinated. No sooner was he outside the temple of the God of peace than he distributed daggers to his retainers, summoned the Duke to his room through a secret door which had just been built at his orders, and had him pierced with a thousand stabs.

People, there is your loyalty, your honour, your religion of kings: beware of their oaths. On the morning of the 19th Louis XVI made a mockery of his.

This perjurer of a king, without faith, without shame, without remorse, this monarch unworthy of a throne, has been restrained only by the fear of being shown up as an infamous beast. The thirst for absolute power that consumes his soul will soon turn him into a ferocious murderer; soon he will be swimming in the blood of his fellow citizens who will refuse to submit to his tyrannous yoke. Mean-

---

* To hear confession from a non-juring priest.
† Montmorin's circular of 23 April. At the time Marat correctly suspected a secret circular contradicting the published one.

while he is laughing at the folly of the Parisians who stupidly took him at his word.

Citizens, the flight of the royal family was prepared from a distance by the traitors in the National Assembly and above all by the *comité des recherches et des rapports* . . .

Only one way remains to drag you back from the precipice where your unworthy leaders have led you, and that is to name immediately a military tribune, a supreme dictator, to remove the principal known traitors. You are lost beyond hope if you continue to heed your present leaders, who will continue to flatter you and set you at ease until your enemies are at your walls. Let the tribune be named today; let your choice fall on that citizen who until now has shown himself to be the most enlightened, the most zealous and the most faithful. Swear to him unswerving loyalty, obey him religiously in everything he commands you to do to defeat your mortal enemies.

Now is the time to have the heads of the ministers and their subordinates, of Mottié, of all the scoundrels of the general staff, and of all the anti-patriotic battalion commanders, of Bailly, of all the municipal counter-revolutionaries; of all the traitors in the National Assembly; begin then by arresting them, if there is still time. Seize the opportunity to destroy the organisation of your National Guard, now lost to liberty: in these times of crisis and alarm you find yourselves abandoned by all your leaders. What need have you of these cowards who hide themselves in time of danger and who show themselves in times of peace only to insult and ill-treat patriotic soldiers, only to betray the motherland? Despatch couriers immediately to ask for aid from the departments; call the Bretons to your assistance, seize the arsenal; disarm the mounted lancers, the guards at the ports, the soldiers at the customs posts: prepare to defend your rights, to avenge your liberty, to exterminate your implacable enemies.

A tribune, a military tribune, or you are lost beyond hope. Until now I have done all that is humanly possible to save you: if you neglect this salutary advice, the last that remains for me to give you, I have no more to say to you, and I will take leave of you for good. Within a few days Louis XVI, assuming once again the tone of a despot will, in an insolent manifesto, treat you as rebels, if you do not willingly submit to his yoke. He will advance on your walls at the head of all the fugitives, of all the malcontents and of the Austrian Legions; he will blockade you! A hundred fiery mouths will threaten to destroy your town with red shot if you offer the least resistance; whilst Mottié, at the head of German Hussars, and perhaps the lancers of the Parisian army, will come to disarm you; all the ardent patriots among you will be arrested, the popular writers will be dragged into the dungeons; *L'Ami du peuple*, whose last gasp will be for the *patrie*, and whose faithful voice still calls

you to liberty, will have for his tomb a fiery furnace. A few more days of
indecision and it will be too late to shake off your lethargy; death will
overtake you in your sleep.

Signed Marat, l'ami du peuple.

L'Ami du peuple, No. 497, 22 June 1791.

60. A Royalist View of the Flight

The king was halted at Varennes near the border on the 22nd and
brought back to Paris on the 25th. The apparent inaction of the
Assembly following his capture gave renewed hope to the counter-
revolutionaries. Royou, like others in the right-wing press, considered that the king deserved praise for his defection: after all he
had only 'acted in the best interests of the people.'

In this critical situation the king, incapable of disarming the neighbouring countries as long as he was held in captivity, conceived, as he
himself has said, the noble and honourable scheme of putting himself
between his people and the powerful enemies threatening them. By one
of those fortunate combinations of political insight and wisdom he
wanted to take advantage of the hostile attitude of the allied powers to
offer really favourable conditions to his subjects and to make them happy
in spite of themselves. Montmédy was, because of its location, a suitable
place to carry out this glorious plan, and since those insolent men who
were holding him captive, and whose position and impunity depended
only on the chaos within the state, would be violently opposed to all
measures which would banish dissension and restore peace, the king
saw himself obliged to break out secretly and to fly those places which
should one day enjoy to the full the fruits of his benevolence. Thus, far
from being condemned as a crime, his flight should, on the contrary,
be acclaimed as a great blessing, and instead of receiving from his
people expressions of hatred and contempt, he should experience at
their hands nothing but love and respect.

To be sure of this, let us compare the state that France would have
been in if the king had reached his chosen refuge, with the state she
was in before his departure, and that into which she has been plunged
again by the renewed captivity of the king. What in effect would have
happened if the king had been able to recover his freedom? Supported
by the impressive forces of his allies, forces he would have been able to
dispose of as he pleased, he would have negotiated with the factions who

today govern the kingdom. The people themselves, whose loyalty was retained in the first days of the Revolution, more than anything else by the very name of the king and by his apparent wishes, would have realised how much better it would have been for them to accept a constitution which would have eliminated both the abuses of the *ancien régime* and the even greater evils of the present Constitution; the well-known love that the king has for his people would have determined him to make sacrifices, in order not to poison the happiness he had offered them by the disaster of a civil war. The people themselves, in order to spare the blood of their brothers and fellow-citizens, would have given up the absurd and fanciful pretensions destined only to perpetuate and aggravate their sufferings, which their real enemies had inspired in them. The result of these negotiations would have been an Assembly that was truly national, so much more solidly founded for being based on the freedom of all the parties concerned. All the factions which today divide France would have been reunited around this solemn charter, which would finally have settled all powers. Hatred, rivalries, dissensions would have disappeared for ever, and we would have become truly a nation of brothers. Trade would have flourished again, obedience to the law would have been re-established, prosperity would have been restored in the home, those who had fled would have returned to our midst, there to enjoy the pleasures of peace and concord; universal harmony would have reigned throughout the empire, the people and the king would at last have found, in their mutual love, a secure prosperity and that happiness of which they have been deprived for so long.

What on the contrary would have happened if the king had not broken free, or will happen if he is not quickly restored to his liberty? The allied powers, concerned for themselves in revenging a king so cruelly oppressed by his subjects, will invade our provinces, bringing death and slaughter among us; we will then see descend on us all the evils which anarchy and chaos bring in their train; citizen armed against citizen, friend against friend, brother against brother, and when victory finally rests with the friends of the constitution at what cost in blood and tears will it have been bought? Is this the road which leads to happiness? Who would not shudder in horror at the sight of a constitution that could only be built on a heap of ruins and corpses . . .

By what crime has he then rendered himself unworthy of this, as it were, hereditary trust which the French people have hitherto accorded to his predecessors, loyalty which he, perhaps more than any of them, has deserved to retain? Assume once again that character of goodness, sweetness and humanity, which used to distinguish you from all the peoples on earth and which causes you to be regarded, and rightly so, as the most agreeable and generous nation in the universe. Return to your king that tutelary power whose usurpation has for so long cost you your peace. Seek in lawful obedience to his legitimate and sacred authority the true liberty which you so vainly chase and which for you has been replaced by a most dangerous and criminal licence. And to render this authority really active, really effective, return also to him that liberty of which he has been so unjustly deprived and without which there can be for you neither constitution, nor law, nor order, nor peace.

L'Ami du Roi–Royou, 28 and 29 June 1791: Walter
op. cit., pp. 186–88, 196.

ASSERTION OF AUTHORITY

On 9 November 1791 the Legislative Assembly issued a decree ordering all émigrés to return to France. The king opposed his veto. Later in the same month he vetoed the decree on non-juring clergy. These became known as the 'rejected decrees'. Louis, of course, was acting within his rights in using his prerogative; it is not quite so certain that he was acting in his best interests. In May and June of the following year he again applied his veto, this time to two of the three 'Revolutionary Decrees'. The two decrees vetoed were that of 27 May subjecting non-juring priests to deportation, and that of 8 June relative to the formation of an army of 20,000 *fédérés*; the third decree, to which he reluctantly assented, was for the dissolution of his personal bodyguard.

Frustrated by this obstruction, Roland read a letter to the Assembly on 13 June complaining, 'in the austere language of truth', of the delay in the sanctioning of decrees. The result was the dismissal of Roland and two other Girondin ministers and their replacement by Feuillants.

61. The Cracks in the Edifice

The editor of the *Révolutions de Paris* is describing the ceremony that brought to an end the Constituent Assembly. A severe critic of the franchise restrictions and of the royal prerogatives, he is still smarting bitterly from the martial law decree brought into effect just two months before on the very field where the new Constitution was now being proclaimed. He quotes the proclamation of the municipal officers.

'Citizens, the National Constituent Assembly for the years 1789, 1790 and 1791, having begun on 17 June 1789 the work of the Constitution, happily concluded it on 3 September 1791. The constitutional act was solemnly accepted and signed by the king, on the 14th of the same month. The National Constituent Assembly entrusts its safekeeping to the fidelity of the legislative body, of the king and judges; to the vigilance of the fathers of families, to wives, to mothers, to the affection of the young citizens, and to the courage of all French people.'

We would have liked to see in this proclamation a little more modesty. Our legislators seem a little too convinced of their infallibility; to listen to them one would think that the whole of human reason is contained in this code, which was however drawn up amidst storms and passions. This 'sacred trust' that they confide to our loyalty, is it then so sacred that we must never touch it? Would they want to make us promise to allow ourselves to be crushed in the collapse of their edifice, rather than put a hand to the weak spots? It is to time, which uncovers all truth, to time, which brings to light the beauties and defects of works that are the product of man's hand or brain, it is to time that they ought rather to have recommended the task of perfecting what they present to us as a masterpiece. Citizens! they ought rather to have said to us, you have asked us for a constitution; here it is. We do not give you a perfect one; you cannot expect such. Such as it is, make use of it, until you secure a better one.

Les Révolutions de Paris, No. 115, 17–24 September 1791.

62. Lemaire on the Veto

> Lemaire was one of the few patriots whose ardent royalism survived the events of June and July 1791. By July of the following year, when this article was written, his patriotism and royalism were at uncomfortable odds.

But, damn it, who is to blame for this? Clearly, the conduct of the king himself, ill-directed, ill-advised; the king, who seemed determined, whether mistakenly or from obstinacy, to struggle constantly against the legislative power; the king, whom I would rather see heaped with blessings, than either pressed by these noisy entreaties, which look like violence, when they are really only the expression of [justified] indignation; or, finally, exposed to the fatal consequences of the despair that he has cast into every soul, by refusing his sanction to the two useful decrees, and by dismissing at the same time ministers whom the nation pays and who have its confidence; ministers whose recall we had a right to demand from him: for if the steward of a house dismisses the servants who are under his orders, the master, who pays the servants, can certainly ask why they were dismissed, especially when he is quite satisfied with them himself.

These disturbances are far from giving pleasure to the Père Duchêne, damn it, who would like to see everything restored to order, and complying with the law; but I am also far from approving resistance to the means taken to suppress the calotted agitators, who are unceasingly leagued against the public good; this fact is attested by all the complaints that arrive from every side against them. I am indeed far from approving that, at a time when great forces threaten us, we are refused permission to summon a greater force for the capital.

This national sovereignty, and I confess it to you with sorrow, is finished with, if with four letters people can play around with it. The *veto* seems to me a monstrosity, especially when the constituents have neglected to determine in which cases it can be applied. For in urgent circumstances, a *veto* which suspends for THREE YEARS the urgent precautions of the legislative body, is a scourge rather than a remedy; and never, I warrant you, will you be able to make the machine work, nor repulse major conspiracies, so long as that terrible weapon is in hands guided by aristocrats interested in paralysing you, or so long as the cases in which the veto can be applied will not be sovereignly determined. You will have, on the one hand, ceaselessly to fear the terrible manoeuvres of our cursed enemies; on the other, the insurrections, which makes two scourges at the one time. While telling ourselves that the Constitution must be respected, if it has not provided a means of remedying the ills that can destroy it, then some means or other must be found; this would not be to attack the Constitution but merely to add to it what is lacking to preserve it. If the legislature has not the right to do this, then there is an immediate need for a NATIONAL CONVENTION: either that or everything goes to the dogs, or we will destroy ourselves without knowing why, or the king will be ceaselessly exposed to the popular movements, or the National Assembly itself will be upended, and with it LIBERTY. For this is the difficulty into which the lack of foresight of the revisers, or their treachery, has landed us, and which today is the cause of our convulsions. Without that alone, we would be cheerful and well disposed, and everything would go to the general satisfaction of the patriots, whom these storms cut to the quick and bring to despair. Again, mark me well, the enemies of the people or even men frightened by its strength, will still accuse it of vigorously showing its strength, whilst they are hardly astonished at the ills which can be engendered by royal resistance to the national will.

One can be delighted, without having a depraved soul, to see a king whom we have given ourselves, delivered to tumultuous scenes, exposed perhaps to the resentment of the masses, and not respected as much AS HE WOULD WISH; but what must truly disturb both Paris and France, is not so much the eruption of the people, as the king's advisers, who bring it about by their infernal obstinacy, which is the sole cause of all the disorders and of all the ills that result from it. This is what I think of the day's events, and it is a friend of truth who says it with deep distress, to those who know well that he is also the friend of the laws.

La Trompette du Père Duchêne, No. 38, pp. 2–5.

63. A Last Word to the King

Louis' initial apathy and constant lack of positive action irritated his friends as well as his enemies. The impetuous Suleau's militancy is matched only by his eloquence.

Moved by a righteous indignation, eager to swell the host of true defenders of the fatherland, I waited for the signal for the battle to begin; I asked for the successor of Henry the Great; I looked for the panache that would show us the road to honour and victory . . . You appeared, and I saw only a slave who dolefully bore the irons upon his unjust hands that a barbarous and sacrilegious troop had manacled.

These terrible signs of your servitude would be eternal trophies erected to your glory, if the God of armies had alone dictated the sentence of your captivity. But what battle has anyone waged for you? . . .

The . . . monarchy is no more, and its death has not even been preceded by the throes of agony . . .

So many crowns accumulated on your head by the hand of time and the love of peoples made you the first sovereign of the world. Also your polity ruled over two hemispheres, when the peoples and the kings of the most distant parts of the known world acknowledged you as the arbiter of their differences. Today the scene has changed. Your people has seated itself on your throne; your people has invaded every authority; your people has declared itself your sovereign. Legislator, magistrate, minister, pontiff and king, it is everything, and you are no longer anything but the plaything of its caprices.

And do not deceive yourself with the vain hope of one day returning to the land of your ancestors: a people corrupted in its morals and dissolute in its principles cannot and must not suffer any domination other than that which it exercises itself, for it is natural for man to set himself under the government that accords best with his vices and his passions, and such is the privilege of democracy.

Let adulation exalt the love of the French for their monarch, let it calm your sadness with the fabulous recital of their fidelity, but I, unable to do other than speak frankly, will tell you: 'This people, whose first need was to love and cherish its kings, today feels only hatred for monarchs and for monarchy; it has changed the objects of its worship; the incense of its sacrifices no longer rises upon the altars of its false gods. Fanaticism of an unbridled independence, which it dares to call by the sacred name of liberty, is the only cult of this impious and savage horde; regicide is the gospel of its bloody religion, and everything that will not bend its knee before Baal will be slaughtered on the pavement of its temples.'

* * * *

Now cast your eye over that country, formerly so flourishing, but today so unrecognisable. What does it offer to your eyes? heaps of ruins, ravaged fields, scaffolds reeking with the blood of the innocent, temples overthrown and trampled underfoot; madmen armed with torches and daggers, running to liberty across the waste and the flames, and threatening with death whosoever will not join in the hatred that they have vowed for their king, whom they have cast in irons in order to torture him at leisure; to the religion that they treat as a chimera, to humanity that they treat as weakness; to justice which they have made the slave of circumstances; to prejudices that they have let run riot; to morals which their corruption no longer regards as anything but tyrants.

Louis, do you now believe that this Empire is still worthy of your regrets? . . .

In this general abandon, Heaven, sensible to your ills, has left you two powerful allies, namely virtue which knows how to scorn, and courage, which knows how to take action . . . Well. Louis, recover as a man that liberty that you lost as a king. Dethroned by those who ought to have strengthened your throne, cast into irons by those who had sworn to uphold your power, hasten to throw off, in the midst of this impious and patricidal horde, these frivolous signs of your past grandeur, which they have left you as a sign of impotency and derision . . .

Louis! this advice, the only one truly worthy of you springs from the most ardent love and desire for your glory, from the intoxication with your goodness and a sense of foreboding for your future. If you hesitate to follow it, remember that it is better to be THE FIRST OF MEN THAN THE LAST OF KINGS.

Le Journal de M. Suleau, No. 2: Hatin, vol. V, pp. 215–18.

64. Appeal

The early hopes of the aristocrats that the Revolution would exhaust itself in anarchy proved unwarranted. Foreign intervention and not time eventually appeared as their only hope.

Note that this document was published at a time when France was at war. Also, as from his number of 13 June, Durosoi displayed his name prominently on the title page of his paper for the first time.

APPEAL

IN THE NAME OF THE FRENCH ÉMIGRÉS, FROM ALL THE ORDERS OF THE STATE

In 1790, there was announced in the *Gazette de Paris* a subscription, whose object was to buy back the demesnes of the king in order to restore them to the most unfortunate, the most beloved of monarchs, whenever the oppression of the usurpers should cease.* A considerable number of faithful royalists from every class and rank made their contribution. Several sent their note payable on sight; all the papers relating to such a reputable operation have been put in safe-keeping— the *sacred* list (*for such is what the whole of Europe calls it*) is deposited in the same place with the relevant notices.

Sensitive as well as faithful royalists, today it is a question of an even more important object than that of repurchasing the demesnes of the Crown: it is a question of coming to the aid of the Crown itself, and perhaps (since we must have the courage to say so) of the sacred head that wears it.

The prince brothers of our good king have armed us for his defence and for the re-establishment of the lawful authority that belongs to him. The justice of our cause, the zeal that inspires our courage, and the support of all Europe, guarantee our success. It is only a matter of spreading our resources further in order to hasten this great enterprise destined to bring back order and public happiness. The nobility, cruelly despoiled of its property and all its resources, does not complain of its own sufferings but bears them: counting as joys the sacrifices that reduce it to the most severe privations, it only aspires before long to walk on the fields of *honour*, beneath the Bourbon standard. But it would regret to see its august leaders exhaust their funds in grants-in-aid; and if it seeks the augmentation of these funds, it is not merely for itself, it is for the sole purpose of serving to multiply the means of acting.

* See Introduction p. 23.

FRENCHMEN, you who make up the *sane part* of the nation, will you see, without bestirring yourselves to participate, the efforts that are being made to save you? Would you refuse to contribute from the resources that are within your power to those which are to be put to such a noble use? Heed our APPEAL, in whatever place in Europe you have made your home; the decisive moment has come. The public cause demands that we gather and assemble together all that can serve to redeem it from the rebels' hands. We have no other aim; no mixture of vindictive sentiment sullies the purity of our intentions; *zeal for Religion, fidelity to the King, love of Country*, these are our only motives . . .

What man would wish to expose himself to the fact that, for lack of *fulfilling his obligation*, his name was effaced from the list of those who will regard *as their first obligation* the duty to come to the re-establishment of the French Monarchy?

One day this SACRED LIST will be published; fathers will then say to their children; 'My name, which is yours, was on the SACRED LIST, and that is the first of your titles.'

Printed at Coblenz, 28 May 1792

La Gazette de Paris, 10 June 1792.

FALL OF THE MONARCHY

Louis' use of the veto and his dismissal of the Girondin ministers provoked a demonstration on 20 June in which petitioners from the Faubourgs St.-Antoine and St.-Michel paraded in armed protest before the Assembly, after which they broke into the Tuileries palace, where they forced Louis to listen to their insults and revolutionary slogans. This event has been seen as a dress rehearsal for the decisive insurrection of the following August when the Jacobins, *fédérés* from the provinces, the Paris Sections, and part of the National Guard combined to capture the Tuileries and bring about the overthrow of the king. Despite the rising danger the royalist press on the whole maintained its verbal onslaught to the end.

65. A Few Thousand Tyrants

One result of the demonstration of 20 June was a resurgence in favour of royalty in many parts of France, indicated by a flood of correspondence into the capital. For André Chénier, as for the right-wing writers in general, it showed the king, whose conduct during the demonstration evoked the praise even of his enemies, as setting a fine example for others to follow.

A magistrate,* whose stupidity and cruelty have become proverbial, was not ashamed to approve of and so show himself an accomplice to the barbarous insolence of a few thousand tyrants who, a few days ago, forced their way into the sanctuary of the hereditary representative of the nation. He was not ashamed to applaud their abominable victory in the very place that had just been desecrated. Before this very king whose life these mad imbeciles had for a long time threatened, and before his wife, whose family had for long shared with him their threats and cowardly taunts, and their vile insults, this magistrate had the sheer effrontery to tell them that they had conducted themselves with the pride and dignity of free men.† The support screeched by the Clubs which made him magistrate and which wanted to make him a judge, together with the obviously malicious subtleties of a few sophists who are today his friends, did not prevent the cries of universal indignation reaching his ear. He heard them. They caused him, if not remorse, at least some embarrassment. He expressed the hope that one day people would give him what he calls justice; and all the good citizens see with joy that true justice has begun to be meted out to him.‡

This day, memorable in so many ways, will evoke not only sad memories, for it has shown to the French the first of its public functionaries, charged with the execution of the laws, fulfilling his duty worthily and at the risk of his own life. All Frenchmen, who have not lost all sense of justice, of equity, of humanity; who indeed cherish and wish to observe the Constitution so often appealed to alike both by good citizens and by hypocrites; who groan to see it daily outraged by its so-called friends, and abused by those whose duty it is to execute it and to see that others execute it; who see with horror the law of royal sanction attacked, and with sorrow the National Assembly too often justify, by its inconsiderate conduct and inexcusable measures, the wisdom of this same law; finally, all those Frenchmen who wish and know how to be free, could only experience a truly patriotic satisfaction on learning of the manly and firm conduct of the king on that

* Pethion.
† Nevertheless they caused no damage and in the end departed peacefully.
‡ Early in July, Pethion was suspended from office, but only for a week.

occasion, and on reading that proclamation in which, without complaining of the attacks upon his person, he binds himself to his duty in
the most noble and civic fashion.

I do not think that there are many minds so dull and souls so
hardened as not to feel and recognise the fine and touching example
given by the king to all the functionaries and to all the magistrates;
let them expose their life in order to justify public confidence, let them
repulse by an unshakable steadfastness the attacks of those who wish
to control the law, and let them no longer seek to excuse their giving
way to harmful whims, by alleging threats made against them and the
dangers incurred. And if all the citizens wish to make sure that this
example is not lost and to encourage, by an enlightened and prompt
obedience, the magistrates to acquit themselves in a manner worthy of
their office and to put down those louts who thrive on disorder and
crime, then it will be possible to date the end of anarchy and the
establishment of government and law from 20 June 1792.

Supplement to *Le Journal de Paris*, 27 June 1792.

66. Arrival of the *Fédérés*

The *fédérés* were delegates to the Festival of Federation held on the
anniversary of the fall of the Bastille. Following the king's veto
of the decree of 8 June for the formation of an army of *fédérés* to
defend Paris, the Assembly overcame this by summoning 20,000
fédérés to the Bastille Day celebrations.

The main incident described here was, according to the *Révolutions
de Paris*, deliberately provoked by a royalist gang, one of whose
ringleaders was Regnault de Saint-Jean d'Angéley, the author of
this article. It further claimed that Regnault was using his columns
in the *Journal de Paris* deliberately to discredit the *fédérés*.

The Marseillaise *fédérés*, numbering five hundred and with two pieces of
cannon, arrived in the capital yesterday. Already several incidents have
made their presence felt. Cockades have been snatched from the
citizens when they were of ribbon, although in the national colours. A
law-abiding citizen was ill-treated at the Palais-Royal, at four
o'clock in the afternoon, for having wanted to protect his ribbon
cockade. Having entered a Hatter's in the Rue St.-Honoré, at the corner
of the Rue St.-Florentin, with their swords in their hands, they overturned his shop and threw the ribbon cockades which he was selling,
into the mud. An even more serious misfortune ended yesterday's events.

A number of National Guard volunteers had gone to dine in the Champs Elysées. Several hundred *fédérés* had assembled there. Some chance remarks caused a brawl, which at first had appeared to end in a friendly fashion. The National Volunteers went back home in small groups. Three of them, one of whom was M. Duhamel, a Lieutenant in the Grenadiers, returned together by the Rue St.-Florentin. They were attacked, it is said, by a large body of *fédérés*; they took out their swords but M. Duhamel was struck several blows and left lying dead in the gutter. Several other National Guards have been attacked, abused, and wounded more or less seriously, both by side-arms as well as by pistol shots fired at them, so one must presume that in defending themselves they also wounded a good number of their assailants. In the evening the alarm was sounded; general consternation spread everywhere, and the shops were closed in the districts near the Tuileries. These facts are beyond reflection: reflection is pointless when one has reached this stage of anarchy, predicted by reason, brought on by weakness, and tolerated by the indifference for which it is the punishment.

In such a frightful moment, when popular murders are cropping up in such a fearful fashion in various parts of the Empire, we can no longer be surprised that the murders find supporters and apologists. We are familiar with those writers who regularly leap to the defence of crimes. Every man, who retains some spark of decency and humanity, cannot read without a shudder the frightful and disgusting gaiety with which the *Patriote français*, in last Saturday's edition, announced the assassination of M. Champion, Minister of the Interior, in the Faubourg St.-Antoine. Some other journalists, equally *patriotic*, doubtless do not believe that they owe justice to those whose beliefs differ from theirs, just as certain Roman casuists do not believe that one must keep faith with heretics. Here is what last Monday's *Chronique* had to say on the assassination of M. d'Esprémesnil: 'Everybody is in agreement in witnessing that M. d'Esprémesnil has been identified in the act of rousing the people against the National Guard. Never has a report been more unanimous.' We thought it our duty to collect information concerning this charge, which we had ourselves denounced in our report on daily events, and we are able to show it to be untrue, according to several trustworthy witnesses and the formal declaration of two citizens who were walking with M. d'Esprémesnil at the time he was attacked. [There follows the declaration by the witnesses.]

Le Journal de Paris, 31 July 1792.

67. Prelude to Silence

There were several calls to arms in the fortnight prior to 10 August (see doc. 66), but these turned out to be false starts. By the evening of 9 August the eventual outcome was never in serious doubt.

(i) *Le Journal de Paris*

An atmosphere of unrest pervaded the Assembly, yet only manifested itself in dull murmurings, arising from private conversations, and from the need to know who was asking all the questions and who was giving the reports. The insults thrown at a large number of deputies on leaving yesterday's session, the acts of violence towards several of them, and the sinister threats that assailed those members who had the courage to speak their minds, had filled almost every heart with a deep and doleful indignation, which, before showing itself openly, manifested itself in the hushed conversations of the majority. During this time another party in the Assembly, the least considerable, appeared sad and anxious.

M. la Marque, in the midst of this disposition of moods, took the floor to discuss the question of the king's deposition: he thought that preparatory measures were necessary and ought to precede that decision, by which the legislative body must, according to the king, answer to the executive power who makes war. We must, he says, watch the capital closely and the traitors who are gathered there; we must strike the ministers already overthrown, and watch out equally for the present ministers to see that they do no harm; all the sessions of the Assembly must be permanent until this matter is settled, all persons actually in Paris and who have not been domiciled there for more than a year, the *fédérés excepted*, must leave or produce a certificate of civism; the municipalities must prohibit journals notoriously known for preaching counter-revolution, and on these bases he proposed the decree be drafted.

It was unlikely that the outrages committed yesterday against the dignity of the Representatives of the People should remain shrouded in silence, that the Assembly should be silent on crimes that had compromised its liberty by attacking the safety of its members.

There follows a list of these outrages.

. . . Several other deputies, including M. Deuzy, have been equally ill-treated, being hit in the back by stones, and injured. They get together to announce it verbally or in writing.

The courage of the decent man, who wants liberty and laws, and execrates anarchy and crime, is ready to give up when he is forced to recount such excesses, which, if they are not repressed, give rise to scenes of blood and horror. His discouragement is at its height, when he hears a deputy, a colleague of those who were attacked the day before, ask, like M. Kersaint, *that they attend to other matters*; when on hearing the account of M. Beaucaron, about to be delivered to the fatal cord, he sees the *unpunished tribunes* break into odious laughter; when he hears this infamous laughter being reinforced by applause, at the recalling of the threat *to cut off M. Dumolard's head*; when he hears a voice from the left ask M. Girardin on which side *he was struck*, as if they did not know that brigands, assassins strike only from the rear, as M. Girardin replied.

Le Journal de Paris, 10 August 1792.

(ii) *L'Ami du Roi*

M. Roederer having ended this distressing account of the present situation of the capital, M. Goujon asked for the return of all the proposals to the Committee of Twelve, and that the Assembly declare itself in permanent session. . . .

Worn out with fatigue, no longer able to hold our pen, we beg our readers to permit us to take some rest, and to postpone for the next issue, the rest of this session.

L'Ami du Roi, No. CCXXII, 10 August 1792.

(iii) *La Gazette de Paris*

Durosoi's final issue opens:

At the moment of writing, all of the hordes, whether those who talk or those who slay, *Republicans, Pétionists, Innovators, Brissotins, Philosophers*, are writing, debating, slandering, sharpening daggers, distributing ammunition, issuing orders, running here and there, bumping into one another; they increase the wages of informers, criminals, libellers and poison-spreaders. . . .

> Much of this last issue is taken up by an account of the proximity of foreign troops: this was the advice given to him by a 'faithful royalist', whose letter is quoted in part here, that the only means left to the supporters of the king was to strike terror in his enemies by a warning of the consequences that would follow an attack on him.

Paris, 6 August 1792

To the author of the Gazette de Paris

'Nothing is more touching, Monsieur, than your invitation to all good Frenchmen to come to the aid of the king next Thursday [10 August].

This act well displays your tender love for that monarch as unfortunate as he is deserving of sympathy [*intéressant*]. But what do you expect of our zeal in the midst of a town corrupt and dominated by a tyrannical Assembly, which is itself the slave of a faction before which even armed force feels itself obliged to yield, and against which there is not even hope. I know of only one answer to the outrage that is being meditated against France in wishing to deprive it of its king in order to deliver it to the dictators; it is to inspire terror of the consequences of this crime in the minds of those unfortunates who are thinking of making themselves guilty of it. . . .'

The issue concludes:

The Procurator-General arrived; he gave details of the new dangers that are menacing Paris; the arrival of a new *Black Band* of brigands is awaited; the new *Marcel* no longer gives assurances regarding the peace of Paris; the Roi de Sicile Section has denounced a decree by the Quatre-vingt Section that says that if the fate of the king has not been decided in the Assembly before midnight, *then the tocsin will be sounded to invite all the citizens to deliberate by themselves*. The Jardin des Plantes Section has passed the same decree; the terrified department has spoken out against the horrors surrounding us; it has invited the Municipality to act in concert with it; but Pétion presides there: at any moment the Saint Bartholomew of the royalists could begin . . .
. . . As I write, the Jacobite and fanatic Condorcet is making the report on the question of the fall. On the new crimes that the day will bring forth is there any need for enlightenment?

La Gazette de Paris, Thursday 10 August 1792.

'LOUIS THE LAST'

Just as the Girondins failed to capitalise on the demonstration of 20 June, allowing the Jacobins to take over the leadership of the popular movement, now they failed to act promptly following the successful demonstration of August. First they hesitated on the fate of the monarchy, then they seemed to temporise on the fate of the king.

Louis' trial opened on 11 December 1792; on 15 January 1793 he was found guilty by the Convention of conspiracy against the public liberty and at the same time it was voted that the plebiscite to the people was unnecessary: on the following day the roll-call for the penalty was taken and on 17 January the death sentence was voted by a clear majority. It was carried out on the 21st.

68. Better Just to Forget Him

Louis Bourbon, Louis XVI, or rather Louis the Last, still lives in the Temple tower. The place is arranged so as to be more suitable for him and his family. His calmness, or rather his dumb apathy, remains the same. He seems to be no more aware of his misfortunes than of his crimes.

It is likely that people will forget him in his prison until victory has forced the enemy to abandon him to justice or to national clemency. The scheme to bring the royal family to trial would be at the present time a fatal one. This is the advice of all the English who have embraced our cause. A king hounded, they say, no longer has supporters; a king killed arouses sympathy, and this compassion gives his family defenders. Tarquin had no successors; Charles I still has them.

La Feuille villageoise, No. 51, 27 September 1792, p. 599.

69. Funeral Oration of Royalty

Temple

Louis XVI, still decorated with his ribbons and other trinkets of royalty, waited patiently for *his highness the Duke of Brunswick* to come and break the barrier that separated him from the throne. Manuel had a conference with him the day before yesterday. He told him that with due regard, not for the tyrant of 10 August, but for his misfortune, that there were no longer in France *either king, or crown, or ribbons, or decorations*; that France henceforth was a *republic*, that the Prussians and the Austrians had no longer any hope of retrieving the bonds of despotism, after having strewn the land of liberty with their corpses; that Spires was in our power; that Savoy belonged to us; that our troops were at the gates of Geneva, and that from its lake to the banks of the Rhine people were crying out *Long live the Republic!* To console him, he told him that *soon there would be no more kings in Europe!* Louis XVI listened to this funeral oration of royalty with the kind of indifference that would, as it were, make one believe that he was a subscriber to the *Gazette de Cologne*, from which the following extract is taken: [the extract tells of the strong position and high morale of the Imperial and Prussian armies] . . . It is not enough that kings have been abolished; we must forget even that *its shade still exists*, and if we are to remember it, it must be only the day when that shade will go to meet those of the Styx, where a place is reserved for it at the side of Ixion. Reports received yesterday tell us that the royal family feigned security and even gaiety; which confirms us in believing [in their] subscription to the *Gazette de Cologne,* printed *with the privilege and permission of His Imperial Majesty.*

Le Courrier des départements, vol. 1, No. 19, 10 October 1792.

70. The Temple of the Owl

It was in this period that Hébert's paper *Le Père Duchesne* was developing to the fullness of its ferocity. On the day following 10 August he had dismissed the thought of the French 'soiling themselves in the blood of a coward', but shortly after this he was demanding the 'monster's' blood at regular intervals and his only regret was that it was such a long and complicated business to 'knock off a tyrant's head'.

Just think, damn it! how surrounded we are with false brothers. All the conspirators were not at Orléans and the Abbey;* their accomplices are still in our midst. These worthy men, in whose name the traitor Mottié wanted to exterminate the patriots, still dwell in Paris. They are concealed by another mask; but at heart they breathe only blood and slaughter. There is not one good citizen who has not at his heels one of these bad angels, who poisons him with his advice, while waiting his chance to plunge his dagger into his heart . . . Yes, damn it! the traitor Louis, shut up like an owl in the Temple tower, would not be so complacent there, if he did not have a strong following in Paris. Already, damn it, they have tried more than one surprise attack to release him. The courtesans, who sneak themselves in everywhere, have more than once got into that famous tower, by greasing the paw of some of his keepers. It is fortunate that we have some sturdy chaps at the Commune, who have their eyes everywhere, and who know all that is going on. Without our agents, damn it, it would have been long since that the brood of howling-toms would have made off for Coblenz. It must not happen that the greatest scoundrel that has ever been should remain unpunished. It is good that the sovereign people become used to judging kings. Oh! the great day! and how I would have hugged myself for joy if our victorious armies had cleaned up all the crowned brigands, if the Mandarin of Prussia and the little Austrian twerp, chained like wild beasts, had been dragged back to Paris by Dumouriez! What a splendid sight to see three guillotines placed in a row with the horny head of paunchy Capet, and those of Frederick and Francis, held in the trap and ready to fall at the one time!

Le Père Duchesne: Hatin, vol. VI, pp. 516–17.

* Scenes of the September massacres.

71. The Day of Decision

The *Sentinelle*, subsidised by the Girondin government, was placarded on the walls of the capital. This extract was reproduced in Gorsas' *Courrier*.

Republicans, Monday is the day that your enemies seek to depict for you in advance as a sad one. Whatever be the judgement that the Convention passes on Capet, think that this is the day of the salvation of the country: it is therefore a day of joy, a day of gladness.

They speak to you of disturbances; they predict them for Monday, because they fear that this day will pass without disturbance: it is then a trap that they are laying for you. It must be avoided.

The Tuileries is no more. The same coffin holds the Bastilles and the palaces of kings. There is therefore no longer any occasion for disturbances, other than an attack upon the sovereignty of the people and its liberty.

On liberty? such an attack is impossible. Where royalty is destroyed, liberty is unshakable. The small tyrants who survive royalty resemble worms squirming in a corpse. With the corpse in dust, the worms will die of want.

On the sovereignty of the people? again an attack is impossible. Whatever be the judgement passed against Capet, your sovereignty is intact.

If he is condemned to death and executed without delay, this will be the decree of your representatives: you have delegated to them the exercise of your sovereignty: it is still yours when they act through it.

If they appeal to you from their judgement, your sovereignty thereby receives still more glory. Thus, if I may make use of this expression, in the first hypothesis, your sovereignty works in private; and in the second it is visible.

But this truth, which your enemies know as well as I, embarrasses their plans, and all their cunning goes into trying to keep it from you.

They tell you that there are two parties in the Convention but they take good care not to tell you that it is not at all a dispute for or against the sovereign will; it is not at all royalism at odds with democracy, it is merely a war of opinions.

Extract from *La Sentinelle* in *Le Courrier des départments*, vol. 4, No. 15, 15 January 1793, pp. 234–35.

72. Louis under Judgement

As to the question of whether it should be put to the people, among the judgements that were given with reasons, we will cite this one–Henri Larivierre: 'I declare that, having participated in the drawing up of the decree which orders Louis to be judged, but having voted against the amendment of this same decree which states that *Louis shall be judged by the National Convention*, I must not pronounce on the *fact*; it is repugnant to my conscience to be at the same time both legislator and jury in an affair that I ask, moreover, should be sent to the sovereign people for decision.'

Gorsas: 'Whereas *royalty* and *kings*, the factious and the factions, will only be truly and legally swept from the territory of the Republic when the people have pronounced that it wants neither kings, nor royalty, nor factions, nor factious, nor any kind of tyranny. Whereas I regard it as an insult to the people, the very suggestion that this vote can excite a civil war. Whereas this vote is on the contrary an act of justice and homage rendered to its sovereignty, which I acknowledge, yes I, much more than they who have it endlessly on their lips. Whereas, finally, it takes courage, in the midst of the dangers of anarchy, to express a view that opposes and upsets the anarchists, I say and must say, whilst waiting to print it, YES.'

> *Le Courrier des départements*, vol 4, No. 17, 17 January 1793, p. 272.

73. On the Eve of Execution

Despite the sinister predictions of some journalists, Paris has never been more calm. Indifference seems to be the most dominant emotion with regard to the decision on the fate of the former king, and we would almost dare to say that the sentence of some individuals condemned to death, even since the Revolution, has made more news than this one, whether it be that our foreseeing the condemnation diminished its effect, or that a kind of public scorn takes the place of resentment against the guilty party, or finally that people have learnt to see only a man in a king, to weigh the value of his existence on no other scale than that of ordinary men. Doubtless there still exist some fanatics of royalty, some superstitious monarchists, some individuals who, to use the expression of Milton, are still prone to *mal de roi*; but the number of such persons is extremely limited. They can be tolerated: they will die of it or they will not die of it, everything leads us to believe that their illness will not become an epidemic.

> *Les Annales patriotiques*, 20 January 1793: Walter, p. 284.

74. Crush the Serpents

On the execution of the king the great joy of the *Père Duchesne* was restrained only by the thought of the remnants of royalty still in France. Marie-Antoinette was to become the object of particularly vitriolic slander from Hébert until her execution in October 1793.

An authority that is powerful enough to dethrone a king commits a crime against humanity if it does not profit from the occasion to exterminate him and his bastard race. What would you say of a fool, who, while working in his field, came upon a nest of vipers, yet was content to crush only the head of the father, and was chicken-hearted enough to spare the rest; if he said to himself: It is a pity to kill a poor mother in the midst of her children: everything small is so tender! Let's take this pretty nest to the house to amuse my brats. Would he not commit, through stupidity, a very great crime? For, damn it, the monsters that he had revived, and whose life he had thus saved, would not fail to recompense him, to bite him, his wife and his brood, who would perish the victims of misplaced pity. No quarter! whenever we can lay our hands on emperors, kings, queens, empresses, let us rid them from the face of the earth. Better to kill the devil than that the devil should kill us. Never will we do as much harm to these monsters as they have done to us and would do to us, damn it.

Le Père Duchesne: Hatin, VI, 518–19.

PART FOUR

The People

Added to the hostility of Church and monarch, the Constituent Assembly had to face after July 1791 the opposition of the 'fourth estate', overlooked in the Assemblies' reforms and finally alienated from it following the 'massacre' on the Champ de Mars.

Fear and hunger are two of the main recurring features of the Revolution. Fear manifested itself in different ways. Prior to July and October of 1789 the main fear of the deputies at the Assembly was fear of counter-revolution. Thereafter this fear became that of continuing revolution. Order became the new watchword, and steps were taken to ensure that the infringements of a liberal egalitarian creed in the interests of bourgeois class rule did not result in civilian protest of a dangerous nature. On 28 October 1789 the Martial Law decree was passed amid the violent opposition of the radicals. But it was not until 17 July 1791 that the Assembly had to apply it. The king's flight had made republicanism a live issue for the first time, but the ferocity with which the National Guard dispersed the petitioners on the Champ de Mars and the cold acceptance by the Assembly of this butchery came as much from fear of the 'fourth estate' as from fear of republicanism.

As it turned out, however, the course of events was merely stemmed. Again the prediction—or rather hope—that 'the Revolution is over', proved false. The 10th of August was the logical conclusion to 14 July and the Declaration of Rights, even if it needed the stupidity of the king and the fear of invasion and counter-revolution to draw it. For the next three years no governing power could afford to neglect the wishes or interests of the people, or the sans-culottes, as they came to be called. The Girondins attempted this and failed. Unable to capitalise on the insurrection of 10 August, wavering over the fate of the king, authors of a war they could not run successfully, they were also unwilling to sacrifice their liberal economic principles to feed the big cities they feared. In this they roused the wrath of the Parisians in particular, whom they were determined to consider as no more than one eighty-third part of France. This deliberate flouting of the pretensions of the people of Paris was a blindness to reality for which they paid dearly. For the fourth time since the Revolution broke out, the intervention of the people of Paris decided events. On 31 May 1793 the Convention was surrounded by the armed Sections and on 2 June the Girondin deputies were expelled.

The sans-culottes proved to be an embarrassment even to their allies. The uneasy alliance of Jacobins and sans-culottes lasted until their social incompatibility and the contradictions of sans-culotte political aspirations and Jacobin war strategy dug a gulf between them. As always, the poorer sections of the community continued to suffer: bearing the brunt of war sacrifice and economic distress, they now suffered from the political pressures of a revolutionary government that they had themselves done so much to create. From a peak of power in the middle of 1793 the sans-culottes were in decline by the end of that year, to sink into apathy in 1794. The attack on Robespierre and his arrest saw the sans-culottes, who could have saved him, stand by passively.

SOVEREIGNTY OF THE PEOPLE

'We were perhaps not even ten republicans in 1789,' remarked Desmoulins once. Indeed as a popular movement republicanism gained no real strength until the middle of 1792. Early in 1791, however, some of its adherents were voicing their opinions. Among the prominent early republicans were Condorcet, Brissot and Desmoulins; also the abbé Fauchet, the Christian socialist who drew his ideas from the Bible and Rousseau's 'Social Contract'. From as early as September 1790, Robert in his *Mercure national* looked forward with great enthusiasm to the day when France would be a republic.

The Champ de Mars petition, initiated in the Jacobin and Cordelier Clubs but from which the Jacobins withdrew their support on the eve of the 'massacre', did not specifically call for a republic, but for the abdication of the king and the formation of a new executive power. It was one of the few purely political demonstrations of the Revolution. However, unemployment had served to cause unrest among the people and rouse fear in the Assembly that the satanic aristocrats might find work for the idle hands of the unemployed.

After Champ de Mars, Brissot, Condorcet and some others founded the first specifically republican paper, the *Républicain*, but it did not have a long career: it was in advance of its time.

75. King or Democracy?

(i) *Brissot's portrait of a democrat*

A democrat or patriot (I equate the two of them) does not say: I love the *people*, I am *the friend of the people*,* and this *pedantry* is as far from his thoughts as from his actions. He defends himself against, and opposes, those who want to tyrannise him, for this tyranny revolts him, as putting him in that immense class that the despots and the aristocrats, and certain popular individuals, insolently place beneath them.

A patriot wants liberty for every man. He wants it without exception or modification. He wishes that the principle be everywhere recognised, although he well knows that the destruction of the work of tyrants cannot everywhere be hastened.

A democrat hates royalty, not for personal reasons, not like Cromwell to replace it with tyranny under another name; but like Cato, or like Hampden, or like Samuel Adam!

> *Le Patriot français*, November 1790: Buchez and Roux,
> *op. cit.*, vol. VIII, p. 76.

. . . and a comment on democracy

The National Assembly has decreed the monarchy, I submit to it; but, even while submitting, I seek to prove that it must give to the representatives of the people such an authority that the executive power or the monarch cannot bring back despotism; I want a popular monarchy, where the balance is always on the side of the people. Such is my democracy.

> *Le Patriot français*, 9 and 12 April 1791:
> Buchez and Roux, vol. IX, p. 436.

(ii) *Suleau's portrait of a democrat*

The democrat's nature is like that of the beaver. The latter is continually cutting down, the former is continually destroying. The one has only one way of building, the other has only one system in politics. The beaver is amphibious, the democrat accommodates himself equally to republican or monarchical sentiments. Finally, both spend their lives in building, the beaver in water, the democrat on sand, and thus have to fear, the one the swift flow of the river, the other the uncertainty of the winds. In general, the democrat has moderate inclinations. Late in his unions, with little foresight, by nature gloomy, he consumes little

---

* Although this description could be applied to Marat, it is Barnave whom Brissot is attacking. At this stage Marat and Brissot were still good friends.

and lives from day to day. Let him be left to level, plaster, erect, demolish, that is all that he asks. These animals are inclined to isolate themselves; but, born fearful and timid, they rarely walk alone; it is fairly common to see them join together in groups. Thus, it is wise to avoid them and to keep some distance between yourself and their grazing grounds; for as much as they are shy in their solitude, so equally do they become bold and enterprising when they find themselves in a big enough group. They have sometimes been seen to leap on passers-by and devour them. The sound of a firearm can prevent these incidents, and is enough to put them to flight.

Le Journal de M. Suleau: Hatin, VII, 220.

. . . and a comment on democracy

Every society that climbs towards republicanism has the same aversion for the depositaries of authority as hydrophobes have for water; so it is, therefore, that be they Mogul or mayor, Inca or militia commandant, it makes little difference, they all inspire the same horror, with the slight difference that while threats are reserved for the one, the noose awaits the others. Leopold as king, Suleau as a bravo or literary power, Lafayette as military dictator, Bailly as civil dictator, appear, beneath their various guises, as being essentially one and the same.

Le Journal de M. Suleau: Hatin, VII, 212.

76. Champ de Mars

Blood has just flowed on the field of the federation; the altar of the fatherland is stained by it; men and women have been murdered; the citizens are in a state of consternation. What will become of liberty? Some say that it is finished, that the counter-revolution is complete; others are certain that liberty has been avenged, that the Revolution has been consolidated in an unshakable manner. Let us examine impartially two such strangely differing views. . . .

The majority of the National Assembly, the department, the Paris municipality, and many of the writers say that the capital is inundated by brigands; that these brigands are paid by the representatives of foreign courts; that they were allied with the factions who secretly conspire against France; that on Sunday, at ten o'clock in the morning, they sacrificed two citizens to their fury; that they insulted, molested and provoked the National Guard; that they assassinated several of the citizen soldiers; that they went so far as to lay hands on M. the

Commandant-General; and finally that they assembled at the Champ de Mars for the sole purpose of disturbing public peace and order, and of carrying to excess what perhaps it would have been hard to restrain two hours later. From this point of view, it is certain that the Paris municipality could and had to take the severe measures that it employed; it is better to sacrifice some thirty wretched vagabonds than to risk the safety of 25 million citizens.

However, if the victims of Champ de Mars were not brigands; if these victims were peaceful citizens with their wives and children; if that terrible scene is but the effect of a formidable coalition against the progress of the Revolution, then liberty is truly in danger, and the execution of martial law is a horrible crime, and the sure precursor of counter-revolution. For the public to form its judgement it will need full knowledge of the facts. So far all the writers have presented garbled versions.

> The writer then goes into details of events since the return of Louis from Varennes, to disprove the hypothesis presented in the first of the 'strangely differing views', and to describe the preparations for the signing of the petition on the Champ de Mars.

[The people] return to the altar of the fatherland, and they continue to sign. Young folk amuse themselves with dances; they go around in circles, singing the refrain *ça ira*. A storm blows up (did heaven intend this as a sign of what was going to rain down on the heads of the citizens?) but the eagerness to sign is undiminished. The rain stops, the sky becomes calm and serene again; in less than two hours there are more than fifty thousand people on the plain; there were even mothers of families, all interested citizens; it was one of those majestic and moving assemblies, such as used to be seen at Athens and at Rome. . . .

You know the field of the federation, you know that it is a vast plain, that the altar of the fatherland is at the centre, that the slopes surrounding the plain are cut at intervals to facilitate entry and exit; one section of the troops enters at the far side of the military school, another comes through the entrance somewhat lower down, and a third by the one that opens on to the Grande Rue de Chaillot; it is there that the red flag was placed. Hardly had those who were at the altar, and there were more than fifteen thousand of them, noticed it, than a discharge of shot was heard: *Let's not shift, they are firing blanks, they must come here to declare the law.* The troops advance, they fire a second time, the look of those who surround the altar is still the same; but when a third round of fire mows down many of their number, the crowd flees; there remain only a group of a hundred people at the altar itself. Alas! they paid dearly for their courage and blind trust in the law. Several men and women, even a child were massacred there; massacred on the altar of the fatherland! Ah! if ever again we hold 'federations', we must choose another place, for this one is profane! What a sight, great God! as this which the last rays of that fatal day did light up! Unarmed citizens fleeing before armed citizens; the husband leading his wife, dragging his children, calling out for his father; a murderous bullet cutting down the old man. Here it was a wife whom death was snatching from her husband; there, it was a child murdered at his mother's breast. What cries! what anguished voices made themselves heard! My wife! my wife! my husband! my son! . . . The cannoneers asked for orders to fire; the cavalry pursued into the fields those who escaped. Eye-witnesses assured us of having seen National Guards throw their sabres at the legs of those whom they could not overtake. One of these brutes had left ranks to pursue his victim; he was stopped by the Grenadiers, who disarmed him, and led him away into the middle of the battalion. Powerful means, despicable methods must have been used to bring the National Guard to this point! Parisians! did you not then remember the story of your unfortunate brothers at Metz and at Nancy. Like you, they were betrayed: if only you had heard their groanings, their burning remorse! Yes, you hear them now; yes, your hearts are already broken: yes, you detest your easy and barbarous victory! Children of the fatherland! what have you done? what use have you made of your arms? There are those among you who have slain your friends, your relations. O new Seides, they have betrayed your courage, they have made you the unfortunate tools of a passion that has never been, is not, and never will be your own.

Les Révolutions de Paris, No. 106, 16–23 July 1791,
pp. 53–55, 63, 65–66.

77. Some Comments on Republicanism

(i) *Hébert*

This number of the *Père Duchesne* was issued on 12 July 1791.

Within ten years there will be not one king, but one sovereign in Europe: in vain has the crowd of jackasses called the Constitutional Committee resolved to reinstate Louis the Traitor on his throne, he will reappear there only to be turned arse up and knocked flat: yes, damn it, from one end of France to the other every citizen is crying out in unison, 'No more kings! No more jackasses!' They will still say that for a big empire monarchy is necessary. Why, damn it all? So that he can devour by himself all the produce of one department?

So that he can undo all the good that has been done? To give an example to nations of perjury and every crime? No, damn it, no, no more kings. But above all no more Capet, no more Louis the Traitor.

> *Le Père Duchesne*, No. 62: cited in J. Godechot,
> *La pensée révolutionnaire 1780–1799*, Armand
> Colin 1964, pp. 233–34.

(ii) *Gorsas*

We made our profession of faith in a *republican France* a long time ago and, after reasoning we considered well-founded, we recounted the fable of the frogs.* We bring that fable to mind here to prove how far we are from wishing to defend republicanism. In rejecting the plan of the committees, we are taking our stand not against the king as such, but against Louis XVI, a prince who has committed treason against his subjects.

> *Le Courrier de Versailles*, 25 July 1791: Hatin, VI, 301.

(iii) *Desmoulins*

If a king is a corrupter, hoarder, crook, savage beast, forger, perjurer, traitor, then this is only part of his nature; he devours the bread of the people and also the people themselves, but I can have no more hatred for him than I can for a wolf that attacks us. Like the tiger when it drains the blood of the traveller, the king animal does no more than follow its instinct when it drains the blood of the people. . . .

> *Les Révolutions de France et de Brabant*, No. 83 *(s.d.)*, pp. 216–17.

(iv) *Robespierre*

Mme Roland tells how following the king's flight Pétion and Brissot wanted to take advantage of the moment to prepare the people for a republic. Robespierre, 'biting his finger nails', is said to have then asked what a republic was. The article from which this extract is taken was issued a year later.

I am republican! Yes, I want to defend the principles of equality and the exercise of the sacred rights guaranteed by the Constitution to the people against the dangerous systems of the intriguers who regard it only as the tool of their ambition. I prefer to see a popular representative assembly, made up of free and respected citizens and with a king, than a people enslaved and debased under the rod of an aristocratic

---

* La Fontaine, *Fables*, Book III, 'Les Grenouilles qui demandent un roi'.

senate or a dictator . . . Is it in the words *republic* or *monarchy* that we have the solution to the great social problem? Is it the definitions invented by the diplomats to classify the diverse forms of government that decide the happiness or otherwise of nations, or is it the combination of laws and institutions that constitute its real nature? All political constitutions are made for the people; all those where the people count for nothing are simply crimes against humanity.

Le Défenseur de la Constitution: Hatin, VI, 284.

THE FOOD CRISES AND THE CROWD

In the six years following the fall of the Bastille, the year 1790 and the spring and summer of 1791 was the only period in which there was no serious food crisis. Indeed the price or availability of bread was a major factor in nearly every political demonstration outside this period. The alliance of bourgeois and sans-culotte was often an affair of necessity, which broke down, once the more political aims of the bourgeois had been achieved. This being so it is not surprising that there were many occasions when, lacking the political direction of the bourgeois, food riots remained no more than an unfortunate incident that temporarily reminded the authorities of the plight of the poor, but which they regarded as beyond their control and an unfortunate interference with the more important task of governing the country. The radical press was not so complacent and its demands for bread and some action against those whom it believed were withholding it kept the issue constantly to the fore. However, it was more popular pressure and the exigencies of war that ultimately forced the government to abandon its liberal *laissez-faire* policies when first in May and then in September of 1793 the 'maximums' were introduced.

78. Justice without Restraint

In their analysis of food riots the aristocrats tended to forget that such outbreaks had been common even in the times of the 'gentle and paternal rule of the king'.

News of a tragic event at Douai spread consternation throughout the Assembly. The people, embittered by misery, angered to see the hope vanish with which they have been beguiled, are always ready to display their discontent by an attack on public order. A ship-load of wheat served to inflame passions on this occasion: doubtless the people of Douai thought that their sustenance was being taken from them. They threw themselves on to the boat and began to loot it. The municipality, asked by the department to proclaim martial law, thought that it could not employ this violent measure without provoking further troubles, and refused to obey. M. de la Noue, the officer in command, wanted to march his troops of the line against the mutineers, but they declared that they would not fire on the people; an officer of the National Guard, who tried to oppose the looting, was strung up, and another citizen, who had provided part of the ship-load of wheat, suffered the same fate. The members of the department were obliged to seek safety in flight, and took refuge at Lille.

It is thus that order is established, despite our Constitution being completed, despite our having set up departments, districts, magistrates, tribunals, justices of the peace, and laws without number.

It is thus that the government assures the peace and prosperity of its citizens: such is the aid that can be expected from a so-called public force, composed of several million armed men; such are the worthy fruits of inflammatory and anti-clerical doctrines preached with so much violence and vigour by the demagogues; such is what must result from a government that is not based on obedience and subordination. It was falsely thought that to ensure the success of the Revolution all that was necessary was to free the people from every restraint; and by that infernal policy they have not established liberty, but have made despotism necessary. This division of powers established by the Constitution is the annihilation of all powers, whilst the departments, districts, and municipalities dispute among themselves, get in each others way, and hold each other in check, the field is always left free for the sedition-mongers and the factions. There will never be other than a single, absolute, and arbitrary authority which can put an end to anarchy; thus for not having been willing to put up with the gentle and paternal rule of our kings, we will fall under the yoke of tyrants, and licence will have led us to servitude.

L'Ami du Roi–Royou, No. CCCV, 21 March 1791.

79. Marat and Grain

As the self-appointed 'friend of the people' it is not surprising to find that Marat's paper constantly raises the question of the food supply. Like so many others, however, he saw 'hoarders' as the true villains of the peace, and 'aristocratic plots' involving a deliberately created scarcity as the main source of the peoples' ills in this regard: as the third extract shows, he was averse to the idea of introducing price controls–in this he was in accord with the other Jacobin leaders.

(i) *A just repartition*

My blood boils in my veins against the so-called fathers of the country, those men without feelings, without decency, who have lavished millions on the king's brothers, dangerous enemies of the country, yet have done nothing for its unfortunate liberators; who have seized the possessions of the Church in order to pay for the pomp, ceremony, and dissipations of the court, yet have not restored a farthing to the poor, to whom it all belongs; who have just sacrificed 80 millions to the dastardly agents of the monarch, yet allow to die of hunger . . . the conquerors of the Bastille and the true restorers of liberty who live in the faubourgs.

My dear friends, you whose want is the fruit of neither vice nor idleness, you have a right to live as Louis XVI and all the well-off types of the century. No, the heir to the throne does not have the right to dine when you lack bread. Form yourselves into an armed body, present yourselves at the National Assembly, and demand that you immediately be given some means of subsistence from the national wealth, which belongs much more rightly to you than to the blood-suckers of the state; demand that the patriotic contribution be applied to improving the lot of the needy of the kingdom; the state does not need it, and, without it, it would go to swell the king's coffers, in order to reforge chains for the nation. If they refuse to grant you immediate aid, gather together in force, join the armed body, the moment has come when it can perhaps understand this language. Share out the lands and wealth of the scoundrels who have buried their gold in order to reduce you by hunger to return to the yoke. Yes, I say to you in all sincerity, you must, in your turn, completely despoil them, for it is a hundred times better that the whole kingdom be completely upturned than that ten million men be reduced to death by hunger.

L'Ami du peuple, No. 306, 10 December 1790.

(ii) *Bourgeois justice*

Here Marat challenges the attempt by Salomon, deputy for Orléans, to get the Assembly to sanction Orléans' request for a special force to keep order.

The municipality of Orléans consists wholly of grain hoarders, who, to shelter from the consequences of the people's uprising, ask for a decree which authorises them to exterminate them; and in order that one should have a plausible excuse to go with it, they concocted the absurd story of a conspiracy of vineyard workers, as if a handful of unarmed peasants would think of attacking a troop armed to the teeth. As for Salomon, he is himself the relative of several monopolists, whose leader is Lambert, commandant for Louis-Phillippe-Joseph d'Orléans. This atrocious individual was the instigator of the disturbances that desolated Orléans thirteen months ago. Nothing better proves how little patriotism Louis-Philippe-Joseph d'Orléans has, than the fact of keeping in his employ this vile scoundrel.

In a footnote Marat cites a particular instance of 'bourgeois justice'.

M. Rimbert, a large vinegar merchant, and a citizen of exceptional honesty, indignant at seeing the municipal officials monopolising the grain, put himself at the head of the inhabitants of a faubourg, in order to force the municipality to sell them some. The municipality dissembled for some time, called out the troops, took poor Rimbert away in the night, gave him a trial that lasted scarcely two hours, and ordered him to be executed immediately. Who would believe that the town hangman was more sensitive than the municipal officials? Revolted by the violence of this procedure, he refused to carry out the execution at night. Five great bourgeois, interested in the grain monopoly, contended for the honour of hanging this unfortunate individual. A wretched surgeon had all the glory. . . . Several executions followed this one. Horrible scenes like these the Orléans municipality will not dare to repeat without a formal decree.

L'Ami du peuple, No. 225, 19 September 1790.

(iii) *Friend of order and peace*

A word to my fellow citizens of the forty-eight Sections of Paris

CITIZENS

About thirty petitioners, calling themselves your deputies, presented themselves two days ago with a petition, printed and signed *Plaisant la*

Hussaye, president, and *Paupel*, secretary, to be admitted to the bar. This petition seeks to present, as the only means of providing for the abuses that are committed in the matter of supplies, the following three measures:

Decree a penalty of six years punishment for those constituted authorities that turn themselves into *shop-keeper administrations*.

Decree the *quintal*, as the *uniform measure* in every part of the Republic.

To fix a 'maximum' for the *quintal*; determined that never, under penalty of six years in irons for the first offence, and death for the second, will it be permitted to any farmer, merchant, proprietor, cultivator, to sell a sack of first-grade grain, weighing 250 pounds, for more than 25 livres, and this in times recognised by the legislative body as *extremely difficult*, such as in the present situation.

This petition was accompanied by a threatening (*comminatoire*) letter in which it was said that if the Convention rejected it, then the forty-eight Sections were ready to act.

Marat considered the petition as ill-conceived, and tells how he personally tried to convince the petitioners to withdraw it. He was unsuccessful.

Le Journal de la République française, No. 121, 12 February 1793.*

Marat had criticised the petition as coming from the enemies of the state, and pointed to the names of the two individuals who had signed it, whom he claimed to be known for their incivism. In his following issue, he reports the presentation of the petition, claiming the petitioners to be the innocent instruments of the Brissotin faction. He sums up his objections:

. . . the measures that have just been proposed to you as the only effective means of remedying the abuses in the control of supplies, and of assuring abundance in the state, are so strange, so violent, so fatal; they are so subversive of all good government, they so obviously tend to destroy the free circulation of grain and freedom of commerce, they seem so carefully calculated to cause trouble, to overturn the state, to light the torches of civil dissension, and to bring about famine, that I find it hard to believe that they came from the mouths of men who consider themselves reasonable beings, as men who call themselves good citizens, friends of order and of peace.

Ibid, No. 122, 14 February 1793.

* Wrongly dated in the original; the correct date is 13 February.

(iv) *Poverty amidst abundance*

It is eight months since you declared war on all the allied powers of Europe; since then you have left the people without bread and without arms: do not doubt that the nation will qualify such conduct with the epithet it deserves, and it will do justice to you. For eight months the starving people have asked you for bread: and you, no longer able to close your ear to its cries, have decreed that you will at last deal with the matter of supplies: and so it is that all your time is spent in listening to encyclopaedic dissertations on the so-called causes of the rise in food prices.

We are dying of hunger in the midst of abundance; who doubts that the artificial scarcity that we have for so long experienced is not the work of the hoarders? The enemies of the fatherland have turned this into a method of counter-revolution: to foil their plot, and to put an end to their machinations, the only effective means are revolutionary laws.

I therefore ask that the people who best know the shops of the hoarders be authorised to go, accompanied by two municipal officers, to have them opened by force in order to supply the markets.

Le Publiciste de la République française, No. 183, 2 May 1793.

80. 'Taxation Populaire'

In January 1792 the price of sugar trebled, partly due to its being withheld by merchants following the troubles in the colonies. Riots broke out during which grocers were forced to sell goods at their former price. This was the first major incident of 'popular price-fixing' in the capital since 1775.

Paris: Wednesday 15 February 1792

The troubles caused by, or at least under pretext of, the high price of sugar, are breaking out again. Yesterday, Tuesday, a waggon laden with 10 to 15 quintals of sugar was stopped in the Faubourg St.-Marceau by several mobs who forced the sale of its provisions at 20 sous a pound. Today in the same district, the disturbances continued; threats were made on several grocers' shops compelling the owners to call in armed force, but in the Sections mobs prevented the leaders of the National Guard from leaving their homes. The tocsin was sounded. The Municipality, after several fruitless attempts to restore order, returned between six and seven o'clock to the Faubourg St.-Marceau, with a strong detachment of Volunteer National Guards and some cannon. We are told that the pikes of the cavalry sent in advance were stopped by a barricade of carts; that an Adjutant-General was stripped, manhandled, and exposed to grave violence; that a Commissioner of Police was injured by a stone thrown at him, but had his wound dressed in the street rather than leave his post; however, at the moment of writing, we can neither enlarge on the details we give, nor guarantee their accuracy; everything now seems very quiet.

We should add that, from the instant the call was made in the various Sections, to provide 50 men per Battalion, the number who rushed fully armed to answer the call far surpassed the required number; and we must give special mention to the fifth Legion which, assembled on the Place Vendôme, by itself proved to be a sufficient force to calm fears about the prolongation of disorder.

Le Journal de Paris, 16 February 1792.

81. Coffee with Sugar

The riots of February 1793 were caused by a serious rise in the price of sugar, candles, coffee and soap, and involved nearly all the Paris Sections. The main riots were on 25 February; the chief victims were the big merchants and wholesalers. But smaller merchants suffered too, and while some rioters left behind what they considered the real value of the goods taken, pillagers who mingled with the distressed left nothing. This was a much more violent and widespread movement of 'popular price-fixing' than that of the previous year.

In the midst of the most frightening storms, there are still some men who retain that traditional sense of humour that made the French so pleasant to know before they became so philosophical. A passer-by, on seeing a grocer's shop being looted, in the Rue de la Huchette, asked what the crowd was up to. 'It is the nation taking its coffee,' a wag replied. 'At least it seems,' answered the passer-by, casting his eyes over the robbers, 'that it does not take it without sugar.'

Le Bulletin national, No. 62: Walter, p. 442.

82. Playing at Pillage

> The leaders of the Jacobins did not approve of rioting for what were considered 'paltry grocers' goods'.

Robespierre read to the Jacobins an address on the causes of the recent looting. The platitude of that address is doubtless due to the despair that Robespierre showed by the fact that *his* people amused itself by such *wretched expeditions* (they are his words). When the people rises, he said to the Jacobins, is it to amuse itself by looting sugar? Much greater projects ought to occupy it; the heads of the guilty must roll in the dust. I denounced to him these guilty ones; they are those who negotiated last year with Brunswick. And they will say that Robespierre does not provoke his people to murder, as does his chief Marat! And they will say that he does not want a sequel to the 2 September!

Le Patriote français, No. MCCCI, 4 March 1793:
Buchez and Roux, vol. XXIV, p. 450.

83. Artificial Scarcity

> Throughout 1793 the food crisis continually worsened. Between June and September the gap between the price of food and the value of the assignat widened considerably.

The artificial scarcity of bread is maintained and increased in a way that is truly alarming. The bakers' shops are besieged from dawn; fortunate is the citizen who, after standing there bored for three or four hours, can succeed in getting some bread without being harmed or crippled by the crowd. A pregnant woman was yesterday trampled underfoot and suffocated. It is most surprising that, during the nine or ten days that this famine has been engineered, no proper steps to remedy the situation have been taken. So far the only measures taken have been to place two sentries at the door of each shop; and what can two citizens do against a crowd, on the one hand excited by hunger, and on the other roused by the provocators, who skilfully incite them to riot and pillage. The majority of the people is deaf, it is true, to their treacherous insinuations; but they find some weak spirits who fall into the trap and a spark is enough to cause a blaze; we feared this yesterday in the Rue Montorgueil. A boarding-house keeper was crossing the street with five or six loaves; on seeing this, those who had none felt how very hard it is to lack bread, but on reflecting that a boarding-house keeper must have bread, they let him pass by in peace. However, a woman, who had all the appearances of being a man in disguise, incited the crowd to take the bread, swearing that the man carrying it was a hoarder. Nothing more was needed: the crowd fell on him, took the bread, tore it in pieces, and the boarding-house keeper was lucky to get away at that. A moment later, a child passed by the market, carrying a loaf; a second woman who had the tricolored cockade in her hat, threw him down, seized the bread, tore it in pieces and threw it away, saying that, since she had none, she did not want others to have any. The citizenesses of the market pointed out to her the indignity of such an act; she screamed abuse at them, telling them that they were aristocrats, and that soon all women over thirty years of age would be guillotined. This time, that messengeress of anarchy received the payment she deserved: they seized her and whipped her until they drew blood. It was too much and too little: they ought to have taken her to the committee of the Section, and there they might have discovered the scoundrels she was working for.

Les Annales françaises, 22 July 1793: Walter, pp.396–97.

84. The Troubles Continue

. . . Pitt and the Brissotins had concentrated all the big guns on forcing us [to offer the French crown to the Duke of York] by reducing us to famine; but, damn it, the sans-culottes solved the problem by putting out of the way all the knaves who sold their bread at four livres.

Some sluts, in spite of the abundance of bread, besieged the doors of some bakers to spread alarm; but the good citizens dispersed them by throwing water over the old rags they had borrowed to ply their trade, while some old gossips lifted the skirts of these filthy intruders and thrashed them soundly. This is the way, damn it, that all the plans of the great Pitt fizzled out; as he sees his castles in the air vanish.

Le Père Duchesne, No. 285, August 1793.

THE CLUBS

Before the Revolution the clubs had played an important part in the social life of the man of affairs: now they played an essential part in the political life of the nation. Many new clubs sprang up and were organised to propagate opinion of every shade. The most important were the Jacobin and Cordelier Clubs.

85. Clubs for the People

Jacques is the father of a typical family of the people. Every morning when he gets up his first thought is for his children, the eldest of whom is only just beginning to walk. How does he provide for them? After some trouble Jacques was able to get permission to put up a small lean-to under which he spends the whole day at a tiring job which returns little profit. On the few occasions when his wife manages to get away from caring for their growing family she sits down at Jacques' side to help him with his work. Jacques, who is a good father, begrudges the half-hour that it takes to eat his meagre meals.

Jacques has his little stall situated almost opposite the house of the Jacobins in the Rue St.-Honoré; he has noticed the crowds of people who arrive there around dusk. He asked what everyone was doing in that house, and at that particular time, three or four times a week. This is what he was told:

Three or four times a week, twelve to fifteen hundred citizens make a point of meeting in the library of the former convent. There, for four or five hours, they discuss, reason, absorb sound principles, and take precautions against pseudo-patriots; in a word they make themselves worthy of the liberty which we have conquered.

Jacques, who has both feelings and good sense, then said to himself, how fortunate they are in there, to be able to set aside three or four hours a day for their instruction! What have I done, then, that I should be condemned to a job which takes up all my time? I feel that I could become, like anyone else, not a better patriot (for I am as good a patriot as any of them) but more enlightened, less easily deceived. Alas! I must reject this idea. My first duty is to my children. Their maintenance is a chain which binds me to this wall. I must waste my abilities on a monotonous and thankless task. Thus will my life be run in the shadows of ignorance while every day I see the torch of instruction pass before my eyes, without once coming into my hands. On hearing of the events which stir up my country I become animated and inflamed. Duped by false news and exaggerated stories I take the side of this or that person, because I have neither the time nor the guidance necessary to clarify my ideas and direct my patriotism. I must blindly follow those who represent me; for this reason they get their own way with their constituents, three-quarters of whom are no better educated than I am. How cruel it is not to be able to enjoy fruitfully and without abusing it, the blessing of liberty, at the conquest of which I played no small part on the 14th of July!

Let others reply to poor Jacques' reflections, and those of 15 millions like him: we do not feel that we have the courage: we will merely say this:

Will nothing ever be done for the people who have done everything? Will they always be forgotten? Without instruction liberty is for them useless and even dangerous. Since they set themselves free has anyone sought ways of instructing them? What are the establishments decreed for this purpose?

> The writer goes on to plead that the people having become sovereign must exercise this sovereignty; that this three-quarters of the population must be given equal education, and a better share in government and in job allocation.

We need clubs for the people. Let every street in every town, let every hamlet have one. The primary assemblies are too solemn and too infrequent to take their place. The people need clubs which are fixed and free, few in number but informal, without regulations or titled officials; such things detract in some way from liberty, waste too much time and engender that selfish spirit so contrary to the public good.

The Jacobin and other clubs serve a purpose but clubs for the use of the people, simply organised and held without pretensions would be of the greatest benefit. Let an honest artisan call together at his house some of his neighbours; see him read by the light of a lamp, burning at common cost, the decrees of the National Assembly, adding to the reading his own reflections or those of some of his attentive neighbours. At the end of the meeting listen as he cheers up his audience, startled by one of Marat's articles, with a reading spiced with the patriotic swear-words of the *Père Duchesne*. . . .

It is most surprising that some wealthy citizens cannot be found who are good enough patriots to offer houses as a centre to which the people of the district could come every Sunday and holiday, to employ usefully the time otherwise wasted in taverns. In this way they could bring themselves up to date with events and make themselves familiar with the principles of the Constitution. In the event of private houses not being made available couldn't the people seize some of these churches rendered vacant by the suppression of the religious orders and the canons? It is said that there has already been formed, in the house of the Capucins in the Rue St.-Honoré, a popular club such as should be set up in every section of the big towns. In the country the porches of the parish churches, or even the churches themselves, could be consecrated to this purpose. Such buildings could only become more respectable.

> *Les Révolutions de Paris*, No. 73, 27 November–4 December 1790, pp. 401–6.

86. Chénier on the Clubs

In 1792 the Jacobin Club was exercising its greatest influence. In the
supplements to the *Journal de Paris* a veritable war was carried out
by several writers against this influence. Although it was denied
by these writers that this was part of a concentrated campaign, the
violence and consistency of these articles, and the known affiliation
of the writers before the Revolution, tend to cast doubt on this.
The most famous of these polemicists was André Chénier, whose
incursion into politics cost him his life in July 1794. His article, from
which this extract is taken, entitled 'On the cause of the disorders
that trouble France and prevent the establishment of liberty',
occupied the entire supplement of this edition of the *Journal de Paris*.

There exists in Paris a large association, which meets frequently, and
is open to all those who are, or claim to be, patriots, governed always by
leaders visible or invisible, who change often, and who mutually
destroy themselves; but who all have the same goal—to rule; and the
same spirit—to rule by any means whatsoever. This society, being formed
at a time when liberty, although its victory was no longer in doubt, yet
was not at that stage firmly founded, naturally attracted a large number
of concerned citizens filled with an ardent love for the good cause.
Several of them had more zeal than enlightenment. Many hypocrites
sneaked in with them, as well as many debtors, idlers, and lazy indigents,
who saw hope in any sort of change. Several just and wise men, who
know that in a well-administered state all of the citizens do not control
public affairs, but that all must look after their domestic affairs, have
since withdrawn. It follows from this that this association must be in the
main composed of a few skilful manipulators who concoct dangers in
order to profit from them; of other minor intriguers for whom greed
and evil-doing take the place of morality, and a great number of men
honest though lazy, but also ignorant and limited, incapable of any bad
intention, but extremely capable of serving, without realising it, the evil
intentions of others.

This society has given birth to an infinity of others: towns, country
centres, and villages are full of them. They are almost all subject to the
orders of the mother society, and they maintain with it a most active
correspondence. There is a main body in Paris, which is head of an even
greater body spread throughout France. It is thus that the Roman
Church *planted its faith*, and governed the world with its congregations of
monks.

This congregation was thought up and brought into being two years
ago by some very popular men, who saw in this a means of increasing
their power, and of putting their popularity to good account, but who

did not see how dangerous and formidable such an instrument can be...

These societies deliberate before an audience that constitutes their strength: and if one considers that busy men never neglect their work to be spectators at a club, and that enlightened men seek the silence of the office, or peaceful conversation, and not the tumult and clamour of these noisy brawls, one can easily judge the habitués who make up these audiences. One can also judge the sort of language necessary to keep in their good graces.

There is one simple phrase that suffices for all others. The Constitution being founded on that eternal truth, the *sovereignty of the people*, one has only to persuade the tribunes of the club that they are the *people*.

This definition is invariably adopted by the publicists, compilers of newspapers, so that a few hundred idlers gathered together in a garden, in a play-house, and some troops of bandits who pillage shops, are brazenly called the *people*; and the most insolent despots at no time received from its most avid courtiers more worthless or wearisome homage than the impure adulation with which two or three thousand usurpers of the national sovereignty are daily intoxicated by the writers and orators of these societies that are throwing France into turmoil.

As the appearance of patriotism is the sole virtue that is useful to them, some men dissipated by a shameful life, rush there to declare a faith in their patriotism by the wrath of their speeches; basing oblivion of the past and hope for the future on turbulent declamations and the passions of the multitude, and buying their way out of opprobrium with impudence.

There one can see daily portrayed sentiments and even principles that threaten every fortune and every property. Under the name of *hoarding* or *monopoly*, industry and commerce are represented as offences. Every rich man is considered a public enemy. Ambition and avarice spare neither honour nor reputation; the most odious suspicions and unbridled slandering are called freedom of opinion. He who asks for proof of an accusation is regarded as a main suspect, an enemy of the people.

There every absurdity is admired, provided it is homicidal; every lie is welcome provided it is heinous. Women go there to applaud the convulsions of a bloody madness . . .

These societies, each guiding the other, each holding the other by the hand, form a sort of electric chain around France. At the same instant, and in every corner of the Empire, they all become agitated, shout the same slogans, create identical disturbances, which they certainly did not have much trouble in predicting in advance.

Their turbulent activity has plunged the government into a frightening inertia; the intrigues and obscure plots of the primary or electoral

Assemblies, together with their scandalous turmoil, have forced many good men to flee . . .

There is the chaos into which they have thrown the empire, and an empire that has a Constitution. That is how, whether by terror or by discouragement, they have reduced talent and integrity to silence; and the man with a just and upright heart (for only he is free), astonished by the disparity between what he is told and what he sees, between the Constitution and those who claim to be its friends, between the law that promises protection and men who speak louder than the law, retires shuddering to his retreat and there tries hard to convince himself that even yet the reign of law and reason might come to gladden a world where oppression is practised in the name of equality, and where the emblem of liberty is no more than the seal that confirms the wishes of a few tyrants . . .

[Chénier concludes] that it is absolutely impossible to establish and consolidate a government alongside such societies; that these clubs are and will continue to be fatal to liberty; that these clubs will destroy the Constitution; that the fanatic horde at Coblenz has no surer allies; that their destruction is the sole remedy for France's ills; and that the day of their demise will be a day of celebration and public rejoicing. They cry out everywhere that the country is in danger. This is unfortunately only too true; and it will remain so as long as they continue to exist.

André CHÉNIER

Supplement to *Le Journal de Paris*, 26 February 1792.

FACTIONS

In Part One we saw how Rivarol feared and despised the people, especially of Paris, and decried the anarchy that he associated with their influence. This was a common cry in the right-wing press. Following the fall of the monarchy it was the turn of the Girondins to voice such fears. Scorning the demagogic appeal of the Jacobins, they waged a campaign against their rivals that often degenerated into mere personal abuse.

87. The New Enemy

This is the first part of a New Prospectus issued by the *Patriote français* in December 1792.

Our wishes are fulfilled; we have achieved the end towards which all our efforts have been constantly directed for four years. The republic is rising on the ruins of the monarchy, of that gothic institution with which the revisers of 1791 had befouled the soil of liberty. The revolution of 10 August, whilst crowning our long endeavours, imposes new ones upon us, and perhaps even greater ones. The patriotic writers have had successively two kinds of enemies to fight: first, there are the counter-revolutionary royalists, the partisans of the parliamentary, patrician and priestly aristocracy, those proud defenders of every abuse and every prejudice, these men who call the Revolution a revolt, and their revolt a holy war; – then there are the constitutional monarchists, the partisans of the aristocracy of property, men who put themselves at the head of the Revolution, either to make it abortive, or to turn it to their profit; these men who wanted neither complete liberty, because they needed a court that paid them, nor complete despotism, because they needed some influence that they could sell to the court.

To these vanquished enemies, even more dangerous ones have succeeded. It is beneath the flags of liberty that they march against her; they call themselves its defenders, in order to make it detested; they stretch it beyond its limits, in order to confuse it with licence; they embrace it in order to stifle it. Flatterers of the people, they despoil it of its sovereignty, and re-invest some hundreds of cheats or imbeciles with it, as a price for their applause. Greedy for power, they wish for anarchy, because anarchy is the rule of intrigue and insolence, in place of which order favours talent and virtue; greedy for money, they wish for unrest, because unrest is the patrimony of those who have nothing, and who cannot enrich themselves by honest means. There is the true portrait of the enemies that remain to be fought. The young republic must crush these hideous serpents who hiss about its cradle.

It is especially in the eyes of nations abroad that we must unmask these vile scoundrels; now that the French armies carry liberty everywhere, it is no longer for France alone that we write, it is also for the peoples among whom the Revolution is beginning or about to begin. We are their elders in liberty, we must aid them by our experience; we are even more their elders in philosophy, we must enlighten them with our light.

Le Patriote français, No. 1230, 23 December 1792, p. 717.

88. A Little Pamphlet, a Lot of Noise

Among the many bizarre characters brought to light by the Revolution, the Prussian Anacharsis Clootz, the 'Orator of the Human Race', occupies a special place.

In his pamphlet referred to here, *Ni Marat, ni Roland*, Clootz included some praise of Marat and an attack on 'federalism'. He sent a justificatory article to the *Chronique de Paris*, but was told to 'take his poisons elsewhere'. He did–to the Jacobins, on 21 November 1792.

But what particular use was it to the republic for the 'orator of the human race' to quit his character of legislator so that he might also descend into the arena and add to the already scandalous number of our political gladiators? What does he want? what is he after, having cited with praise that maxim consecrated by the Convention: 'let us finish with personalities and get back to business'. Is it part of the day's business to know that Roland is cross-eyed, and Marat is wild-eyed; that Guadet has sometimes over-eaten; that the presence and graces of Madame Roland would make the house of the Minister of the Interior most agreeable, if a stupid raillery against Paris did not render her table obnoxious; that Buzot is ascetic, and Kersaint a shaker; that Rebecqui sells liquor; that the patriotism of Barbaroux is as pure as the look on his face; that Roland runs the dictatorship through the spirit of the *Bouche de Fer*, the nation's cash, and twelve to fifteen secretaries; that he, Anacharsis Clootz would like Brissot enough etc. etc.

Let our readers be the judges. Where do all these trivialities lead? and ought they to be given any importance? Will anyone believe that this wretched pamphlet has just disturbed the whole of Paris? The Minister of the Interior is in convulsions. Letters rain down in the Brissotin journals and others, and the very society of the Jacobins has for a long time weighed in its wisdom what it ought to decree on *neither Roland, nor Marat*.

Les Révolutions de Paris, No. 176, 17–24 November 1792.

89. Robespierre—Organ of the People

Paris

Wednesday, 5 December 1792

This evening the Jacobins broke the bust of Mirabeau in their hall. It was on the motion of Robespierre that this 'execution' was carried out, and it was on the motion of Robespierre that the honours of he

Panthéon were accorded to Mirabeau. Pétion reproached Robespierre for this on the same day in the presence of the writer of this article. 'It is true that I despise Mirabeau,' replied Robespierre, 'but the Sections have asked that he have this honour and I have to be the organ of the people.' This word characterises Robespierre, and the flexibility of his *popular conscience* . . . In such a manner do the demagogues pay homage to the popular idols in order to please their admirers, and then break these idols in order to replace them. Moreover, Robespierre could without fear chase Mirabeau from the Panthéon, for no one will ever retaliate against him. While they were in this iconoclasm at the Jacobins, they also broke the bust of Helvétius. Several decent men of the society asked if he was a member of the faction from the Gironde. He was a philosopher, which comes to the same thing!

Le Patriote français, No. 1213, 6 December 1792, p. 647.

90. Robespierre at the Convention

Gorsas has been quoting parts of a speech by Robespierre criticising Roland, the Minister of the Interior.

Robespierre then goes into his usual banal performance; he accuses the minister of circulating libels in the departments, as well as some pamphlets, which depict good patriots like *himself* as agitators and partisans; yes, the defenders, the true friends of the people like *himself* . . . 'No one wants the Sections to be permanent; it is again a result of the plot,' he continues; 'because that is where the worthy citizens gather together . . . Perhaps they would like to violate the Temple deposit* and have him killed illegally. You are going to see them,' continues Robespierre, 'these so-called virtuous men like Lafayette, mount the tribune in order to accuse the TRUE PATRIOTS;' (there is scornful laughter)–'I shall not accuse the true patriot Robespierre,' says Barbaroux, 'but I shall remark that, having asked yesterday, yes I, for the closure of the debate on the matter of Louis, Marat and Robespierre, who were so anxious to have it done, opposed it; I leave the Convention to consider this change of tactics.'–Several members wanted the right to speak. 'If anyone must have it,' said the president, 'it will be me; but I leave it to the vote to judge between Robespierre and me.'

Roland at last got the right to speak: 'I shall not reply,' he said,

---

* Louis XVI.

'to the personal charges levelled at me; I shall merely remark that of all these allegations of Maximilien Robespierre, not one of them affects me: I defy him to prove a single one of them; they are, like so many others, lies; I attach no importance to them'—He then went on with the reading of his report.

La Courrier des départements, vol. 4, No. 8, 8 January 1793, pp. 124–25.

91. The Arrogance of the Capital

The abuses of power by some Parisians, their readiness to rule over the people of that city, and the despotism that they dared to exercise in the departments, created discontent against Paris itself. People were afraid that this great city wanted to arrogate to itself a supremacy that is not in keeping with republican government, and that, proud of its revolutions, it acquired from them a dangerous habit. Capitals are like kings, they do not like to climb down from their grandeur.

But Paris will see that it must view itself as no more than a municipality, and that the more it would like to affect superiority, the more will its republican principles be lost. We shall not consider then taking refuge in federated republics, which would before long give the advantage to the seaports, the commercial towns, to the wine and grain districts, and would reduce Paris to great deserted streets.

The agitators [i.e. those opposed to the unity of France] have not finished: they will try again to make disturbances among this great mass of people; but there is no immediate danger of a simultaneous and general uprising, so that the people of Paris will be given enough time to become enlightened enough to realise that Paris is France, that France is Paris, that all distinctions lead to its ruin, and that at the federation of the Champ de Mars, it was not in vain that we all swore to be brothers.

La Chronique de Paris, No. 298, 18 October 1792, p. 1168.

ANGER OF THE PEOPLE

The Declaration of the Rights of Man offered promises that never materialised for many sections of the population. The Revolution cleared away the abuses of the old régime, but in building the new, the bourgeois deputies incorporated within it a plutocratic system of privilege that the popular press was willing to equate with the enemy just overturned. From the earliest days of the Revolution personal interpretations of the Declaration might be held by some individuals to be above the law, but it was not until 1793 that these people as a group represented a powerful independent force.

92. Liberty on the Rampage

The two following extracts are from letters typical of those pub-lished by the aristocratic press.

Extracts from a Letter to the Editors

I have not the honour of being either a gentleman or a priest: I am a good plebeian, the father of a family, and I have worked for thirty years to turn to good account a quite considerable estate inherited from my forebears. I regularly support twenty labourers whom I employ on my property; often I employ more than forty.

Until the Revolution these good people always treated me as a father and benefactor. How times have changed!

No sooner had the new doctrine of equality and the unrestricted liberty of man been announced in our district than my peasants, who worked from dawn till dusk, made it known that henceforth they wanted three hours off during the day; and when I put it to them that by reducing their working day by a quarter it was only fair that I, in turn, should reduce their wages by a quarter, they declared that, if I reduced their wages by a farthing they would ruin my property and set fire to my house. I yielded to such powerful arguments and I now realised that the new liberty which has been given to us is only freedom to use force and oppression against weakness.

The seigneurs in my neighbourhood . . . had a levy imposed on them, and all were subjected to outrageous and most violent excesses; their only salvation lay in flight.

I thought that as I was not a seigneur I would be exempted from attacks of this kind; but I was wrong. Mobs came one after the other. Groups of six, eight and ten men, made up of masons, iron-workers, carpenters, and peasants, who had worked for me for twenty years, and whose dismissal notices had been given to me, under pretext, some that they hadn't earned enough on the rates I had fixed with them; the others that their daily wages were not enough, demanded in threatening tones, 15, 20, 30 and even 50 louis. I saw no other alternative, if I was not to be completely despoiled, but to take into my pay a dozen armed men and to meet force with force. This show of force made an impression on the evil-doers; from then on they left me in peace. My only fear now is of being denounced before the *comité des recherches*, and of being accused, like M. de Bussy, of hatching a counter-revolutionary plot with my dozen armed men.

Signed U.D.V.A.

Sommières, 21 November 1790.

L'Ami du Roi, No. CCXII, 31 December 1790.

93. Reclamation of Rights

Letter to the Editors

Marseilles, 24 October 1790

The missionaries of our legislators and of the gospel of the day, Messieurs, have their greatest success here. The spirit of equality spreads in an ever increasing and obvious manner, and the *loi agraire* comes ever closer. Here is an actual event that I believe may well convince you of this.

A merchant of this town, owner of a quite considerable estate, while at supper in his country house, receives a visit from a farm hand whom he had employed for fourteen years and whom he plied every day with fresh favours. In the most friendly fashion, he invites him in to have a drink; but the peasant, who no doubt had just read or had heard explained the Rights of Man, is by no means satisfied with that friendly invitation; instead he takes a chair and sets himself down abruptly at his master's table, repeating several times, *we are all equal, the National Assembly so wishes it*. The merchant merely laughs and hastens to serve him.

You may think, perhaps, that the guest stops at that; not at all; he has even greater pretensions, which he does not delay in expressing. *Monsieur*, he says to the merchant, *for fourteen years I have farmed your estate, therefore, a half belongs to me*. The merchant at first bursts into laughter and looks on it as a joke; but the peasant persists, and speaks in a tone that is hardly a joking one. He loses his temper, he threatens, and the proprietor, anxious to rid himself of this dangerous person, gives way to his demand . . . [subsequently, the merchant manages to have the peasant brought to justice. In his defence the peasant replies] that he wants only what is just, that he appeals to *the Rights of Man* and above all to the comments on them by Camille Desmoulins, the Marats, the Prudhommes, the Merciers, etc. and finally ends by saying to the crown prosecutor, *that he is a f* * * aristocratic pig*. The magistrate can only groan at the accused's madness and he confines his remarks to telling him that he will answer with his head for everything that might happen to the merchant.

The farm worker swore to ruin the merchant; he is still at large in the neighbourhood, and the proprietor is forced to go into hiding, for fear of being killed.

There, doubtless, Messieurs, is a *very active* citizen and a good patriot in the sense of the Revolution.

One of your subscribers.

L'Ami du Roi, 3 November 1790.

94. 'We do not lack Hostages'

What will be the results of all these attempts at counter-revolution? Here they are: bankruptcy, then civil war, the war of those who have nothing or almost nothing against those who have everything, the death or expulsion of the aristocrats, and the sharing of their possessions among those whom they have made aware of the gross inequality of wealth. It is, therefore, at least as much in the interest of the aristocrats as it is of the patriots to work for the general pacification. Moreover, whatever are the inclinations, designs and resources of our enemies, let us never forget, citizens, that we do not lack hostages.

Les Révolutions de Paris, No. 38, 30 March–6 April 1790.

95. Provocation to Pillage

(i) *Hang them from their doors*

The appearance of this number by Marat coincided with the grocery riots of 25 February 1793. The next day Marat was attacked in the Convention, and demands were made for his arrest. The debate ended in a farce with Marat turning the accusation against his accusers. In the end the Girondins had to make do with a face-saving compromise.

It is beyond question that the capitalists, the speculators, the monopolists, the dealers in luxury goods, the quibblers, the hangers-on, the ex-nobles etc. are all, practically every man of them, supporters of the *ancien régime*, who long for the abuses from which they profited in order to enrich themselves at the public expense. How then could they agree in good faith to the establishment of the rule of liberty and equality? In the impossibility of bringing about a change of heart, seeing the futility of the means hitherto employed to recall them to this task, and despairing of seeing the legislator take serious measures to force them to it, I now see only the utter destruction of that cursed brood as the sole means of restoring peace to the state, which they will continue to trouble as long as they are alive. Today they redouble their efforts to afflict the people by the exorbitant rise in the price of basic necessities, and by the fear of famine.

While waiting for the nation, exhausted by these disgusting disorders, to take upon itself the task of purging the land of the licence of that criminal race, which its cowardly representatives encourage to crime with impunity, one ought not to find it strange that the people in every town, in the depths of despair, are taking the law into their own hands. Wherever the rights of the people are not empty titles ostentatiously catalogued in a simple declaration, the ransacking of a few shops and the hanging of the monopolists at their door,* would soon put a stop to these frauds, which reduce five million men to despair, and which make thousands perish from want! Will the people's deputies ever do more than talk about these wrongs, without ever suggesting a remedy?

Let us forget about the repressive measures of the laws: it is only too evident that they have always been and always will be ineffective; the only effective means are revolutionary measures . . .

A little patience and the people will finally grasp that great truth, that it must always save itself. The scoundrels who seek to replace its chains, to punish it for ridding itself of a bunch of traitors on the 2nd, 3rd and 4th of September, let them tremble at the thought of themselves being put among the number of rotten members, whom it will judge necessary to excise from the body politic.

Now I know of only one other means that can be adopted to our feeble conceptions, if we are not to invest the present committee of general security, which is composed wholly of good patriots, with the power to hunt out the principal speculators and to hand them over to a state tribunal consisting of five men taken from those men best known for their integrity and severity, to judge them as traitors to the country . . .

I know one other means which would very well suit this purpose: it would be for the well-off citizens to form associations in order to import from abroad basic commodities and to sell them at cost price, in order to bring down the current high prices until they reach a reasonable

---

* This is the phrase which was thrown back at Marat, then and many times later. It loses its ferocity when considered in context, and especially with his explanatory article. (See doc. 95 (ii).)

level; but the execution of this plan supposes virtues not to be found in a country where cheats dominate, and where they only act the good citizen better to deceive the fools and plunder the people. However, these disorders cannot continue.

L'Ami du peuple, No. 133, 25 February 1793.

(ii) *Marat explains*

In fact Marat disapproved of the riots (see doc. 79(iii), p. 167). His statements in the issue of 25 February were in part to match the popularity that the *enragé* Jacques Roux was enjoying: Roux was in fact a participant in the riots, if not an instigator.

Indignant at seeing the enemies of the commonweal eternally plotting against the people, revolted at seeing hoarders uniting to reduce the people to despair by distress and hunger, desolated to see that the measures taken* by the Convention to stop these conspiracies did not attain their purpose, tired of the groanings of the unfortunates who come each morning to ask me for bread, while accusing the Convention of letting them perish of hunger; I take my pen to air the best means of putting an end to the conspiracies of the public enemies, and to the sufferings of the people. The simplest ideas are the ones that first present themselves to a well-meaning mind, that seeks only the general welfare without any return for itself: I ask myself, then, why we did not use against those public brigands the same means that they employed to ruin the people and to destroy liberty? As a result, I observe that, in a country where the rights of the people are not empty titles, ostentatiously set out in a simple declaration, the pillage of a few shops and the stringing up of the hoarders in their doorways, would soon put an end to these frauds! What do they do, these ringleaders of the faction of statesmen; they eagerly seize this phrase, then they hasten to send agents among the women grouped in front of the bakers' shops, to urge them to seize at cost price the soap, candles and sugar from the retail grocers' shops, while these agents themselves loot the shops of poor patriotic grocers. Next, these scoundrels keep quiet all day, but at night they plot together in their secret assembly held in the Rue de Rouen, at the house of the counter-revolutionary whore Valazé, and they come the next day to denounce me to the tribune, as an instigator of the excesses of which they are the first authors. Sales,

* The denounced number was written, composed and printed, before the decree, assuring supplies for Paris, had been passed: 'for all my numbers are in the press 36 hours before appearing.' Moreover, the riots had begun before Marat's first edition was on sale.

the former comte de Sales, who acts as their spokesman, had seized the moment when I was absent to consummate that treachery.

Le Journal de la République française, No. 136,
28 February 1793.

96. Paris under Surveillance

On 10 March 1793 Roux's fellow *enragé*, Jean Varlet, tried to stage an insurrection against the Convention with the aim of introducing the death penalty for hoarders and eliminating Roland and Brissot. Lacking the support of the Jacobin Club, the Commune, and the Faubourg St.-Antoine it proved abortive. The Jacobins were as yet afraid of a movement that they might not be able to control. Nevertheless the threat to the Girondins was growing.

(i) *Tuesday 26 March*

They are saying that there will be violent disturbances this week; they say that there will be another attempt to revive the 10 March conspiracy. Citizens, watch over the National Convention, watch over liberty.

Le Patriote français, No. MCCCXXII: Buchez and Roux,
XXV, 155.

(ii) *Wednesday 27 March*

The disturbances that we warned you about are becoming more and more likely. The talk is of a great meeting that will take place on the Champ de Mars. Santerre should be praised for having taken precautions against this event, which would produce at Paris the same outbreaks that are tearing apart the departments of the north-west. Santerre, it is on you that the peace of Paris rests. What a terrible responsibility on the one hand, what glory on the other!

Ibid. No. MCCCXXIII: Buchez and Roux, XXV, 155

(iii) *Thursday 28 March*

This has been a fine day for Paris. The whole town has risen up, but only against the aristocrats. The call to arms began from day-break; all the Sections assembled. The sentries over the public coffers and over the prisons were reinforced; strong patrols were carried out. However, the house-to-house searches, necessary for disarming suspects, were performed in orderly fashion. A large number of men without civic cards were arrested, and we must hope that among them we will discover some émigrés and agitators. Also the citizens in the tribunes of the Convention were inspected.

Ibid. No. MCCCXXIV: Buchez and Roux, XXV, 155.

(iv) *Friday 29 March*

Peace reigns in Paris, and the plans of the *septembristes* were even better foiled yesterday than those of the aristocrats, whose mask they used to murder the people. Yesterday's events proved that morale was high in the Paris Sections; let them rise and the brigands are finished! The good decrees passed today prove it. It will, however, be difficult to bring the Paris Municipality back to obeying the law. Yesterday's decree ordered that the customs gates should be watched over for only twenty-four hours, and this evening the gates are still being watched. How can you expect the people to respect the law and the Convention when its magistrates violate it?

Ibid. No. MCCCXXV: Buchez and Roux, XXV, 155.

(v) *Saturday 30 March*

The extraordinary tribunal was installed yesterday. You will get some idea of the doctrine preached in the Jacobin Club at Paris, by reading the following extract from a speech of the priest Chasles, which we copy verbatim from the *Journal des débats*. 'We announced,' he said, 'to the citizens in the country that, by means of the war tax, the poor would be nourished by the rich, and that *they should find enough in the wallets of the egoists to provide for their needs.*'

Ibid. No. MCCCXXVI: Buchez and Roux, XXV, 156.

SANS-CULOTTE ASCENDANCY

From April 1793 the Jacobin–sans-culotte alliance was forged for the final rounds of the death struggle. The Girondins struck first, but clumsily, by trying to arrest Marat: they did not take warning, but repeated their error, this time arresting Hébert. Shortly after this they were eliminated. Following the May/June days the sans-culottes were at the peak of their power (see also Part Seven, The Safety of the People, pp. 277–80) but to some extent their very success was to result in their decline, for by the end of the year they represented a threat to the government they had installed, and measures were taken to clip their wings, and remove their leaders.

97. Marat's Impeachment and Triumph

On 12 April the Girondins impeached Marat. Twelve days later he was acquitted. Paris thus declared itself against the Girondins.

The crime absolved and crowned, the audacious infringer of the laws carried in triumph in the midst of the sanctuary of the laws; this respectable sanctuary soiled by the impure gathering of drunken men and women of ill-fame, a worthy procession for the triumphant Marat; these are the events of the day, a day of mourning for all virtuous men, for all the friends of liberty!

... No one took seriously the question of discussing the act of accusation; they were in a hurry to finish the matter; they finished by acquitting Marat. Then followed great acclamations, loud applause, a civic crowning of Marat; two municipal ushers grasp him and lead him into the streets; he is followed by a large band of adulators who proclaim him *the father of the people*; they take him to the Convention. Danton prevents Lasource from closing the session. The procession enters the hall, and installs itself in the seats of a large number of deputies who had withdrawn. Marat is carried to the tribune, and pronounces a harangue, half-modest, half-triumphant. Danton says that it has been a fine day and they all leave.

Le Patriote français, No. MCCCLI: Buchez and Roux, XXVI, 148–49.

98. Hébert Appeals to the Sans-culottes

A month after their attempt to have Marat arrested the Girondins tried to silence Hébert. He was arrested following the publication of the number from which the following extract is taken.

The great denunciation by the Père Duchesne, to all the sans-culottes of the departments, on the subject of the plots formed by the Brissotins, Girondins, Rolandins, Buzotins, Pétionistes, and all the damned crowd of the accomplices of Capet and Dumouriez, to have them massacre the brave Montagnards, Jacobins, the Paris Commune, in order to give the death blow to liberty, and to re-establish royalty. His good advice to the brave lads of the faubourgs, to disarm all the imbeciles who piss cold water on the patriots and who, instead of defending the Republic, seek to set alight civil war between Paris and the departments.

Everywhere our armies make the enemies of the Republic dance. These bands of wild beasts that the crowned brigands have unleashed against France, have not yet taken an inch of our territory, despite the treacheries of Dumouriez and Roland. The imbeciles and the scoundrels who, for the love of the good Lord, have ravaged the departments of la Vendée, Deux-Sèvres and Loire-Inférieure, murdered women and children, burned towns and villages, run like hares at the approach of our brave volunteers. In a few days, the so-called Christian army will be scattered, and its cannon will be no more dangerous than those of the pope. Each day our affairs get better and better. We have no more enemies to fear other than those in our midst, damn it.

It is in the Convention, yes, damn it, it is among the representatives of the people that there still exists the source of the counter-revolution. The accomplices of Capet and Dumouriez move heaven and earth to inflame civil war and to arm the citizens of the departments against the Parisians. For a long time the fire has smouldered beneath the ashes; the Mandrins of the Gironde, the Brissotin cartridges, have worked from a distance to bring about this dastardly plot. To prepare in advance all their batteries, they first had 24 millions handed over to old Roland, under the pretext of it being to buy supplies; but, damn it, these millions, on the contrary, were used only to starve us, to supply the counter-revolutionaries, and to grease the paw of these vile manufacturers and dealers in journals filled with lies, calumnies and atrocities against the best patriots.

. . . The audacity of the Brissotins has redoubled itself; the jackasses think that they are approaching the longed-for moment of the counter-revolution; they threaten, they insult the Montagnards, they recruit in Paris an army of errand-boys and louts to chase the sans-culottes from the Sections; the sugar merchants of Rouen, Bordeaux, and Marseilles invent petitions of the same kind as those that threatened the sans-culottes, when the sans-culottes demanded the fall of Capet. He was none the less cut short, the scoundrel, despite so many thousands of jackasses who made their whip crack so loud in his support last June. Ah well, damn it, it will cost no more to annihilate the traitors who conspire against the Republic. Their death knell has sounded when their tainted blood has been spilt, the carpers among the aristocracy will return to their cellars as on 10 August.

Brave sans-culottes, your enemies are only audacious because you remain with your arms folded; wake up, damn it; get up, and you will sec them at your feet. Disarm all the imbeciles who piss cold water on the patriots and who do not want to take any part in the Revolution. The poison of the moderates is more dangerous than the steel of the Austrians. Be victorious, and all the departments will approve you; but above all strike while the iron is hot. If you sleep even for a few moments, fear lest you wake up slaves, damn it.

> *Le Père Duchesne*, No. 239, May 1793: Buchez and Roux, XXVII, 208–9, 211–12.

99. The End of the Infamous Clique

The Great Joy of the Père Duchesne on the subject of the great revolution that has just damned to hell the infamous clique of Brissotins and Girondins, who will now take their turn to sniff the guillotine. A Great Judgement of the people to make these cheats cough up.

The heaps of gold they have received from England to keep up the civil war, and the assignats that they have stolen from the nation. His good advice to the brave Montagnards so that they will make up for lost time and give us a good constitution.

The pitcher goes so often to the well that at last it breaks. I had certainly predicted, Girondins, Brissotins, Rolandins, Buzotins, Pétion-istcs, that your reign would not last long, that you would end up like a moth burning itself at the candle. You thought you were in a strong position because your pockets were well filled with the guineas of King George the Ninny and your wallets stuffed with the assignats that old Roland and his companion Clavière had ladled out by the fistful. You saw the republic as a milch cow that you wanted to suck dry. Ravenous wolves, devouring wolves, you who have covered yourselves in sheep's clothing, for some time you succeeded in pulling the wool over the eyes of our brothers in the departments, who were poisoned with all the insipid newspapers of your making.

> The article continues with accusations that the Girondins were in fact doing what they accused the Jacobins of doing–collaborating with Austria and Britain.

> *Le Père Duchesne*, No. 242.

100. 'The Earth Belongs to All Men'

I am always hearing preached respect for property; that is all well and good; but the first property, is it not existence? Is there any power on earth that can rob us of it? The earth, like the air and water, belongs to all men. Ought not the rich to be satisfied with having three-quarters of the cake, and do they want to prevent the poor from gleaning, when they themselves have had such a good harvest? Again, the man with a famished stomach has no ears. Starvers of the people, fear his despair. [Why get rid of the old aristocratic tyrants and let new oppressors take their place?]

The first article of the Declaration of the Rights of Man is resistance to oppression, and even if the Convention had not decreed it, this principle is written in the hearts of all men. The slave often crushes with his irons the tyrant who demands more from him that he can give.

What then is your hope, enemies of equality? Do you believe that, through making us suffer, we will fall at your feet and beg you to give us charity [*caristade*], while, damn it, we still have arms to snatch from your claws the gold that you have hoarded and the keys of the granary that you refuse to give up? People, formidable giant, wake up! Crush beneath your feet all these dwarfs who profit from your sleep to enchain you. What next, after having put paid to all the petty squires of the *ancien régime*; after having made all the marquises, dames, princes, monks, bishops, archbishops and cardinals dance the *Carmagnole*; after having cut short the subsidy of the long-eared animal called pope; after having forced all those bewigged and brainless heads of the *parlements* to hang up their red robes; after having cut back the talons of the financial birds of prey; after having destroyed the Tuileries menagerie and made the head of the misshapen monster called King of France and Navarre roll on the scaffold, you still find yourselves at morning prayers. All that you do good and useful is in the instant destroyed. New cheats replace the old ones. New vermin want to devour you. A million damnations! I am consumed with rage when I think of all the evils that overwhelm us, whilst, damn it, it is so easy to remedy matters.

Where then is that revolutionary army that was to have marched in all the departments with the sacred guillotine, to purge the republic of its hoarders, traitors, conspirators? Ought it not, damn it, to have been formed the very day that the Convention decreed it? What then is the reason for the delay in executing these most salutary measures? Who then are the dolts that paralyse the arm of the republic when it is going to strike its most deadly enemies? Ah, damn it, if the sans-culottes were as active as the aristocrats, France would soon be swept clean of all the scoundrels within it. They stand no nonsense, they are only a handful, yet they daily find a thousand means to plague and torment us.

However, we must finish them off. Misery is at its height. Our wealth is in the hands of the counter-revolutionaries. Throughout the departments, the sans-culottes languish. Well, damn it, let the sans-culottes arise; let them seize from all the proprietors, from the great hoarding farmers, let them threaten to make them lose their taste for bread, if the scarcity continues. Soon, damn it, wheat will be abundant in the markets and we shall live, damn it.

Le Père Duchesne, No. 289: Walter, pp. 321–23.

101. The Revolution is Over

This extract is from the final number of the *Révolutions de Paris*. Despite his plea, Prudhomme had in fact been for some time threatened with the guillotine.

The ruin of my health, after five years of demanding work, makes it physically impossible for me to continue my newspaper regularly. Therefore, this Number 225 is the last of my collection. Nevertheless I am too much the friend of the liberty of my country not to be always, as far as in me lies, its most ardent supporter, and its martyr, if need be.

I shall publish, in order to complete the history of the Revolution, a SUPPLEMENT, which will contain, in addition, the ERRATA of the unavoidable errors found in a weekly newspaper. In the meantime, I shall complete the collection of the crimes of all the crowned tyrants, and I shall give the impartial history of France in 12 volumes in 8vo announced three years ago.

I should deserve to be hung, if the counter-revolution were possible.

I have sworn to cease my *Révolutions de Paris* only when my country was free; I have kept my word.

My country is free, since the French have sworn liberty, equality and indivisibility.

My country is free, since the head of the last tyrant of the French has fallen.

My country is free, since we have a Constitution truly republican, worthy of serving as a model to all peoples who want to cease being slaves.

My country is free, since the French make all despots tremble.

My country is free, since the French are able to procure liberty for all other peoples.

My country is free, since none of the abuses of the *ancien régime* exists any more. No more feudalism, no more monarchy, and soon no more superstition.

My country is free, since federalism is destroyed.

My country is free, since the patriots have come to the end of all the enemies of liberty.

My country is free, since the sans-culottes have won their rights and now occupy all positions.

My country is free, since the Convention has decreed that there should be no more begging, and that the needy patriots shall have compensation from the goods of the enemies of the Revolution, and patriots who are disabled, from their territorial possessions.

The Revolution is over, since the epigraph that I put in my newspaper, and which I have religiously kept, has finally its full and complete effect. The people is no longer on its knees, it has risen, and has reduced the 'great' to their true *stature*.

The Revolution can and must be regarded as over, if the sans-culottes never depart from its principles, if they exert themselves and do not allow any kind of tyranny; for to abuse liberty is to fall back into slavery.

The Revolution is over, if the Convention does not divide itself, and if the patriots always rally round it.

The Revolution is over, if the patriots know how to be patient in times of shortage of supplies, following the example of those battalions of the army of the Nord, who, on learning that there was a shortage of meat in Paris, asked to receive only a quarter of their ration.

The Revolution is over, if the sans-culottes examine and learn how to distinguish the true from the false patriot.

The Revolution is over, if the sans-culottes do not tolerate illtreatment of the true friends of liberty, who have for long given proof of their patriotism.

The Revolution is over, if the virtuous poor are no longer at the mercy of the selfish rich.

The Revolution is over, if the father, responsible for the family, is aided by the nation, not as an act of charity, but as an obligation.

The Revolution is over, if the nation finds work for the able-bodied citizens.

The Revolution is over, since the nation forces the return of fortunes usurped from the people.

The Revolution is over, if the patriots and true republicans, always united, conserve their energy and their love for liberty. The ardour that they put into manufacturing saltpetre in order to crush the remainder of the slaves proves that they will only cease to fight when there will be no one left to conquer.

The Revolution is over, if the sans-culottes are always persuaded of the great advantages that result from the unrestricted exercise of freedom of speech and of the press, contained in the Declaration of Rights, as well as of resistance to oppression.

The Revolution is over, since the Convention has decreed that all patriots imprisoned shall be set at liberty.

The Revolution is over, if the French people truly take to heart the beauties of republican government.

Les Révolutions de Paris, No. 225, 25 Pluviôse–10 Ventôse, Year II (13–28 February 1794), pp. 521–23.

THE SANS-CULOTTES

The word 'sans-culotte' was first used by the aristocrats as a term of ridicule. Gautier talked of the 'sans-culotte army' in his number of 28 February 1791, and thereafter used it fairly frequently. The *Actes des Apôtres* also used it: for example, in early May 1791, in their No. 263, they remarked that they did not have, 'like messieurs the Jacobins, the support of forty-four thousand societies and an army of sans-culottes to give [their] fantasies the force of law'. It was more commonly used after the massacre on the Champ de Mars, and still in a derogatory sense. For instance, Desmoulins in a letter to Prudhomme, published in the *Révolutions de Paris* of 20–27 August 1791, exclaimed in horror: 'God forbid that I should insult [the nudity of hardworking folk] by the atrocious word sans-culotte.' Even as late as the middle of April 1792, the writer for the *Révolutions de Paris* asked the pardon of his readers for using 'that ignoble word'.

Part Four ends with some documents more specifically illustrative of the spirit and ideals of the sans-culottes as they appeared to contemporaries.

102. It's the Man who Counts

Marat's writing is not without humour, although it is usually bitterly ironic or satirical. Here he is in a more pleasant mood, ridiculing the exaggerated respect for social position or authority that the rise of the sans-culottes would put temporarily in eclipse.

To the Ami du peuple

15 January 1790

Today's *Journal de Paris* has taken the trouble to give us a bulletin on the condition of M. Necker. I ask you, Sir, to be so good as to publish in your paper the bulletin on the illness of my coachman, who was at the siege of the Bastille, and who has deserved as much of his country as the first minister of finance.

'Pierre le Brun yesterday evening had a violent attack of hepatitis, which lasted almost all the night; he then slept fitfully, about seven minutes at a time. His urine is still infrequent; there are nauseating vomitings; his pulse is still poor.' SIXTE-QUINT.

I hope that all good patriots will interest themselves in the health of an excellent French citizen: 'Vice alone is lowly, virtue determines rank.'

Signed le chevalier DE BLAVILLE

L'Ami du peuple, No. 102, 19 January 1790.

103. On the Abuse of Words

When it is considered that the greatest number of men of all classes are governed by words, one cannot be indifferent to the sense that they accidentally acquire and which often perverts their original meaning.

Permit me to bring to your notice a trivial word that is being used on the one side as an insipid pleasantry and on the other as absurd or perfidious declamations. When the word 'sans-culotte' is introduced into conversation, some men make use of it rather skilfully to attract to their side all the concern that poverty inspires and to charge those who do not do so, with all the hatred that wealth, proud and pitiless, deserves. Would to God that poverty should never become the object of such odious banter! that the sight of rags should ever excite derision! The man who jokes at the misfortune of his equal, whatever party he belongs to, whatever his beliefs, is surely a wretch unworthy of the name of man. Without being a Jacobin, without decorating oneself with the title, today too ostentatious, of 'sans-culotte', one can still know that misfortune has a right, not only to compassion, to concern, but even to respect.

Res est sacra miser

By indulging in light-hearted banter, imprudent and in poor enough taste, it is by no means poverty that one has intended to make light of, it is the affectation and apishness of those who lower themselves to the level of the poor in order to acquire elevation and wealth, who cover themselves with the rags of indigence in order to come to places of profit or honour; or who, if they are in good faith, imitate the proud humility of the Cynic who trampled underfoot the display of Plato with a yet greater display. To unmask the so-called 'sans-culottes' let us not ignore that this term has only become ridiculous or insulting since they converted it to their own use; since they made of it the rallying word for their agents and since it became synonymous with *brigand* and *burner of houses*. It no longer designates one who lacks essential clothing, but one who, independently of the clothing which he has, still wants to appropriate that of his neighbour. To take the clothes off the poor man whilst running after the joys of luxury and opulence is a ridiculous parody, a criminal profanity, extremely insulting to the real poor; it is a mean piece of flattery insulting to their reason. It was thus that the courtesans of our kings and princes, not content with adopting in a servile fashion their opinions, passions, and tastes, even took on their colours. Let us give the French people the credit of believing that to seduce it there is need of a less clumsy artifice.

If in the eyes of some men nudism appears as a sign of patriotism, it is hardly surprising that wealth has become the synonym for aristocracy . . . [The writer goes on to enlarge on this theme.]

Supplement to *Le Journal de Paris*, 21 April 1792, p. 2.

104. Christt the first Sans-culotte

Already in July 1789 the abbé Fauchet had preached a sermon in which the virtues of the common man were compared to the teachings of Christ. The notion reappears in Hébert's homilies. In the number from which this extract is taken Hébert has been preaching the necessity for a good education to reform the individuals in society. Liberty and equality were to be the child's first words and the Constitution his only catechism; the history of kings would engender a hatred of monarchy, but each child would be encouraged to choose the religion that suited him best, be it Judaism, Hinduism or whatever. In particular he would not mind if every child chose to be a Quaker, for these 'good chaps hold bloodshed in horror'. Yet they are Christians, he points out, and draw their humanitarian principles from the same gospel as the blood-thirsty Catholics. In fact it is only the priests who destroy the beauty of this book, which contains the perfect model for life 'in the Sans-Culotte who made [it]'.

(i) I know no better Jacobin than this man Jesus. He is the founder of all popular societies. He did not want them to be too large, for he knows that large assemblies almost always degenerate into a rabble and that sooner or later the Brissotins, the Rolandins, the Buzotins worm their way in. The club that he created consisted of only twelve members, all of them poor sans-culottes; yet, even into this small number, a false brethren insinuated himself, namely, Judas, whose name signifies, in the Hebrew language, a Pétion. With his eleven Jacobins, Jesus taught obedience to the laws, preached equality, liberty, charity, fraternity, waged eternal war on priests, financiers, destroyed the religion of the Jews, which was a bloody cult; he taught men to despise wealth, to respect old age, to forgive wrongs. All the sans-culotterie soon gathered about him. The more that kings and emperors persecuted his disciples, the more did their number grow. Unfortunately, damn it, the tares are mixed with the good wheat. Other Judases succeeded to the one who sold him, and, after his death, they crucified him again by becoming popes, cardinals, bishops, abbés, monks and canons. This wretched gang, in the name of this divine lawgiver who loved only poverty, enriched itself on the spoils of the fools by inventing a purgatory, a hell, by selling indulgences for their weight in gold. In the same way, I avow, did the Feuillants, like the priests, seek to lose liberty by dishonouring it and robbing it of everything it has.

Le Père Duchesne, No. 277.

(ii) *To the 'poor chaps' incited to revolt by the priests*

Ah! If the good sans-culotte Jesus came back to earth he would be every bit as angry as the Père Duchesne at seeing such rascals use his name to commit the worst of crimes. 'Read my gospel, bloody and lying priests,' he would say to them, 'and you will see there that I have always preached liberty and equality; that I have ceaselessly protected the poor against the rich; in my time I was the most enraged Jacobin in Judaea . . . In my life consecrated to virtue and good deeds I was called an incendiary, agitator, and anarchist (*désorganisateur*) . . .' [and so the parallel is continued to the crucifixion on false charges].

Le Père Duchesne, No. 252.

105. Origins and Definition of the Sans-culottes

A number of our readers ask us for a definition of the sans-culottes, the history of their origin, and a precise and true list of the manners and virtues of these patriots *par excellence*, of these born republicans. We could content ourselves by replying that every citizen who is neither royalist, nor aristocrat, nor idle rich, nor selfish, nor moderate, deserves to be saluted by the honourable title of sans-culotte. But we think that it is not without some value to enter into a few details on this quite new subject, although the term itself is in common enough use. So many people, today, out of fear or for even less excusable motives, take on the cloak of sans-culottism in order to hide themselves or in order better to deceive the nation which they rob and betray!

> The writer dismisses contemporary revolutions in other countries as paltry affairs.

The *Journal des Révolutions de Paris* was the first which, from 1790, spoke of the sans-culottes (which we then called the *bonnets de laine*), that is to say, the true revolutionary people, who did its duty in working clothes, despite the scorn that they, whom they at the time called the *habits bleu-de-roi* and the *fayetistes*, affected for them. From then on the newspaper had the honour of being denounced to the public prosecutor, because it said, or rather because it prophesied, that these *bonnets de laine*, whom people scorned, whom they kept out of the good offices, would become the sole supports of France reborn; the day will come, it said, when the *habits bleu-de-roi*, and the *fayetistes* will go back into the dust, as soon as the *bonnets de laine* or the sans-culottes rise up. . . .

As you see, the origin of the sans-culottes goes a long way back, it dates from the first days of the Revolution; they were the first to show themselves, and they have faithfully followed it and supported it in its different stages. . . .

The court's excesses and the abuses of arbitrary power having reached a climax, there suddenly awakened sans-culottism which had slept for so many centuries in the bottom ranks of the Third Estate. It did not arise at once. Surprised, it first opened its eyes, looked around, listened to what was going on about it, then finally, we saw it stand up on its two feet. No one believed that it was so great, so formidable. It did not know nor did it exert all its force until it suddenly found itself upright . . . until then the Revolution had only been, so to say, like rose-water: but from the beginning of 1791, as we have already said above, we forecast that it would not remain so for long. . . . [The author then claims the Constitution of 1791 to have been a 'royal charter'.]

Are we then more free, more content? They call us sovereign, yet we still have a king; they tell us that all men are equal, have equal right to live, yet we continue to die of hunger, in the midst of abundance, beneath the eyes of the rich who sneer at us. It is still we who work the land and gather the harvest, and a minority consume it or allow it to rot rather than share it with their brothers. It is too much! What kind of revolution is it that leaves everything on one side and nothing on the other? Let's march; let us re-establish the natural order of things, and without any false piety or criminal weakness let us make a clean sweep of all who refuse to go along with us. At this cry of reason, too long stifled; at this demand for justice, too long outraged or blinded; those who are not sans-culottes become seriously alarmed, and say to themselves in their turn: the storm is rumbling and drawing near; the sans-culottes are people who put words into action. . . . Do you know what a sans-culotte is?

He is not the equivocating type, the person without character who lets himself go with the tide of events; who, as it is said, howls with the wolves in order not to be devoured by them.

Nor is he the smug egoist who has no other country than the inside of his house, and who, like the snail, withdraws into its shell while the tempest blows, and who swims near the surface.

He is not at all the man who, warned of his danger by the imprudences of several of his former aristocratic comrades in arms, has endlessly upon his lips the tune of the hymn of liberty, and repeats deep down and from the bottom of his heart, O Richard, O my king! [Nor is he the sybarite in disguise . . . nor the greedy rich fearful for his fortune, . . . nor the speculator . . . nor the privileged members of society . . .]

Where then will the true sans-culotte be found? By saying what he is, one will know where to find him.

The true sans-culotte is a man of nature, or one who has preserved all his energy in the heart of civil society regenerated by the Revolution. He is a patriot strong in mind and body, who has always shown himself openly and taken a step ahead, consequently he has not waited for the country to summon him to her. It is this artisan, this head of the family, endowed with good sense, who, far from giving to the service of the republic the spare part of his time, regarded himself, from 12 July 1789, as permanently requisitioned, both in his person and in his abilities. A true sans-culotte is what one used to call the man of the people, open, cordial, sometimes rough and ready but always humane, even in those revolutionary moments when a veil is thrown over the statue of humanity. The true sans-culotte desired the death of the despot and of all the conspirators; he is seen where traitors pass on their way to execution; he is seen even pressing about their scaffold, because his humanity does not exclude justice. . . .

He carries the sense and love of justice to a point that distressed the moderates, the undecided, the temporisers, all those who compromise with their principles. The true sans-culotte loves to get to the heart of the matter, even if he has to forgo his interests, provided it is in the public interest; thus no sans-culotte becomes or remains a rich man. *Rich and sans-culotte!* The two terms never go together. . . . He is hard-working, economical, but at the same time he is the opposite to selfish and dislikes those who are such. Selfishness is the curse of patriotic virtues and generous sentiments. . . . Love of work and frugality justifies, more than enough, the sans-culottes slandered; the share they take in the affairs of their country makes them deaf to the comforts of life that they could get for themselves, like so many others. They are neither less active nor less intelligent; but they are less selfish. . . .

It has been said and often repeated that religious practices, the offices of the Church, the ideas associated with the god of the priests, would serve as a consolation and spectacle for the people in its misery. The sans-culottes prove at this moment that they need other spectacles. . . .

This fine and sudden revolution in religious ideas had its source in the awareness of their dignity, with which the sans-culottes have been imbued since they declared the Rights of Man. The sans-culottes will be honoured now in their own eyes, and soon will force all Europe to honour them likewise. . . .

One must not confuse the sans-culottes of the French Republic with the *shoeless* of England, and the *beggars* of Holland. . . . The sans-culottes have no leader at their head. They give themselves plenty of protection and have no need of it. They are not sectarians who lay claim to a separate law and class, or to be set apart. What is understood by sans-culottes, is, in the final analysis, the free people, who has won its rights, who is not of a temper to be deprived of them, and who sooner or later must bring into its mass all those who, at this very moment, seem unable to appreciate it. In a word, all which is not sans-culotte is illegal, provisional and momentary. Finally, who says the word sans-culotte, means a republican born above the events and the needs of the time, who has only one passion, the love of order and of equality, of independence and fraternity. All the factions, and the parties, all the sects will pass away; the *people*, the sans-culottes, will last as long as nature whose laws they follow, as long as reason which alone they worship, as long as liberty, on whose behalf they will forever fight.

Lés Révolutions de Paris, No. 214, 15–22 Brumaire, an deuxième de la République française (5–12 November 1793), pp. 177–83; No. 215, 23–30 Brumaire, Year II (13–20 November), pp. 202–7.

PART FIVE

War

If it had not been for the outbreak of war it is possible that the main divisive forces acting against the Revolution could have been contained, allowing for the gradual acceptance of the reforms. War gave new hope to the counter-revolutionaries, and with France's initial reverses fear and anger gripped the patriots. Without war there probably would have been no Terror.

To what extent was war inevitable? Was war forced on the Revolution or did the Revolution force war on Europe? In the initial stages of the Revolution war seemed remote. The revolutionaries proclaimed their fraternity with the peoples of the world while the major foreign courts ignored or enjoyed the embarrassment of France's former ruler. Poland and Turkey occupied centre stage in the international scene. However, there was implicit in the revolutionaries' declaration of friendship a threat to the established order in Europe, for the revolutionaries' appeal was to the ruled and not to the rulers. The successful example of the Revolution and the subversive ideas contained in the Declaration of Rights could be a threat to any régime that allowed the free infiltration and discussion of such ideas and events within its borders. In France the guilt of stolen fruit might give rise to fear of retribution, but while the revolutionaries answered bellicosely any threat from abroad, the possibility of initiation of war by France was remote.

The flight of the king altered this situation. Louis had publicly demonstrated his opinion of the Revolution and advertised the fact of his unwilling residence in Paris. The fears of the revolutionaries increased, and in the Declaration of Pillnitz (27 August 1791) they saw more than a face-saving proclamation by Louis' brother monarchs. By this time, too, Louis was willing to countenance the armed intervention he had formerly disavowed.

In the opening months of the Legislative Assembly the issue of war dominated all others. With the exception of Robespierre and Marat, who saw the main danger as being internal, and, on the right, Mallet du Pan in the *Mercure*, and Duponte de Nemour's *correspondance patriotique*, who saw the danger to the king, all other factions favoured war: Brissot, supposedly, as a crusade against the crowned heads of Europe; the War Minister, Narbonne, in the hope of establishing a military dictatorship; Louis in the hope that 'the inevitable defeat' of France would result in his being restored to his former absolutism.

At the same time the situation in Europe added to the climate favouring war. After several half-hearted attempts from as early as 1790 to direct the attentions of the European monarchs towards France, Marie-Antoinette's brother Leopold, Emperor of Austria, died, to be succeeded in March 1792 by the more aggressive Francis II, an ardent opponent of the Revolution. Following an exchange of ultimatums and insults, France declared war on Austria on 20 April 1792. On 1 May Prussia joined Austria.

France was badly prepared for the war and suffered severe setbacks until Brunswick's army was blocked at Valmy (20 September 1792) and the Prussians were forced to leave French soil. By the late autumn defence was being turned into attack, as first Savoy and Nice were occupied (late September). Then following France's first major victory, at Jemappes (6 November 1792), Belgium was under French control and Holland threatened.

The theatre of war widened. Britain might express righteous anger at the deposition of the king, the September massacres, and the execution of Louis, but she could not stand by and watch the threat to her mercantile interests in Holland and the Rhineland grow unchecked. On 1 February 1793 the Convention anticipated the British government, by declaring war on it and Holland.

At war with virtually the whole of Europe, France was also divided against itself, especially after the outbreak of the long simmering war in the Vendée, which followed the decree of 24 February for a levy of 300,000 men. To this burden was added treachery when Dumouriez, following his defeat by the Austrians at Neerwinden (18 March 1793) and Louvain (21 March 1793), fled to the enemy. These events, however, had their most serious repercussions on the home front, as extraordinary measures were taken to meet the crises.

The victories of late 1792 had presented France with the new problem of 'imperialism'. The Propagandist Decrees of November and December 1792 rang discordantly alongside the May 1790 'no annexation' declaration that had been incorporated in the 1791 Constitution. Before long it was apparent that the French 'armed missionaries' were not going to be welcomed with the enthusiasm they expected. It is with this issue that the final section in Part Five ends.

NO MORE WAR

The Nootka Sound crisis of May 1790 between Britain and Spain threatened to bring France, as the dynastic ally of Spain, into a war that did not interest her. The debate on this issue resulted in the declaration of the Assembly that France would 'refuse to undertake any war of conquest' or interfere with the 'liberty of any people'. It also gave rise to the debate on whether the right to declare war should belong to the king or the people. Both before and after these matters were being debated, the revolutionaries alternated between declarations of pacifism and threats against interference.

106. The Right of War and Peace

Towards the end of May 1790 the first issue of Fréron's *Orateur du peuple* appeared. The exaggeration that typified it can be judged by this extract from his second number. Moreover, his sentiments are hardly justified by the event he is praising.

If the right of war and peace had been granted to the king, we would have been finished; civil war would have broken out on the night of the Saturday or Sunday, and today Paris would have been swimming in blood. At midnight, the tocsin would have called the citizens to arms; the château of the Tuileries would have gone up in flames; the people would have taken under its protection the monarch and his family; but Saint-Priest, and Necker, and Montmorin, and la Luzerne would have been strung up, and their heads paraded throughout the capital. Imagine all the crimes that such a night would have covered with its shadow, the massacres, the robberies, the sound of the bells, the crash of artillery, the rattle of arms, the gleam of the torches, the noise, the confusion, the cries of women and children; no aristocrat would have escaped from the fury and resentment of the people, which would have made of the constitution a solemn hecatomb. Yes, these are all the evils, all the horrors that the ministers were preparing for us, and from which the National Assembly has saved us. In vain would the National Guard have tried to oppose itself to a people aroused; it would have led to the outbreak of conflicts among the citizens. There is no doubt that they were expecting some frightful outbreak, for more than 400 cartridges per company had been distributed . . .

L'Orateur du peuple, No. 2, May 1790:
Buchez and Roux, VI, 132–33.

107. Peace among Nations

The *Annales patriotiques* was to become one of the most ardent proponents of war in 1792.

(i) *Patriotism and fraternity*

One may be sure that on 15 March there already existed a treaty between the Court of the Tuileries and the new King of Hungary, to help him to bring the Belgian provinces back under the infamous Austrian yoke: some very active movements took place between the French ministers and the Courts of Madrid and Naples. Some Spanish squadrons cross into the Mediterranean and into the gulf of Gascony; the commandants of the forts on the Provence coast, especially at Marseilles, make preparations for war. The national militia of that maritime city have no arms at all, and they are refused them; the king has again not accepted the constitutional decree on the organisation of the army, although it is almost a month since the decree was brought in . . . If the Spaniards or the Neapolitans invade or land in our provinces, we shall first send them the decrees of the National Assembly, translated into their own language, then, if they persist and do not come to drink to universal liberty, by taking our cockade, we shall send their death certificates to their relations. As for the Belgians, we shall defend them . . . As for our army, we shall organise it by the sentiment of patriotism and the magnetism of fraternity . . . Friends! let us redouble our courage, our commitment, our vigilance, and our patriotism. A nation such as ours, with 30 million individuals, cannot perish. It is its enemies who shall perish.

Les Annales patriotiques, 15 March 1790:
Buchez and Roux, V, 144.

(ii) *Family pact of nations*

City merchants, national confederate guards, brave soldiers of the troops of line, worthy municipal officers, and you citizens, who have formed patriotic societies, let us all unite together; let us raise one deadly voice against this treacherous plan of the ministers, against the ministers themselves. Let us drive them from the presence of a king whom they ceaselessly infect with their aristocratic venom. Why do we wait to hunt out these stupid and insolent beings? Have they not gone too far in wanting to involve us in a foreign war? Why do we wait to declare that we wish to be the friends of all nations, the enemies of all tyrants, and that we acknowledge no family pact other than the pacts of national families?

Les Annales patriotiques, No. 226, May 1790:
Buchez and Roux, VI, 37.

108. Why Interfere with Suicide?

The aristocrats enjoyed the sight of what they regarded as revolutionaries 'frightened by their own shadows'. Royou's analysis bears comparison with the scornful claims later made famous by Burke, that the Revolution had benefited the British as rivals (to the French) more than twenty Ramillies or Blenheims.

(i) *Frightened of their shadows*

England and Holland are making extraordinary preparations. But do we not know that the first of these powers has, as the fundamental maxim of its policy, to be in a perfect state of war before declaring it? and is not its interest in extorting from Spain a treaty of commercial advantage a strong enough reason to engage England in developing all its sea power? If its arming has not as its only aim to impose itself on Spain by a display of force, then these two powers must have some agreement between them and be secretly allied against France. But why then these enormous expenditures on useless ships? for it is land forces that are needed for our so-called counter-revolutionaries. But there is not the slightest movement, not the shadow of activity among the troops on Spanish soil. Therefore there is not the slightest need for anxiety on our part.

Sardinia, you will say, is making preparations. But the insults made by the French to its flag, and the threats made by the National Guards of Marseilles and Toulon of attacking Nice, the fears inspired by the numerous apostles of revolt and sedition, sent by one of our clubs throughout their territory, are they not themselves sufficiently plausible reasons for the feeble arming of the Sardinians, without supposing the design of attacking a powerful empire, which, with one breath, could overturn and destroy them?

The King of Hungary is no doubt strongly enough aroused to undertake the defence of the German princes, whose rights have been compromised by the decrees of the Assembly.* But the Turkish war, the insurrection of Brabant and the Low Countries, the claims of the King of Prussia, do they not dominate Leopold's leisure, and do they leave him time to concern himself with French affairs?

In a word, despite the peaceful views of the Assembly, the writers and the incendiary clubs have done everything necessary, as we would say today, to raise up against us all the European powers; but we still see nothing that indicates that they are thinking of profiting by our

---

* The rights of the German princes in Alsace had been a thorny problem since the night of 4 August. Although Alsace was French territory, the land rights were derived from and guaranteed by the Emperor.

weakness. These powers, especially England and Prussia, are too informed to want, by a declaration of war, to put an end to the cruel divisions that rend the bosom of that unfortunate country, much more deeply than any one enemy could do.

They take good care not to attack us, since we inflict on ourselves all the evils that the ambition and hatred of our cruellest enemies could wish on us. They would not be impolitic enough to divert us from destroying ourselves by our own hands, by presenting us with foreign armies that could reunite us; by wanting to lose in a ruinous war the fruit of the immense profits that the ruin of our trade produces for them; and to run, by the risk of fighting, the danger of losing the preponderance that our political ineffectiveness assures to them.

L'Ami du Roi, No. LX, 30 July 1790.

(ii) *An aggregation of suicides*

Moreover, all of that *forced* homily* seems to me to be perfectly useless. If the foreign princes want to form a league with the throne of France in order to maintain the balance of Europe, it won't be that declaration that will prevent them. If, on the contrary, they want to abandon this country to putrefaction and dissolution, the ministerial jeremiad will have served only too well to confirm them in their wish . . .

The French Revolution is nothing but an aggregation of suicides. *The king killed himself: the clergy killed itself; the nobility killed itself; the Estates-General killed itself; a few more days and the National Assembly will have killed itself.*

Les Actes des Apôtres, vol. II, No. 261, p. 15.

109. Arming for Peace

The desire of the Assembly for peace, but its fear of being caught unprepared, is reflected even in the moderate *Journal de Paris* throughout 1791.

(i) *Imitate the Spartans*

However, if there existed among the princes or among the peoples of Europe any whose madness and iniquity had wanted to attack France at the moment when it had, as it were, made itself sacred by its declaration of peace to the human race and by the example of liberty it gives

* Montmorin's circular of 23 April 1791 in the name of the king, to the French ambassadors in Europe, proclaiming the king's attachment to the Revolution.

to all peoples, you will soon learn what position it will adopt in the
face of such mad and iniquitous onslaughts. It was by arming themselves from head to foot, by covering themselves with iron, that the
Spartans renounced conquests: those who do not believe the genius of
Lycurgus to be a fable, at least believe it a prodigy that had to be
eternally unique: in this regard, at least, it is revived in France.

Le Journal de Paris, 30 January 1791.

(ii) '*No more Pyrenees*'

On news from the department of the Pyrenees interpreted to give
hope that the Revolution might spread to Spain.

This news is as wonderful for Spain as it is for France: is the time very
far off when we can say, but in a different sense from Louis XIV, *there are
no more Pyrenees?*

Le Journal de Paris, 13 February 1791.

(iii) *Threat removed*

You will recall that the National Assembly decreed that enquiries be
made of the Minister of Foreign Affairs for elucidation and definite
facts on the attitude of the European powers towards France. A letter on
this matter from M. de Montmorin, written to the President of the
Diplomatic Committee, was read to the Assembly. We shall print it in
its entirety, because there is no single Frenchman but who should
ponder with the greatest interest over its every word, and because it
gives hope that henceforth France does not have a great deal to dread
from without, and that she has nothing to fear from within.

Le Journal de Paris, 15 March 1791.

(iv) '*No booty other than ashes, corpses and blood*'

To put itself in a state of defence, the department of the Lower-Rhine
asks the National Assembly to send 5,000 *volunteers*. The nation and,
what is the same thing, its representatives, can easily satisfy this request.
All the National Guards of the kingdom are without a doubt *volunteers*;
one can swear to it for those of Metz who shed their blood before
Nancy, for those of Bordeaux who marched with so much ardour to
Montauban. How much greater then must be the strength of feeling
that will inspire every Frenchman to repulse a foreign invasion! Just
let any foreigners interfere in the affairs of a nation that is creating its
constitution and its liberty! While supposing, what we believe impossible, that such great iniquity could have some success, the nation

which has shown itself so proud would be the most vile of nations, if, throughout the length and breadth of its territory, it left as booty for its victorious enemies anything other than ashes, corpses and blood. For the future these are the spoils on which tyrants must sing their *Te Deum*. But the very request of the department of the Lower-Rhine proves how greatly exaggerated are all these ideas of foreign invasions. Would it have asked for only five thousand men, if the danger were very real or very great?

Le Journal de Paris, 30 May 1791.

THREATS FROM ABROAD

Suspicions of the king's plans for escape, and of secret appeals to foreign powers, were unfortunately too well founded; and the so-called Austrian Committee was no mere fantasy of over-anxious democrats. Not until after Varennes, however, did foreign powers openly threaten the security of France.

110. *Le Comité Autrichien*

> This extract is from an article that appeared under the headlines: *Horrible manoeuvres of the Austrian Committee at the Tuileries to bring to life civil war with outside aid—imminent departure of Louis XVI for Saint-Cloud.*

We are assured that there are at present at Barcelona a number of aristocrats and discontented Frenchmen. They work in Spain against the glorious revolution of their country, and get the Court of Madrid to redouble its precautions against French pamphlets. But they are wasting their time, liberty will arrive sooner or later in that country.

There exists, however, a large intelligence system between Paris and Madrid. Numerous couriers pass between them. Among those arrived in Paris from Spain is one who is a great Spanish lord. He travels *incognito* but he is perfectly known and a close watch is kept on his movements.

The talk is of two Spanish squadrons destined, according to the rumour, one to cruise off the coast of Gascony, the other off those of Languedoc and Provence.

The King of Sardinia is raising troops that are suspected to be destined for the invasion of France.

The King of Naples is making preparations as though to bombard Algiers. From all this news, it appears that the movements of these various powers have as their object to aid the French ministry, whose evil intentions are known, to overturn the constitution and to bring about a counter-revolution . . .

Moreover, it is known that MM the ambassadors of Naples, Spain and Sardinia go almost daily to the château of the Tuileries; that they arrive there at ten in the morning and leave only at midnight, often even later; which must naturally lead one to believe that there is something important in these negotiations between our court and theirs, and that their purpose is certainly not to favour the new régime but indeed to restore the old.

It is also certain that there meets at the Tuileries, under the king's wife, a committee composed of M. the Keeper of the Seals, M. de Saint-Priest, M. le comte de Merci, the ambassador of the Emperor, M. the count of Reuss, secret but well-known agent of the Court of Vienna. We are assured that MM the ambassadors of Naples, Spain and Sardinia are sometimes summoned to it.

This committee could be called the 'Austrian Committee', because they say that the decision has been taken there, against the best interests of France, to renew the alliance with the Court of Vienna, and to try to make the Low Countries return to Austrian domination. M. de Montmorin is not a party to these political arrangements; furthermore, he is in bad favour with the queen.

Les Révolutions de France et de Brabant,
No. 18, pp. 137–40.

111. Tyranny on the March

You are walking on the edge of a volcano; you know the peace of the King of Prussia and of Leopold. In the first place they only pretended to take up arms against one another in order the better to deceive you, in order the better to disguise their combined movements against you. Do not doubt it, this attempt is part of the Austrian policy of the Tuileries, where are to be found the true allies of these crowned puppets; and there are the royal displays that have always been used to beguile the people! Soon you will see them descend upon Brabant, in order to conceal from you again the real object against which they want to strike; for tyrants never pursue a straight path. Already Belgian liberty is at its last extremity: the cannon of the imperial troops has pounded its legions into the dust; terror is at the gates of Brussels, and the hideous standard of despotism flies over the ramparts of Namur. Internecine divisions have been fomented among them only in order to weaken them and to massacre them. What a lesson for you, brave Parisians! patriot soldiers! But, with Brabant conquered, will you wait to see this torrent of vandals flood the kingdom? Do victorious troops lack any pretexts? If need be, the aristocrats will well be able to furnish them! Know then the height of their treachery! The King of Prussia, this fact is definite, under the prompting of our ministers, has just written to the French king, to demand from him, as Imperial Vicar, the redress of wrongs caused by the decrees of the National Assembly, to several German princes, who have possessions in Alsace. He says that he will not be able to exempt himself from upholding their rights! what an execrable ministerial trick! Notice how this leader of assassins does not recognise the nation's sovereignty, and that he condescends to treat only with its delegate. Why then ignore it? You can well expect, in a very short time, the inevitable scourge of war.

L'Orateur du peuple, No. XII: Buchez and Roux, VI, 320–21.

112. Beware the Prophets of Peace

The flight of the king was thought to herald imminent invasion. A wave of panic swept the country. On 29 June, Bouillé, who was to have escorted Louis across the border, sent a threatening letter to the Assembly. Here Hébert echoes the people's fear.

Yes, damn it, I am leaving; adieu furnaces,* adieu writings, it's all over; there's no time for trifles when the fatherland is in danger. God's thunder! Thousands of brave chaps flying to the defence of the frontiers and yet the Père Duchesne remains at his fire-side? No, damn it, quick, bring my big sword, pistols and carbine. Eh! Come along then, damn it! Hurry it up there, my bag, my cartridge pouch: and above all don't forget my pipe and tobacco.

'Where are you off to in such a hurry then?' a blackguard of an appeaser [*endormeur*] . . . will ask me. 'Do you think there is going to be war?–What do you mean, damn it, do I think? Is there any doubt about it?–False alarm, Père Duchesne, the foreign powers have no intention of attacking us.–In the name of the devil am I not to believe what I see?' But it is for a long time now that I have been waiting for this stab in the back; is it possible to believe that all the jackasses called

* The Père Duchesne was always characterised as a dealer in furnaces.

kings and princes can coldly contemplate a Revolution that kicks them into the gutter, that they don't fear that what is going on here will come to their own country and that they would not shift their arses or lift a finger to bowl over our constitution?

> *Le Père Duchesne*, No. 62: cited in J. Godechot,
> *La pensée révolutionnaire 1780–1799*, pp. 230–31.

113. Search for Alliance?

M. Talleyrand-Périgord, former Bishop of Autun, departed from here, last Tuesday, for England. It is generally believed that he has been entrusted with special negotiations with the London Court. There is no doubt that an alliance with a nation which has been made the first power in the world by the energy of its government and by the spirit of liberty animating and directing it would be very desirable for us; the success of the Revolution would no longer be in doubt with such an ally; and it is most natural to show some confidence in the only government in Europe that, by a remarkable singularity, has maintained down to the present, in regard to our Revolution, a perfect neutrality.

> *Le Journal de Paris*, 21 January 1792.

FRANCE DECLARES WAR

The documents presented here are brief extracts from the many pages of speeches and articles on the necessity, advisability or otherwise, of declaring war. This issue dominated every other in the Legislative Assembly from the time in October 1791 when Brissot first preached his 'crusade against the crowned heads of Europe'.

114. Opinions

(i) *Robespierre—caution*

M. Robespierre

It seems that those who desired to provoke war adopted this view only because they did not pay sufficient attention to the nature of the war that we shall undertake and to the circumstances in which we today find ourselves. We put our efforts into attacking the enemies of the Constitution, because we believe that we have at hand the means of directing the forces, because we think that the courage of the nation will be guided by pure hands, and the troops directed in an open and loyal fashion: if that were so, it would be necessary to declare war on those who would like to support our émigrés, and their protectors would no longer exist. But considering the difficulty of entrusting yourselves to the agents of the executive power, it would be better to wait for the enemy to provoke the war. I shall not deal now with the question of dictatorship; I am dealing with government merely as it is, and I leave it to circumstances to fetch the extraordinary measures that the safety of the people could demand. Until then, I prefer to keep quiet: and I do not in any way seek to anticipate events. I say then that to know which is the better course of action, it is necessary to examine what kind of war can threaten us; will this be a war of one nation against other nations? Will it be a war of a king against other kings? No, it will be a war of all the enemies of the French Constitution against the French Revolution. These enemies, who are they? They are of two kinds; the enemies within and the enemies without. Is it reasonable to look for the court and the agents of the executive power among the internal enemies? I cannot in any way resolve that question; but I will observe that the external enemies, the French rebels, and those who could be counted among their supporters, claim that they are only the defenders of the court of France and of the French nobility.

I should like to examine a little what has passed until now, from the time of the minister who wanted to annihilate the National Assembly, to the last of his successors. . . . Can we fear to find the internal enemies of the French Revolution, and to find among these enemies the court and the agents of the executive power? If you reply in the affirmative, I shall say to you: To whom will you entrust the conduct of this war? to the agents of the executive power? By this act you will abandon the security of the empire to those who wish to destroy you. It follows from all this that what we have most to fear is war . . . War gives opportunity for terror, danger, retaliation, treason and finally loss. The people grow weary. Is it necessary, they will say, to sacrifice the public treasury for empty titles? Would we be any worse off with counts, marquises, etc.? The parties come together; they slander the National Assembly, if it is severe; they blame it for the misfortunes of the war. Finally they capitulate.

Le Journal des débats des Amis de la Constitution, 13–14 December 1791: Buchez and Roux, XII, 406–9.

(ii) *Brissot—consummation*

M. Brissot

'The question under discussion is to know whether we should attack the German princes, who support the emigrants, or whether we should await their invasion . . .

For six months and ever since the Revolution I have been considering which side to take. Even the most cunning sorcery on the part of our adversaries will not in any way see me abandon it. It is by force of reason and fact that I am persuaded that a people that has conquered liberty after ten centuries of slavery has need of war. It needs war to consolidate its victory, it needs it to purge itself of the vices of despotism, it needs it to dispel from its bosom the men who could corrupt it. Thank heaven for the way it has favoured you and for the fact that it has given you time to settle your Constitution. You have to chastise the rebels, you have the force to do it; be resolved then to do it. . . . For two years, France has exhausted all the peaceful means to bring back the rebels into its bosom; all the attempts, all the requests have been fruitless; they persist in their revolt; foreign princes persist in supporting them; can we hesitate to attack them? our honour, our public credit, the need to moralise and to consolidate our revolution, everything makes it imperative; for would not France be dishonoured if, the Constitution being finished, it tolerated a handful of dissidents who insulted its constituted authorities; would it not be dishonoured if it endured outrages that a despot would not have put up with for a fortnight? A Louis XIV declared war on Spain, because his ambassador had been insulted by that of Spain; and we who are free would hesitate for a moment!

What do you want them to think of it? That we are incapable of acting against foreign powers, or that the rebels are getting the better of us? This they will regard as the result of our anarchy. Meanwhile what will be the effect of that war: it will either avenge us or make us the object of opprobrium of every nation. We must avenge ourselves by destroying that horde of brigands, or consent to see perpetuated among us the factions, the conspiracies and the conflagrations and to see the insolence of our aristocrats become bolder than ever. They trust in the army of Coblenz; it is from there that stems the obstinacy of our fanatics. Do you want to destroy in a single blow the aristocracy, the refractory, the discontented: then destroy Coblenz. The leader of the nation will be forced to rule by the Constitution, because he will see that his safety lies only in his attachment to the Constitution, and in directing his step nowhere but in accordance with it.'

There is a demand for the printing of M. Brissot's speech. M. Robespierre proposes the postponement of the printing until the end of the debate; after a long discussion, printing was ordered.

Ibid: Buchez and Roux, XII, 410–11.

(iii) *Marat–deception*

Here at last is war declared against the French by the powers sworn to oppose liberty. Now who does not see that all these so-called ministerial negotiations with foreign courts had no other purpose than to deceive the nation and to gain time, until all their batteries were ready and in position. Who does not see that all these warlike preparations, ordered by the Assembly, had no other purpose than to lull the nation into a false sense of security? Who does not see that all these references to the executive power, the denunciations, the fraudulent ministers, and these complaints of the citizen soldiers, crammed up at the frontiers, and left without munitions, without weapons, without clothing, without pay, had no other purpose than to leave the country defenceless; to leave the state a prey to the machinations of the court, to the enterprises of the fugitive conspirators, to the attacks of foreign satellites?

Will war break out? Everyone believes it will. We are assured that this opinion has finally prevailed in the cabinet, following the representations of the sieur Mottié, who no doubt has made it out to be the only way of distracting the nation from its internal affairs so as to occupy it with foreign ones, to make it forget internecine dissension in favour of events abroad; to squander the national wealth on military preparations, instead of using it to liberate the state and to help the people; to crush the state under the burden of taxation, and to slaughter the army at the front as well as the citizen army, by leading them to butchery, under pretext of defending the frontiers of the Empire. There is no doubt that, in urging the monarch to negotiate no longer and to order the opening of the campaign, he does so because he regards this as a way in which to end his career honourably, if there is no other means of regaining the confidence of the nation by new acts of seduction and by his hypocritical devotion to the cause of liberty.

Led astray by the captious speeches of Brissot, of Lemontey, of Girardin, of Lacroix, of Gouvion, of Buvras, and other rascals sold to the court; seduced by a false picture of the national strength; intoxicated by the fumes of Gallican boasting, the people seem no less anxious than its implacable enemies to have war. Three years ago I pointed out that this would be the last resource of the counter-revolutionaries and since then I have not ceased in my efforts to destroy the various measures taken by the cabinet to bring it about.

L'Ami du peuple, No. 634, 19 April 1792.

(iv) *Durosoi—vengeance and delivery*

While waiting for the moment when the princes and the French warriors of every order can avenge their country and deliver their king, they wish to call down on their arms the protection of the God of Armies. A great number of venerable priests who have escaped their hangman, have arrived in Flanders and in Brabant, overcome by most abject want and poverty. The numerous cantonments of Ath and Enghien have *unanimously* decided to receive in their midst these venerable victims of the unsolicited scourge of the French Church. Each of the French *chevaliers* wanted to be included in the voluntary and individual tax levied among them to come to the aid of the Ministers of the Altar outlawed by the *Fauchet*, the *Pontard*, the *Gobel*, the *Dumouchel*, by all the mob of the new *Mathan*. We are even now expecting many others of these exiles: if the *chevaliers* were able to find out the date of their arrival, they would walk at their head, holding in their hand the white panache, symbol of the purity of their conscience and of their vows for France and for their king.

Finally, never has the emigration been so large: the peasants, the artisans hasten in crowds to the post of honour. They come to swell the host of Frenchmen, faithful to their sovereign as well as to their religion.

La Gazette de Paris, 17 February 1792.

(v) *A foreigner*

Of a series of letters on how to avoid war published in the supplements of the *Journal de Paris* the fourth was returned unpublished, the proprietors deeming it 'useless to discuss the means of avoiding war when war is already solemnly declared'. The author then changed his tack and wrote the article from which the following extract is taken.

For the present let us see the motives that forced you to this and how you have been prepared to justify it.

There is no point in my repeating here what I have already said or what has been demonstrated for every man versed in the political dispositions of Europe; namely, that no one wanted to make war on you, and that in order not to have it, it was enough for you not to have begun it. The facts support this assertion; it is now well known that, not only did the government of Brussels not think of attacking you, but even that it was in no way ready to defend itself: it was with a great deal of haste that they got together the troops with which your attacks on Mons and Tournay were repulsed. When General Beaulieu heard that you had begun to move on Valenciennes, he was forced to send post-haste to look for cannon at Brussels. This fact is definite, and such lack of foresight can only be explained by the little likelihood there was that you would take your madness to the point of actually commencing hostilities; in effect, it is only since the installation of your present government that people began to think that it was possible.

Your declaration of war, however, seemed so strange here, that I hardly dare tell you what direction it gave to the suspicious; it was thought that those who had provoked it with so much ardour were in alliance with your most exalted émigrés, who, impatient with the fact that the Courts of Vienna and Berlin were not fulfilling the part they wanted, and despairing of bringing them to it, had thought to get you to attack them. In order to do this, it was said that they turned to men who never completely closed their ear to certain proposals; they found them all the more ready to listen to their plans, since an increase of violence and confusion in France fitted in very well with their own intentions. Thus, it was said that they found a double advantage in serving your émigrés; hence, it is added, the overthrow of the old ministry, the composition of the present one, and everything that followed from it. You well know that I do not attach any great importance to these rumours that I have mentioned other than as proof of the astonishment that your conduct produced. For this extraordinary event it is easy enough to look for bizarre causes, but let us pursue our examination of the means taken by you to prepare yourselves for war. . . .

If I cast my eyes over your conduct abroad, it seems to me even more strange; you adopted towards all the powers of Europe (England excepted) a tone, not of dignity, but of despotism, which Louis XIV did not dare to adopt even when he was at the height of his glory. In your clubs you daily insult the sovereigns, and even do so in the very heart of your Assembly; and whenever some insult can be made heard, some violent declamation against them, there are endless cheers and applause, and shouts demanding the printing of the nonsense that has been circulated. Such are at the least the scenes whose descriptions we read daily in your official papers.

Almost all the courts are filled with your emissaries who bestir themselves to spread your newspapers and your Jacobin pamphlets; believe me, Monsieur, that all these efforts, all these movements have no other effect than to irritate us against your nation, which I see with sorrow is often confused with the vile and damnable intriguers employed by your factions. Your journalists and your emissaries will for the future receive a cold hearing; the position into which you have put yourselves is the most powerful antidote to the poison that they seek to spread.

Supplement to *Le Journal de Paris*, 2 June 1792.

DEFEAT, DEFECTION AND REPERCUSSIONS

The tide of war again turned against France soon after she was faced by the combined forces of Austria, Prussia, Britain, Holland, Spain, Naples, Rome, Venice and Sardinia in the spring of 1793. On 5 March, the French general, Miranda, withdrew from the blockade of Maestricht, merely on hearing of the enemies' approach: on the 8th Danton and Lacroix, commissioners of the army near Belgium, told the Convention of the rout and accused the generals of not having carried out their duty.

Dumouriez, who was already demonstrating anti-revolutionary sentiments, suffered defeats at Neerwinden (18 March) and Louvain (21 March) and then entered into negotiations with the enemy. He announced on the 28th that he would march on Paris and restore the Constitution of 1791. Two days later the Convention ordered his arrest. The deputies sent to arrest him were themselves arrested by Dumouriez and handed over to the enemy. Failing to coerce his troops to march on Paris he crossed to the enemy on 3 April.

As an associate of the Girondins, Dumouriez' defeats and treachery discredited them. Before his treason was clearly established, Marat was boldly announcing it, but his claims were ridiculed in the Girondin press. However, the optimism of the Girondins was no substitute for reality when the truth was made known.

115. Prophecy Fulfilled

The war into which we are entering and which no doubt more wisdom, more sense of value, of prudence, would have avoided, but which, under whatever pretext our enemies colour it, is no other than the continuation of the ancient struggle of the nobles and kings against the people, this war is going to open a new source for intrigues, plots, and passions, perhaps to the aggrandisement of that league of confraternities that controls France.

When such congregations exist, the views of their leaders are cast aside as personal opinions when they are unsuccessful; but in cases of success, the opposite process happens, they are all taken to be the views of the society. Thus let us not doubt that, whatever happens, it is their interests that will benefit by it. They will so arrange things as to ensure their own success in the general success or defeat. Our gains or our losses will increase either their power or their credit, and they will continue to call themselves insolently the French People.

If the war is a disaster, they will say: we saw what was going to happen, we did not want the war, and they will quote some nonsense from one of their learned men.

If it is successful, they will say: it was we who made the war; and they will again quote something or other.

If the war is successful; if French impetuosity, inspired by the natural enthusiasm of men who fight for the liberty of their country, should win some immediate victory, then what cries! what suspicions! what conspiracies to be discovered! This victory will not have been won over the enemy, but over the Constitution; M. Lafayette will be marching against Paris at the head of his army; and Caesar and the Rubicon will fill the pages of a thousand eloquent pamphlets.

If, on the contrary, the indiscipline of our troops, their disunity and various other causes shall lead first to defeat, there will be other cries, other fears; accusations daily; our soldiers will have been betrayed; our generals will be traitors, sold out to the enemies, sold out to the court; it will be necessary to make sure of the one, to imprison the other etc.

Notice that at the present time, when war has not yet begun, most of these things have already been said.

André CHÉNIER

Supplement to *Le Journal de Paris*, 29 April 1792.

116. Not by Terror, but by Hatred of Tyrants

Paris: 8 March 1793

Is it by fearful panic, is it from a treacherous intention, that the evil-wishers take pleasure in exaggerating the bad news? This evening it was deliberately spread abroad, in the groups, in the Sections, that Liège and Brussels had fallen, that the enemy was marching towards France, that Dumouriez was lost . . . and this news was followed by exhortations to get rid of the traitors, to cut off their heads, etc.

Good citizens cannot be too much on their guard against these horrible insinuations. In a position to know the truth, we can affirm, according to men who knew the facts, that if Liège is evacuated, Liège is not taken (at least nothing is known of it); that if the enemy can march on Liège, it can also, by that march, expose itself to defeat, and thus there is still hope for the city. We can affirm, according to experts, that it is impossible for the enemy to break through into Belgium. We can finally affirm that the enemy is not as large as they say, that it is inferior to our army, that Dumouriez is not at all cut off and continues his expedition to Holland.

No, it is certainly not by terror that recruitment must be encouraged, but by hatred of tyrants, by the need to crush them in a campaign. Terror! does it not dishonour free men? and, from this point of view, ought we not to regard with indignation the Municipality's orders to close the theatres for this evening? Is it then a retreat that fills you with consternation?

> *Le Patriote français*, No. MCCCV: Buchez and Roux, XXV, 14–15.

117. Treason of the Generals

(i) *Marat comments*

The painful news announced by our commissioners* is unfortunately only too well founded. I hear at this very time that Miranda's advance guard has been sacrificed by the treachery of the generals, Laneau, [Miagenski] and Stengel, the last of whom has emigrated. We have lost at least three thousand men to the enemy's steel, and twelve pieces of cannon.

Far from lessening our courage this set-back must increase it and must make us be doubly on the watch; all good citizens must unite to demand trial of the generals who betrayed the country as well as the removal of Beurnonville,† for having left these traitors at the head of the army. Our plan of campaign must also be changed so that we go onto the defensive: unless we follow the strategy of seizing the Dutch dikes–a surprise attack that would have soon put an end to this war, whose beginning has already been disastrous.

> *Le Journal de la République française*, No. 142, 9 March 1793.

(ii) *Exaggeration*

Today, since early morning, the avenues of the Convention, and especially the terrace of the Feuillants, were covered with the pro-claimers of massacres. Marat's newspaper, which was published with this title: *great treason of our generals*, was the subject of the harangues. They spoke only of cutting off the head of the Minister of War, of the generals, of a section of the representatives of the people, of the journa-lists, who don't go along with Marat; and it must be vowed that Duhem's motion had singularly prepared people's minds. Pétion, who contributed

---

* Danton and Lacroix.
† Minister of War and friend of Dumouriez.

most to the revolution of 10 August, whilst struggling courageously against the treachery of the court–the republican, the popular Pétion had been pursued by more than two hundred scoundrels. Beurnonville was insulted and threatened.

These fatal attitudes were strengthened by the false news that was deliberately spread around. It was not enough to announce, like the Municipality, the capture of Liège and of Brussels, for they spread the rumour of the desertion of Dumouriez, of the majority of the generals, and of the siege of Valenciennes. They announced (and the plan was actually formed for this) that they were going to thrash the general, sound the tocsin, and fire the alarm cannon.

What will be the consequence of these horrible signs? Republicans, it depends on you. When will you learn to recognise your own strength? When will you put your courage to use? When do you want to save the country, and liberty, without which there can be no country? For us, at least, we await events with concern for the public good, without any for ourselves. Who is the good citizen who could dread the fate of the Barnevelds or of the Sydneys?

> *Le Patriote français*, No. MCCCVI, 9 March 1793:
> Buchez and Roux, XXV, 26–27.

(iii) *Another prophecy fulfilled?*

On 11 and 12 March Dumouriez defied orders from the Convention and then accused them of being responsible for the loss of Holland. In Belgium he reversed many revolutionary reforms, and when met by Danton and Lacroix, who were sent out to reprimand him, two days after Neerwinden, he remained obdurate.

Finally, when he entered Belgium, and when, instead of putting arms into the hands of the citizens against their oppressors, he tried only to maintain the creatures of the Emperor in their positions, and to create the people's representative assembly from enfeoffed aristocrats, titled nobles and upper clergy, I saw in him only a conspirator sold out to the Vienna office, as well as to Berlin; a traitor who sacrificed the liberty of the Belgians to his own ambition, an atrocious scoundrel who made the treasure and armies of France service his own advancement, a guilty ambitious type who sold his country in order to be duke of Brabant.

Since the death of the tyrant, he has aimed his sights higher: he wants to be sovereign of a united Belgium and of Holland; he has discarded his mask, and his crimes appear in the open–despite the veil under which his accomplices in the Convention are still forced to keep them . . .

[If Dumouriez turns the tables on the commissioners sent to arrest him], it will put the seal on the prediction that I made about him, namely, that contained in my paper of 13 October 1792. Here it is.

'Perfidious leaders, atrocious plotters, you hope to cover your criminal plots with a hypocritical veil: but you will not escape from the penetrating glances of the *Ami du peuple*, he has torn aside your mask, he will print on your brows the stamp of opprobrium; he will bring you to the altars of justice; to escape your punishment he will force you to flee, if you do not take the wise course of anticipating the storm.

'A hundred to one that d'Harville, Chazot and Dumouriez, emigrate before next March.'

Le Publiciste de la République française, No. 148,
20 March 1793.

(iv) *An Answer by* Le Patriote

Paris, 21 March

While they were reading at the National Convention the letters that confirmed the success of Dumouriez, Marat, still the journalist, peddled from the terrace of the Feuillants one issue with this title: *great treason of General Dumouriez*. The indignation was such that they chased away the newspaper-sellers. Marat appeared a short time after and, on that very terrace, where he was carried in triumph ten days ago, he saw himself hissed, insulted and even threatened. Citizens, you have forgotten yourselves; if Marat was only a vile libeller, only a cowardly conspirator, only a disgrace to the human race; if, in a word, he was only *Marat*, I would say to you don't waste your hisses on him; do not honour him with your indignation, do not stir up the filth into which he has plunged. But citizens, Marat, the real *Marat* that is, is a representative of the people; the hisses against him are practically a crime, threats are a crime. Let Marat's only penalty be for him to hear passers-by say: Look out, here comes Marat.

Le Patriote français, No. MCCCXVII: Buchez and
Roux, XXV, 154.

118. Paris must Defend itself

This is from a speech by Robespierre reported in the Jacobins' official newspaper following Dumouriez' treason. The relationship between war and the Terror is clearly shown.

A revolutionary army must be raised; this army must be composed of all the patriots, of all the sans-culottes; the faubourgs must constitute the strength and nucleus of this army. I will not say that we must sharpen our swords to kill the *calotins*; they are enemies beneath our contempt, and these fanatics would desire nothing better than an excuse to cry out.

We must mercilessly hunt from our Sections all those who have been distinguished by their moderation; we must disarm, not just the nobles and the *calotins*, but all doubtful citizens, all the intriguers, all those who have proved to lack public spirit: measures have been taken at Marseilles. Dumouriez has to arrive in Paris before the battalions from Marseilles; that is why he hastens his march. Paris threatened must defend itself. There is no one who could oppose these measures without declaring himself a bad citizen.

The time has come to compromise with the despots or to die for liberty. I have taken my stand; let all the citizens imitate me. (Applause.) Let all Paris arm itself, let the Sections and the people be on their guard, let the Convention declare itself the people. I declare that as long as the post is in the hands of the counter-revolutionaries; as long as treacherous newspapers, which praise Dumouriez, corrupt public opinion, there will be no hope of safety. But the spirit of liberty will triumph; patriotism and the people must win and win everywhere. (Loud applause.)

Le Journal du Club des Jacobins, No. 388:
Buchez and Roux, XXV, 272–73.

THE REVOLUTION AND EUROPE

Success in the war presented France with new problems. Strategic necessity and political idealism demanded that France advance the war beyond her own frontiers. Moreover, could she ignore the call of patriots demanding release from clerical and monarchical despotism? Already she had released Avignon from papal domination and Alsace from the claims of the German princes. Now Savoy and Nice, part of the kingdom of Sardinia, asked that they be incorporated into France. After some hesitation Savoy was annexed on 27 November 1792 and Nice on 31 January 1793.

But what of Belgium and beyond? What if the patriots were only a minority? What if the liberated countries objected to French reforms? And who was to pay the cost of this liberty? It was soon apparent that the armed missionaries were not always welcome, that the 'liberated' did not always have the proper republican hatred of kings, and even those who were at first favourable to French intervention objected when it turned out that they were financing French wars. The liberators soon appeared as conquerors; temptation and disillusionment turned the idealism of the opening crusades into simple exploitation.

119. A Word from Thomas Paine

> This is the concluding part to one of the many letters printed in the Girondin press by the famous publicist of the American war of independence, now a naturalised Frenchman and deputy at the Convention.

The scene that now opens before France will stretch well beyond its territory. All nations are going to become its allies, and every court its enemy. It is now the case of all peoples against kings. The terror that seized the despots has secretly given rise to this confederation among the crowned brigands, and the real reason for the attacks on France is to snuff out the internal disturbances that they themselves fear in their own states.

In advancing on this stage, a greater one than any on which any nation has ever shone, let us say to those who are alarmed: Be calm. Let us punish by spreading the light rather than taking vengeance. Let us begin this new era by unfolding its grandeur, its generosity; and let us think only to maintain unity and to win hearts, in order to ensure our success. Your fellow citizen,

Thomas Paine
La Chronique de Paris, No. 303, 23 October 1792, p. 1183.

120. Pure as the Cause of Liberty

(i) *Savoy*

Savoy asks to become part of France. The National Convention must not close its eyes to this honorable proposition. We want in no way to bind peoples by fire and flame, by right of might. But because a rich citizen has sworn to have no slaves in his house, do you forbid him to adopt an abandoned child who has been ill-treated by a barbarous master and who now throws himself into his arms?

Savoy if left to itself would sooner or later be crushed by the Piedmontese who, in league with the tyrants of Bern and Austria, would descend on her and bury her under her own débris . . . Switzerland proposes to add her to the Helvetic Confederation and to make of her a fourth canton. I will add that Savoy, eldest daughter of the King of Sardinia, has no national debt; she emerges a virgin from her mountains and brings us rich hope [*de riches espérances*] in offering us her hand. It is no small matter to add, by a single decree, 3 millions a year to our finances, 10,000 men to our front-line troops, 40,000 volunteers to guard our frontiers; an expanse of territory to exploit by commerce, manufacture and the arts; to have the Alps as a barrier to the Republic, and Mont Blanc as pedestal for the tricolor, standard of liberty.

Le Patriote français, No. 1172, 24 October 1792, p. 472.

(ii) *Nice*

The Convention has decreed, on the proposal of its committees of war and diplomacy, that emissaries appointed from its midst should be sent to Nice and neighbouring districts in order to gather information on the excesses that have been committed and in order to devise means of having their authors promptly brought to justice.

The Convention wants the conduct of the French armies to be as pure as the cause of liberty for which they are fighting; no people will have to reproach it with having tolerated excesses or disorders which would not have been an inevitable consequence of the war, and which it would have been within its power to prevent, or at least to make good. Even the most dedicated enemies of liberty will only have to suffer penalties demanded by justice or enjoined by the law of reprisals.

La Chronique de Paris, No. 330, 19 November 1792, p. 1293.

121. A Lesson for the People of Europe

With the execution of Louis, France lost most of the sympathy that it still had in Europe. The revolutionaries tried not to see it this way.

Today there has been decided that great truth that the prejudices of so many centuries had stifled; today we have just convinced ourselves that a king is only a man, and that no man is above the laws. Capet is no more. Peoples of Europe! Peoples of the earth! Look at the thrones, you can see that they are but dust!

France has just given a great example to the peoples and a great lesson to kings for the good of mankind. They can both profit by it!

Le Républicain, 22 January 1793: Walter, 286–87.

122. Conquest and Devastation

Let our victorious armies pursue their conquests into Belgium, and not mess around with trifles by planting in every town a tree of liberty that will never take root in that ungrateful country: let stupid Belgians who lent a hand to the infamous Dumouriez to massacre the good chaps who were fighting to set them free, let these vile soldiers be disarmed; let all the shops in the towns we are about to reduce, serve to clothe our battalions; let all the property of the rich, the gold and silver of the churches, compensate us for the cost of the war. When we have made a vast desert from our frontiers to Brussels, let our booty-laden battalions return to our war-torn towns (*villes de guerre*) to spend the winter to await firm-footed, until next spring, the satellites of the despots–that is if they again take it into their heads to come and attack us.

Le Père Duchesne, No. 306 (mid October 1793).

123. A British View of the Revolution

(i) *On the occasion of the fall of the Bastille*

REBELLION
AND
CIVIL WAR
IN
FRANCE

They [the present violent commotions] began on the Monday morning, and have continued unremittingly ever since. It cannot now be said that the present violences are the effect of a mere unlicensed mob. The concurrent voice of the nation demands a new constitution, nor do we foresee that any power can resist it.

On Monday the people joined in greater numbers than they had hitherto done, and seemed determined to be revenged for the insult they said was offered to them, by removing M. Necker. Previous thereto the mob had destroyed several of the toll-gates belonging to the Government in the vicinity of Paris, as well as the books belonging to the Excise Officers by which very large entries of goods passed without paying the revenue, and every part of the metropolis exhibited a scene of riot.

The regular troops held for the protection of Paris were persuaded to join the people; they were encamped in the Champ de Mars, to the number of 5,000 men, and marched to the Hotel of Invalids, a building in the outskirts of the city. The Invalids joined the rest, and brought away all the great guns, and other ammunition, belonging to the Hospital. With this reinforcement the people then attacked the Bastille Prison, which they soon made themselves masters of, and released all the state prisoners confined there, among whom was Lord Mazarine, an Irish Nobleman, who has been confined for debt near 30 years. The prisoners in the other goals [*sic*] were freed in like manner, except such as were under sentence of death, whom they hung up within the prisons. This seemed to argue a premeditated design, as well as great caution.

On attacking the Bastille they secured the Governor, the MARQUIS DE L'AUNEY, and the Commandant of the Garrison, whom they conducted to the Place de Grève, the place of public execution, where they beheaded them, stuck their heads on tent poles, and carried them in triumph to the Palais-Royal, and through the streets of Paris. The MARQUIS DE L'AUNEY was particularly odious to the people, from the nature of his employment, and it is therefore no wonder that he should be singled out amongst the first victims of their resentment.

The Times, Monday 20 July 1789, p. 2, col. 3–4.

This spirit of LIBERTY, which so long lay in a state of death, oppressed by the hand of power, received its first spark of returning animation, by the incautious and impolitic assistance afforded to America. The French soldier on his return from that emancipated continent, told a glorious tale to his countrymen – 'That the arms of France had given freedom to THIRTEEN UNITED STATES, and planted the STANDARD OF LIBERTY on the battlements of New York and Philadelphia.' The idea of such a noble deed became a general object of admiration, the facets of a similar state were eagerly longed for by all ranks of people, and the *vox populi* had this form of argument. – 'If France gives freedom to America, why should she not unchain the arbitrary fetters which bind her own people?'

Such we may venture to say was the original cause of that important struggle, to the event of which surrounding empires look with impatient anxiety–for the victory of the people must seriously affect the different interests of all Europe.

The Times, Tuesday 21 July 1789, p. 2, col. 4.

(ii) *On the occasion of the execution of the king*

By an express which arrived yesterday morning from Messrs. Fector and Co. at Dover, we learn the following particulars of the king's execution. . . .

After the execution, the people threw their hats up in the air, and cried out *Vive la Nation!* Some of them endeavoured to seize the body, but it was removed by a strong guard to the Temple, and the lifeless remains of the king were excepted from those outrages which His Majesty had experienced during his life.

The king was attended on the scaffold by an Irish priest as his confessor, not choosing to be accompanied by one who had taken the national oath. He was dressed in a brown great coat, white waistcoat and black breeches, and his hair was powdered. . . .

Long in the habit of supporting the virtues of this unhappy victim of savage republicans; and, steady in persevering to declare, THAT HIS HIGHEST AMBITION WAS THE HAPPINESS OF HIS PEOPLE, we hold ourselves justified, from the universal indignation which has marked this last act of cruelty exercised against him, to pay our sorrowing tribute to his memory, and join with the united millions of Europe, in supplicating the wrath of heaven, and the vengeance of mankind, to extend to his unnatural murderers the most exemplary punishment.

Posterity, in condemning these infamous judges who have sacrificed Louis to the fury and ambition of the vilest of men, will extend their censures yet further; and in the warmth of virtuous indignation, will not refrain from blasting the memory of that minister [Necker], who to gratify a selfish vanity, directed the royal victim to make the first step towards that precipice, from the brink of which he is now precipitated.

Posterity will condemn those members of the Constituent Assembly, who allured by the meteor of false philosophy, madly burst asunder the bonds of popular subordination; tore down the pillars of monarchy and religion, and left Louis defenceless, forsaken, and abandoned to those hordes of Monsters, who, under the different appellations of Legislative Assemblies, Clubs, and Sections, have inflicted upon their miserable victim a thousand agonising deaths and apprehensions before they delivered him up to the axe of the executioner. . . .

Unquestionably, the blood of this unfortunate monarch will invoke vengeance on his murderers. This is not the cause of monarchs only.

229

it is the cause of every nation on the face of the earth. All potentates owe it to their individual honour, but still more strongly to the happiness of their people, collectively to crush these savage regicides in their dens, who aim at the ruin of all nations, and the destruction of all governments. It is not by feeble efforts only that we can hope to exterminate these inhuman wretches. Experience has proved them to be ineffectual. Armed with fire and sword, we must penetrate into the recesses of this land of blood and carnage. Louis might still have been living had neighbouring princes acted with that energy and expedition which the case required.

The Times, 25 January 1793, p. 2, col. 3–4.

PART SIX

Ideals

The previous Parts have indicated the generation of opposites and clash of contradictions that characterised so much of the reforming zeal of the revolutionaries; in the realm of ideas this was no less so. The early years of the Revolution stressed the universal rights of man and the doctrine of progress. Heaven was to be brought from the hereafter to the here and now. Evil in every form was to be eradicated from the earth. The opponents of the Revolution blamed the new 'philosophy' for the turmoil they claimed was ruining France, and they commented cynically on the reforms that were destroying their vested interests or cherished ideals. Yet the reformers at the Assembly were essentially practical men, but blinded by enthusiasm for a new ideal to the value of tradition and forced by events to forgo gradual change. The political reforms of the constitution-makers were the least successful. Of other progressive measures much was destroyed by war. War, too, gave rise to the feeling of nationalism that was to curse later centuries and which was so much at odds with the basic universalism and egalitarianism of the Revolution.

The French press of the early Revolution abounds in the expression of ideals that ranged from one extreme to another; issues which are still live ones today were then debated furiously; others have since been absorbed into everyday life; still others have been banished to the limbo of mere chimera.

Some idea of the breadth and depth of this free interplay of opinion may be judged by the extracts which follow.

THE NEW SOCIETY

Racial equality, equality of the sexes, regeneration of the soul and purification of the morals of society were just some of the hopes held by some revolutionaries of what would be achieved after the sweeping away of the old abuses.

124. Progress

(i) *France is free*

In this extract from Desmoulins' pamphlet *La France libre* the writer has been listing the evils of each of France's kings. In July 1789 he sees the very principle of monarchy struck at its roots and looks forward to the ultimate republic.

How changed is the face of that empire! with what gigantic steps have we moved towards liberty! Thirsty with a thirst of twelve centuries, we have flung ourselves towards its source as soon as it was pointed out to us. A few years ago, I was looking everywhere for republican spirits; I despaired of not having been born a Greek or Roman, and yet I could not persuade myself to depart from my native land, from the nation which, even in my servitude, I could not prevent myself from loving and esteeming. But today it is foreigners who are going to regret not being Frenchmen! We shall outdo those Englishmen so proud of their constitution, and who used to insult our slavery. No more magistrates for money, no more nobility for money, no more hereditary nobility, no more financial privileges, no more hereditary privileges, no more *lettres de cachet*, no more decrees, no more arbitrary prohibitions, no more secret criminal procedures. Freedom of trade, freedom of conscience, freedom of writing and freedom of speech. No more oppressive ministers, no more predatory ministers, no more vice-despots of intendants, no more trials by commissioners, no more Richelieu, no more Terrai, no more Laubardemont, no more Catharine de Médicis, no more Isabella of Bavaria, no more Charles IX, no more Louis XI. No more of those sales of offices and honours at the house of Dubarry, at Polignac's. All the robbers' dens will be destroyed, that of the informer, and that of the attorney, those of the speculators and those of the monopolists, those of the ushers-snuffers and those of the ushers-blowers. The breaking of the Council that has broken so much. The extinction of the *parlements* that enregistered so much, decreed so much, destroyed so much, and so much lorded it over us; let both their name and their memory perish. Suppression of the arbitrary tribunal of the marshals of France. Suppression of the tribunals of exception, suppression of seigneurial justices. One law for everybody. Let all the books of feudal jurisprudence, of fiscal jurisprudence, of tithe jurisprudence, of hunt jurisprudence, provide a bonfire for next Saint Joan! It will be truly a bonfire of joy and the finest that has ever been given to the peoples . . . The Bastille will be razed and in its place will be erected the temple of liberty, *the palace of the National Assembly*.

La France libre, 3rd edition, 1789, pp. 69–70, 72.

(ii) *The illusion*

The excessive praise for the Revolution by some sections of the democratic press, and the tendency to consider all that was good in France as emanating from it, left them open to the jibes of their opponents. The extreme Right was just as anxious to blame all of France's evils on the Revolution.

You would do me a favour also to advise the *Chronique de Paris* to be more sparing in its praise for the National Guard for the few murders committed this winter, as well as for the few accidents caused by carriages, unless this paper is also grateful to them for the little snow that has fallen, and for the fine weather we have been having up to now. The donkey in *La pucelle* can well say that he kept his virginity for a thousand years in paradise, for there weren't any female donkeys. I recommend the *Chronique* to imitate this logic, and to agree that if no one has been run over in Paris it is because there are no more carriages; and if one is less exposed to danger in the streets, then it is because there are a few more policemen than passers-by. Paris bears a remarkable likeness to a college with more teachers than pupils.

Les Actes des Apôtres, No. 33, pp. 12–13.

125. Paris—Sink of Iniquity

Saturday 5 February 1791

Frightful depravity of the capital's morals, and especially of the representatives of the nation—Inevitable loss of liberty through the natural influence of these vices.

To the Ami du peuple

Yes, my dear Marat, you predicted seventeen months ago that the gentlemen of the robe, the king's men, the lawyers and the tight-fisted attorneys would harm the commonweal. A little after the Revolution these vile supporters of legal chicanery took possession of all the offices in the districts, then of all the offices in the Sections, the municipalities and the directories of the departments. No longer able to defraud their clients, they defraud the public, they swindle the fools, fleece the gambling dens, pillage the citizens, hold up the course of justice, and put a gag on the laws. In the midst of the frightful anarchy into which they have plunged the state, they rail at the outbursts of despair of an indignant people, they reprimand it for taking justice into its own hands, then, to add insult to injury, they send it back to appeal before the tribunals that they have crippled: today, people are openly murdered in the streets, yet they keep silent. Merciful heaven, what God will have pity on us, since the people is stupid enough to close its ears to the wise advice that you gave it so many times? When laws are powerless to protect the people against their oppressors, it is up to them to take the law into their own hands: to re-establish order by murdering their unworthy mandatories and by ignominiously removing from office those who have escaped their righteous fury; alas! we are lost beyond hope, if they do not finally come to grasp this great truth.

Method of getting rich quickly

The shortest road to wealth is to buy the protection of the divine Bailly, and hire the apartment of a tart at the Palais-Royal, in order to put on a game of *biribi*; and to have an experienced caller: with that, you can dispense with the *treatise of Condorcet on odds of games of chance*, a precious work in an absolute government, founded upon vices, and which produced for its worthy author a pension of two thousand *écus*.

Daily costs of a game of biribi

Hire of apartment	96 livres
The hostess and savoir-faire, at least	96
Experienced caller	24
Three counter-checkers, one at 12, two others at 9	30
Bag carrier	9
Two bouncers	24
Four assistant-bouncers	24
Two porters or ticket keepers	12
Four boys for holding the scoops for taking the counters	12
Eight pimps going from house to house with their invitation cards	36
A waiter	6
Refreshments (any old kind)	36
Illuminations	24
Apartment cleaner	3
Wages of the protecting committee	48
Costs of registration, inspection and protection money	24
Total	504 livres

Judge what a banker must win or rather steal with his thousand *écus* by making in eight or ten months a fortune of three to four hundred thousand livres after having paid out expenses at 500 livres a day. . . .

Marat comments on this letter with his 'address to the honest people . . .'

Paris is the sink of all the vices, yet its inhabitants claim to be free! No, no, let them not deceive themselves: to be free, it is necessary to have enlightenment, courage, virtues. Men who are ignorant, frivolous, cowardly, servile, given up to dissipation, to effeminacy, to pleasures, to gambling and wantonness, and whose leaders have a rotten heart, such men are made to be slaves despite their stupid boasting; this is so today more than ever before. They call themselves sovereign, yet their representatives have sold them out to the despot! They call them their agents, yet these agents pillage them, ill-treat them, oppress them, taunt them and make fun of their meaningless cries.

They have taken arms to defend their rights, yet they are only blind satellites, devoted to the orders of these scoundrels who conspire to bring them back into chains.

Poor people, object of their eternal disdain, of their injustices, of their outrages, you whom they have condemned to misery, are nothing in their eyes. If any hope remains for us then it rests entirely on you. Save your country which is on the brink of ruin. Hasten as a body to the senate, denounce at the top of your voices the municipal traitors among the police; demand that every gambling house, these veritable dens of thieves, be shut down; demand that the wealth of the poor no longer be held a prey to a horde of rogues; fill the air with your sad wailing: perhaps this will rouse any scrap of decency left in your 'conscript fathers' to force them to see that you get justice. Only by abolishing these dens of iniquity will they prove to France that they do not retain them as a means of counter-revolution.

L'Ami du peuple, No. 362, 5 February 1791.

126. Hébert's Moral Conscience

This is one of the earliest outbursts of the Père Duchesne (February 1791). His protest is just a short time after that by Marat. The *Révolutions de Paris* ran similar articles in this period.

A thousand million damnations! What gets into the head of our municipal officials that they take no steps to remedy excesses that lead to such a thousand misfortunes? Speak then, gentlemen with the sash! Will you wait for all the citizens to be robbed before you open your eyes? And you, great Bailly, who know so well how to read the stars, how do you fail to see the abuses that are committed in a town entrusted to your care? And all your damned police agents, what are they doing . . . ? Ah, blast it! they boast to us of a revolution that is going to bring back a sense of decency into our morals, yet they tolerate with impunity everything that can corrupt them. I am afraid, gentlemen of intelligence, that you are neither up with your administration nor your politics. You are villains who give us fine speeches but not from the heart, as they say, and whenever you have been applauded, you get lost in the clouds, without a thought for what is going on in the streets of Paris, which should be your main concern.

Well, my fine friends, so you say nothing! you remain indifferent while this city is swamped with the infamous gambling dens [*tripots*] of a truly cut-throat character, in which youth, maturity, even old age, ruin themselves daily; in which the debauched son gambles and loses the money that he has stolen from his father; where the father, deprived of all natural feelings, gambles and loses the fortune of his children, the husband the dowry of his wife, and the merchant his shop! Ah! blast it! do we not have here the true cause of the robberies, bankruptcies, suicides, and murders! We certainly do. The Municipality is aware of these disorders, yet it keeps quiet, and it appears, from its guilty silence, to authorise these wretched games that desolate families! A thousand damnations! how much longer will they last, these tombs of virtue, morals, honesty, industry, work and fortunes!

Le Père Duchesne: Hatin, VI, 521–22.

127. Equality of the Sexes

This is part of the report of a speech by a Dutchwoman, Madame Palm d'Aelders, read to the confederation of the 'Friends of Truth'.

Justice must be the first virtue of free men, and justice demands that the laws be common to all beings as the air and the sun; and yet everywhere the laws are in favour of men, at the expense of women, because everywhere power is in your hands. What! free men, an enlightened people, would they consecrate, in a century of enlightenment and philosophy, what has been the abuse of power in a century of ignorance? Be fair towards us, Messieurs, you that nature created very superior in physical strength; you have kept for yourself all the ease and enjoyment of vice, while to us, who have so fragile an existence, whose collective ills are enormous, you have given all the difficulty of virtue as our share; and this delicate formation of nature has made your injustice all the more profound, since instead of remedying it by education and by laws in our favour, it seems that you form us only for your pleasures, whilst it would be so sweet, so easy, to associate us in your glory! The prejudices that have surrounded our sex are based on unjust laws, which grant us only a secondary role in society, and often force us to the humiliating necessity of conquering the wicked nature or savage character of a man, who, having become our master through the greed of our parents, has caused to change for us the sweetest, the most sacred of duties, that of spouse and mother, into a painful slavery. Yes, Messieurs, there is nothing more humiliating than to demand as a right what it would be glorious to obtain by choice; to get by guile what is so sweet to own only by sentiment; to acquire your heart, your hand, the association of a companion for life, of another self, by a pose that is not our own, by a blind submission to the wishes of our parents, and by making a special study of coquetry in order to soften our captivity; for, I must tell you, Messieurs, that it is more often by simpering, by trifles, and the beauty-box, I almost said even by vice, that we win your approval and affection rather than for a lofty mind, a great genius, a heart both truly feeling, as well as delicate and virtuous . . .

Madame Palm then tries to prove by examples from history that if nature gave men greater physical strength, it made women their superior in moral force, in delicacy of sentiment, and generosity of soul, etc. Then she concludes by saying:

Would that our sacred Revolution which is due to the progress of philosophy, would work a second revolution in our morals: that the instruments of severity so weighted against us, and which true philosophy condemns, would give place to the sweet, just and natural law;

that your love, your friendship, your approbation would be henceforth the recompense of virtuous citizenesses; that civic crowns replace
on these attractive heads the wretched pompons, symbols of frivolity
and shameful signs of our servitude.

> *La Bouche de Fer*, 3 January 1791 : Buchez
> and Roux, VIII, 425–27.

128. On Racial Equality

The Declaration of Rights and the slave trade, an important source
of French commercial wealth, raised one of the most obvious
clashes of principle and practice. Eventually the problem of the
political status of the coloureds was left to the colonies themselves
to solve [see doc. 141, p. 259]. After the outbreak of war the issue was
pushed into the background.

(i) *No colour bar*

However, we do not think that the patriots of the colonies are yet at
the level of the principles of the French Revolution. Everybody wants
them to have liberty; yet they refuse the right of citizenship to coloured
people; they want to perpetuate slavery and the slave trade. Certainly,
the aristocrats have included in their party coloured people; but they
do so only in order to oppress the friends of the constitution, firmly
resolved to leave them in contempt, and to add to their chains when
they think they can do without them.

As for the slave trade and negro slavery, the European governments
will find it useless to oppose the cries of philosophy, the principles of
universal liberty that germinate and spread throughout nations. Let
them learn that it is never in vain that peoples are shown the truth; once
the impulse is given, it must absolutely give way to the flood that is
going to sweep away the ancient abuses, and the new order of things
will raise itself despite all the precautions that have been taken to prevent
its establishment. Yes! we dare to forecast with confidence that the time
will come, and that day is not far off, when you will see an African,
with frizzy hair, with no other recommendation than his good sense and
his virtues, come to take part in the legislation in the heart of our national
assemblies.

> *Les Révolutions de Paris*, No. 63, 18–25
> September 1790, pp. 523–24.

(ii) *Born to slavery?*

But negroes, you will say, are a kind of men born to slavery; they are dull, lying and wicked; they themselves agree about white superiority, and almost about the legality of their rule.

It is not true that negroes are dull; experience proves that they were successful in all branches of knowledge; and if the brutalised condition into which they are sunk makes them believe that whites are a superior race, liberty will soon bring them up to their level. As for what people say of their wickedness, it will never equal the cruelty of their masters.

Les Révolutions de Paris, No. 66, 9–16 October 1790.

TOWARDS UTOPIA

Education and law reform were the main means that were used by the reformers to inaugurate the new society. The extracts on education chosen from different periods of the Revolution show the constant concern of the revolutionaries for universal education. The extracts on law reform illustrate opposite opinions on two of the more spectacular issues, capital punishment and the guillotine.

129. The Light of Reason

This extract is from the first number of the *Feuille villageoise*; it explains the motives that led to its being founded and the principles on which it would be based.

It is for you that we write, O peaceful inhabitant of the country; it is time that education came to you. Previously, it was restricted to the towns, where good books imperceptibly enlightened people, and prepared the Revolution from which you received the first benefits. It is by reading that those brave men were produced whom you charged to represent you and to defend your rights: it is by reading that you yourselves will learn to know your rights, and to preserve them. Doubtless you have not the ambition or at least the leisure to aspire to very detailed knowledge; but there is some knowledge that must be held precious by all French people, and which it is indispensable for you to acquire. We have seen the time when people were not ashamed to insist that ignorance must be your lot; the reason being that ignorance on the part of those who are ruled seems to ensure the safety of those who rule; the powerful who abuse always fear to be noticed. This time of obscurity is no more. A new government is going to succeed the one that, from abuse to abuse, had heaped up its wrongs upon every class in society.

. . . Country dwellers, you take part in this government. You have the right to elect those who represent you, you yourselves can be elected; your fellow citizens can entrust to you some share in the administration of your everyday affairs; and even if you do not aspire to any of these honourable positions, you ought to know their duties and functions, in order to obey those who have been raised to them, in order to judge whether they are worthy of your trust. Finally, the right and the duty of each one of you is to study its laws, in order to learn how to obey them.

Previously the peasant, still attached to the soil, knew nothing of the relations of France with her neighbours, or he received only false ideas in this regard. Every inhabitant of a free country must, however, be instructed in the interests of his country . . .

Persuaded finally that light is born from light, and that the mind is enlightened in proportion to that which is enlightened, we shall present you, country dwellers, with all sorts of useful discoveries which will make your lot better, will enrich your leisure, lighten your work, and instruct you in the arts and trades that open up new sources of wealth to you. You are everything to us. Those who concern themselves with the happiness of the country workers, do so to the good of the nation, for the rural areas are the source of the state's wealth, and it is the enlightened tiller of the soil who enriches this source. Receive then the light; let it spread in your soul as joy swells in the heart: and never forget, that if liberty is gained by force, it is preserved by education.

La Feuille villageoise, No. 1, 30 September 1790, pp. 3–6.

130. Hébert on Education

Issued in February 1794, this is one of the last 'great angers' of Hébert.

The great anger of the Père Duchesne at seeing public education limping along and the existence of intellectual monopolists who do not wish the people to be educated, in order that beggars should continue to tramp the streets. His good advice to all the popular societies that they should put all their efforts into educating the sans-culottes, in order to crush once and for all fanaticism and tyranny.

The greatest evil for man is ignorance, damn it! It is the cause of almost every act of stupidity and every crime committed on earth. It is this, damn it, that has brought about all the wrongs that afflict us. Despotism is its work, and fanaticism its masterpiece; for, damn it, if men had had common sense, they would never have been duped by the trickery of the culotted charlatans, and they would not have let themselves be bound, strangled and muzzled for so many centuries by the dummies who dare to call themselves princes, kings, emperors. The first to be a priest was a rogue a little more slick than the savages with whom he lived. He had noticed that his cat twitched its nose or his ass moved its ear every time the weather was about to change. Quite proud of having made this great discovery, he used it to deceive and rob the others, by telling them that the Eternal Father or even the devil blew in his ear to announce to him that rain or fine weather was coming. How well we know, damn it, that it is only the first step that takes all the effort. The impostor, after having once found his dupes, conjured up other trifles to plague the fools who listened to him. He then allied with other cheats who acted as his jesters, and who thought up other tricks to throw dust in their eyes. There, damn it, is the true origin of the calotin's trade, which paid off so well for those who exercised it and cost so dearly the peoples who let themselves be duped by such mountebanks. It's because, damn it, these poor fools, who didn't know A from B, had not examined why cats scratch themselves, it is because they did not know all the science to be found in the ears of an ass, that there came into being priests, and the canker of fanaticism has for so long gnawed at mankind . . .

> Hébert then goes back to the origins of kings and their crowns, and finds ignorance at the source. Aware of what their authority rested on, the kings maintained the people in this state. Hébert blames the Constituent Assembly for not setting up primary schools, and now asks that the Convention make up for this lost time.

O patriotic societies what a fine task I propose to you! Appoint all men that are pure and enlightened to fill the places in the primary schools; take it upon yourselves to educate the sans-culottes, and open, every *decadi*, courses of instruction for the poor sans-culottes; give prizes to those who draw up the best works for this educational programme, and for the elementary textbooks that the Convention has decreed; oblige each of your members to pay the tribute that he owes to the country. When all men who can think and write have put down their ideas on paper, gather together everything that you find good. Damn it, it is you who have founded liberty; but that is not enough, you must now teach us how to preserve it. Deliver us then from lies and ignorance, and you will give the *coup de grâce* to every kind of tyranny, damn it!

Le Père Duchesne, No. 349 (*s.d.* February 1794).

131. The Death Penalty

(i) *Loustallot*

Much of Loustallot's comment here refers to Book II, Chapter V, of Rousseau's *Social Contract.*

This question [why there are hangmen] depends on the other, namely, can the death penalty be lawfully imposed on criminals? If we were to find that no power on earth has the right to order the death penalty, it would follow that there would be no need whatsoever of executioners.

Now, so far from that question being put to the National Assembly in that manner, it was proposed to it, on the contrary, that it should decree that those who had been condemned to death should be beheaded by means of *a simple mechanism.*

On what then can be founded the right attributed to sovereign powers of imposing the death penalty? It may be supposed that, in the social contract, everyone has consented to the loss of his life, when it is expedient to the state that he should die.

It is a sophism on the part of Beccaria,* to say that man, not having the right to dispose of his life, could not have conferred the right on the sovereign, but it is also a sophism on the part of J.J. [Rousseau] to compare the criminal condemned to death to the soldier who moves into battle.

The sovereign has the right to force the individual to *risk* his life for the defence of the state, because then it is true that he risks it both for his own advantage and for the public good, which is one of the conditions of association; the sovereign thus uses the right that has been conferred on him by the subject: namely, the right to defend his life.

But to say that it is in order *that we may not fall victim to a murderer that we consent to die if we ourselves become murderers,* is to suppose that by this consent we really protect ourselves from being murdered; which is clearly false, since this guarantee, on the part of the sovereign, cannot be executed by any human agency; for, in effect, instead of giving protection from murder, the sovereign does nothing else but punish the murderer, if he is caught: it is evident that this is not the same thing.

If the sovereign could protect the subject from being murdered, by the latter consenting to die if he became a murderer, there would be no doubt that this agreement could be made between the sovereign and the subject; but as the agreement of the subject is fixed and certain, namely, that he will die if he becomes a murderer; while that of the sovereign, on the contrary, is only conditional and probable, that is to

* Italian criminologist, economist and jurist (1738–94). His *Essay on Crime and Punishment* (1764) was one of the first arguments against capital punishment and inhumane treatment of criminals.

say, that he will guarantee it if he can, then there is no proper balance between the obligations, no proportion between the price and the object; it follows therefore that this cannot be one of the conditions of the social contract.

It must be observed that Rousseau does not say definitely that the case of the criminal condemned to death is comparable to that of the citizen sent into battle, he merely says that it *can to some extent* be considered from the same viewpoint; the authority of Rousseau is therefore *slightly* in favour of the death penalty. The difference is enormous from the one to the other case. The right of sending the citizen into battle derives from the right that every man has to defend himself when he is attacked; and this right has been pooled at the time of the social pact: the citizen consents to fight, but not to die. If he is killed, it is against his will and against that of his sovereign. But in the other case, the criminal would be put to death by virtue of a will that it is not possible for him to have, and by virtue of the sovereign who would be committed to protecting him against all others from a crime that he could not prevent him from committing against another.

Well, all the death sentences that have been passed, are only judicial murders? Precisely; and what is more, they cannot be justified on the grounds of either necessity or of usefulness.

> Loustallot rejects the claim that capital punishment is necessary to prevent the wrong-doer repeating his crime, or that it is useful as a deterrent to others. Nor does it serve as a punishment, he continues, for the guilty is merely removed from the living, without having to reflect on his crime.

I speak of the most ordinary of punishments, for I do not wish to know, for the honour of France, that it uses some punishments in which the art of prolonging life and pain is employed with an atrocious skill, worthy of the most cruel cannibals.

Yet, if you were to give the choice to a criminal, either death or life imprisonment, he will not hesitate to die. He would live only for remorse and suffering. Death for him is a blessed relief.

I do not intend to speak of the 'hard-labour' of those prisons where the murderer is chained with the smuggler, and the robber with one who has killed a partridge, where scoundrels corrupt the guilty, and put an eternal barrier in the way of their returning to a decent life, where indeed by a strangeness worthy of our corruption and of our former government, the privileges have been distributed, not in proportion to age and to weakness, not to the least criminal and to the most repentant, but to convicts who, by whatever industry, by whatever trade, can work to their advantage and satisfy the greed of those who rule over these terrible establishments.

If the death penalty is neither useful to deter the wicked, nor necessary to prevent the culprit from relapsing into crime; if, on the contrary, imprisonment fulfils perfectly both these aims, then the French nation will without any doubt advance almost to the ranks of the humane nations, by abolishing this punishment. The Declaration of Rights says: 'The law must establish only strict and evidently necessary laws.' It is clear that the death penalty is not necessary and that, in a government which has such great power and such vast means, it is cowardice on the part of those who govern to have recourse to it.

Les Révolutions de Paris, No. 24, 19–26 December 1789, pp. 8–10, 11, 12.

(ii) *Royou*

They resumed the debate on the death penalty: it is on such topics that the demagogues, protectors born of scoundrels and brigands, display, completely at their ease, their regrettable popularity and their pernicious sophisms: but one cannot find in their vain parade of humanity a single solid piece of reasoning and not even a specious one: the authority of the greatest statesmen, of the most profound philosophers utterly crushes them. The constant custom of all the republics, the experience of all the centuries condemn them; but, with an impudence and a fanaticism that you would have thought until now was reserved for the most uncouth and ignorant of men, they scorn the witness of history, the lessons of philosophy, the voice of reason, the opinion of J–J. Rousseau, of Montesquieu, of all the statesmen and legislators the world has ever known, slavishly to follow the marquis de Beccaria, whose work enjoyed celebrity for its novelty and for its flattery of the fashionable current enthusiasm for humanity, much more a sign of frailty than tenderness of feeling . . .

First, they claim that society has no right to take away the life of a criminal, especially when it has made it impossible for him to fear it. They compare the judge who condemns a murderer to death to a victor who cuts the throat of his captives, to a grown man who kills an obstinate child. To listen to them, you would think that the laws must not punish the crime, but only correct the guilty; they want the magistrates to treat the brigands like a kind father treats a well-born son whom the ardour of youth has plunged into some fault: one could hardly push further their goodness and their indulgence, or better, their madness and extravagance. We must expose these absurdities to the scorn and ridicule they deserve, but without doing them the honour of seriously refuting them.

L'Ami du Roi, 2 June 1791.

132. The Guillotine

(i) *Début*

Yesterday, at half-past three, there was used for the first time the machine destined to cut off the heads of criminals condemned to death. The condemned man was one named Nicolas-Jacques Pelletier, an habitual criminal, finally convicted for assaulting a private citizen with a cudgel and stealing from him a wallet containing 800 livres in assignats, and several other effects.

The novelty of the instrument of execution attracted a particularly large crowd of those people who are drawn by a cruel compassion to such dismal spectacles.

This machine was rightfully preferred to the other forms of execution; it in no way soils the hand of the man who murders his fellow-man, and the promptness with which it strikes the condemned is more in the spirit of the law, which may often be stern, but must never be cruel.

La Chronique de Paris, 26 April 1792: Hatin, VII, 53–54.

(ii) *Denigration*

Legislation and the arts become every day more perfect. Thanks to the latest anatomical discoveries, our criminal jurisprudence is about to take on a new brilliance, and if philosophy still permits the spilling of human blood, then at least the ingenious and gentle manner in which it will be spilled in the future will serve in time to come as a model for all the legislators in the world. It was reserved for M. Guillotin, deputy from Paris, as skilful a doctor as he is an accomplished mechanic, to present to the world the design of a *machine for cutting off heads* that will spread the glory of the French name as far as the banks of the Bosphorus . . .

And how superior will this prompt and expeditious device prove to the methods adopted by the English! this ferocious people who seem to have preserved all the customs for which Tacitus reproached them?

1° The pomp and beauty of the spectacle will attract more people to the place of execution; the sight will be more striking and the law better respected.

2° This method of killing will allow the criminal to face death with a bold front, to defy in some way the scythe of time that he sees suspended above his head. The next day all the gazettes will present their readers with the details of the glorious death, and every dying hero will at least be able to say as he dies: *Non omnis moriar* [not all of me dies].

3° Anatomy will derive from it inestimable advantages for experiments on the seat of the soul [*siège de l'âme*] and will perfect the suitability [*perfectionner la gradation*] of the machine for the different heads.

4° People will be able to speak of the noose with impunity before the whole world; and this is no small matter, as everyone knows, above all when it is a question of destroying every trace of the former aristocratic judiciary.

A great difficulty arose as to the name that the machine should be given. Shall it be given the name of its inventor so as to enrich the language? Shall it be the name of the president who pronounces the will of the Assembly on this matter? Or will it be Themis' first victim?

Those who favour the inventor's name have no trouble in arriving at the soft, flowing denomination of *Guillotine*.

There follows a discussion on various names for the machine, playing on the names of certain members of the Assembly.

They say that a new candidate is putting his name up to share the honours of this machine *supplicielle*. It is well known the ardour with which M. de Mirabeau has up till now seized every chance to strike home the greatest blows against tyranny. His so well-known attempts at criminal jurisprudence gave him incontestable rights on the proposed monument. With a slight amendment the honourable member could take this machine *sous œuvre* and the name *Mirabelle* could replace, to the great satisfaction of all good Frenchmen, that of *Guillotine*.

The subject is brought to a close with the verses of a song to the tune of 'the solemn minuet *Exaudet*', the first verse of which is given with a literal translation.

Guillotin	
Médecin	(Guillotin, a doctor, and shrewd, fancies
Politique	one fine morning, that to hang is inhuman,
Imagine un beau matin	and not very patriotic.
Que pendre est inhumain	
Et peu patriotique.	
Aussitôt	Immediately, he must have a punishment
Il lui faut	which, with neither rope nor gallows,
Un supplice	will deprive the hangman of his office.)
Qui sans corde ni poteau	
Supprime de Bourreau	
L'office.	

Les Actes des Apôtres, vol. I, No. 10, *s.d.*
pp. 11–16.

PRIVILEGE AND PUBLIC ORDER

Needless to say, the issues of privilege and of public order, which were of supreme importance in 1789, continued to be brought before the public and the authorities: the extracts chosen here reflect on the claim, being voiced as early as August 1789, that a plutocracy was replacing an aristocracy, and on the opinion of the nobility when this body was formally abolished in 1790. The final extract presents a condemnation by the chief spokesman for the people on the 'justice of the streets'.

133. Aristocracy of Wealth

One of the early acts of the Constituent Assembly was to establish a basis for franchise restrictions. Sieyès introduced the idea of 'active' and 'passive' citizens, by which the former enjoyed natural and civic rights, but only the latter were to enjoy political rights. The distinction was based on ownership of property and payment of taxes. A decision that aroused even greater protest, and which was fully publicised in the press, was the decree requiring that to be eligible to become a deputy one had to pay a silver mark in taxes and possess landed property of some sort. In the revision of the Constitution the qualifications on becoming an elector were slackened at the same time as qualifications to become an 'active' citizen were tightened.

(i) *Loustallot*

It seems a contradiction that a person can neither be an elector nor eligible for the primary assemblies until the age of twenty-five yet he can be included on the electoral roll of citizens at the age of twenty-one. There is no such thing as a half citizen. This status, once it is received, carries the exercise of all the rights of the citizen, and if the civic listing confers no right, since it is only an empty ceremony, then the great effects that are properly expected of it will be altogether missing. Now, what other right can it confer, but that of being an elector or eligible for the primary assemblies; it will not be that of carrying arms, for a citizen is liable for military service from eighteen years of age, and it is policy to summon him to it as soon as he can perform it.

These contradictions are heart-rending for those who ardently engage themselves in everything that has a bearing on morals and liberty; they saw with joy the bankrupts and insolvent debtors excluded from civil functions; but if they hoped that this decree would make commerce flourish again, and would restore good faith in our midst, their hopes surely were dashed when they saw that a man needed some sort of property and had to pay a contribution of a silver mark to be able to be a deputy in the National Assembly?

There, then, is your aristocracy of wealth consecrated by a national decree; but I am mistaken, I should say by a decree of the representatives of the nation. If the nation itself had pronounced that unfortunate decision, I would have had the courage to tell it with every respect that a citizen owes to a nation, even when it goes astray, that decreeing a mark's contribution before being appointed to the National Assembly is the greatest scourge of morals that it would be possible to find. Thus two-thirds of the nation is precluded from holding the most honoured position of deputy.

Civil functions in the primary and secondary assemblies, although honourable in themselves, are no more than steps towards becoming a representative of the nation. Thus, being despoiled of their greatest charm for those who do not pay the silver mark contribution, there exists from the birth of the Constitution no bond strong enough to unite every private will in a single goal. Because of this no public spirit will emerge, and patriotism will die in its cradle.

You will probably laugh at my prediction but I give it to you all the same: within ten years, this article will lead us back under the yoke of despotism, or it will cause a revolution, which will have for its object the *lois agraires*.

Les Révolutions de Paris, No. 17, 31 October–7 November 1789.

(ii) *Desmoulins*

Desmoulins claims that all Paris and soon all France will cry out against the Silver Mark decree, the absurdity of which, he argues, is exposed by the fact that it would have excluded Rousseau, Corneille and Mably; this argument was used also by the anti-philosophic *Année littéraire* as being in favour of the decree.

In particular Desmoulins takes offence at a priest who welcomed the decree.

. . . Do you not see then that your God would not have been eligible. Jesus Christ of whom you make a God in your pulpits, in the tribune you would have him relegated to the rabble! And you wish that I should respect you, priests of a proletarian God, and who was not even an *active citizen*! Respect then the poverty that he ennobled. But what do you mean by this oft-repeated phrase 'active citizen'? The active citizens are those who took the Bastille, they are those who clear the fields while the idlers of court and clergy, despite the immensity of their vast domains, are no more than vegetating plants.

Les Révolutions de France et de Brabant, No. 3, p. 109.

134. Extinction of Nobility—a Protest

On 19 July 1790 the Assembly decreed the abolition of hereditary nobility and titles. It was the logical outcome of the August declarations, but a pointless provocation to a class of citizens whose powers had already been considerably reduced. The right-wing press came out solidly against the decree and opened its columns to letters of protest.

Everything that reminds a nation of the antiquity and continuity of the services of an honoured race is a distinction that nothing can destroy; and just as the nation is united by the bonds of gratitude, so do those who, in all classes of society, hope to serve their country well, and those who have already had the honour of doing so, have an interest in respecting this transmission of titles or tokens of remembrance, the finest of all heritages that can be passed on to their children.

If this authority, without a doubt the most important they can use, had not been capable of repelling every attack against a property that will be forever above every power, they would have argued that the abolition of hereditary nobility would be, in regard to gentlemen, a degradation which, in our customs and according to existing laws, could only be pronounced as the penalty for the most serious crimes; that far from having anything with which to reproach the nobility, one could in the heart of the National Assembly not even refuse to pay homage to the generosity with which it conducted itself in recent times by a show of the patriotism that never ceased to inspire it; that it is quite impossible not to accord recognition to the free sacrifice made by the nobility, of the several advantages, whose origin could only make them infinitely precious; *that the extinction of the nobility*, if it were possible, far from being useful to France, would be a scourge to her, because it would be necessarily followed by a considerable emigration which would deprive the country of thousands of whole-hearted defenders, just as it would take from agriculture, from commerce, from the arts, and from all kinds of industry a great part of the specie that sustains and supports them; that the gentlemen who see themselves forced to look for a foreign land would surely live in unhappy circumstances, since everywhere they would be overwhelmed by the grievous memory of being separated from a country that would never cease to be dear to them, but that they would still find some consolation in their fidelity to honour.

That if these motives, and so many others, did not suffice to deter the Assembly from pronouncing its decree, the undersigned would oppose to it: first, Article 6 of the Declaration of the Rights of Man and of the citizen, where it is said: 'All citizens being equal in the eyes [of the law] are equally admissible to all the offices, places, and public employ, according to their capacity and *without any distinction* other than that of their talents and abilities'; second, the eleventh article of those decreed the night of 4 August, which orders 'all citizens, *without distinction of birth*, shall be able to be admitted to every employ and office—ecclesiastical, civil and military—and no useful profession *will involve loss of rank [dérogeance]*'; that it is evident that these two depositions necessarily suppose the existence of the nobility in the kingdom, since, otherwise, they would be void of meaning and would have no application; that, moreover, these two articles have been included by the National Assembly among constitutional laws, which it is no more in its power to contradict than to revoke; that the last article of the Declaration of Rights orders, 'property being an inviolable and sacred right no one can be deprived of it, unless it be when legally constituted necessity evidently demands it, provided it is just and previously compensated.'

That the nobility is the first property, the most precious patrimony of French gentlemen, for whom it is proof of the goodness that their ancestors had in consecrating their lives and their fortune to the defence of the country; that, consequently, by the terms of this last article, one could not deprive of nobility those who possess it.

The undersigned will never swerve from the deep respect that they have vowed to the National Assembly; but pressed by the most commanding sentiment for Frenchmen, honour; and by the various considerations that they have just expressed, they beseech the National Assembly that they may give them official notice of their constant opposition to the decree that was passed in the session of 19 June, and of the protestation that they now renew at this time in the most formal and most authentic manner. At Paris, 22 June 1790.

Signed Crussol d'Amboise, le chevalier de la Coudraye, du Bouex, de Villemort, Irland de Bazoges, Lamberty, Darsac de Ternay, Jouslard d'Iversay, Claude de la Châtre.

L'Ami du Roi, No. XXIX, 29 June 1790.

135. Pavements for the Poor

The Assembly decreed the suppression of the titles of *count, duke, noble* etc. It is a fine decree, or rather it is a fine result of its earlier decrees; but it would have been a good decree to force these citizens to exact declarations of their goods, and to subject their parks, châteaux, and other lands that they foolishly leave uncultivated, to the same heavy taxes as if they had been cultivated.

It is a fine decree to put an end to livery; but it would be a good one to establish a tax on the number of domestic servants, and by this means to cause to return to the country some of the good-for-nothings that the former nobles support in idleness.

It is a fine decree to have the statues of the tyrants knocked down. It is a good decree to have established pavements for the poor, who carry burdens, and to protect pedestrians against the despotism of coachmen.

Les Révolutions de Paris, No. 50, 19–26 June 1790, p. 638.

136. Loustallot on Public Order

The opening remarks of this extract follow the report of the burning of some editions of the *Actes des Apôtres and of the Gazette de Paris*.

Firstly, it is a violation *of the freedom of the press*. Must the people do by open force what despotism formerly did by *lettres de cachet*? Certainly not! yet what else has it done? Despotism avenged itself, the people have been avenged; it destroyed work that displeased it; they have destroyed two works that displeased them.

It is an attack on *property*? Well, people have no more right to take from a bookseller the edition of a dangerous work than to take from an apothecary all the materials that contain poison. If they feared the evil that these works could produce, then they ought to denounce their authors and their distributors to the public authority; if they wanted vengeance for a wrong already done, they ought to seek it from the public authority.

To execute one's own justice is to decry the good cause. If the principles of the Revolution are good, they will triumph in the spirits of those who have no direct interest in reviling it in their own presence. If the principles are just, they have to fear neither debate, nor sarcasms, nor sophisms, nor calumnies.

Three thieves, caught by some civilians and handed over to the police, boasted that they would soon be set free by the Châtelet.

Inflamed by this reminder of what Loustallot calls the triple 'aristocratic infection'–judges, privileged, and pensioners–of that establishment, the crowd seized the thieves and hanged them.

I know citizens, just how far the sad inaction of justice justifies your frenzy. But do not expect me to participate in your crime by cowardly complacency. What have you done? You have violated not only the laws, but justice and equity. This is all very well in cases where the laws are silent. When you sacrificed the de Launays, the Flesselles, the Beaussets, the Voisins, you used the right of *legitimate defence*, you were saving the state and yourselves. Between giving and receiving death, you chose the part that was laid down for you by necessity, public good and nature. But when, for a theft of silver plate or of kerchiefs, you make yourselves the judges and executioners of the accused, do not deceive yourselves that you are anything but murderers.

The tribunal that you thought to replace, and the law of which you have made yourselves the executioners, would have condemned the guilty only to confinement, to branding, to a few years in the galleys, yet you inflict death on them. Where is the justice? Where is the humanity?

In his conclusion Loustallot reveals his underlying fear of these outbursts, namely that they are incited by or used by enemies of the Revolution for their own ends, ultimately to foment civil war.

You expose yourselves to making an innocent man perish, and you draw down on each of yourselves that horrible doubt. 'I could be put to death at any moment, without being *judged or tried*. I could be deprived at any moment of the most fundamental *of the rights of a man and citizen*: it is enough that I have some enemy, a debtor in bad faith, a relative greedy for my inheritance, for him to label me a *thief*; for him to have the skill to make me all confused by such an accusation, or to convince the masses of it; for him to be clever enough to plant some pieces of evidence on me, such as a snuff-box, or a kerchief, *and I am done for.*' . . .

It is much better to save an innocent person than to punish ten guilty ones. This fine maxim was a prodigious effort of reason under the old régime; it must be the first idea of distributive justice under the empire of liberty. It belongs only to despotism and to anarchy to strike blindly and to delight indiscriminately in the blood of innocent and guilty alike.

Les Révolutions de Paris, No. 46, 22–29 May 1790, pp. 425–26, 432, 433–34.

PRINCIPLES, PROPERTY AND PROFITS

Inevitably, the revolutionaries became aware of the fact that not all men shared equally in the material rewards of the Revolution. Likewise those in power realised that government–even the most idealistically based–cannot be carried on without financial stability. The history of the assignats reveals both the strength and weakness of the new rulers, for at their inception they helped to save the country from bankruptcy but later, when the notes were over-issued in an attempt to finance the war, they led to depreciation and to the inflationary crisis of 1793. In such an atmosphere individual speculators flourished and became identified with the economic ills that the nation had to endure. As for the French colonies, their fate reveals that revolutionary ideals do not always triumph over national self-interest.

137. *La Loi Agraire*

It is said that some stupid, or wicked, orators have in certain places tried to lead the people astray by offering them the hope of a so-called *'loi agraire'*. We have noticed that a number of people use this term without understanding it. They attach to it the idea of an equal and universal partition of all territorial possessions; now, not only did such an extravagant notion never enter into the heads of the Romans, from whom came the expression *'loi agraire'*, but it does not present to anyone who reflects on it anything other than a dream impossible to realise, a project incapable of being put into practice, and a scheme whose attempted institution would destroy society itself, to the extent of starving several generations.

We will come back to this subject: we wish that even he who possesses nothing be aware that his greatest interest is to respect the possessions of others: the reasons that included the exclusive right of property among the rights of man are abstract and profound; we will make them real and understandable to everyone. Meanwhile the extract which follows will suffice to give a clear meaning to a word which has been ridiculously abused.

> There follows an extract from some 'notes by the citizen Brosselard', in his 'Translation of the Offices of Cicero, or the Duties of Man'.

> *La Feuille villageoise*, vol. 4, 25 October 1792, p. 75.

138. Concession to Finance

The opening of this session presented a memorable example *of the conscience that the Assembly*, always right, makes for itself, when it is afraid. The excise clerks and other employees of the *ferme générale* could have formed a formidable army, whose discontent and despair would have had the most dangerous consequences. In view of this danger, the pitiless hearts of MM. Camus and Bouche were softened for the first time; they saw in the *employees* no more than *honest servants of the country*, nothing but *respectable fathers of families*; it seemed to them as contrary to justice as to humanity, to reduce to beggary men who had given such outstanding services to the state: the old maxims—*that it is impossible to achieve the general good without individual suffering; that a great revolution cannot be effective without some disorder of fortunes; that the nation finds itself unable to make good all the temporary evils that the Revolution necessitates*—these maxims, always invoked successfully by M. Camus, whenever his pity was sought for old soldiers, covered with wounds, weighed down by infirmities, who sacrificed their fortune, their health, in the service of their country, and poured out their blood in its defence; for the magistrates and ministerial officers of justice, who gave up their night's rest to the maintenance of the laws—these maxims seemed offensive in regard to the customs and excise clerks. M. Camus himself recognised the justice, or, at least, the need to compensate these victims of the Revolution for the losses that the suppression of their offices is going to cause them. He asks for, and obtains, that in the new financial administration only the former agents of the *ferme générale* will be employed, and, that, while waiting to be placed in the new administration, they should each receive a pension of 50 livres a month.

I am very far from blaming this act of sympathy and, perhaps, of justice; my complaint is that the same principles did not guide the Assembly in respect of the soldiers, the ecclesiastics, the magistrates, attorneys, etc. and that, so kind or so just towards men who, formerly, were the object of a practically universal hatred, it has shown itself unyielding and barbarous in regard to people formerly honoured by public esteem.

L'Ami du Roi–Royou, No. CCXCIV, 10 March 1791.

139. The Speculators

This cursed race which emerged from the wounds of the country, like maggots born in a dung heap, does more harm to the peace and general prosperity, damn it, than the incurable aristocracy.

Greed like a true plague has so spread its contagion into every heart that people no longer think of anything but money.

There is not one trick that these miserable beings, who speculate on public disasters, do not employ in order to succeed in casting distrust into every head. Just like birds of ill omen, they are the first to spread and to exaggerate bad news. And, damn it, they do so even when none exists.

Distrust, citizens, all the fairy tales that they spread about in order to lull your credulity, to deceive your good faith, they are the work of these bloodsuckers who leave no stone unturned to ensure that the fortune of their victims falls into their hands. Today they will spread the rumour that Monsieur is dead, tomorrow, it is the king who abdicates, another time it will be other and even more ridiculous nonsense, and the simpletons who believe everything, are soon caught like fools in their nets.

I would have no trouble in believing that great speculators would be the instigators of riots in conjunction with our enraged aristocrats, for there are some poor devils of aristocrats very peaceable and very stupid, who grumble a lot, but that is all. To cause such a din, money was needed, and these grabbers of crowns and gold *louis* have plenty of that.

Forged *louis* and forged assignats are still a resource for these *honest men*, who swallow up and absorb everything.

In my opinion the greatest scourge for a state is this ant-hill of insatiable rogues, who increase the prices of everything, who paralyse everything, who devour everything, to the point that the poor devil of a father of a family, restricted by his small fixed income, can, damn it, no longer dress himself, nor feed either himself or his unfortunate family.

But, damn it, you are aware of nothing. It will be much worse in time to come if we do not employ a big enough remedy for so many abuses.

What is certain is that so long as this execrable, ruinous and criminal intrigue lasts; which will gradually absorb into the hands of a few insatiable wretches, every resource and every fortune, then we must never count on national prosperity. It will never be anything but an empty name, so long as the laws do not, damn it, condemn this infamous and devouring trade that will spread abuse and consternation throughout the Empire within six months, if we are not careful. It is up to the National Assembly to get down to the job and to give serious thought to this important matter, and to sweep away entirely all these disastrous plagues that steadily undermine the foundations of liberty, which they have already begun to make detested; for the man who suffers all these wants at one time, would prefer to carry the chain of a slave and to feed his wife and children under a master who would be just as odious, than to see his children die for want of bread.

Kick out this ravenous pack; let a stringent and well-executed law pulverise with one blow both the speculators, the money dealers, and the bankers who PUMP EVERYTHING, and the damned touts wicked enough to imitate these double cheats.

Yes, damn it, if you could expose the abominable resources that these assassins use to gratify their monstrous greed, you would be astounded at so many repulsive horrors.

Good citizens, if we want peace and happiness within the kingdom, if we want to avoid soon having to pay for cloth at 20 crowns the ell, 12 francs for shoes, and generally exorbitant prices for all necessities, then, by Jove, let us wage war on these financial executioners who strangle us and couldn't even care less about it.

Trois cent quarante-sixième Lettre du véritable Père Duchêne, pp. 2–5.

140. Lessons from History—the Story of the Assignats

Comparison of the circumstances which preceded and accompanied bank-notes and assignats

Bank-notes	*Assignats*
The notes known under the name of bank-notes became legal tender during the minority of Louis XV. M. le duc d'Orléans, regent of the kingdom, governed the finances.	The assignats gained currency as money under Louis XVI. The National Assembly, as the legislative body, governed and administered exclusively the finances of the kingdom.
The wars that Louis the Great had waged at the end of his reign, to maintain for France its preponderance in Europe, and to place one of his descendants on the throne of Spain, had increased the debt and had thrown the finances into disorder.	The war of the insurgents that Louis XVI waged for four years, occasioned some borrowings which had thrown the finances into considerable disorder.
Law, protestant and banker and a foreigner, had won the confidence of the regent to whom he promised the liquidation of the debts; he obtained control of the bank, and the *notes of state* that preceded the bank-notes . . .	M. Necker, protestant and banker and a foreigner, promised the re-establishment of the finances by public credit; he won the confidence of the king in his first ministry; both as the inventor of the *Caisse d'escompte*,* and of

* Established by Turgot during his ministry but extended in scope under Necker and collapsed under Brienne.

Bank-notes	Assignats

its notes which preceded the assignats.

To give special preference to the bank-notes it was ordered that they could be reimbursed only by *livres tournois*;* they mortgaged all the revenues of the government; the West India Company monopoly was given to the bank as well as that of the right to mint money.

The National Assembly, to give special preference to the assignats, decreed that they would be received in all payments of acquisitions of national goods; they mortgaged for them especially the goods of the Church, those of the Crown's demesne and the fruits of these goods, until they could be sold . . .

The first issues of bank-notes were to the amount of 400 millions. 12 September 1717, 120 millions were added, a like sum on 24 October following, and on 28 December of the same year, 360 million, which made, with those already created, a *milliard*. An express clause of the decree of the council ordered that this sum could in no way be exceeded in future.

The issue of assignats, from 16 and 17 April 1790, was for 400 millions; 29 September the same year 800 millions were added, the decree of the National Assembly expressly stated that it could never exceed 1200 millions in circulation.

This great mass of paper notes frightened the capitalists, especially foreigners and foreseeing Frenchmen; they sought at any price the exchange of their paper for coin, which increased the rate of exchange.

The second issue of assignats, rejected by the opinion of the main commercial towns, doubtless determined the capitalists to exchange those that they had; the rate of exchange increased considerably.

Government expenses demanded new issues. The council decree which fixed the quantity of the bank-notes to be put into circulation was broken, forgeries had already increased the number.

Government needs and the drop in receipts forced them to break the decree of 29 December 1790, which fixed at 1,200 millions the assignats in circulation; 19 June 1791, 600 millions were added; the new Assembly issued 300 millions. It has been accepted that forgeries had increased this figure; on 1 January,

5 October 1721, it was recognised that there had been burnt a *milliard* 837 millions 327 thousand

* Franc minted at Tours of 20 sous value.

Bank-notes	*Assignats*
467 livres, and that there still remained in circulation a milliard 169 millions 72 thousand livres.	369 millions had been burnt, yet there still remained in circulation a milliard 393 millions 782 thousand 634 livres.

Despite all the means taken by the government to maintain the bank-notes, on 5 May 1721, they lost 50 per cent in exchange for silver, and in the month of the following October, the exchange was at 90 per cent discount.

Gold and silver having disappeared, the holders of bank-notes exchanged them for silver-plate, pearls, diamonds, which prodigiously increased in value. Merchants tripled their prices when they were paid in paper, the price of various goods and foodstuffs rose in proportion.

M. de Forbonnais attributes the great disfavour for bank-notes and their rapid depreciation, to the issue of 20- and 10-livre notes, which linked with public credit the least fortunate class of society, always too bold or too timid in its dealings.

The total loss of the bank-notes determined the government to suppress their circulation, by a council decree, on 5 October 1721. It was ordered that they would be legal tender only until 1 November following, that what would remain at issue would be converted into annuities [*actions rentières*]; such was the end of this deplorable system.

The assignats depreciated on 1 February 1792 by some 45 to 48 per cent, their depreciation increased each day at a frightening rate; on 6 February you could only get 100 livres in specie for 160 livres in assignats.

Pearls, diamonds, silver-plate, increased considerably in value. Merchants were forced to increase all their goods; cloth which sold before the Revolution at 30 livres was being sold for 40 to 42 livres. Goods and foodstuffs, despite the suppression of tolls into the towns, are much dearer than before.

The depreciation of assignats is attributed to their excessive issue, and the disappearance of coin must be the result of the printing of 5- livre and of small patriotic notes, which made every individual and every commodity participate in the circulation of assignats.

The final parallel of this article remains to be seen; but the circumstances that preceded the assignats make one fear that they may finally have the same unfortunate end as that of the bank-notes.

L'Ami du Roi, Nos. LXXIV & LXXV, 14–15 March 1792.

141. Perish the Colonies

On 7 May 1791 it was proposed that the colonial assemblies, which were composed entirely of whites, should be given exclusive legislative power in the colonies. Thus not only the negro slaves, who made up the bulk of the population, but the free negroes and mulattoes, who had been seeking representation at the Assembly since it first met, were to be left to the mercy of the colonists.

The proposal excited a violent debate, during which Robespierre (12 May) compared the inequality in the colonies to the situation that had existed in France before the Revolution: the abbé Maury made sombre prediction that the colonies would perish if they were not controlled by the whites. The famous expression, 'Perish the colonies rather than a principle!' was not used by any one orator, although it was implicit in the speeches given by Robespierre and Dupont de Nemours. In the final outcome, self-interest won over principle, although in the concluding debate on 15 May, Robespierre gained a slight concession for the mulattoes. But even this was lost on 24 September 1791 when further pressure from the colonists forced the Assembly to reconsider its decree.

In the press Desmoulins actually used the expression quoted. The extract chosen here gives a glimpse of Durosoi's opinion. From the first he had opposed any reform affecting the colonies, claiming the national interest as the supreme law: his columns were always open for the expression of pro-colonial opinion.

In my number of the 15th I gave you the full details of the affair concerning the mulattoes. I told you how the abbé Maury, by dint of power and eloquence, triumphed over the sophisms of these factious metaphysicians and republicans who use the cause of the blacks or mulattoes only to promote their own schemes and their own insurrection against all legitimate authority . . . errors, lies, sophisms and anachronisms are heaped together to support a scheme that is as dangerous as it is culpable. There is, moreover, a great truth that we must set before us, and which has not been mentioned by one of the orators. What was the mission of these unfaithful mandatories? It was to re-establish the prosperity of the kingdom. They are told and it is repeated: 'If you follow your scheme you threaten us with the loss of our colonies. You will destroy our commerce and our shipping. We will become the weakest and most wretched of peoples'. To that sad and too truthful assertion these men, eaten up by the rage of a legislative despotism, reply, 'Better that your colonies perish than that the slightest blow be struck at your Constitution, your glory, your sublime

Declaration of the Rights of Man'; and that orator, nephew of Damiens,*
spoke loudest of Glory and the Rights of Man.

Bloodthirsty innovators, your secret is revealed . . .

La Gazette de Paris, 22 May 1791.

THE IDEALISTS

The most extreme expression of the ideals of the Revolution were
usually founded on an individual interpretation of the writings of the
philosophes. It was in the later years of the Revolution that an attempt
was made to implement such ideas: by this time the more trenchant
opponents of the *philosophes*, who prided themselves on their 'realism'
and 'true' knowledge of human nature, had been silenced. Royou's
fears of 'philosophical fanaticism' appear to have been partly justified.

142. Man and Nature

They reply to me that man has pleasures and enjoyments proportionate
to his ills. Animals are condemned to browse on grass, whilst we savour
the most exquisite dishes. Yes, damn it! but to sate our devouring
appetite, war must be made on all nature; the dove must be killed in
order to devour its flesh; the lamb must have its throat cut for us to eat
its entrails. We have fine palaces in which abundance reigns; but
alongside is the poor man's hut, where the most frightful poverty
dwells. We build ships; but only in order to look for gold and silver in
the far-off Indies, and with these treasures we have been brought corruption. We read in the stars to predict eclipses, rain and fine weather;
but we do not see on the ground the precipice towards which we are
hastening at every step. We have invented writing and printing; but
are we better educated, are we the better off for it? The great book of
nature lies open: it is this which we ought to consult; it would enlighten
us more than all the musings of these mind merchants.

Le Père Duchesne: Hatin, VI, 529.

* Robert François Damiens, quartered in 1757 for striking Louis XV with a knife.
The reference is to Robespierre. It was a common practice to refer to Robespierre as
the nephew of this would-be regicide, accusing him in this way of wishing to do away
with Louis or the Monarchy.

143. Royou on Voltaire

On 30 May 1791, the anniversary of the death of Voltaire, the Assembly decreed the transfer of his remains from Seillière Abbey to the Panthéon.

Session of Monday morning 30 May 1791

When Voltaire, still living, was crowned at Paris, in a full theatre; when a hired pit publicly adored him, as the god of the French stage, this excessive and fanatic cult had at least some foundation; the temple where he received such homage in reality had been embellished by his talents; it was not strange to see young enthusiasts, actors and actresses, bend their knee before the author of *Alzire* and *Mahomet*; but that the legislators of a great nation; that an Areopagus of solemn senators should make a great man out of this hero of the theatre, and canonise the author of *La pucelle*: that it should chase the patroness of Paris from the temple raised to her by the piety of the nation, in order to replace her with the public enemy of the Christian religion–this is a scandalous profanity and an odious sacrilege, made to fill the cup of indignation of honest folk.

I do not, however, know if Voltaire would be very honored to be put alongside Mirabeau; although he has done greater harm to the country, his private life and his personal qualities did not assuredly merit that he be given such a neighbour; by the first choice it has made, the Assembly has soiled and debased itself from the honours that it wanted to give to the heroes of the country; it outrages all those that it brings into association with such an infamous person.

M. Gossin, who was only known in the Assembly by his copious distributions of justices of peace, and trade tribunals, has suddenly been immortalised by the proposition that he made to disinter Voltaire, and to bring him to Ste.-Geneviève, to make him the patron of Paris. He much praises *this great man*, for the zeal and courage with which he dared to attack *the abuses of a corrupt court*. It is, however, notorious that Voltaire was one of the most vile flatterers of this corrupt court, and that his despair was always due to being ignored by it. The speaker exalts what he has done *to deliver the world from the darkness of fanaticism*. Voltaire began to write in a century of vitality, gaiety and luxury: if he had lived in a time of fanaticism, he would have been one of its most ardent apostles, following his wise maxim of never offending public opinion, and of always favouring the moods of the day; he insulted religion only to amuse the great, the wealthy, the women, and all the libertines to whom its yoke was most inconvenient; he wrote against religious fanaticism, then despised by the well bred; but he produced philosophical fanaticism, much more deadly and even more intolerant.

It must be agreed that Voltaire is one of the men to whom the majority of the Assembly owes most acknowledgment; he was their precursor, he has, so to say, prepared the way for them; he made ready the nation for the irons with which it is today overwhelmed. Never could the Revolution have been brought about, if the French people with its morality and religion had kept some spark of common sense; when they convoked the Estates-General, it had been a long time since the pamphlets and facetious remarks of Voltaire had corrupted the spirit and destroyed the heart of youth: he spread throughout the entire kingdom the poison of impiety, introduced egotism, pride and ignorance, debased and degraded the moral fibre of the nation, founded a religion, murderous and destructive of virtues, arts and talents. In the eyes of all men of sense, of every impartial *philosophe*, Voltaire is the greatest scourge that has ever existed in Europe; he is the most dangerous seducer, the most formidable enemy of society and of humanity, since it is established that religion and morals are the first bases of public prosperity: this is not here a declamation, but a geometrical proof to which neither M. Gossin nor any demagogue can make any reasonable objection: the Assembly, which dares, in the face of the nation, to consecrate, in the first temple of the capital, the memory of a man, whose very name alarms piety and modesty, dishonours itself. It dishonours the nation whose interpreter it is, and proves to all Europe at what point it is incapable of giving laws to a great Empire, since it does not know how scandalous and criminal the abuse of talents is and what influence religion and morals have on the government.

L'Ami du Roi–Royou, 1 June 1791.

144. The End of the Old World

The abbé Fauchet, socialistic priest, demagogic revolutionary and associate in the republican *Bouche de Fer*, launched a new paper on 6 June 1793. By this time he had become a moderate, and was espousing the Girondin cause, for which he would be executed in October of that year.

Yes, the universe will be free; all the thrones will be overturned; the strength of peoples is making itself felt; the age of reason for humanity draws near. We are experiencing the last storms of the youth of the world. Social wisdom will raise itself on the remains of the tyrannical and servile passions that ruled the ignorance of nations. Happiness will be born from the alliance of light and truth. Society will embrace nature. Delivered from all chains we shall be happy with all things. Fraternity will unite the human family, and equality of rights will finally make man king of the earth; it is for him, and not just for the few, that it has been given him in domain; he is the greater, he will lay hold of his empire and will fulfil his destiny.

We experience the worst extremes, and we are tempted to believe that we are far from such great happiness; yet we are approaching it, we are separated from it only by the torrent of anarchy that rolls through the ruins; but it will dry up. These are the final downpours of the tempests of all the expiring despotisms and of the vapours of all the sinks of iniquity gouged out by the long servitude of the peoples. The fire of liberty makes them boil with violence; but soon it will have dried them out; this is the infallible effect of its divine warmth. After this purification, it will give forth only waves of light and it will let flow only the gold of virtue. . . .

On the moral position of France and the
destinies of the human race

The old world is coming to an end. Soon it will end up by dissolving itself; a second chaos is going to precede the new creation; in order to usher in a true society, the parts of the social order must mix, vie and overwhelm one another. It is universal war that is going to bring to birth the peace of the universe; it is the complete dissolution of morality that is going to create the virtue of nations; it is misfortune of all that is going to necessitate general happiness.

At present we are in the most terrible crisis of humanity. I believed that that philosophy, which laid the way for it, would be able to soften it, to make less painful this second travail of nature. But philosophy, which is invoked by all, has still no hold over the hearts of men; one feels the need of it everywhere, yet one finds the reality nowhere. Nothing is more opposed to philosophy than those domineering and pretentious legislative heads, who have not even the elements of morality and the principles of common sense. With materialism, you have the morality of brutes; with irreligion, you have the very break-down of social values: with habitual failure to think, comes inability to make stable laws and to form a government: with all passions un-bridled, you have all the uncurable evils. Thus, we are approaching the end of human affairs . . .

Le Journal des Amis: Hatin, VI, 410-11.

145. Comments on the New Calendar

The old almanac was a piece of patch-work, composed of Greek and Latin, Arabic and French words. We would have thought that the new authors would have avoided the inconvenience of a similar medley. But apparently they did not have sufficient respect for people's reason. They judged people to be as one-tracked [*routinier*], as enslaved by their customs as before, and in order to make it easier for them to understand and follow it, they decided to use no French at all. As a result, they tortured themselves to compose a barbarous nomenclature for it, but terminated in rhymes, hoping in this way to help the memory and to efface the old impressions.

But instead of calling *October* the month Vendémiaire,

November, Brumaire
December, Frimaire

why not say quite simply and in good French, the month of vintage or of the grapes, the month of fogs, the month of frosts, and so on? They call

January,	Nivos	*June*,	Préréal
February,	Ventos	*July*,	Messidor
March,	Pluvios	*August*,	Fervidor
April,	Germinal	*September*,	Fructidor
May,	Floréal		

Why not say the month of snows, of winds, of sap, of flowers, of meadows or of grass, of corn or of the harvest, of the warmth, of the fruits?

This terminology that we propose is really so much better, particularly since the committee made no changes at all in the names of the seasons; these are still winter, spring, summer and autumn.

Another consideration would have stopped the members of the committee naming the months after natural things. This is that, by them, the month formerly July is not that of harvests throughout the Republic; nor October, that of the vintage, etc.

Would it not have been better to stick to numerical denomination, or even better, to compose a whole 'political' calendar: to call, for example, the month of January that of the justice of the people, because of the punishment of Capet; July, the month of the Bastille; September, the month of the Republic, and so on. We cannot hope to familiarise too much the coming generation with the epochs of our Revolution.

The names of the days of the *décade* are numbered, it is true; but they smack of the barbarity of the century when one thought up *Lundi, mardi*, etc. Let us add to this the fact that they do not have the merit of the former names as far as softness and ease of pronunciation is concerned:

1.	Primidi	6.	Sextidi
2.	Duodi	7.	Septidi
3.	Tridi	8.	Octodi
4.	Quartidi	9.	Nonodi
5.	Quintidi	10.	Décadi

The object of the feast of the five complementary days (or *épagomènes*) make a more fortunate choice:

> The Virtues [*Les Vertus*]
> Genius [*Le Génie*]
> Work [*Le Travail*]
> Opinion [*L'Opinion*]
> Recompenses [*La Récompense*]

Perhaps these five feasts are not placed in their most natural order; *work* ought to come before *genius*, which should come after *recompenses*, and then follow *genius* with *opinion*:

> *La Vertu,* and not *les Vertus*
> *Le Travail*
> *La Récompense*
> *Le Génie*
> And *l'Opinion*

The feast of the people, or of the *sans-culottide*, every four years, the *jour bissextillaire*, is very well planned; it could also have been called the feast of the Revolution, of that revolution *par excellence*, which perhaps within four years, will become that of all the world.

> *Les Révolutions de Paris*, No. 213, septidi Brumaire/quartidi Brumaire Year II (28 October–4 November 1793), pp. 138–39.

PART SEVEN

The Terror

The Terror was an emergency system of government inaugurated to deal with the exigencies of war. War revived counter-revolutionary hopes and sharpened existing tensions, provoking counter-measures and breeding extremism. War upset the economy, causing inflation and a rise in the cost of food. Defeat in war increased suspicion and fear and gave sanction to the suspension of normal government. The Terror aimed at mobilising the nation against enemies, internal and external, and ensuring a regular food supply at controlled prices. The crisis of war gave birth to the basic instruments of the later Revolutionary Government: the Revolutionary Tribunal; the Committee of Public Safety; the Watch Committees; and the Representatives on Mission.

Nevertheless there had been present since the fall of the Bastille the 'popular' terror, the terror of the streets, in which civilians took the law into their own hands and meted out what they considered revolutionary justice. Yet in total, and before the September massacres, the incidence of such action was comparatively slight. The great revolutionary 'days' certainly intimidated their victims, but they were remarkably free from retributive justice. It was the authorities who first exhibited this aspect of the Terror when in the massacre on the Champ de Mars they spilled more innocent blood than the people had done in two years. Nevertheless the frequent appeals to the sovereign people, the fanaticism generated by the purge of other 'fanaticisms', and the quasi-religious cult developed by the revolutionaries, together with the ever present fear and hunger, formed a well-spring from which might gush forth in moments of crisis or weak government, spontaneous popular action. The provisional government that took over after the June 'days' of 1793 was declared on 10 October of that year 'revolutionary until the peace'. On the following 4 December, the so-called 'Constitution of the Terror' firmly defined the basis of the government that ruled until the fall of Robespierre. In this way the Terror became institutionalised and centrally directed.

The documents already cited have illustrated more particularly the 'popular' aspect of the Terror, especially in the first years of the Revolution. Those in this section concentrate on the later years, and on the actual implementation of the demands for strong government. As the press during the period of the main Terror was not spared the emasculation of thought and speech, and indeed lost or had already lost many of its leading editors, the documents tend to be allusive rather than direct. There is no need to justify the inclusion of a whole section on the *Vieux Cordelier*, but in order to balance this attack on the Terror a short section is included on the rationale of the Terror as seen by some of its main proponents.

THE SWORD OF JUSTICE

In the first days of September 1792 the Prussian advance on Paris seemed assured by the fall of Verdun, less than two hundred miles from the capital. The call for volunteers to meet the threat was answered enthusiastically, but fear was expressed of a rumoured royalist rising from the prisons, swollen by the arrests following the insurrection of 10 August. In face of the dual threat of foreign invasion and counter-revolution, a panic broke out in which the prisons were purged of political suspects and common criminals alike, sometimes after a hasty trial or just as often without. The slaughter continued over 2 and 3 September, and then gradually petered out. Although some people in authority were willing to justify the deed at the time, the epithet '*septembriseur*' came to be a weapon of abuse in the developing faction fight. In the press, Prudhomme and Gorsas were prominent with their praise of the murders. Horrifying though they may have been, they left the volunteers free to meet the Prussians without fear of a stab in the back.

146. Marat Calls for Heads

Marat's part in the September massacres has often been debated. Whatever the extent of his personal involvement, it is even more difficult to assign the part played by his paper. The following extracts show Marat at his most extreme, the final one having been held in evidence against him as the instigator of the massacres. Yet it will be noted that this is no more violent than any of the other extracts, none of which had a recognised effect. Moreover, Marat was in hiding from 4 May to 10 August and in this period his influence was not great. Note too that his paper did not appear between 22 August and 7 September.

(i) 'A hundred thousand heads'

The bribed bunglers cry out murder when I counsel you to take a jump on the monsters who would cut your throats. A year ago by cutting off five or six hundred heads you would have set yourself free and happy for ever. Today it would need ten thousand; within a few months perhaps you will need to cut off a hundred thousand, and you will do a fine job; for there is no peace for you until you have exterminated the implacable enemies of the *patrie* down to their last member.

L'Ami du peuple, No. 313, 17 December 1790.

(ii) *The edge of the sword*

. . . No, it is not on the frontiers, but in the capital that we must rain down our blows. Stop wasting time thinking up means of defence; there is only one means of defence for you. That which I have recommended so many times: *a general insurrection and popular executions*. Begin then by making sure of the king, the dauphin and the royal family: put them under a strong guard and let their heads answer for events. Follow this up by cutting off, without hesitation, the general's head, and those of the counter-revolutionary ministers and ex-ministers; those of the mayor and the anti-revolutionary municipal councillors; then put all the Parisian general staff, all the 'blacks' and all the 'ministerials' of the National Assembly, all the known supporters of despotism, on the edge of the sword. I tell you again, this is the only way which remains for you to save the country. Six months ago five or six hundred heads would have been enough to pull you back from the abyss. Today because you have stupidly let your implacable enemies conspire among themselves and gather strength, perhaps we will have to cut off five or six thousand; but even if it need twenty thousand, there is no time for hesitation.

L'Ami du peuple, No. 314, 18 December 1790.

(iii) *Sacrifice for salvation*

My poor citizens it is not with sticks that you will defeat the hordes of scoundrels conspiring against your happiness, of scoundrels bent on your destruction. If they were stronger than you they would cut your throats without pity; consequently you should stab them without mercy. Let Chapellier, Rabeau, Eméry, Duport, Bureau-de-Pusy, Barnave, Desmeuniers, Malouet, Goupil, Thouret, Target, Fréteau, Prugnon, Regnault, Sieyès, Dupont, d'André, Montlosier, Bailly, Mottié, be your first victims!* Perhaps these bloody sacrifices will ensure you your salvation.

L'Ami du peuple, No. 522, 18 July 1791.

(iv) *The vision of a statesman*

Marat is telling of an interview he had with Robespierre in which the latter accused him of destroying the 'prodigious influence of [his] newspaper on the Revolution' by bloodthirsty exaggeration. What follows is the conclusion of Marat's reply.

. . . let it be known that if I could have counted on the people of the capital after the horrible decree against the Nancy garrison, I would have decimated the barbarous deputies who passed it. Let it be known that after the Châtelet inquiry into the events of 5 and 6 October, I would have roasted at the stake the iniquitous judges of that infamous tribunal. Let it be known that after the massacre on the Champ de Mars if I had found two thousand men burning with the thoughts that filled my breast, I would have been at their head to stab the general in the midst of his battalions of brigands, to burn the despot in his palace, and to impale our atrocious deputies to their seats, as I told them at the time. Robespierre listened to me in fear, paled, and remained silent for a while. That interview confirmed me in the opinion that I have always had of him; that he combines with the enlightenment of a wise senator, the integrity of an upright man and the zeal of a true patriot; but that he lacks both the vision and the audacity of a statesman.

L'Ami du peuple, No. 648, 3 May 1792.

(v) *The people's duty*

What is the people's duty? . . . In the last resort, indeed the surest and wisest measure it can take, is to present itself armed at the Abbaye, to pull the traitors out from within it, particularly the Swiss officers and their accomplices, and to put them under the edge of the sword. What stupidity to consider trying them! It's all over; you took them prisoner arms in hand against the *patrie*, and you massacred the soldiers; why then spare their officers, incomparably more culpable? The stupid thing is to have listened to the appeasers [*endormeurs*], who advised taking them prisoner of war. They are traitors who must be immolated immediately, for they could never be considered from any other point of view.

L'Ami du peuple, No. 680, 19 August 1792.

* Deputies at the National Assembly, most of whom were to become Feuillants. Malouet and Montlosier were already clearly on the right.

And as a post-script, from the edition of three days earlier.

(Hurry ahead with the judgement of the prisoners at the Abbaye.) If the sword of justice at last strikes down the intriguers and the traitors, you will no more hear me speak of popular executions, a cruel expedient that only the law of necessity can command of a people reduced to despair, and that the wilful torpor of the laws always justifies.

L'Ami du peuple, No. 679, 16 August 1792.

147. Let them Perish!

Within a short time Gorsas was decrying the event he glorifies here. On 15 May 1793 Chaumette proposed that Paris be placarded with posters showing the opinion of Gorsas in two columns: 'The Gorsas of September: the Gorsas of today.'

The terrible moment has arrived. Hordes of cannibals, greedy for blood and pillage, have violated the asylum of liberty; they do not conceal the fact that they have friends on the inside on whom they can count . . . They want the death of the patriots . . . It is therefore today a fight to the death! . . . Let them perish! . . . We are in open conflict with the enemies of our liberty: either we must perish at their hands or they must perish by ours. Such is the cruel dilemma in which we find ourselves.

While a hundred thousand citizens flew to their arms in order to go to the frontiers, a hundred thousand others, or rather all Paris, betook themselves to the prisons, packed with brigands, with the intention of sacrificing everything to the public safety. But a sense of justice soon put a curb on this initial fervour. A jury is formed; the jail registers are brought out; prisoners examined: all the innocent, all the wretches arrested for debts, all the victims of a moment's *error* or *imprudence*, are taken home in triumph, and crime alone perishes. The Force, the Conciergerie, the Châtelet, Bicêtre, indeed all the abodes of crime, have no longer anything but walls; all the conspirators, all the rascals, have seen their last, all the innocents are saved . . .*

Doubtless no one expects us to recall here all that had happened in these various abodes of wickedness and of crime; these details are too painful, and the humane man turns his face away, even when he knows that it is the blood of scoundrels that has flowed, and this blood alone that has flowed.

Le Courrier des départements: Hatin VI, 307–308.

* It has been estimated that only one quarter of the victims were 'political' prisoners.

And a postscript from Hébert.

We are continually having the massacres of the 2nd and 3rd of September shoved in our faces, despite these massacres having been made by foreigners; and in any case, damn it, who was it who perished in these massacres? Wasn't it the greatest of all the rogues, monsters who had themselves slaughtered thousands of good citizens? Has it been forgotten that Gorsas and Brissot who today spill tears over the death of Montmorin and all the members of the Austrian Committee, and who would like to lick the arses of the refractory priests, bishops and archbishops who perished in these last few days, themselves praised these massacres? Just compare what they were writing then with what they are writing today and you will see that little faith can be put in such weathercocks who turn with every breeze if it means picking up a bit of money or a few assignats.

Le Père Duchesne, No. 245.

148. The Glory of being French

Prudhomme, unlike Gorsas, reiterated at intervals throughout 1793 the necessity and justice of the massacres. This is the conclusion to an article on the military and political state of France.

Magnanimous nation! such are your destinies: you made the first revolution for the kings, but the kings did not wish to profit by it, now you are going to make it for the people. They say that a group of plotters thought they would profit from your sublime courage to give a successor to Louis XVI; they say that a section of the National Assembly itself wanted to offer the crown, either to Brunswick, or to the son of the King of England;* it is pointed out that the Prussians, sure of this information, commit no excess, neither on the march, nor in the towns that have been delivered to them, whilst the Austrians commit the most unheard-of cruelties everywhere that they appear; all of which can be said to provide material proof of this new conspiracy: but what can a few villainous conspirators do in the immensity of a nation fully armed for the conquest and defence of its rights? These contemptible conspirators are swallowed up in the mass; none even bothers to notice that they exist or that they conspire; the nation is heading straight for liberty and it will arrive there before the name of the traitors can be made known.

Such is the state of our armies, such is the political state of France; this empire is at the highest degree of glory that could ever be reached;

* The Duke of York. The accusation was made against the Girondins, Carra in particular.

the axe of the people has done justice to the conspirators within the nation; soon their guilty leader will fall beneath the axe of the laws; yet sooner, will the armies of the conspiring despots be repulsed or cut to pieces. The people are going to remain in permanent insurrection until the perfect establishment of universal liberty. How glorious it is to be French!

Les Révolutions de Paris, No. 165, 1–8 September 1792.

PARIS AND THE PROVINCES

As a town five or six times larger than any other in France and regarded throughout Europe as the centre of arts and manners, Paris had always exercised influence over the rest of the country. Before the Revolution it was accused of gobbling up all the nation's produce, during the Revolution it was feared that it was monopolising the nation's political power. In their attitude to the capital the Girondins in some way were the successors to Rivarol. They feared Paris, and upheld the theory of 'federalism', whereby the central authority of Paris would be replaced by a loose federation of the provinces. Following their proscription in June 1793 many of them escaped to the provinces, and federalism became the programme of an armed insurrection which was exploited by the royalist and clerical counter-revolution. Rapidly the revolt spread to more than sixty departments, and action taken to repress this crime against the 'republic one and indivisible' became an integral part of the Terror.

149. Paris the Pigeon-run

Tremble then, National Assembly, that France does not become cruel, and that its capital, which has drained and corrupted it for so many centuries, will not succeed in dishonouring it. It is you alone who will be to blame for all our ills, since you have invaded every power. . . . What do they not, in effect, expect from an Assembly that has overturned the throne? They will ask you for agrarian laws. To satisfy them, you will have to divide France into equal shares, like a vast chess-board and this is where they will lead you, those whom you have been too long filling with ideas of equality; for legislators also have their indiscretions and the little people are always ready to profit by them. You will have armed the man who has only a thatched cottage against the fortunate possessor of a house, and the simple boatman against the master of a ship; the have-nots will rise up against the haves, that is to say, the greater number against the smaller. Licence, that frightening phantom of liberty, will pursue you into that very hall, beneath those very vaults where, like Samson, you summoned all the people, and you will bury yourselves, like him, beneath the ruins of the temple, and this because you shook its strongest columns, *personal safety and property* . . .

It is mainly for Paris that the National Assembly must show concern. One can count, in this wretched city, forty or fifty thousand men whose existence and intentions are unknown; and these men are armed! and they are rubbing shoulders with the bourgeois whom they could murder whenever they please. Even supposing that this misfortune does not happen, is the capital aware of its own interests, when it remains under arms? Is Paris then a city at war? Is it not, on the contrary, a city of luxury and pleasure? Meeting-place for France and Europe, Paris is the fatherland of no one; and you can only laugh at a man who calls himself a citizen of Paris. Is he a citizen of a dance or of a theatre? A capital is only a vast pigeon-run that must be open at all times . . .

Ah! if ever the provinces open their eyes! if one day they discover how much their interests are, I will not say different, but opposed to the interests of Paris, how that town will be forsaken. How its merchants will complain for having expelled the many customers who make them rich, for raising that absurd militia that ruins them! Was it then for you to begin an insurrection, insane city! your Palais-Royal has pushed you towards a precipice from which your town-hall will not save you; the grass will soon grow in your filthy streets. To ruin you, there is no need to capture you; it is only necessary to leave you alone; it is for the provinces to besiege you from a distance; by a blockade as good for them as it is bad for you, let them cease to send you their supplies that you consume, their silver that you dissipate, their children whom you corrupt; let them cease this for a single day, and you are finished!

Le Journal politique national, (edition of 1790), vol. I, No. 10, *s.d.*, pp. 98–102.

150. Town v. Country

(i) *Greed of the country*

The people of Paris, angry at not being able to procure bread except with a great deal of trouble and great loss of time; worn-out, moreover, and no longer having the means to pay excessive prices for basic necessities, the people betook itself on Thursday to several markets and demanded a quarternon of eggs at 25 sous; a pound of meat at 15 sous.

Can anyone make a crime out of this illegal measure? Is it not terrible that one must pay 25 sous for two quarts of dried haricot beans, 12 sous for an artichoke, and the same for other articles of consumption, indispensable and in daily use!

The assignats, it is true, and the dry season, have certainly contributed to this sudden and enormous rise in prices, but we can also put some blame on the inhabitants of the surrounding countryside, for profiting from the circumstance to quadruple their profit. If they had had a little patriotism and humanity, would they have conducted themselves in such a fashion with their brothers who made the Revolution, and who bear all its weight? The citizens of the surrounding communes, ought they not to have been content with an honest profit? Far from that, they even come to steal the bread that is being distributed at Paris at a moderate price, thanks to a tax that the Parisians alone have to bear. In truth, country people are very much to blame, and especially since the benefits of the Revolution have practically fallen on none but themselves. The towns paid all the costs, the country districts have taken all its fruit.

Les Révolutions de Paris, No. 211, 20 July–3 August 1793, p. 58.

(ii) *All are equal*

No doubt there is no man more useful, more respectable, than he who works the earth and waters it with the sweat of his brow, in order to nourish his fellow man. I love with all my heart the man who plants the vine, who raises and fattens the flocks that are used to nourish and clothe us; but, damn it, the sans-culotte who yarns the countryman's wool, who makes it into clothing, who forges the ploughshare and the arms that exterminate the enemies of the Republic, are they not also good chaps and equally precious men? All men who work are equal before the law; it must protect them. The country dwellers have no more right to starve their brothers from the towns than this latter have to exhaust the country-side and to fatten themselves on the blood of the farmers. We are now all one family; the rich must share with the poor; the strong must aid the weak; the enlightened must enlighten, and instruct those unfortunates who do not know their ABC; it is essential, damn it, that all good republicans hold each other by the hand and that they be united like brothers.

> Hébert goes on to smash this idyllic picture by growling that too few people think this way, and ends with a denunciation of 'the rich, the merchants, the big farmers,' and the 'starvers of the people'.

> *Le Père Duchesne*, No. 341.

151. La Vendée

The tenth of March 1793 was the date set for the first enrolments in accordance with the decree of 24 February for the conscription of 300,000 men. It was the signal in the Vendée for a revolt that was to last sporadically throughout the Revolution.

(i) *'Vive le roi; rendez-nous nos prêtres'*

The public enemies have just relit the flame of revolt in the departments of the Vendée, Mayenne et Loire, of the lower Loire and of Morbihan. At the same instant, formidable uprisings broke out in various places. The recruiting was the pretext for the uprising. *Vive le roi, rendez-nous nos prêtres!* is the cry of the seditious. The white flag is at their head; they wear the white cockade. Large bands of peasants roused to fanaticism and intermingled with brigands and émigrés, scour the countryside, falling unexpectedly upon the towns, devastating and pillaging them. The small towns of Monglonne in the department of Mayenne et Loire, of Roche-Bernard in the Morbihan, even St. Florent, are prey to the rebels. Several magistrates have been hacked to pieces; the administrative registers burnt; never has the counter-revolution shown its hideous face so insolently. Some of these mobs have clever leaders, guns and cannons. The towns of Angers, Nantes, la Rochelle, and Vannes have put into the field small armies, which have in turn been repulsed and victorious. However, new forces are on the move; the patriotism of the cities, and the firmness of the administrations will re-establish order and liberty. Those who best know these regions deplore the disasters more than fear them. Doubtless, the English ministry, accomplice of these horrors, is waiting for the time to attack and to set ablaze the coasts of a country whose interior will have been inflamed with civil war. But they are making a mistake; the majority of these wretches would be the first to repel an invasion. The sight of an Englishman would restore their patriotism, as the sight of a priest restores their fanaticism.

La Feuille villageoise, No. 25, 21 March 1793, p. 597.

(ii) *The milch cow*

The least observant have noticed that the war in the Vendée was an excellent milch cow for most of our generals and for the civil leaders, who, like Goupilleau, had to manipulate everybody. It is known that, at Paris, in addition to the accomplices of the rebels with which our forces are infiltrated, in addition to the Feuillants and the moderates who have been put into our armies by the good intentions of some and the malevolence of others, many clever rascals pilfer the funds, multiply costs, insult the poverty of the people by exposing to view all the vices and all the accessories of proud opulence . . .

They have exaggerated our defeats and our successes; they have increased and diminished the strength of the rebels. This army, which fifteen days ago they said was in extreme destitution, is today composed of fifty thousand well-armed men. The women are on the look-out; they help to surprise our posts and shelter the enemy troops. When this army is beaten, we believe it to be destroyed. It seems suddenly to be reborn, arises *en masse*, surprises our troops, who are either raw or not expecting so much resistance, and snatches victory. The poor organisation of our army corps, the lack of supplies, the knavery of the administrators, the ease with which the English can provide help to the brigands, the jealousy and hatred that vanity and self-interest have aroused among the generals, the lack of unity that ensues in the military operations, the failure to enforce laws and measures for public safety; all these causes have together favoured the progress of the enemies, and have provided fuel for a war that could have been ended in its first days.

L'Anti-Fédéraliste, 3 October 1793: Walter, 320.

152. Will Paris save the Republic?

Whatever you say, whatever you do, whatever the cost, *ça ira*! The Revolution must be accomplished; nothing will prevail against it, and it is Paris that will have the glory of ending it, as it has that of giving it the first push. Yes, if we were to be defeated, Paris by itself would again save the commonweal.

Citizens of the departments do not despair then for the safety of the fatherland on hearing of events in the heart of the Convention and in the Paris Sections. If I may use the following figure of speech, ought not nascent liberty first *blow off steam*; it will perform better afterwards.

The recruiting for the Vendée produced at Paris an effect that, at first sight, seems hardly to the credit of that great city; one would say that there is no more public spirit. They vie with each other not to leave, say the ill-willed, whose secret and well-paid mission is to malign that part of the republic where there is still the most patriotism as well as the most enlightenment and resources. It needed immediate help, they say; they asked for several thousand men within three days; after a fortnight they had scarcely found a few hundred. Paris is tired or disheartened; it has lost all its energy; nothing more can be got from it; the example of the department of Hérault and of several others has in no way pricked its honour. Have not cries of *vive un roi, à bas la république* already been heard?

Be quiet, slanderers, and learn that if there were a third revolution to be made, Paris would make it again. It is true that it is no longer so easy to carry it to the shameful excesses advised by some people; because of poverty and provocation we would certainly like to arouse in Paris those tumultuous disturbances of which it has only too often been the centre. The patience of courage and the peace of wisdom reign for the past two months within its walls, to the great astonishment, to the great regret of persons hired to stir up trouble. Daily becoming more shrewd, learning by the very mistakes that they have been made to commit, the citizens are no longer so credulous. They will leave, have no doubt about that, to fight and destroy the rebels; but they are not to be deceived: before joining up and leaving, they want the Convention, by changing its locale,* to change also its conduct: they want to see the executive council pursue a straighter course; at the head of the troops, they want more expert generals and ones they can trust. They would have preferred the front-line troops not to have been left inactive for so long, when they wanted only to conquer. They know the danger that waits them in the Vendée; as though to discourage them, care has been taken to repeat to them that the rebels are strong and numerous, and that they give no quarter; that their army is composed of men who will stop at nothing; they are vindictive lordlings, wild priests, game-keepers without pity, valets, clerks, and a quantity of fanatic peasants, for whom crime has become an act of virtue. Jesus Christ and the virgin, Louis XVII and his mother, are their war-cries. This rabble, which grows at every step, forces the patriots to walk ahead of them in pairs, bound and pinioned, and exposed to the first hail of fire from their brothers coming to their aid.

Les Révolutions de Paris, No. 200, 4–11 May 1793.

THE SAFETY OF THE PEOPLE

On 17 August 1792 a special court was set up to judge 'the crimes committed on the 10th of August current, and other crimes relative thereto, everything depending on legal action'. This court proved in-efficient, was unable to prevent the September massacres, and was disbanded on 29 November of the same year. It was revived in the following year in the form of the more famous Revolutionary Tribunal

* On 10 May the Assembly moved from the Manège to the Salle des Machines at the Tuileries.

proposed by Danton on 10 March 1793, one of the first measures of 'public safety'. Eleven days later the committees to be known as Watch Committees were instituted, although they did not at that time have the powers that were to make them one of the most powerful organs of the Terror government, particularly in their domination of local authorities.

By April the two famous Committees of General Security and Public Safety were in existence. The Committee of General Security had been formed on 17 October 1792, to perform mainly police functions, and it is likely that its influence equalled or excelled that of its more openly effective junior brother. The Committee of Public Safety grew out of the Committee of General Security, which suffered from overwieldy administration and was rendered partially ineffective by having to hold public sessions. It was reformed on 6 April 1793 into the Committee of Public Safety, which, from its origins as a link to ensure greater and more effective co-operation between the legislature and the executive, eventually came to dominate the Convention to which it was supposedly responsible.

The institution of the Representatives on Mission (9 April 1793) formalised an activity already fully practised: it also completed the foundations for the government of the Terror.

153. The Revolutionary Tribunals

The newspaper from which this extract is taken began on 6 April 1793 to let posterity know 'how much their [posterity's] liberty had cost their fathers'.

The most odious plots against liberty had exhausted the patience of a generous people; the people created, on the 17th of August 1792, an extraordinary tribunal. They deluded themselves by thinking that the prompt and severe punishment of a few culprits would frighten, intimidate, or bring back to the fold those of its children who are either deaf to or rebel at the voice of the fatherland. That institution survived only a few months, and even when it was suppressed it had been partially infected by the gangrene of the aristocrats.

Scarcely had the people stayed the revolutionary blade than infamous treason broke out in every shape and form. It was necessary again to bring into play the axe of vengeance; circumstances determined the laws and prescribed their mode of application; it became imperative that the ferocious beast that nothing could tame should be destroyed: a new tribunal was created.

It is the decisions of this tribunal that I feel I must pass on to my fellow citizens; they must serve the history of our Revolution; they must vindicate both the nation and the agents of this redoubtable tribunal against the odious reproaches made against them–but only by these vile creatures who regret the old régime for no more than personal interests.

Reader, run through the list of the condemned; see who they are; weigh up their crime, and do not forget that the judgements I have gathered together are made by a people who desired liberty or death, that they are made at a time when a coalition of all the tyrants has forced millions of slaves to choose between despotism and liberty, at a time, finally, when even the English dishonoured themselves by the most infamous violation of the rights of peoples, by the death of the representative of a nation whose sole crime, towards its adversaries, was to want to live in its own way and under the sole dominion of laws it considered as suitable to itself. Read, and let your conscience be the judge!

Le Bulletin du Tribunal révolutionnaire: Hatin, VII, 172–3.

154. Dictators for a Day

They wanted to rule, and they still want to . . . you need only to have once had a taste of power and you never want to let go of it . . . Like those northern wolves that follow the armies to devour the corpses, and want to live on nothing but human flesh having once tasted it, so do tyrants of a single day wish to remain such for the rest of their lives; their imagination no longer knows how to feed itself except on exquisite pleasures, on the atrocious delights of tyranny.

THEY WANTED TO RULE, AND THEY STILL WANT TO . . . for they have need to be kings, whatever form this might take, in order to escape punishment for the crimes that their desire to rule has made them commit. If the law should finally triumph, their guilty heads will fall beneath its sword; at the least they have no hope other than in national clemency. However, a dishonourable pardon does not suit them any more: their brows, impressed with the seal of their crime, when the disorders cease to exist, would inspire terror in the very people they have misled; *they could live*, but *they would linger on, despised and accursed, in a nothingness worse than death*. They must be KINGS or they must be NOTHING: by means of crime they must recover the power that their atrocious crimes had in the first place procured for them; they must, in short, take their fill in order to live without fear and without remorse.

Le Courrier des départements, 26 February 1793:
Hatin, VI, 311–12.

155. Six Good Patriots

The measure taken in Paris to disarm, by virtue of a decree of the Convention, the ex-nobles and refractory priests, and to arrest suspects, has failed completely; they seized hardly any arms: this could hardly have been otherwise, for this measure, taken in the heart of the National Assembly, in the presence of a large public, could have no other effect than to warn the culprits to hide their arms and to hide themselves. Everyone knows that for this measure to succeed it ought to have been taken in secret by the police; and executed without any delay, during the night, and simultaneously throughout the town.

But listen to the Convention, or rather to the faction of the statesmen, entrusting the above matter to the cares of a patriotic mayor; it is like crying for the moon: for how will he be able to save us from the machinations of the agents and spies of the émigré Capets and of the enemy powers?

What grieves me is that the Convention never passes any decree, revolutionary in appearance, that is not utterly illusory, or better, derisory. One would believe that the deputies of the people have not the slightest idea of politics: for it is absurd that the legislator directs a police operation to make it fail.

For the safety of the people and to put an end to the mocking raillery of our enemies I shall not cease to repeat that it is absolutely necessary that the Convention establish a committee of six good patriots, and that it invests it with the power and the means to have arrested all the public enemies, to seize their papers, and to hand them over to the Revolutionary Tribunal.

Le Publiciste de la République française, No. 157, 1 April 1793.

A NATION ARMED

Having, with the Parisian sans-culottes, rid the Convention of the Girondins, the Jacobins took over the framework of government they left, extended and strengthened it, clothed it in the rhetoric of revolutionary patriotism, and prepared to wage a war on the enemy who threatened on all sides. On 23 August 1793 the Convention passed the decree authorising the *levée en masse*, and for the first time in history the entire human and physical resources of a country were requisitioned in the name of the nation. In September pressure from the sans-culottes forced further revolutionary measures on the Convention. Following the insurrection of 4–5 September the Revolutionary Army was set on foot, on the 17th the Law of Suspects was passed, and, most significantly of all, the sans-culottes forced the government to accept the General Maximum on the 29th. The government thus weathered the domestic and foreign crisis of the summer and autumn, but it still faced continuing drought and a cruel winter. Moreover the enemy had only been repulsed, not defeated.

The sans-culottes were still to discover that their victories concealed a sting that they themselves would feel. The Terror continued: indeed intensified: a silent press would be one of the witnesses of that.

156. Plea for a Maximum

On 26 July 1793 the Convention issued a decree against profiteers which made monopoly a capital crime. This measure, a precursor to the General Maximum, is here impatiently criticised as a half measure.

It is with good reason that hoarding has been included among the capital crimes. That is also a conclusion from the great principles, which the Constituent Assembly would not have drawn, if all those, who, since the Revolution, have shown more concern for the wealthy class than for the masses or for the entire people impoverished by the rich; if these had not ceased to demand freedom of trade, right of property, as if liberty was something other than the right to do anything that does not harm another, as if property, always badly defined, even by the Convention, in its best days, that is, in the days of the creation of the Constitution, was something other than the right to lawfully enjoy goods lawfully acquired. Liberty, property–do they give the right to assassinate me? Well, what difference do you make between the man who takes my life and the one who deprives me of the means of existence; between the one who plunges his dagger into my breast, and the one who deprives me of basic necessities . . ?

A further measure was still necessary after having forced all the proprietors to put up for sale everything that they have no use for; as we have said several times before, a *maximum* had to be fixed for all provisions. We foretold this, and unfortunately time has only too well proved us right, that, fixing only the price of grain could have no other effect that to make it scarcer. Likewise by forcing proprietors to sell their surplus, you will achieve nothing if you do not fix the price, for all these rich men, who have the time to wait, have only to price their goods too high so as to be certain of not selling them; they will, in fact, monopolise, and yet according to law they will not be guilty, since they will always be able to tell you that they put them on sale daily and openly, and that it is not their fault if they do not find any buyers. . . .

We must at the same time take all necessary measures, and clamp down like lightning on all the abuses, without giving [the ill-willed] time to help each other to recover. The excess of assignats was one of the main and obvious causes of the rise; it is essential to decrease the amount. The lack of free circulation contributes to it somewhat; every cause that opposes it must be removed. Some hoarders will hide their goods; we must force their hand. Some greedy merchants profit from these circumstances to overcharge and to sell necessities at an exorbitant price; we must put a curb on their greed by fixing prices, and all this must be declared at the same time, that is to say in the same session. It is a formidable enemy that has to be attacked in one go and from all sides at the same sign. If we had followed this system, the only good one, the only saviour of the country, then everything would have been brought back to the normal price a long time ago. The speculators would have been dazed by the blow. It would have been impossible for them to have re-established all the old abuses immediately; instead it has not been difficult for them to repair the few breaches that a piecemeal policy of attack has made in them.

Les Révolutions de Paris, No. 211, 20 July–3 August 1793, pp. 54–58.

157. Appeal to the Guillotine

> Leclerc, the author of the paper from which this extract is taken, shared with his fellow *enragé*, Jacques Roux, the claim to be the successor of Marat. Both attacked the government of the day as sacrificing the interests of the people to the pretensions of the bourgeoisie.

If the National Convention really desires the salvation of the fatherland, let it prove it by at once conscripting all the sans-culottes of that immense city, without distinction of rank or age;* let the toll-gates be closed, as well as the shops; let all activity cease except for the manufacture of arms and, above all, once the people are on their feet, see that they are not forced to withdraw, as happened on the evening of 29 May, exhausted from want, and collapsing from fatigue and inanition; let the popular tribunals be provided with the best of the citizens and

---

* The *levée en masse* was declared the same day as this number was issued.

be formed up at once and let them set up two guillotines permanently on the Place de la Révolution. Then with a decree or without a decree, according to the orders of a revolutionary committee which, I hope, will not be composed as is usually the case of weak or wrongly intentioned individuals, the armed force will betake itself in platoons to the homes of all the hoarders, speculators, suspects, egoists, persons who have grown rich since the Revolution, the plunderers of the Revolution in general, whatever be their mask, and we will say to them:

To the hoarders
'Pitiless bloodsuckers, grown fat on the needs of the people, too long have you abused the patience of the French nation; you have founded upon their needs your odious speculations; you have dared everything to reduce them to perish from want and hunger: well then, it is for the Republic that you made your fortune.'

It will not be enough merely to make them restore their ill-gotten goods; if they have bought up the basic foodstuffs before the promulgation of the law forbidding monopolies, then let them be imprisoned until the end of the war; but if they have had the audacity to disobey the law, let them be sentenced on the spot, no quarter, no delay, and straightaway to the guillotine.

To the speculators
'By infamous dealing you have cast on our assignats an attitude of mistrust and lack of confidence; now, the man who discredits face values is as wicked as the one who by forgery increases the quantity. Your judgement is decided by this simple logic; to the guillotine.'

To the suspects
If, after having made the most exhaustive searches of their homes, any papers have been found that indicate they have been in correspondence with the counter-revolutionaries, say to them:

'The time of the people's rising is that of the death of men of your type: to the guillotine.'

To the egoists
'The people are tired of carrying on by themselves the weight of a terrible war. The time is past, when, by making financial sacrifices, a man could buy the right to perpetuate his shameful uselessness. Without being excused from paying proportionately to your fortune and progressively the immense expenses occasioned by the war, you will come in person to defend the cause of liberty. Take your choice: take the road either to the frontiers or to the Place de la Révolution where the guillotine awaits you.'

To the scoundrels who, under the mask of patriotism, have squandered the resources of the Republic

'You have abused the people's trust, you have gorged yourself on their gold, you have appropriated to yourself the spoils of their enemies, you have been more wicked than the counter-revolutionaries who have been exposed. Therefore, no mercy: to the guillotine.'

All these measures could be executed legally, if there did not dwell in the breast of the Convention a spirit of moderation, which is hopeless for the public good; yes, I dare to say it, I begin to assume that, if this state of affairs continues, the mountain in labour will bring forth a mouse, and the people will be reduced to acting as its own saviour.

L'Ami du peuple, 23 August 1793: Walter, 306–308.

158. The Task of the Convention

The 'good sans-culotte Audouin', much to the pleasure of the Père Duchesne who 'appreciates the praise of the true republicans', has in his paper addressed the Père Duchesne in the words with which this extract opens.

'Well, Père Duchesne, are you pleased with the Convention? It has decreed the Revolutionary Army, it has decreed a *maximum* for grain, it has decreed the incarceration of all the rogues, it has passed great measures, it has decreed a tax on foodstuffs [*denrées*], it has re-organised the Revolutionary Tribunal, in a word it has decided to conduct itself with a truly republican energy. Press on then, with execution of all these decrees; for what use are they if they are not carried out . . . [Of these laws] either they will be obeyed by those whom they strike or they won't be. In the first case the good they promise will materialise, in the second the people will recognise that the Convention has done its duty and that it is up to the people themselves to follow the road implicitly pointed out to them by the Convention. The people do not need glasses to see what it has to do if the rogues whom the Convention wishes to strike continue to act as rogues.' My answer to my comrade Audouin is that I never cease to say or repeat just exactly what he says to me: like him, damn it, I render justice to the Convention; on the whole, it is excellent; it wants to save the Republic, and its will would be done if all its decrees were executed; but unfortunately there are still many jackasses who put a spoke in the wheels. The ambitious, cheats, and traitors destroy all the good and useful things that it does; but with time it will snuff out all its enemies and ours. Patience, damn it, Paris wasn't built in a day; but once and for all if the Republic wants to be well served then let it be pitiless in guillotining those who cheat it; it bores me stiff to see the way the jackasses who have already humbugged it a hundred times and who are bursting with fat through feasting on the blood of the people, continue worse than ever to make hay while the sun shines despite the voice of the people crying for vengeance. [Why then has there been no action against Dumouriez' agents, against the former 'toads of the marsh', against the former Girondins now professing to be Jacobins, and other turncoats, such as Barère, whose conversion is worth no more than the religion of Henry IV.*]

There, comrade Audouin, is my profession of faith; you will never get white flour from a bag of coal; once a drunkard always a drunkard; once a jackass always a jackass. We will spoil everything if we sit on the fence; you are right to say that the people do not need glasses to see what has to be done; but the Convention needs a very strong pair to see what is surrounding it and to examine every word and deed of the rogues who despise its decrees and who bugger it up from inside. It would make me hellish and happy to see all the muscadins and muscadines† arrested; but my joy would be complete if I were to see the board cleared of all the big intriguers and the big as well as the little cheats. Let the Convention remain at its post without losing any ground until it has saved the Republic; but for it to reach its goal more quickly and with more certainty, let it once and for all take the bit between its teeth, exterminate the traitors and have its laws carried out, damn it.

Le Père Duchesne, No. 292.

* Reference to Henry's '*Paris vaut bien une messe*'.
† Name first applied to Royalists in 1793.

159. The 'Armée révolutionnaire'

Suggestions for a revolutionary army had been made by Danton on 5 April 1793 and were supported by Robespierre a few days later (cf. doc. 118, p. 224). Following the September 'days' this was at last decreed, but it was not until 30 October that Barère could assure the Convention that 1,500 men were ready to set out to requisition supplies of grain and foodstuffs from the surrounding countryside. This instrument of the Terror, the special creation of the sans-culottes who often raised armies without the Convention's permission, did not survive the deaths of their leaders: three days after the execution of Ronsin, its commander in chief (24 March 1794), the Revolutionary Army was disbanded.

(i) *Tremble the enemies of equality!*

The paper from which this extract is taken is one of the many ephemeral publications of which not even the name of the author is known. It appeared, placarded, in folio.

Here they are then at last those terrible legions that are going to pursue, almost into their last hide-outs, all our internal enemies. Tremble! Yes, tremble, all you that equality kills, who look on liberty and the Republic as chimeras; tremble public bloodsuckers, who build colossal fortunes on the needs and sustenance of the people. Hitherto you have eluded the law, escaped, if not the judgement, at least from the enquiries of the magistrates. Hitherto you believed that the number of the guilty persons would bring impunity. But the number of the victims who suffer is infinitely greater; and it will not be said that twenty-three million men will allow a million to grow fat on them. Can you envisage it, that Revolutionary Army invading your shops, sweeping down with a single blow those sacrilegious piles of provisions and goods so essential for life, bringing back into the markets joy and plenty? Do you see it again watching, night and day, your impious conventicles, dispersing your meetings, breaking the thread of your intrigues, unearthing your treasures, catching in the act your manufacturers or distributors of forged assignats? Tremble, I tell you, secret enemies of the happiness of the world! Your final hour has come. You will no longer corrupt with gold that army that the fatherland regards as its strongest support. You will not frighten it, you will not paralyse it, you will not bend it by any of the methods so familiar to the aristocracy. Every guilty person will be dragged by it into the sanctuary of the laws, every suspect person arrested on the instant, every hypocrite unmasked, every hoarder delivered to public vengeance. O you, you who give yourselves to this perilous and sublime ministry, you who are going to enrol beneath the flags of sans-culottism, and to form these new legions; you, the scourge of the aristocracy, the hope of true republicans, you, our defenders, our brothers and our friends, do not dash our hopes. New Curtius, gain immortality by a devotion which adds to the glory of the French name. Pursue with a firm step the future that opens up before you. Red bonnet on head, pike in hand, dagger at the side, swear, on the altar of the fatherland, not to rest until it shall have triumphed over all its enemies. Prove by deeds that it is no longer *terror which is the order of the day*,* but the avenging sword of the laws, and the guillotine consecrated by heavenly justice.

Le Révolutionnaire, No. 1, 18 Brumaire, Year II
(8 November 1793): Walter, 324–25.

(ii) *A letter from Ronsin*

*The General-in-Chief of the Revolutionary Army, to his
brothers and friends the Cordeliers*

The Revolutionary Army on 5 Frimaire [25 November 1793] entered that guilty city, so wrongly called *Commune Affranchie*.† Terror was painted on every brow; and the complete silence that I had taken care to impose on our brave soldiers, made their march even more menacing, more terrible; most of the shops were closed: some women stood alongside our route; one read in their eyes more indignation than fear. The men remained hidden in their dens from which they had sallied forth, during the siege, only to assassinate the true friends of liberty.

The guillotine and the firing squad did justice to more than four hundred rebels. But a new revolutionary commission has just been established, consisting of true sans-culottes: my colleague Parein is its president, and in a few days the grape-shot, fired by our cannoneers, will have delivered to us, in one single moment, more than four thousand conspirators. It is time to cut down the procedure! delay can awaken, I will not say courage, but the despair of traitors who are still hidden among the débris of that impious town. The Republic has need of a great example–the Rhône, reddened with blood, must carry to its banks and to the sea, the corpses of those cowards who murdered our

---

* On 5 September 1793 it had been declared that 'Terror is the order of the day'. This was formalised by the 10 October declaration that 'the provisional government of France is revolutionary until the peace'.
† On 12 October 1793 the destruction of Lyons was decreed and a memorial column set up with the inscription: *Lyons made war on liberty, Lyons is no more.* Under the instruction of the same decree its remaining buildings were to be called *Commune Affranchie.*

brothers; and whilst the thunderbolt, which must exterminate them in an instant, will carry terror into the departments where the seed of rebellion was sown, it is necessary that the flames from their devastated dens proclaim far and wide the punishment that is destined for those who try to imitate them.

These measures are all the more urgent because, in that commune of one hundred and twenty thousand inhabitants, you would scarcely find, I shall not say fifteen hundred patriots, but fifteen hundred men who had not been accomplices of the rebellion; but thanks to the representatives of the people and to the Jacobins, sent into the commune, the vigilance of the constituted authorities everywhere pursues suspect persons and paralyses, as it were, with fear, the great number of those who secretly aspire only to plunge their knives into us. Already the cowards have assassinated one of our revolutionary soldiers during the night: decide, then, brothers and friends, if it is not time to use the most prompt and most terrible means of justice! this great event is being prepared, and we hope that, before the end of Frimaire, all the authors and accomplices of the rebellion will have paid for their crimes.

Salut et fraternité. RONSIN

Les Révolutions de Paris, No. 218, 18–27 Frimaire, Year II (8–17 December 1793), pp. 335–36.

THE TERROR UNDER ATTACK

The threat posed by the sans-culottes to the Jacobin government was paralleled by a threat from the right, from the Citras, or Indulgents. These Indulgents, whose chief spokesman was Danton, aimed at relaxing the rigours of revolutionary government, removing the restrictions on commerce, and negotiating a peace. To Danton's oratorical eloquence Desmoulins added his rapier pen, but he made the mistake of engaging two enemies at once. It is clear from the first number of the *Vieux Cordelier* that Desmoulins intended to attack the government; yet his first two numbers were directed at the Hébertists, and in the title 'Old Cordelier' he drew comparisons that were unfavourable to the 'new Cordeliers' or Hébertists.

160. The Truth Must be Heard

Desmoulins' first two numbers, incorporating exaggerated praise of Robespierre, were submitted to the latter for scrutiny.

. . . No longer do we have a paper that tells the truth, or at least the whole truth. I re-enter the arena with all the honesty and courage for which I am known.

A year ago we were ridiculing, and with good reason, the so-called freedom of the English, who do not have unrestricted freedom of the press, and yet what honest man would today dare to compare France with England as regards freedom of the press? See with what audacity the *Morning Chronicle* attacks Pitt and his conduct of the war. What journalist in France would dare to criticise the blunders of our committees, of the generals, of the Jacobins, of the ministers, and of the Commune, in the way that the opposition criticise that of the British ministry? And I, a Frenchman, I, Camille Desmoulins, cannot have the freedom of an English journalist! I feel indignant at this. And do not tell me that we are in the middle of a revolution and that in a revolution it is necessary to suspend the liberty of the press . . .

I have a storehouse of truths, which I will not open up entirely, but I will dispense just enough to save France and the Republic, one and indivisible.

Le Vieux Cordelier, No. 1, quintidi Frimaire, 2ᵉ décade, Year II (5 December 1793), pp. 5–6, 7.

161. 'Suspect!'

Encouraged by the success of his first two numbers, Desmoulins then launched an attack on the revolutionary government, and the Law of Suspects in particular, under the guise of a translation of Tacitus. He did not seek the prior permission of Robespierre for this number.

In the fight to the death in which the republic and the monarchy are engaged in our midst, and in the necessity that one or the other triumph in bloody victory, who would regret the republic's triumph, after having seen what history has told us of the triumph of monarchy, after having glanced at the brief and rough outline of events as depicted by Tacitus that I am going to present to the honourable circle of my subscribers.

. . . There was formerly at Rome, says Tacitus, a law that specified crimes against the state and a law of treason, which carried the death penalty. These crimes of treason, under the republic, were reduced to four kinds: for deserting one's army in enemy territory; for fomenting sedition; for maladministration by ministers of public affairs and funds; for degrading the majesty of the Roman people. The emperors had only to add a few extra articles to this law so as to include both the citizens and entire cities in the proscription. Augustus was the first to extend this law of treason by including in it what he called counter-revolutionary writings. Under his successors, it did not take long for these extensions to become unlimited. From the moment when mere talk became an offence against the state, it was but a short step to make a crime out of the simplest of expressions, out of sadness, compassion, sighs, even silence . . .

[It was] a crime of counter-revolution to complain of the misfortunes of the time for to do so was to put the government on trial. Crime of counter-revolution not to invoke the divine genius of Caligula. To fail in this respect caused a great number of citizens to be hacked to pieces, condemned to the mines or to the lions; some were even cut in two . . .

It was necessary to feign pleasure at the death of a friend or a relative, if one wished to avoid death oneself. . . At least it was necessary to put on a look of contentment, a look open and calm. One feared that fear itself might make one guilty.

Everything gave offence to the tyrant. A citizen was popular; this made him a rival of the prince, one who could excite civil war. *Studia civium in se verteret et si multi idem audeant, bellum esse.* Suspect.

On the other hand, if one shunned popularity, keeping to one's own fireside, then this withdrawal brought attention on you and singled you out. *Quanto metu occultior, tanto famae adeptus.* Suspect.

You are rich; then there's an imminent danger that you will corrupt people with your wealth. *Auri vim atque opes Plauti principi infensas.* Suspect.

You are poor; well then! invincible emperor, you must keep close watch on this man. There's no one more enterprising than a man who has nothing. *Sylvam inopem, unde praecipuam audaciam.* Suspect.

You are of a sombre, melancholy character, or slovenly dressed; what pains you is that public affairs are going well. *Hominem bonis publicis moestum.* Suspect.

If, on the contrary, a citizen gives himself up to good times and overeating . . . Suspect.

Because of this it was impossible to have any quality, short of making oneself a tool of the despot, which did not arouse the despot's jealousy and which did not expose one to a certain death. It was a crime to hold high office, or to resign from it; but the greatest of all crimes was to be incorruptible . . .

Le Vieux Cordelier, No. 3, quintidi Frimaire, 3e décade, Year II (15 December 1793).

162. Terror—Sole Instrument of Despots

Don't let the royalists come and tell me that this account proves nothing, that the reign of Louis XVI in no way resembled that of the Caesars. If it in no way resembled them, this is merely because, with us, tyranny for so long dormant in the lap of pleasure, and for so long resting on the strength of the chains that our fathers had worn for fifteen hundred years, believed there was no longer the need for terror, the sole instrument of despots, according to Machiavelli, and the all-powerful instrument against those unworthy souls, timid and fit only for slavery. But now that the people have woken up, now that the sword of the Republic has been drawn against the monarchies, let royalty reset its foot in France, and it is then that those portraits of tyranny, so well painted by Tacitus, and which I have just set before the eyes of my fellow citizens, will be the living image of the sort of ills they shall have to suffer for the next fifty years. And is it necessary to look so far back for examples? The massacres of the Champ de Mars and of Nancy; what Robespierre described the other day at the Jacobins, of the horrors that the Austrians have committed at the frontier, the English at Genoa, the royalists at Fougères and in the Vendée, and the very violence of the partisans, all these demonstrate easily enough that despotism once it has returned enraged to its destroyed possessions has no other means of strengthening its position but by ruling like an Octavius or a Nero. In this duel between liberty and servitude, and in the cruel alternative of a defeat a thousand times more bloody than our victory, *to carry the Revolution to excess had therefore less danger and was still better than standing still*, as Danton said, and it was above all essential for the Republic to win confidence on the field of battle . . .

> Desmoulins goes on to show that Pitt, unable to prevent the establishment of liberty in France by open warfare, seeks to dishonour it by using the language and dress of the Revolution in a manner that would make the Revolution appear tyrannical.*

Although as a result of this plan [Pitt] gave all his agents, all the aristocrats, the secret order always to wear a red bonnet, to change their hose [*culottes*] for trousers and to turn themselves into fervent patriots; although the patriot Pitt, who had become a Jacobin, in his orders to the invisible army that he maintains among us, has adjured it to ask, as did the marquis de Montaut, for *five hundred heads in the*

---

* Note that Danton's associate, Fabre d'Eglantine, in order to draw a veil over his own shady financial dealing, had played on Robespierre's fears of a foreign plot in order to accuse the left extremists of acting under the orders of Pitt, who was said to pay them to discredit and destroy the Republic.

Convention, and that *the army of the Rhine should shoot the garrison at Mainz*;
to ask, as a definite petition, that *nine hundred thousand heads should fall*; as a
definite request, that half the French nation be imprisoned, as suspect;
and as a definite motion that barrels be put under these countless
prisons, and an ever-ready spark by their side; although the 'sans-
culotte' Pitt has demanded that, at the very least, by way of punishment,
all the prisoners be treated with the utmost severity and that they be
denied all necessities of life, even to go so far as to deny sight of their
fathers, their wives and their children, to leave them and their family
open to terror and to despair; although this skilful enemy has everywhere
aroused a threatening crowd of rivals in the Convention, and although
there are today, in France, but twelve hundred thousand men in our
armies, who, most fortunately, do not make laws—for the Commissaries
of the Convention make the laws; the departments, the districts, the
municipalities, the Sections, the revolutionary committees make the
laws; and, may God forgive me, I believe that the fraternal societies
make them as well; despite, I say, all the efforts that Pitt has made to
render our Republic odious in the eyes of Europe; to give arms to the
ministerial party against the opposition party, at the reopening of
parliament; in a word, to refute the sublime manifesto of Robespierre . . .

Ibid.

163. Better that some Culprits go Free

> Desmoulins concludes his No. 3 with a plea for clemency. Shortly
> after the issue of this number a crowd of women petitioned the
> Assembly to release wrongly accused persons. On 22 December
> Robespierre appointed a committee to review arrests, but it was
> suppressed four days later.

Doubtless, the motto of republics is that *it is better not to punish several
culprits than that one single innocent should suffer.* But is it not true that, in
time of revolution, this maxim so full of reason and humanity serves to
encourage traitors to the fatherland, because the extent of proof that a
law favourable to the innocent demands is such that the cunning
culprit avoids punishment? Such is the encouragement that a free
people allows to its own disadvantage. It is an illness of republics,
which derives, as we see, from the goodness of their nature. The motto
of despotism is, to the contrary, that *it is better that several innocents
should perish than that a single culprit should escape.* It is this maxim, said
Gordon on Tacitus, which makes for the strength and security of kings.
The Committee of Public Safety knew it well enough; and it believed

that, to establish the Republic, it needed for the time the legal outlook of the despots. It thought, with Machiavelli, that in cases of political conscience, the greater good effaces the lesser evil. For some time therefore it drew a veil over the statue of liberty. But shall one confuse this transparent gauze veil, with the covering of the Clootz, the Coupés, the Montauts, and this shroud beneath which one did not realise that principles were laid to rest? Shall one confuse the Constitution, daughter of the Mountain, with the superfetations of Pitt; the errors of patriotism, with the crimes of the foreign party; the request of the procurator of the Commune concerning the *certificates of civism*, the closing of churches, and its definition of *suspects*, with the tutelary decrees of the Convention, which have maintained freedom of religion and its principles?

I have not in this issue claimed to be referring to any particular person. It would not be my fault, if M. Vincent, the Pitt of Georges Bouchotte,* chanced to recognise certain characteristics in this issue. My dear and brave colleague Philippeaux† has not taken so many detours to direct at him even harsher truths. It is up to those who, on reading these lively portraits of tyranny, happen to see unfortunate resemblance in them, to do something about correcting it; one shall never be persuaded that the portrait of a tyrant, traced by the hand of the greatest artist of antiquity, and by the historian of the *philosophes*, can become a true portrait of a Cato and of a Brutus, and that what Tacitus called despotism and the worst of governments, twelve centuries ago, can today be called liberty, and the best of possible worlds.

Ibid.

164. Attack Renewed

Emboldened by the reception of his No. 3, Desmoulins tore aside the mask of Tacitus, abandoned his ambiguous attack, and stepped up his demands for clemency.

(i) *An excess of revolution*

Some people have disapproved of my No. 3 where they say I took pleasure in making reproaches that tend to cast disfavour on the Revolution and on the patriots: they ought rather to speak on the

* Vincent was arrested with Ronsin following his denunciation by Fabre; Bouchotte was Minister for War.
† Philippeaux had been recalled from the Vendée because of his conduct of the war there. He then accused his critics of needlessly prolonging the war by their cruelties, attacked the Committee of Public Safety, and repeated his denunciations in the Convention. He was arrested and executed with the Dantonists.

excesses of the Revolution, and of professional patriots. They believe that number refuted, and everything justified by this single phrase: '*It is well known that the present state is not that of liberty, but be patient, one day you will be free.*'

These people apparently think that liberty, like childhood, has to pass through crying and tears in order to reach maturity. It is on the contrary the very nature of liberty that, in order to possess it, it is enough to desire it. A people is free the moment it wants to be such (you may recall that this was Lafayette's saying); it entered into the fullness of its rights, from 14 July. Liberty has neither age nor youth. It has only one age, that of strength and vigour.

Le Vieux Cordelier, No. 4, 30 Frimaire, Year II
(20 December 1793).*

(ii) *One death = 10 enemies*

You want to remove all your enemies by means of the guillotine! Has there ever been such great folly? Could you make a single man perish on the scaffold, without making ten enemies for yourself from his family or his friends? Do you believe that these women, these old men, these weaklings, these egoists, these stragglers of the Revolution, whom you imprison, are really dangerous? Of your enemies, there remain among you only the cowardly and the sick. The strong and the brave have emigrated. They have perished at Lyons or in the Vendée; the remainder do not merit your wrath. This crowd of Feuillants, of rentiers, of shop-keepers, whom you imprison in the conflict between monarchy and the republic, resembles only the Roman populace, whose indifference Tacitus described, in the combat between Vitellius and Vespasian.

Ibid.

(iii) *Committee of clemency*

I think quite differently from those who tell you that terror must remain the order of the day. I am sure, on the contrary, that liberty would be strengthened, and Europe conquered, if you had a *committee of clemency*. Such a committee would finish the Revolution; for clemency is also a revolutionary measure, and the most effective of all, when it is wisely distributed. Let imbeciles and rascals call me a moderate, if they want to. I am certainly not ashamed not to be more outraged than M. Brutus; yet this is what Brutus wrote: *You would do better, my dear Cicero, to put more effort into cutting short the civil wars than in losing your temper, and pursuing your personal resentments against the vanquished . . .*

---

* But did not come on sale until the 24th.

At this expression *committee of clemency*, what patriot would not feel deeply moved? for patriotism is the plenitude of all the virtues, and consequently cannot exist where there is neither humanity, nor philanthropy, but instead a spirit barren and parched by its own egoism. Oh! my dear Robespierre! It is to you that I address these words; for I have seen the time when Pitt had none left but you to conquer, when, without you, our Argo would have foundered, the Republic would have fallen into chaos, and the clubs of the Jacobins and the Mountain would have become a tower of babel. O my old college comrade, you whose eloquent speeches will be read by posterity remember well these lessons of history and of philosophy: that love is stronger and more lasting than fear; that admiration and religion are born from good deeds; the acts of clemency are the ladder of lies, as Tertullian tells us, by which the members of the Committees of Public Safety have been raised to heaven, and that no one has ever ascended there by bloody steps.

... To those who accuse me of being too moderate in this fourth issue, I will for the present reply as Marat did, when, on a very different occasion, we reproached him with having been excessive in his paper: You have understood nothing of what I have been saying; Oh! my God! let me merely say this: you'll change your opinion soon enough.

Ibid.

165. Camille, Hébert and the Jacobins

Warned after the publication of his fourth number that he was 'skirting the guillotine', Desmoulins turned to a personal attack on Hébert. Hébert had denounced the 'champion of all the jackasses who are in quod', and accused Desmoulins of marrying a rich wife. In turn Desmoulins armed himself with information from the official records concerning payments to the *Père Duchesne* and indicted Hébert for theft against the nation. Hébert was unable to account successfully for the money he had received to help pay for his paper, and so replied with further invective of a personal nature. The exchange of polemics was carried out by Hébert and Desmoulins in the club as well as in their papers.

Camille will stay in the Jacobin Club, despite the faults of his frankness. By revoking their resolution that excluded Camille, the Jacobins have paid striking homage to the principle of unrestricted freedom of opinion and of the press. Also, it would have been ungrateful to have acted so severely towards a patriot who gave his services to the Revolution; and, moreover, it would have been a real triumph for the aristocrats who are never more content than when they see the best patriots tearing each other to pieces, being disunited and mutually excluding each other from the popular assemblies. They have already had enough pleasure in reading the commonplaces that *le Vieux Cordelier* and *le Père Duchesne* write in the face of the whole Republic. Doubtless, these two are good citizens who, wiser than the heroes of Homer, should only feast themselves when the country has no further need of them. What have they to reproach themselves with? At the most with the errors, and exaggerations, the product perhaps only of a mind too exalted or of a soul too sensitive. Camille, for example, was wrong to accuse Hébert of swindling. As for Hébert, was he not obviously exaggerating the affair when he called Camille a counter-revolutionary, another Brissot, for having demanded liberty for the patriots imprisoned among the suspects? Is Camille not to be forgiven for desiring that we be the last to punish traitors and conspirators? It would be proof that the French Republic was fully consolidated. Camille thinks that it is only despots who are at all greedy for blood. His mistake lies in having said this too soon. A day will come when the death penalty will be abolished; in principle, it has already been accepted. But that splendid law, so worthy of a republican people, cannot, must not receive its application before its time. Peace for the good is only the result of war on the wicked.

Camille also thought that it must be a most painful task for the Revolutionary Tribunal to have to pronounce so many executions. Ah! no doubt, these patriotic judges ardently desire to reach the end of their sitting. It is hard on them having only death verdicts to pronounce. Their love of justice has by no means excluded from their hearts the sentiment of humanity, and the looks that they give to the condemned show this to be so. Camille would deserve more than the burning of his newspapers if he had proposed that pardon be granted to the royalists, counter-revolutionaries, cheats, and enemies of the Republic . . .

We shall conclude by congratulating Camille, for having held so strongly to unlimited freedom of opinion and of the press; he knows the full consequence of this. He knows that the public welfare depends on it. And, doubtless, it is this that made Robespierre suddenly change his mind. The great legislators, and history does not count many of them until now, never feared the despotism of thought. It is only the tyrant that must suffer in a powerful and enlightened republic, which is not afraid, as one was afraid under the monarchy, that truth be shouted from the roof-tops.

Les Révolutions de Paris, No. 221, 14–23 Nivôse, Year II
(3–12 January 1794), pp. 425–26, 427.

'AN EMANATION OF VIRTUE'

The Terror has often been regarded as synonymous with the aims and ideals of the Revolution, rather than an aberration thereof. Yet it was never regarded as other than a temporary measure–except by a few zealots. Robespierre, who tried to prolong it beyond the period of emergency, paid for his error.

166. Towards the Reign of Eternal Justice

This speech, delivered by Robespierre to the Convention on 5 February 1794, was occasioned in part by the struggle with the 'citras' and 'ultras'. In it he justifies the policies of the government and outlines its aims. Entitled 'Report on the Principles of Public Morality', it followed a speech where Robespierre claimed that 'The Revolution owes its enemies nothing but death'.

What is the goal towards which we are heading? The peaceful enjoyment of liberty and equality, the reign of that eternal justice from which the laws have been engraved not on marble and stone but in the hearts of all men, even in the heart of the slave who forgets them or of the tyrant who denies them.

We want an order of things in which all base and cruel passions will be unknown, and all generous and charitable feelings watched over by the laws; where ambition is the desire to merit glory and to serve the country; where distinctions are born only of equality itself; where the citizen is responsible to the magistrate and the magistrate to the people, and the people to justice; where the country assures the well-being of each individual, and where each individual enjoys with pride the prosperity and glory of the fatherland; where all its members grow by constant exchange of republican sentiments and by the need to merit the esteem of a great people; where the arts are decorations of the liberty that ennobles them; commerce, the source of public prosperity, and not just of the monstrous opulence of a few families.

In our country, we want to substitute morality for egotism, probity for honour, principles for customs, duties for proprieties, the rule of reason for the tyranny of fashion, contempt of vice for contempt of misfortune, pride for insolence, greatness of soul for vanity, love of glory for love of money, good folk for good company, merit for intrigue, genius for wit, truth for brilliance, the charm of happiness for the boredom of sensuousness, the greatness of man for the pettiness of the great; a people magnanimous, powerful, happy, for a people amiable, frivolous and wretched, that is to say, all the virtues and all the miracles of the republic for all the vices and all the absurdities of the monarchy . . . Now what is the fundamental principle of democratic or popular government, that is to say, the essential force that maintains and inspires it? It is virtue: I am speaking of public virtue, which brought about so many wonders in Greece and Rome, and which must produce even more astounding ones in republican France: of that virtue that is none other than love of the fatherland and of its laws. . . .

If the mainspring of popular government in time of peace is virtue, the mainspring of popular government in time of revolution is at the same time virtue and terror; virtue, without which terror is intolerable; terror, without which virtue is powerless. Terror is nothing other than justice, prompt, stern and inflexible; it is therefore an emanation of virtue; it is not so much a particular principle as a consequence of the general principle of democracy applied to the most urgent needs of our country. It has been said that terror is the mainspring of despotic government. Would ours then resemble a despotism? Yes, just as the sword that shines in the hand of the heroes of liberty resembles that with which the satellites of tyranny are armed. If the despot rules his brutalised subjects by terror, he is right as a despot. Tame the enemies of liberty by terror, and you will be right as the founders of the Republic. The government of the Revolution is the despotism of liberty against tyranny.

> *La Gazette nationale* (or *Le Moniteur universel*), No. 139, 19 Pluviôse, Year II (7 February 1794); 3rd series, vol. 6, pp. 402 and 404.

167. 'Not Cruel like Kings and their Ministers'

We are sure that all the revolutionary or vigilance committees of the Republic would not have asked for anything better [than that the Committee of General Security examine the case of each suspect]; for if they put so much zeal and rigour into the arrests, who could doubt that it was not with the best intention in the world? Good sans-culottes can be mistaken, but they are in no way vindictive, unjust and cruel like kings and their ministers. Certainly, nothing was more urgent, more necessary than that measure, and the Republic plucked from it glorious enough fruits; but if it had been taken immediately after 10 August, a great deal of blood would have been saved, all the blood spilt in la Vendée, at Lyons, at Toulon, and even on our frontiers. Let us put our trust in the Convention which, doubtless, will not fail to seize the right moment to have the reign of terror replaced by that of justice. The sans-culottes are far from deceiving themselves that there are some innocent victims among the great number of detainees, and they hasten to correct the involuntary and inevitable mistakes that occur, when they bring the criminals to the tribunals. For it is necessary to distinguish carefully the conduct of a Committee of Twelve, who before 31 May had Hébert arrested, and had imprisoned the best patriots, from that which has been forced to be held since. The Committee of Twelve wanted the counter-revolution and, at the least, federalism. Our committee wants only the unity of the Republic.

Les Révolutions de Paris, No. 221, 14–23 Nivôse,
Year II (3–12 January 1794), p. 426.

168. The First Law—the Safety of the People

This extract is from the manuscript for Desmoulins' No. 7, which Desenne his bookseller was afraid to publish. Desmoulins has been discussing the virtues of freedom of the press–'Let there be freedom of the press at Moscow, and tomorrow Moscow will be a republic'– 'To say that liberty is dangerous to the Republic is as stupid as if one were to say that beauty can be afraid of setting itself before a mirror'.

.

But however incontestable these principles are, freedom of speech and of writing is not an article of the Declaration of Rights more sacred than others, all of which are entirely subordinate to the most compelling, the first of the laws, namely, *the safety of the people*; freedom of coming and going is also one of the articles of this Declaration of Rights, yet will anyone say that the émigrés have the right to come and go, of leaving the Republic and returning? The Declaration of Rights says also that all men are born and die equal, yet will anyone conclude from this that the Republic must overlook the *ci-devant* and not treat him as suspect; that all the citizens are equal before the Committees of General Security; that would be absurd; it would be equally so, if the revolutionary government had not the right to restrict the liberty of possessions, of opinion and of the press, the freedom of crying, *vive le roi* or *aux armes, et l'insurrection* against the Convention and the Republic. I have especially doubted the theory of my No. 4 on the unrestricted freedom of the press, even in a time of revolution, when I saw Plato, that mind so well ordered, so full of politics, of laws and of knowledge of rules of government, demand as a prior condition (in his treatise on

Laws, Book 4) that, in the city for which it is proposed to make laws, there be a tyrant (which is certainly very different from a Committee of Public Safety and of General Security), and that *the citizens need a preliminary government to succeed in making them happy and free*.

Le Vieux Cordelier, No. 7, quintidi Pluviôse, Year II, (3 February 1794).

169. Hébert Justifies his Ferocity

Hébert's reasoning on the need for severe measures closely follows Marat's. Compare, for example, Marat's plea in his edition of 2 June 1790: 'Can I be accused of being cruel, I who cannot bear to see an insect suffer? But when I think that, in order to spare a few drops of blood, we expose ourselves to spilling it in great waves, I get indignant, despite myself, at our false principles of humanity, and of our stupid trials for our cruel enemies.'

You speak only of choking, killing, beheading, massacring, the Feuillants will tell me! You have a great thirst for blood, you miserable dealer in furnaces. Haven't you spilt enough? Too much, damn it! But whose fault is that? It's yours, you blasted dim-wits who held back the arm of the people when it was time to strike. If they had strung up a few hundred rogues in the early days of the Revolution, there would not have perished since more than a million Frenchmen. . . . We have acted like milk-sops; we have given our enemies time to strengthen themselves, to arm themselves to the teeth, and, to our cost, to divide us. It was only a snowball to begin with; but this ball became an enormous mass which only just failed to crush us. Let the past be a lesson to you; profit from the mistakes we made in order not to commit more in the future. No more mercy for these scoundrels, whom we dealt with leniently for too long, who would not do the same to us if they could once get their claws into us. A fight to the death between the men of the people and the enemies of the people has begun: it can only end when one of the two sides has destroyed the other. . . .

Le Père Duchesne: Hatin, VI, 520–21

170. To the Future Generations

This extract is from the final number of the *Révolutions de Paris*.

You generations that will succeed us, more blessed than we, having learnt from our mistakes and become wise by our follies, it will doubtless be enough to have charted for you the main reefs. O my children, we shall leave you only roses to pick; your fathers will have had nothing but the thorns.

Children more blessed than your fathers, we have been forced to tolerate, to endure many things that would be loathsome to you, but which will remain unknown to you. In the first place, as public affairs become, in time, less numerous, less complicated, you will not see the National Assembly dividing off into small groups, who solve their difficulties by getting away from the eye of the sovereign people. Next, you will doubtless completely abolish payment for public officials, or indeed all positions will be paid the same. Where is the equality in paying one citizen more than another? Such differences in salary still smack of aristocracy. With a free people there are no first and last places. . . .

For too long have we allowed women to leave their homes to be present at the deliberations of the legislators, at the debates of the popular societies. You will recall their true, their unique vocation, and not permit them to deviate from it any more. They will continue to adorn the national feasts, but they will no longer interfere in public affairs . . .

You will look into what goes on in the detention houses: pending trial, you will scrupulously observe the law, which lays down that a detainee be heard within a day, and if it is possible at the very time of his detention. If the crime is the kind that detains the accused for some time, you will not leave him to languish in idleness.

We have all been soldiers in order to conquer liberty and to reduce its enemies to silence. But the morals of a camp are not those that are needed to put to good use all the advantages that the republican government promises and guarantees. More blessed than we, you are almost certain to avoid that military spirit, inevitable during the storms of a long revolution.

Under the government that we bequeath as a heritage to you, you will have for its execution no need of all those violent means that typify even today the republic of Venice, which prolongs its precarious existence only by means of spies and informers, of hangmen and state inquisitors. Everything will work of its own accord, everything will flow from principles. The motherland will be neither a vixen nor a stepmother. You will see in her only a good mother of her family. You will love her, you will adore her. Every government, as wise as one would wish it, cannot long exist if it does not make itself loved. Every citizen must love the Republic as his mistress.

More blessed than we, you future generations who come after us, you will cling to the principles of republican government, as nature, whose example it is ever necessary to come back on, clings to the principles of its system: it is its slave. The constitution that we leave you is the most perfect thing that one could conceive to hold men together. Some people will perhaps still create circumstances and occasions to cover these principles with a veil, a veil suited to the intriguers and the ambitious. Tear this veil down immediately with an indignant hand, and punish the first among you who would dare to propose to silence for one moment those principles. They have been silent long enough; they have had only too much difficulty in making themselves heard above the cries of the suffering and in the midst of the tempests that have raged during the inauguration of the statue of liberty.

Finally, the republican government is a strong oak that we planted to give shade to our children. As soon as it has taken root, nothing must, nothing can shake it. It must protect and cover all Europe with its welcoming shade, and it must last as long as the soil that preserves and nourishes it.

Les Révolutions de Paris, No. 225, 25 Pluviôse–10 Ventôse,
Year II (13–28 February 1794).

Glossary*

Abbaye

Parisian prison built between 1631 and 1635. It began as the prison of the monastery of Saint-Germain-des-Près and was later converted into a military prison. A principal scene of the September massacres of 1792; demolished in 1857.

Active Citizens

Although the Declaration of Rights (26 August 1789) had recognised the right for 'all' citizens to take part in the making of laws, the Constituent Assembly established a representative system. However, not everyone had the right to vote in the elections. The Constitution divided citizens into two classes: 'passive' and 'active' citizens. The latter excluded domestic servants and all those who did not pay taxes equal to at least three days' labour. In 1791, out of a total population of 26 million, there were some 4,298,360 'active' citizens. This meant that 3 million poor were excluded from the vote. The 'active' citizens were also divided into grades. The primary assembly could choose as their 'electors' only those persons who held estate of specified amount–such men were to be chosen in proportion of one to a hundred members. These persons met at the departmental capital and formed the electoral assembly and elected to the main offices, including the National Assembly. (See also doc. 133.)

Aiguillon, Armand De Vignerot du Plessis de Richelieu, duc d'

b. Paris, 1761–d. Hamburg, 1800.
Deputy of the nobility to the Estates-General, he voted with the constitutionals and played an important role in the events of the night of 4 August 1789. He was in the Army of the Rhine in 1792, but after 10 August he fled abroad because the Legislative Assembly had accused him of having disapproved of certain of its measures. His name was subsequently removed from the list of émigrés but he died before he could return to France.

Anacharsis Clootz

See Clootz, Jean Baptiste

---

* Names of newspapers and editors covered in the Introduction are not included in the Glossary. The Index should be consulted for these and other more general references, as well as for location of actual terms included in the Glossary.

Glossary

Annates

> A tax on the first year's income of an ecclesiastical benefice paid to the papacy. During the Middle Ages there had been constant opposition to such payments, but they had been confirmed by the concordat between Francis I and Pope Leo X (1516). The Constituent Assembly abolished them on 4 August 1789.

Assignats

> Paper money used in France between 1789 and 1796. Initially issued as bonds, carrying interest, in order to avoid bankruptcy (2 November 1789), they soon became, in effect, a forced paper currency, whose excessive issue led to inflation. They were discontinued 19 February 1796.

Audouin, François-Xavier

> b. Limoges, 1766–d. Paris, 1837.
> A zealous Jacobin, he became a member of the Revolutionary Commune, 9–10 August 1792, and subsequently a member of the Committee of General Security. However, he was excluded when the Committee was reorganised in January 1793. With Barère, he proposed a motion that a commission should be appointed for the purpose of preparing the organic laws of 'The Republican Constitution', 24 Brumaire, Year III (14 November 1794). Imprisoned because of his intemperate civism, and freed after 13 Vendémiaire, Year IV (14 October 1795), he was, under the Consulate, secretary of the department of forests.

Autun, Bishop of

> *See* Talleyrand

Avignon

> A town situated on the Rhône, in the department of Vaucluse. From 1309–76 it was the residence of the popes. It was sold by Joanna I, Queen of Sicily, to Clement VI in 1348 and it remained in papal possession after the popes returned to Rome. It was governed by papal legates and vice-legates until the Revolution. On 12 June 1790, Avignon voted its annexation to France. The decree of 14 September 1791 confirmed this vote. Bonaparte made it into a bishopric in 1802 and it returned to an archbishopric only in 1821.

Bailly, Jean Sylvain

> b. Paris, 1736–d. 1793.
> Savant and politician, member of the 'Académie des Sciences' (1763), and author of works on astronomy. In 1783 he entered the 'Académie Française'. On 12 May 1789 he was elected first deputy of Paris to the Estates-General. On 3 June he

became president of the National Assembly. He was the first
to take the Tennis Court Oath (20 June), and as head of the
Assembly he refused to accede to Louis XVI's orders of 23 June.
On 15 July he was appointed Mayor of Paris. With Necker and
Lafayette he was one of the three popular heroes of 1789; like
them he fell foul of the radical press, and from 1790 was being
continually attacked, especially by Marat. It was he, as Mayor
of Paris, who proclaimed the Martial Law of 17 July 1791 that
led to the massacre on the Champ de Mars. Thereafter his reputation in the eyes of the democrats was irretrievably ruined.
He resigned his post on 12 November 1791. On 11 November
1793 he was himself condemned to death and executed.

Barbaroux, Charles Jean Marie

b. Marseilles, 1767–d. Bordeaux, 1794.
Deputy for Marseilles to the Assembly, and member of the
Jacobin Club where he was a prominent associate of the
Brissotins. He published *L'Observateur Marseillais*. As a Girondin,
he was proscribed with them on 31 May 1793. He fled to Caen,
where he tried to organise resistance to the Jacobin government. Later he went to Bordeaux, where he was discovered at
the same time as Buzot and Pétion, and guillotined.

Barnave, Antoine Pierre Joseph-Marie

b. Grenoble, 1761–d. Paris, 1793.
A successful lawyer at Grenoble and member of the Third
Estate of the Dauphiné, which met in 1788. Member of the
Constituent Assembly, his influence and reputation as an
orator rivalled that of Mirabeau. He was constantly ridiculed
by the aristocratic press for his reaction to the murders of
Foulon and Berthier, 'Is their blood then so pure?' With
Dupont and the Lameth, he was to become a leader of the
Feuillant party and chief advocate of the revision of the
Constitution. At this time he became a secret adviser to
the Crown, a role formerly filled by Mirabeau.

After 10 August, he was accused with Guadet of forming a
plan for counter-revolution and after imprisonment at the
Abbaye and then at the Conciergerie was executed on 29
October 1793 aged only 32. In 1792 he wrote an *Introduction à
la Révolution française* (published 1843).

Bastille

A fortress built in the east of Paris towards the end of the 14th
century. Extended and enlarged in the 16th and 17th centuries,
it served from the first as a state prison. It became the symbol
of royal absolutism. Rectangular in shape, its flanks were cut
by eight great towers of five storeys each. Its upper gallery was
filled with cannon that could be turned against attack from
within or without. It stood astride the Rue St.-Antoine, lying
towards the Porte St.-Antoine. Each tower had several
prisons and underground dungeons. It held usually seventy to

eighty prisoners, but this number rose under Louis XIV and Louis XV. Many were imprisoned on the *lettres de cachet* (q.v.), for political or religious reasons. At the time of its fall, it held seven prisoners.

Besenval, Pierre, baron de

b. Soleure in Switzerland, 1721–d. Paris, 1791.
General in charge of the troops surrounding Paris in July 1789; he fled on the morning of the 14th, but was captured and three months later tried at the Châtelet. The main reason for the hatred of the people against him was an order to De Launay (q.v.) that he must hold out by any means whatever until replacements were sent to him. The radical press demanded his execution, but court intrigue and the skill of his lawyer, De Sèze, secured his release.

Bicêtre

Important hospice for the aged. A corruption of the name 'Wincestre', i.e. a castle built in 1285 by John of Pontoise, Bishop of Winchester. Destroyed in 1632 by Louis XIII, it was replaced by a new building to give shelter to wounded soldiers. After the construction of the Invalides, it was turned into a prison for vagabonds, madmen and galley-slaves. *See also* Hôpital général.

Blacks (*noirs*)

Term of abuse for the opponents of the Revolution who seated themselves at the extreme right in the Constituent Assembly (usually aristocrats and priests). Marat used expressions such as 'half-blacks' (*demi-noirs*), or 'browns' (*bruns*), for the moderate right, otherwise known as Impartials.

Bourdon de l'Oise, François Louis

b. Rouy-le-Petit, 1751–d. Sinnamary, Fr. Guiana, 1798.
A former procurator at the Paris *parlement,* he took part in the uprising of 10 August. In the Convention he fully supported the Terror. However, on 9 Thermidor, Year II (27 July 1794), he headed the troops that arrested Robespierre. He became so reactionary and pro-royalist that the Directory deported him after 18 Fructidor, Year V (4 September 1797).

Brissotins

Name of the group that formed itself around Brissot in the Legislative Assembly. In the Convention they became known as Girondins, taking their name from the department of the Gironde, from which many of their members came.

Brunswick, Ferdinand, Duke of

b. Wolfenbüttel, 1735–d. Ottensen, near Altona, 1806.
Leader of the coalition armies against France. On 25 July

1792 he published the famous *manifeste* which threatened to destroy Paris, if Louis XVI was harmed. Brunswick was defeated at Valmy (September 1792) and soon after he was relieved of his command. He returned to active service in 1806 and was mortally wounded at Auerstadt.

Buzot, François

b. Evreux, 1760–d. Saint-Magne, Gironde, 1794.
Lawyer; with Robespierre and Pétion gained great popularity in the Constituent Assembly for his democratic opinions. He later became a leader of the Girondins, and was enamoured with Mme Roland. After the 2 June 1793, he raised an army of 4,000 men in Normandy, but was defeated and took refuge in the Gironde. His decayed body was discovered alongside that of Pétion's in July 1794. He has left us his *Mémoires sur la Révolution française*.

Ça ira

A song of the revolutionary period. Ladre adapted the words to the tune of the *Carillon National* of Bécourt. The origins of the phrase is said to come from Benjamin Franklin. In Paris during the American War of Independence (1776–83), he was asked how the war was progressing: his short reply was '*Ça ira!*'

Calotins

Those who observe religious prescriptions or those who belong to the clerical order.

Camus, Armand

b. Paris, 1740–d. 1804.
Advocate of the clergy at the Paris *parlement*, and a Jansenist, he was elected to the Estates-General and took a major part in drawing up the Civil Constitution of the Clergy. At the Convention, he was one of the Commissioners sent to enquire into the conduct of Dumouriez. Arrested and handed over to the Austrians, he was returned to France in 1795. He was largely responsible for the formation of the National Archives.

Capet

The name given as a term of insult to Louis XVI and his family, particularly after the abolition of hereditary titles. Desmoulins was particularly fond of addressing the king as Louis Capet, or just Capet.

Carmagnole

A song and dance adapted by the revolutionaries, but prohibited under the Consulate. The authors are not known. It originated in August 1792 and was successively added to in 1830, 1848, 1863–4, and 1882–3.

Glossary

Casuel

Revenues, lay or ecclesiastical, paid for services not regularly given, such as for burial and marriage services.

Chambre d'union (de réunions)

A term given to the special courts instituted by Louis XIV, in 1679, in the *parlements* of Metz and of Besançon, whose purpose was to recover dependencies ceded by France at the Treaties of Westphalia and Nimwegen.

Charenton

A hospice founded in 1641 and maintained by the Brothers of the Charity of St. John of God. Until the abolition of *lettres de cachet* it received persons so put away by their families and others sent on the king's orders. It was suppressed in 1795 and re-established in 1797 as a national asylum.

Champ de Mars

A plain on the left bank of the Seine where the Eiffel Tower stands today. It was the chief military parade-ground of Paris (1770–89). During the Revolution it was used as a main centre for such civic festivals as the celebration of the anniversary of the fall of the Bastille and for the Festival of the Supreme Being (8 June 1794). It was here that the famous petitions of 16–17 July 1791 and 6 August 1792 were drawn up.

Charles IX

Name of the play by M. J. Chénier that enjoyed immense popularity in the early days of the Revolution. Its plot centred around the massacre of St. Bartholomew's day, 1572; its message is anti-clerical, while the part played in it by the unfortunate king, Charles IX, highlights the perfidy of kings and their counsellors.

Châteauvieux, Regiment of

See Nancy.

Châtelet

Former Paris castle, standing on the right bank of the Seine, which, until the Revolution, was the seat of royal justice. It also served as a prison. Like the Bastille, a reminder of the old régime, it was constantly denounced by the radical press as a refuge for the aristocracy. It was demolished in 1802.

Clootz, Jean Baptiste du Val-de-Grâce (*dit* Anacharsis)

b. Gnadenthal, 1755–d. Paris, 1794.
Born into great wealth, he donated large parts of his fortune to the Revolution, and besieged many newspapers with his letters and articles. A fanatic advocate of aggressive war by

France in 1792, he became associated with the Girondins.
Declared a French citizen and elected to the Convention, he
tried to get in favour with the Roland clique but was rejected.
He then became a Jacobin and, after 2 June, a wholehearted
sans-culotte. But his association with the worship of Reason
and his foreign birth brought on him the suspicions of Robespierre, and so, despite his acceptance of the Revolution at
every turn, he in the end mounted the guillotine (24 March
1794).

Club Monarchique

Formed in Paris as an attempt to counteract Jacobin influence.
It gave charitable relief but was eventually forced to close its
doors under Jacobin pressure.

Coblenz

Town at confluence of the Moselle and Rhine. It became the
main rallying place of French émigrés under the leadership of
Condé from as early as July 1789. In November 1791, 60,000
émigrés were enrolled in the army there. The streets of Coblenz at that time are said to have resembled a miniature
Versailles.

Cockade (Fr. *cocarde*)

A ribbon or knot of ribbon or rosette of leather, worn in the
hat as a badge of a political party. In 1767 a regulation ordered
soldiers to wear a white cockade, and in 1782 cockades were
forbidden to all but soldiers. The king's gendarmes wore black
cockades. After the fall of the Bastille, the National Guard was
granted a cockade (27 July 1789), made of a white ribbon
edged with blue and red, colours of the city. The wearing of
this cockade was extended to all citizens and became a
patriotic duty.

Committees (*recherches, aliénation and constitution*)

The work of the National Assembly was done largely in committee. There were thirty-one standing committees of which
the most important met almost daily. The *rapports* of such committees could initiate legislation. Thus the *comité des recherches*
issued warrants of arrest. The *comité d'aliénation* attended to the
sale of the *biens nationaux*. The *comité de constitution* was charged
with the task of drafting a constitution to implement the
Declaration of Rights.

'Common-Sense': (pamphlet)

See Paine, Thomas.

Commune

In this context, the name given to the municipal government
of Paris from 1789 to 1795. On 13 July 1789, some thirty-six

electors of the Third Estate illegally took over some of the municipal power and formed the *comité permanent*. On 30 July they took the title of *Commune de Paris* and named Bailly (q.v.) as Mayor. The following year a regular government was elected by the active citizens of the forty-eight Sections. The subsequent history of the Commune mirrored and was part of the political events of the Revolution.

Conciergerie

At Paris, the Conciergerie is a part of the Palais de Justice, which was the royal residence from Saint Louis to Charles V. It then became a prison. Under the Terror, it became the ante-chamber of the scaffold. Sometimes it held as many as 1,200 victims, who included Marie-Antoinette, Mme du Barry, the Girondins, Danton, and Robespierre.

Condorcet, Marie Jean Antoine Nicholas de Caritat, marquis de

b. Ribemont, 1743–d. Bourg-la-Reine, 1794. One of the most famous of the writers and philosophers of the late 18th century; a member of the great Dauphiné family. Elected a member of the 'Académie des Sciences' in 1769. In 1782 elected to the 'Académie Française'; was recognised as the chief of the *idéologues*. During the Revolution he played an important part in many newspapers, and was variously associated with the *Bouche de Fer, Républicain, Journal de Paris, Chronique de Paris*, and others. He was deputy for Paris in the Legislative Assembly (1791/2). His moderate opinions and attacks on the Jacobins in the papers to which he contributed, brought him under fire from the extreme left in 1793. Outlawed by the Jacobin government he was imprisoned at Bourg-la-Reine, 27 March 1794. The next day he was found dead, either from poison, or from exhaustion.

Cordeliers, Club des

Revolutionary club founded at Paris in July 1790, under the name of *Société des droits de l'homme et du citoyen*. Its headquarters were in the former monastery of the branch of Franciscans known as the Cordeliers. Its leaders included Danton, Camille Desmoulins, Marat, Chaumette, Ronsin and Hébert. It had a more popular recruitment than the Jacobins due to its low subscription; it also adopted more advanced ideas. It had special influence over the workers in the Faubourgs St.-Antoine and St.-Marceau. It spread the republican movement after the Varennes incident in 1791. The Cordeliers disappeared politically when the Hébertists, who had taken a leading role in the club, were sent to the scaffold in March 1794.

Corvée

Labour service performed by the peasant on his lord's demesne, without payment. The royal *corvée* expanded under Louis XV and was performed as road building and maintenance. Under Louis XVI, royal *corvée* could be substituted by a tax. Both kinds were abolished on 4 August 1789 and by the law of 15 March 1790.

Danton, Georges Jacques

b. Arcis-sur-Aube, 1759–d. Paris, 1794.
Studied at Troyes and Rheims, graduating in law. He founded the Cordeliers (q.v.) in 1790 and was one of the great popular leaders of the Revolution, also one of the few who were not directly associated with a newspaper; was president of the Cordelier district in January 1790 when that district defended Marat against the Parisian authorities; was accused of being an instigator of the September massacres–he had, in fact, neither urged nor forbidden them, but he went on to justify the use of force. Deputy for Paris in the Convention he sat with the Mountain and voted the death of Louis XVI. In April 1793 he was the virtual head of the first Committee of Public Safety, but refused to join the second (July). Subsequently he became the centre of opposition to the Terror. Robespierre attacked him and had him guillotined in April 1794. His venality is today generally admitted. He was a committed supporter of the Revolution and safeguarded it at such times as the threat of Prussian invasion (September 1792).

Dérogeance

Action which led a person to lose his quality of nobility under the old régime. This included the pursuit of a trade and such like. A person could exploit his own estates without loss of status, but not those of another. Unlike *déchéance* (loss of title or deposition from office), the loss was not definitive. It ceased as soon as the disqualifying trade was renounced. Furthermore, children who were born after such acts were committed, were not deprived of their noble status.

Districts of Paris

For the elections to the Estates-General an ordinance of 15 April 1789 divided the sixteen quarters of Paris into sixty districts. The headquarters served as an electoral centre. Like the assembly of electors, the district assemblies took an active part in the politics and administration of the city. In June 1790, the sixty districts were replaced by forty-eight Sections.

Dumouriez (Charles François du Périer, dit)

b. Cambrai, 1739–d. Oxfordshire, England, 1823.
French General. After a varied military and diplomatic career, he became Minister of Foreign Affairs (11 March 1792) and a member of the Girondin ministry. After the dismissal of the Girondin ministers on 13 June 1792 he was put in charge of the army of the north. His early victories at Valmy and

Jemappes fed his ambition of becoming master of France and led him to intrigue against the Revolution. Defeated at Neerwinden (18 March 1793), he refused to yield his command and he handed over the Commissioners of the Convention to the enemy. He finally went over himself to the Austrians. Despite his defection, he failed to secure royalist confidence. He was not allowed to return to France at the Restoration.

Duport, Adrien Jean François

b. Paris, 1759–d. Appenzell, Switzerland, 1798.
In 1789 he was deputy of the Paris nobility to the Estates-General and an influential member of the National Assembly, allying himself with the Third Estate. With Barnave and Alexandre de Lameth he formed the famous 'triumvirate'. After the return from Varennes, he defended the royal prerogatives. A distinguished jurist, he was named president of the criminal tribunal of Paris, but he fled the day after 10 August. He was arrested but escaped and finally settled in Switzerland.

Enragés

The name given in 1793 to a party of extreme revolutionaries, whose leaders were Jacques Roux, Varlet, Claire Lacombe, Chalier and Leclerc. The group was especially concerned with food costs and proposed such measures as the requisition of foodstuffs, help for the poor, a tax on the wealthy. They opposed the Girondins, and influenced the Montagnards. Their extremism roused the anger of Robespierre. Roux and Varlet were arrested in September 1793 by order of the Committee of Public Safety. The Hébertists were their successors on the political scene.

As early as 1789 the right-wing press used the term *enragé* when referring to their opponents.

Esprémesnil, Jean-Jacques Duval d'

b. Pondichéry, 1746–d. Paris, 1794.
In the Paris *parlement* of 1788, he opposed any reform of privileges and he was one of the inspirers of the events of May 1788, which forced the summoning of the Estates-General. Elected to that body as deputy for the nobility of Paris-outside-the-walls, he proved one of the most dedicated defenders of privilege. Condemned to death by the Revolutionary Tribunal, he was executed in 1794.

Faubourg

Those parts of a city lying outside the city proper, beyond the gates or walls. By 1789 the faubourgs had all become enclosed within the city boundaries. The most famous among them were the Faubourg St.-Antoine and the Faubourg St.-Marceau. Applied also to the working-class population of the faubourgs and (wrongly) to denote working-class districts.

Fayettistes

See under Lafayette.

Federalism

Provincial discontent with Parisian rule expressed itself in the creation of revolutionary committees of the departments (September 1792), and then with federal revolutionary committees. After 2 June 1793, the Girondin deputies who had taken refuge in the country at large encouraged a series of uprisings against the 'dictatorship' of the capital. The Jacobins denounced their separatist tendencies. Sixty departments were involved in one way or another. The Convention acted firmly to suppress the movements.

Fédérés

Representatives sent to the Festival of the Federation on 14 July 1790. Used particularly of the battalion of volunteers who, in 1792, were raised in the provinces and sent to the capital where they played a significant part in the insurrection of 10 August.

Feuillants, Club des

Took its name from the place of its headquarters in Paris, which was the former Cistercian monastery situated between the Rue St.-Honoré and the Terrace of the Tuileries. The religious were dissolved in 1791. Already the Constituent Assembly had occupied some of its property. On 16 July 1791 it became the meeting place for those who split with the Jacobin Club after the dispute concerning the king's fate following his flight. This group was led by Lafayette, Sieyès, Barnave, Duport, and de Lameth. They sought to maintain the 1791 Constitution. 264 deputies were members and they formed the right wing of the Legislative Assembly until 20 August 1792. They became divided among themselves (Lamethistes and Fayettistes), and they were put down by the Jacobin/Girondin alliance. 10 August marked their end, just as it marked that of royalty. The designation Feuillant, however, continued to be applied to any 'moderates'.

Franc-fief

(a) a fief which carried obligations worthy only of a free man.
(b) the tax payable by a commoner who acquired property of nobles. The tax was first imposed by Phillip III in 1275.

Gabelle

A salt-tax (under the old régime) theoretically imposed on everybody, but from which numerous classes were exempted, e.g. clerics, nobles, royal officials. Sale of salt was a monopoly except in a few provinces and severe penalties were imposed on those who broke the law. The tax was extremely unpopular, and the existence of a host of *gabelous*, whose job it was to detect fraud, increased the ill-feeling. It was suppressed in 1790 and reimposed in 1806.

Gallican Church *or* Gallicanism

The term given to a body of thought within the Roman Catholic Church that recognised papal primacy, but asserted certain rights of the national Church. For political reasons, it was encouraged by the monarchy in its struggle with the papacy. It may be said to have originated in the 13th century, but the classic formulation was in the four so-called 'Gallican articles' passed by the assembly of the French Clergy in 1682. The papacy condemned them but they continued through the 18th century. Napoleon added them to the concordat of 1801. They were finally ended by the Vatican Council of 1870.

Guadet, Marguerite Elie

b. Saint-Emilion, Gironde, 1758–d. Bordeaux, 1794.
Deputy from the Gironde at the Legislative Assembly (1791) and a member of the Jacobin Club. A member of the Convention, he was one of the most eloquent of the Girondins, bitterly attacking Robespierre and Marat. After 2 June, he fled to the provinces, but after the failure of the appeal to arms at Caen (13 June), he was eventually captured and executed at Bordeaux.

Guillotin, Joseph Ignace

b. Saintes, 1738–d. Paris, 1814.
A doctor and member of the Constituent Assembly after whom the guillotine is named. He did not invent the guillotine, but only proposed its introduction as a humane and egalitarian form of execution.

Hôpital général

Known also under the name of Salpêtrière. Established 1656–7 as a remedy for the increasing poverty in Paris. It was under ecclesiastical control, it had large revenues and included ten 'houses' among which was the 'Enfants trouvés' and 'Bicêtre'.

Hôtel-de-Ville (Paris)

Seat of municipal government, begun in the 16th century and completed in 1623. It was destroyed by fire in 1871 and reconstructed. During the Revolution it served as the headquarters of the Commune (q.v.).

Jacobins

See Society of the Friends of the Constitution.

Glossary

Jansenist

The name given to a supporter or holder of the doctrines of the Dutch Theologian, Cornelius Jansen (1585–1638), who taught a special doctrine of justification. Despite condemnation in 1642, 1653, 1693 and 1713, the Jansenists survived in France. Among their defenders had been Pascal (1623–62), and Pasquier Quesnel. The movement's headquarters were at the abbey of Port-Royal, near Paris. Jansenist influence was behind much of the religious reform of the Constituent Assembly.

Jardin des Plantes

Name given to the botanic garden of Paris, founded in 1636, to which were added in 1693 a museum of natural history, then a menagerie. Later changes were made under the intendant Buffon (1739–88).

Kersaint, Armand Guy Simon de Coetnempren, Count of

b. Le Havre, 1742–d. Paris, 1793.
Naval officer. In 1789 he attacked privileged orders in a pamphlet *le Bons Sens* and suggested a plan of reform of the Marine. A Paris deputy to the Legislative Assembly, he was a Girondin. In 1793 he was arrested as a suspect, condemned to death and executed.

Lafayette, Marie Joseph Paul Yves Roch Gilbert Motier, marquis de

b. Chavaniac, Auvergne, 1757–d. Paris, 1834.
Fought for the Americans in the War of Independence and helped to secure French aid for them. A liberal noble of great wealth; was elected to the Estates-General in 1789. He became first commander of the National Guard; helped to found the Feuillant Club in 1791. However, his favour of the crown after the flight to Varennes and his opening fire on the participants in the Champ de Mars petition (July 1791), lost him popularity. Even prior to this and as early as 1789, he was constantly being ridiculed in the pages of the *Ami du peuple*, *Révolutions de Paris*, *Orateur du peuple* and *Révolutions de France et de Brabant*, often under the derisory name Mottié. In 1792 he became a commandant at the frontier and he denounced the influence of the clubs. He failed to secure the support of his troops to march on Paris and crossed over to the enemy (August 19). He was imprisoned in Austria until 1797. Subsequently, he lived in retirement until after Waterloo when he became more active. He lived long enough to command the National Guard again in 1830 and to help Louis Philippe ascend the throne.

La Force

A Paris prison, formerly the residence of the duc de la Force, from which it took its name. It became a debtors' prison in

1780, was turned into a political prison in August 1792 and lasted till its destruction in 1850. It was one of the main prisons in the September 'massacre' and its most famous victim was the princess de Lamballe. It was situated between the Rue Pavée and the Rue de Roi-de-Sicile.

Lambesc, prince de (Elbeuf, Charles-Eugène de Lorraine, duc d')

b. Versailles, 1751–d. Vienna, 1825.
Colonel of the Royal-Allemand regiment in 1789. He was responsible for the attack of 12 July on the Parisian demonstrators. He fled the country and served in the Austrian army.

Lameth, Alexandre, chevalier de

b. Paris, 1760–d. Paris, 1829.

and Charles, comte de

b. Paris, 1757–d. Paris, 1832
Aristocratic brothers who professed liberal views. Alexandre de Lameth formed with Barnave and Duport the famous 'triumvirate' who were influential in the Constituent Assembly, The brothers left France after the fall of the king.

La lanterne

The cry '*À la lanterne*' (cf. '*Ah! ça ira, ça ira! Les aristocrates à la lanterne!*') was an incitement to hang someone from the street lamp. The *lanterne* of the Place de Grève, at the corner of the Rue de la Vannerie, served specially as an improvised gallows. Despite the horror affected by the aristocratic press at the incidence of popular justice involving '*la lanterne*', its influence as a threat by far outweighed its use as a means of execution.

De Launay, Bernard Jordan

b. Paris 1740–d. 1789.
Succeeded his father as Commandant of the Bastille in 1776. He was governor there when it was besieged by the Parisians on 14 July. He was accused by them of treachery and for this was massacred and his head carried in triumph on a pike on the return to Paris.

Leopold II

b. Vienna, 1747–d. 1792.
Emperor, Archduke of Austria, brother of Queen Marie-Antoinette of France. At first he hesitated to intervene in the Revolution, but after the flight of the king he issued his Declaration of Pillnitz (27 August 1791) which was, however, more a face-saver than a direct threat. The revolutionaries demanded that he intervene against the émigrés whom he tolerated at Coblenz (q.v.). Leopold rejected the French ultimatum (25 January 1792) and then made a military pact

with Prussia (7 February 1792). The war was about to break out when he died (1 March 1792).

Lettres de cachet

Letters, signed by the king (but often by a secretary), and closed with the royal seal. They were a special instrument of royal power (imprisonments, orders for exile, revoking of orders, etc.), and as such were hated especially by the nobles, who were the most frequent victims. They were suppressed on 16 March 1790.

Ligueurs

Term of abuse used during the Revolution. The expression derives from members of the Catholic confederation founded by the duc de Guise in 1576 to defend the Catholic religion against the Huguenots and, as a means of doing so, dethroning Henry III in favour of the Guises. The Ligue, discredited by its alliance with Philip II of Spain, was dissolved by Henry IV. The epithet *'ligueurs'* was often used with that of *'frondeur'*, this latter referring to the revolt against royal authority in the Frondes of 1648–52.

Mainmorte

A payment required to a landlord, when land was granted to an institution, lay or ecclesiastical, that was continuous, and did not pay inheritance tax on the death of an owner. A gift of land to the Church did not change hands, and was called property 'mainmorte' with usually agreement to pay the fee of mainmorte at stated intervals. Most such tenures date from the Middle Ages or prior to the eighteenth century.

Malouet, Pierre-Victor

b. Riom 1740–d. Paris, 1814.
One of the first leaders of the Revolution, especially in the events prior to the fall of the Bastille. The leader of the moderate right in the Constituent Assembly, he fell foul of the radicals for his support of the king's prerogatives and the retention of real power in the hands of the executive. Founder of the Impartials' club, or the Monarchical club; a leading spokesman for the moderate right he was respected by all but the extremists He emigrated to Britain after 10 August and returned to France under the Consulate.

Manège, La Salle de la

At Paris, near the Tuileries; it was converted into the meeting place for the main assemblies of the Revolution, from the Constituent Assembly to the Council of Five-Hundred. It was demolished in 1810.

Maury, abbé Jean Siffrein

b. Valréas, 1746–d. Rome, 1817.
Deputy to the Estates-General in 1789. As the most eloquent spokesman for the opinions of the extreme right, and for the

obstructionist policies he pursued throughout the period of the Constituent Assembly, he was one of the main enemies of the radical press. Despite this he was not a great favourite with some sections of the right-wing press. He emigrated to Rome in 1792, became Cardinal in 1794 and was named Archbishop of Paris under Napoleon (1810), but was not instituted.

Ministerials

Also Malouétins, Impartials, supporters of the Constitutional monarchy, favouring the absolute veto and often a bicameral Legislature.

Mottié

See Lafayette.

Mounier, Jean Joseph

b. Grenoble, 1758–d. 1806.
Like Malouet a popular leader in the events prior to 14 July–Mounier proposed the Tennis Court Oath. He resigned from his position as deputy following the October days, and returned to his home province, Dauphiné, where he unsuccessfully tried to stir up counter-revolution. He left for Geneva (May 1790) and then went to Britain two years later. Returned to France after 18 Brumaire, Year VIII (9 November 1799).

Nancy

A town on the River Meurthe, in Lorraine. On 31 August 1790, the garrison rebelled against their aristocratic officers. The rebellion was harshly suppressed by the marquis de Bouillé, who condemned several men to death and sent twenty-one Swiss, of the regiment of Châteauvieux, to the galleys. The name was thereafter invoked by the radical press as a symbol of martyrdom or counter-revolution.

Necker, Jacques

b. Geneva 1732–d. Coppet, near Geneva, 1804.
Financier, who was sent to Paris in 1747 where he established his position as a banker. He entered public life in 1772, and published several essays on economic affairs. In 1776 he became Director General of the Royal Treasury and then of Finance in 1777. His administrative reforms roused the hostility of the *parlements*. In 1781 he published his famous *Compte rendu au Roi*, which attacked royal expenditures and which by its optimism on the state of finances assured his popularity. He had to resign his post on 19 May 1781. He continued to press for reforms. On the acceptance of the fact of bankruptcy (16 August 1788), the king recalled Necker, but the situation was beyond recovery. His apparent support for the vote by head and reunion of the three orders added further to his popularity.

On 11 July 1789, Louis XVI dismissed Necker, which roused popular wrath and helped to bring about the attack on the Bastille. He was recalled again on 16 July and remained in office until September 1790. As it did with LaFayette and Bailly, the radical press defied popular opinion in its frequent attacks on the abilities of Necker. In September 1790 he was forced to leave France in disgrace.

Paine, Thomas

b. Thetford, Norfolk, England 1737–d. New York, 1809.
Emigrated to America in 1774 and became an ardent supporter of Independence. His pamphlet *Common Sense* (10 January 1776), was not merely a powerful expression of his views, but a document cited by the later French revolutionaries. In 1791 and 1792 he published his *Rights of Man* in answer to Burke's *Reflections on the Revolution*. Pitt had him indicted for treason, but he escaped to France and was elected to the Convention. He subsequently incurred the suspicion of Robespierre and was imprisoned from 28 December 1793 to 4 November 1794. He was released and returned to America after 9 Thermidor, Year II (27 July 1794).

Palais-Royal

An assembly of buildings and gardens, on the Rue St.-Honoré, which became known as such in 1643. It passed into the hands of the Orléans family in 1672. In 1780 it was opened to the public in a reconstructed form. It became the amusement centre of Paris. Public meetings were held there in the Revolution and it was there (12 July 1789), that Desmoulins, one among many, made his celebrated appeal to arms. Opposite the Palais-Royal was the Lycée, founded in 1785 as a centre for free lectures, concerts and exhibitions. It was open to the public from 9 a.m. to midnight, daily. As well as the books in its library, current periodicals were available for study.

Panthéon

Constructed to replace the former abbey of Ste.-Geneviève. Construction lasted from 1764 to 1812. The Constituent Assembly changed it from a church into a temple (April 1791), to shelter the remains of famous men—such as Mirabeau, Voltaire, Rousseau. It reverted to a church in 1806 and finally, in 1885, became a temple once more.

Parlements

The name given before the Revolution to certain sovereign courts that had final right of decision in civil and criminal cases. Fourteen such courts existed of which the *parlement de Paris* was the best known. The Paris *parlement* had administrative and political jurisdiction. It had also acquired the right to register royal decrees. Frequent opposition to royal wishes led to suppression or diminution of power and offices on part of the *parlements* in 1771. The Paris *parlement* alternated between defence of its privileges against monarchy and a desire to represent the new ideas. It came into opposition to the reforming movement in 1788 and 1789, so that from 3 November 1789, it was prorogued indefinitely.

Pétion de Villeneuve, Jérôme

b. Chartres, 1756–d. Saint-Emilion, 1794.
Lawyer, elected to the Estates-General in 1789; with Robespierre the most popular of the democrats. At the close of the Constituent Assembly he was elected Mayor of Paris over Lafayette and subsequently he became the first president of the Convention. By this time he had allied himself with the Girondins. He was one of the twenty-two Girondin deputies named in the May/June insurrection. He tried to raise Normandy against the Convention, but failed. Subsequently he committed suicide in the Gironde (1794).

Philippeaux, Pierre

b. Ferrières 1754–d. Paris, 1794.
Lawyer and deputy in 1792; Representative-on-Mission to the Vendée (June–October 1793). A friend of Danton and Desmoulins, he was executed with them in 1794.

Rabaut-Saint-Étienne, Jean-Paul

b. Nîmes, 1743–d. Paris, 1793.
Protestant pastor. In 1787 he negotiated for an edict of tolerance for Protestants. Deputy for the Third Estate at Nîmes in the Constituent Assembly (1789), he had freedom of conscience inscribed in the Declaration of the Rights of Man. In the Convention (1792), he sat with the Girondins and was a member of the Commission of Twelve. He was executed on 5 December 1793. He helped Cérutti found the *Feuille villageoise*, and collaborated in the *Chronique de Paris*.

Rentiers

The holders of national stock, on which the annual interest by 1789 consumed about one-half of the nation's revenue.

Robe (nobility of)

Those who had their noble origin from the purchase of offices of state.

Roland de la Platière, Jean-Marie

b. Thizy, Beaujolais, 1734–d. near Fleury-Sur-Andelle, 1793.
Economist and author of several works on manufacture. At Lyons he was elected notable of the general council of the commune (1790). In February 1791, he came to Paris, where

he later allied himself to the Brissotins and was a member of Dumouriez's ministry (March 1792). He became a member of the Convention and determined to protect it against the Commune. He defended the monarchy and left the ministry in January 1793. Continually attacked by Marat, his arrest was ordered, but he escaped. He committed suicide 10 November 1793.

Roland, Marie-Jeanne Phlipon, Mme

b. Paris 1754–d. 1793.
Wife of the former, whom she surpassed in intelligence and ability. Her dinner-parties were favourite meeting places for the Girondins. Her *Mémoires* written during her five months' imprisonment are the most famous of their kind. She was executed on 8 November 1793.

Ronsin, Charles Philippe

b. Soissons, 1752–d. Paris, 1794.
National Guard Officer, member, and later prominent leader of the Cordeliers Club, and War Commissioner (1792); later became general; he fought in the Vendée and defied La Rochejaquelin at Doué in August 1793. Later he was recalled and arrested, but freed on the intervention of Danton. He was subsequently executed with the Hébertistes.

Rossignol, Jean Antoine

b. Paris, 1759–d. Anjouan, 1802.
Revolutionary general and friend of Robespierre. He joined in the conspiracy of Babeuf, but was acquitted. He took part in the *coup d'état* of 18 Fructidor, Year V (4 September 1797). Bonaparte had him deported in 1801.

Royal-Allemand, Regiment of

See Lambesc.

Rue Vivienne

The financial centre of Paris.

Saint Bartholomew's Massacre

A slaughter of Huguenots begun in Paris, 24 August 1572, which was largely the outcome of the policy of Catharine de Médicis. Some 3,000 to 4,000 were killed. Provincial towns followed the example of Paris. The central event in M. J. Chénier's *Charles IX* (q.v.), it was constantly recalled in the press of the Revolution.

St. Lazare

Former leprosary established in the Faubourg St.-Martin, at Paris, –became a house of correction in 1775 and a celebrated prison under the Revolution, where the suspects were imprisoned while waiting for judgment. Subsequently it became a women's prison.

Salpêtrière

See Hôpital général.

Santerre, Antoine Joseph

b. Paris 1752–d. 1809.
Brewer in the Faubourg St.-Antoine and a generous benefactor. He took a prominent part in the fall of the Bastille and in the risings of 20 June and 10 August 1792. As commandant of the Paris National Guard (1792), he protected the royal family. He disowned the September massacres. As a divisional general in 1793 he went to the Vendée, but was eventually defeated near Cholet and imprisoned. He was saved by the events of 9 Thermidor (27 July 1794) and resigned.

Sections (*Sections parisiennes*)

Forty-eight Sections created by the decree of 21 May 1790 to replace the sixty districts (q.v.) instituted for the elections of 1789. The Legislative Assembly guaranteed their meetings on 25 July 1792 and to these were gradually admitted the 'passive' citizens aged twenty-five and above. Forty-seven Sections urged the deposition of the king. The Section of the Faubourg St.-Antoine was prominent in the organisation of the events of 10 August 1792. The Sections were then (17 August) invited to elect a special tribunal to try the suspects. In 1793 the Sections of the eastern districts supported the Jacobins and then helped in the downfall of the Girondins. After 9 Thermidor, the moderate Sections of the western region played the main role, especially in 13 Vendémiaire, Year IV (5 October 1795). The Sections disappeared when the Directory came to power.

Seides

A character in the *Tragedy of Mahomet* by Voltaire. He is so dedicated to the prophet that he is ready to commit an assassination on his orders.

Septembristes

Those who took part in the massacres of 2–5 September 1792. Also called 'Septembriseurs'.

Society of the Friends of the Constitution

Commonly known as the Jacobin Club, this was a middle-class body, consisting of 'active' citizens (q.v.). It was established in 1789 and, after the move of the Assembly from Versailles to Paris, it set up its headquarters in the library of the Jacobin Convent in the Rue St.-Honoré, close to the

Assembly's meeting place. It became the most famous of the clubs, and much of the legislation passed in the Assemblies had previously been initiated and ratified in the session of this club.

Talleyrand, comte de (Charles Maurice de Talleyrand-Périgord)

b. Paris, 1754–d. 1838.

Deputy for the clergy at Autun in the Constituent Assembly; French Foreign Minister and diplomat in the Napoleonic and Restoration periods. He was ordained priest in 1779 and eventually Bishop of Autun (2 November 1788). In the Revolution he sought to transform the Bourbon monarchy into a constitutional form along the lines of the English monarchy. He played a prominent role in the nationalisation of Church lands, and was one of the two bishops who took the oath to the Constitution. He resigned his bishopric and was excommunicated in 1792. He helped to found the Feuillant Club. Ineligible for election to the Legislative Assembly, he became a diplomat, pursuing missions in England. Suspected of duplicity, his name was included in the official list of émigrés (March 1793). He went to the United States and was allowed to return to France in 1796. He became Foreign Minister in 1797 and served until 1807. Played a large part in the restoration of the monarchy in 1814.

Temple tower, at Paris

Formerly the residence of the Order of Templars in France, built in 1212 and later the property of the Hospitallers. The main tower was used as a prison during the Revolution, Louis XVI and his family were imprisoned there on 11 August 1792. It was demolished in 1811.

Tithe

The most important source of ecclesiastical revenue, normally one-tenth of all produce, paid by landowners and peasants, but in different form by the Catholics living in towns, cities or castles.

Tocsin

Before the Revolution the tocsin was sounded on occasions such as the birth and death of royalty; in case of major fires or revolt. During the Revolution the sounding of the tocsin usually acted as an alarm-signal preceding an insurrection.

Town-hall (Paris)

See Hôtel-de-Ville.

Tribune

Prior to 1789 there was only a president's chair (*chaire*) and a bar in the big assemblies. The Constituent Assembly introduced a tribune from which parliamentary speeches were made. The tribune was the scene of many great oratorical triumphs, also many unsavoury incidents.

Tribunes

That section of the Assembly where the public or journalists were permitted as spectators or reporters.

Tuileries

Former residence of the French monarchy situated between the Louvre and the Place de la Concorde. Built 1564. The gardens were begun in 1600. The kings, however, preferred the Louvre or Versailles. After the events of 5 and 6 October 1789, the king was reinstalled in the palace. In 1792 the Convention set itself up there.

Ultramontane principles

The term 'ultramontanism' signifies a body of opinions or doctrines favourable to papal authority. Such principles were opposed to Gallicanism (q.v.).

Varennes-en-Argonne

A town on the River Aire, Varennes was the end of Louis XVI's ill-fated attempt to cross the frontier in June 1791.

Vincennes (tower)

The castle and tower-prison of Vincennes was built from 1337 to 1370. From the time of Louis XI, the tower became the state prison. From Louis XIV onward the castle was no longer used as a domicile. It became an annex of the Bastille until 14 July 1789, and like it it was regarded as a symbol of the old despotism.

Vincent, François-Nicolas

b. Paris, 1767–d. 1794.
Secretary of the Section of the Théâtre Français. One of the most violent members of the Cordeliers. Tried and executed with the Hébertistes (24 March 1794).

Vincent, Pierre Charles Victor

Deputy for Seine-Inférieure at the Convention. A Girondin, proscribed after 2 June. Returned to the Convention after the fall of Robespierre, sat in the Ancients, but after 1797, retired from politics.

Index

(Titles of individual journals, newspapers and pamphlets are listed under Press)

Index